# PROJECTING PARANOIA

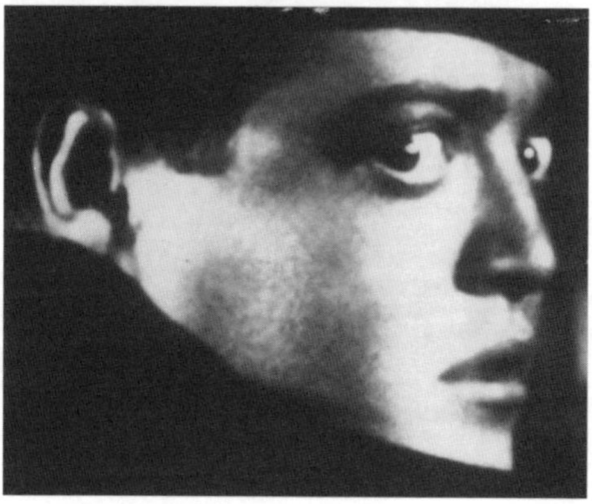

**CultureAmerica**

Karal Ann Marling

Erika Doss

SERIES EDITORS

# PROJECTING PARANOIA

## Conspiratorial Visions in American Film

Ray Pratt

University Press of Kansas

Published by the University Press of Kansas (Lawrence, Kansas 66049), which was organized by the Kansas Board of Regents and is operated and funded by Emporia State University, Fort Hays State University, Kansas State University, Pittsburg State University, the University of Kansas, and Wichita State University



Library of Congress Cataloging-in-Publication Data
Pratt, Ray.
Projecting paranoia : conspiratorial visions in American film / Ray Pratt.
p. cm. — (CultureAmerica)
Includes bibliographical references and index.
ISBN 0-7006-1148-7 (alk. paper) — ISBN 0-7006-1150-9 (pbk. : alk. paper)
1. Motion pictures—Political aspects—United States.
I. Title. II. Culture America.
PN1995.9.P6 P72 2001
791.43'658—dc21 2001002319

British Library Cataloguing in Publication Data is available.

Printed in the United States of America

10 9 8 7 6 5 4 3 2

The paper used in this publication meets the minimum requirements of the American National Standard for Permanence of Paper for Printed Library Materials Z39.48-1984.

# Contents

# Illustrations

*A photo gallery follows chapter 5 (p. 144).*

# Acknowledgments

Many of the insights about the films discussed in this book arose from teaching a course—American Political Thought and Popular Culture—in which from thirty-five to fifty bright minds engaged in discussions and writing assignments centered on a group of films, many of them included here. Since I started teaching the course in 1989, each time I review a paper on a film I have looked at as many as a dozen times, I still get some remarkably fresh insights from students who are always capable of seeing something anew.

Sara Goulden has been a supportive companion throughout this project, watching and rewatching bad copies of very old films and commenting on my often turgid prose. Carl Boggs, a colleague for over thirty years, has read and commented on most of the chapters at various stages. Douglas Kellner—thanks to several stimulating talks at the Popular Culture Association and after reading his books *Camera Politica, Media Culture,* and *Television and the Crisis of Democracy*—has helped me see film in new ways. George Lipsitz, who provided his usual perceptive and thoughtful comments on the original book proposal, has for several years offered suggestions and comments on my work, thereby always improving its general tone and direction. Dan Flory, a philosophy colleague at Montana State University, has enriched my understanding of film noir and provided many useful suggestions that came of informal hallway conversations. Jerry Calvert, my department head during the project, helped me get a reduced teaching load in the fall of 1999 to complete an early draft of the manuscript. James Maxfield made some helpful comments on early drafts of chapters 7 and 8. Chrisopher Sharrett made suggestive comments on chapter 10 as well as other portions of the manuscript. Mike Briggs had the foresight to suggest the project in the first place and has, more than anyone, worked to make it happen. It is to the memory of my late father, Raymond W. Pratt—who introduced me to the sheer pleasure of watching movies by taking his ten-year-old son to such now almost forgotten features as Fritz Lang's *House by the River*—that I dedicate this book.

# Introduction

Happy Hollywood endings have never completely hidden the darker side of American democracy from the viewing public. From classic postwar film noir through television's *X-Files,* the deepest fears of receptive audiences have found effective expression. For much of the past sixty years, Americans—feeling powerless and distrustful of government and experiencing social transformations and threats imperfectly understood—have looked to movies to exorcise their fears, which are often dismissed as "paranoia." Such feelings, on closer examination, seem to mirror longer-term yet largely hidden programs of state surveillance, covert manipulation, and even coordinated repression by national, state, and local political-intelligence systems, all of which can be considered forms of organized conspiracy.

Simultaneously, such public apprehensions also reflect the emergence of the postmodern situation, with its loss of sense of what is "true" and "real," as well as the erosion of traditional liberal notions of citizenship, individuality, and *agency.*[1] Conspiracy theory is often symptomatic of more pervasive anxiety among individuals concerning their ability to control their lives. This seems especially true in the United States, with its political culture so much a product of the grand narrative of classical liberalism—what C. B. Macpherson has termed "possessive individualism."[2] As Louis Hartz argued in his classic study *The Liberal Tradition in America,* American political thought begins and ends—indeed is virtually coextensive—with classical liberal ideology.[3] Imbued with an individualist ideology reinforced by such cultural documents as Emerson's essay on "Self-Reliance," Americans may be more prone than citizens of other cultures to experience peculiarly intense kinds of anxiety over what they perceive as a "loss of autonomy, the conviction someone's actions are being controlled by someone else, or that one has been 'constructed' by powerful, external agents," producing a contemporary and quintessentially postmodern psychological phenomenon Timothy Melley has labeled "agency panic."[4]

American films—distinctive and formative reflections of the nation's political culture—are products of complex teams consisting of producers, writers, directors, cinematographers, set designers, and actors—including "stars" commanding such huge financial returns (twenty million dollars or more, in some cases) that they may now virtually function as "auteurs," dictating all aspects of a film, from script to final cut. Nevertheless, at any historical moment one can find in film images and narratives systematic critiques of individuals, institutions, and movements; and even more far-reaching calls for utopian alternatives to the existing political economy and society. In this sense, film texts can be seen, in Fredric Jameson's phrase, as "socially symbolic acts,"[5] reflecting, albeit indirectly, one of the grand narratives of the nineteenth and twentieth centuries: the quest for individual and social liberation. In Jameson's terms, this quest is seen in its specifically Marxist "single great collective story . . . the collective struggle to wrest a realm of Freedom from a realm of Necessity."[6] Throughout much of the period encompassed in this study, the political films described may be seen as unconscious reflections of state-supported repression of movements for human emancipation, or the belief among significant sectors of the public that their lives are no longer under their own control.

Popular or *media* cultural texts, of course, not only reflect and express, but also influence social trends and the ways people think about them. Among other narrative trends, during the last century, Max Weber's master narrative of rationalization—the growth of bureaucracy and its complex division of labor, and hierarchical organizational structures in business and government—has predominated. Another, perhaps less recognized, narrative is what Marshall Berman eloquently described as the "tragedy of development"—the onward march of a consolidating and globalizing capitalism—involving the "emptying-out" of thousands of "little worlds" as families, neighborhoods, rural communities, and once-thriving businesses and industries are all eventually transformed or destroyed.[7]

Tragically, throughout the recent history of the United States, the longer-term quest for utopian social-political alternatives to the latter trends in the name of human emancipation has resulted in a failed and ultimately fruitless search. In significant ways, state repression contributed to that failure, though greater causal weight might be placed on the decisions and tactics of many radical movements and, most significant of all, on the abundance—compared with nineteenth-century Europe and the twentieth-century third world—of the blandishments of the consumer society created by the very capitalist system such movements sought to change.

Anticipated by nineteenth-century "populism," throughout the twentieth century significant minority political movements in the United States sought new kinds of social organization to realize narratives of human liberation: socialism, communism, visions of decentralized social anarchism. Specific organizations and alternative parties to the dominant factions of the free-enterprise party (known as the Republican and Democratic parties) played a major role early on. These included the Socialist Party of America and the Industrial Workers of the World (IWW), the latter being one of the most romantic and influential American radical movements of the early twentieth century. These were followed by the Communist Party of the United States, active from the 1920s through the 1950s, whose members and supporters were involved in organizing the many and diverse forms of industrial unions from the 1920s onward. In the 1950s and '60s the civil rights movement emerged, having grown out of earlier movements and the black church. It contributed to the massive peace/anti–Vietnam War movements, and grew synergistically with the New Left and its only real organization, Students for a Democratic Society (SDS). Feminism in the period reflected both longer-term influences and—as Sara Evans recorded in *Personal Politics*—the reaction of women to the male domination and sexism of other movements.[8] The diverse environmental movements also grew exponentially, following such works as Rachel Carson's *Silent Spring* and such widely viewed ecological disasters as the 1969 Santa Barbara oil spill. All of these movements, evidently, were the objects of the closest observation, surveillance, and infiltration by agencies of the national, state, and local government, together with often allied private security and investigative organizations working for ever-evolving and increasingly concentrated corporate capitalism.[9]

Surveillance of radical movements by government agencies on a systematic basis became intense during and following World War I, increasing as a result of the bloody struggles to organize industrial unions in the 1930s and then to expel Communists in the 1940s, finally intensifying in the cold war period after World War II. During the cold war, the FBI and various civilian and military intelligence agencies carried out complex programs of surveillance and harassment of radicals, including Communists, union organizers, entertainment figures, educators, and journalists. This trend continued in the complex programs of surveillance of such civil rights leaders as Martin Luther King Jr.—possibly even leading to his death[10]; in systematic programs directed against antiwar activists from the 1960s through the '70s[11]; and finally against advocates for peaceful and just policies toward Central America—particularly El Salvador and Nicaragua—in the 1980s and '90s.[12] It continues into the new century with anti-"terrorist" programs and legislation.

In a variety of ways, movie culture imperfectly reflected these trends. Exploration of the complex manner in which film texts reflect, represent, and inflect these movements is a central concern of this book. Its title suggests that what is commonly deprecated and dismissed as irrational and without foundation—

sheer "paranoia"—actually represents visionary expressions illuminating what Foucault has termed "subjugated knowledge" of largely hidden, repressive trends in American life, known in detail only to their victims and perpetrators.[13] Presented in this study are glimpses, by way of film, of such trends over a period of sixty years. This does not pretend to be a comprehensive and explicitly detailed compendium of all "conspiracy" and "paranoia" films; there are simply too many examples. Because of complex influences in the system of production, movies—often as unconscious expressions of repressed struggles and more ill-defined anxieties—imperfectly reflected the trends of surveillance and repression extending throughout the twentieth century and into the twenty-first. Such attempts at revealing underlying trends through film nonetheless may influence—and even help create—political ideology and movements, sometimes providing insights that further enhance and heighten radical critique or magnify and amplify distrust. Filmic visions usually follow chronologically the historical events they represent, but the films considered here also suggest often extraordinary artistic prescience: they may anticipate or even *prefigure* historical events.

This study began as an exploration of conspiracy—theories about conspiracy thinking, and thinking about the possibility of great conspiracies as explanations of historical events.[14] Conspiracy thinking, as has often been noted, has been endemic in U.S. political discourse throughout our national history.[15] While more recent and contemporary versions of conspiratorial visions date from the 1963 assassination of John F. Kennedy, modern right-wing conspiracy theory can be traced back to the cold war—at least to what is now called "McCarthyism" but in the post–World War II period could more accurately be termed "Truman-McCarthyism.[16] If one identified such repressive developments with a single individual—from the great "Red Scare" of the World War I period through the Vietnam War—it could well be termed, as I argue in chapter one, "J. Edgar Hooverism," reflecting the importance of the late FBI director's coordination and intimate involvement in surveillance of domestic radical and oppositional politics throughout his career and right up to his death in 1972.

A largely hidden yet massively repressive government-organized, anti-progressive, state-sponsored conspiratorial mind-set has been a consistently recurring feature of the American political system since the radical political movements of the World War I period, up to and including the campaigns against alleged domestic "terrorism" and passage of a major terrorism act in 1996,[17] which was largely ignored by the major media. The pattern has continued, with diverse forms of surveillance of oppositional and separatist groups, into the twenty-first century. The trajectory of political film is seen as mirroring—usually following—the overall pattern of such internal surveillance and repression. If it is a perspective reflective of "paranoia," the events and programs from which it developed are documented in numerous scholarly historical and analytical surveys.[18]

In *The Racial Contract* philosopher Charles W. Mills describes a society—a world—profoundly skewed in favor of the white race. Most whites, of course, do not believe they occupy such a position of privilege, one based upon the domination and subjection of the world's nonwhite races. They participate in what Mills describes as a shared "epistemology of ignorance"—a cognitive model precluding genuine understanding of the system of social realities that accords them such a position of privilege among the world's peoples. It is "an invented delusional world, a racial fantasyland."[19] It is very much, as William Gibson has characterized cyberspace, a "consensual hallucination," albeit located in the very real spaces where hundreds of millions live.[20] While the journeys of the individuals who are characters in the films discussed in this study might seem to be experiencing perceptions of danger, menace, and threats, their filmically represented, artistically created perceptions may also be taken as clues. What might be dismissed as their paranoia might also signal heightened awareness and anticipation of emergent, potentially repressive trends. While the films I discuss only occasionally touch directly on race—except for several dealing explicity with African-American experiences at the hands of law enforcement agencies—the perceptions and epistemology of ignorance in which so many in the society participate speak directly to the central dynamics of racism—the mechanisms used to maintain power and to exclude, threaten, and repress. All these films involve forms of systemic domination and privilege, of which racism might be seen—together with class, sex, and the multiple, proliferating forms of bureaucratic and police power—as representative.

# "Our Greatest Export Is Paranoia"

## Visionary Paranoia

In *The End of Violence* (1997, Wim Wenders),[1] a man sits above Los Angeles in the Griffith Park Observatory, spying through a network of video cameras set up throughout the whole city. The man (Gabriel Byrne), an expert in satellite surveillance trained by the National Security Agency (NSA), is part of a secret plan within the U.S. government to pretest a sophisticated system of total personal surveillance. Through satellites and remote-controlled video cameras, all exteriors on any street in Los Angeles can be monitored. A mysterious e-mail dropped into the computer of producer Mike Max (Bill Pullman) provides details of the secret pilot project under the control of a sinister "man-in-black" (Daniel Benzali), who has the power to eliminate anyone who seeks to expose the project, which would so deter street crime that it could mean "the end to violence."

In *Enemy of the State* (1998, Tony Scott), privacy becomes obsolete as electronic eavesdropping, communication satellites, and computer hacking are utilized to track a private citizen (a lawyer played by Will Smith) and eventually to fabricate news stories, freeze his bank account, and extract information from his (or any) computer through hacking, or through electronic bugs in his home and on his person—a fate previously befalling Sandra Bullock in *The Net* (1995, Irwin Winkler) and Michael Douglas in *The Game* (1997, David Fincher). In *Enemy of the State,* a terrifying dystopian vision of the ultimate surveillance society, there are no such things as unmonitored phone conversations or even buttonholes without secret video cameras. An NSA senior official (John Voight) controls a legion of computer geeks and robotic, tireless "men-in-black" who even kill a U.S. congressman. A whole satellite is dedicated to finding Will Smith and the information he inadvertently possesses. His only friend turns out to a shadowy figure named Brill (Gene Hackman), before 1980 a U.S. spy and since then a secret operative at the fringes of intelligence and surveillance. While he has a new name, he could literally be "Harry Caul," the role he played in Francis Ford Coppola's 1974 techno-paranoia film *The Conversation.*

He has almost exactly the same workshop in a similar old warehouse. His ID photos are identical to those of Harry Caul. Emerging from the Watergate era past of illicit corporate and government surveillance, he has changed with the times, knowingly telling Smith about how the government can listen in on any conversation, gain all types of information, and observe anyone anywhere.

Both films provide terrifying portraits of an emerging society of total surveillance and unlimited government access, obliterating any illusions of the possibility of a free, private, personal space. Both illustrate the potential, all-pervasive nature of government power, demonstrating how data about you could be used against you, how your slightest suspicions could be actual clues, and how what you think is paranoia might be a heightened awareness of real possibilities. This is visionary paranoia.

## Paranoia and the Popular Media

In this study "visionary" cultural paranoia—widespread in American films, television, and popular novels—is viewed as a subjective reflection of the perceived powerlessness of the American public. Because popular cultural analogues of paranoia are so much in evidence, and there are so many indications in public opinion surveys of precursor attitudes, paranoid thinking increasingly seems widespread among the U.S. population. It has been said that this postmodern era is an "age of paranoia."[2] Paranoia, in one sense, is a crisis in interpretation, a desire to make sense of what does not make sense. Clinically, paranoia reveals distortions in the minds of subjects, involving feelings of persecution (threatening aspects of life seem greater than is justified) and delusions (creating alternative beliefs to replace those elements seen as threatening). Both involve creating what is regarded by others as a "false" sense of the world. Yet, as the advertising for the film *Enemy of the State* suggested, "It's not paranoia if they really are after you." Actual surveillance of the streets of London and other cities in Britain now takes place via video cameras, surpassing the fictional visions of Los Angeles surveillance in *The End of Violence.* In the United States cameras now stare at everyone browsing at a Barnes and Noble bookstore or renting videos at a Blockbuster outlet. Everyone is under surveillance while shopping, while on the Internet, while crossing under freeway overpasses, while entering schools and any public buildings. Visible cameras are backed by hidden ones, concealed in tinted domes or behind mirrors, which peer through pinhole-size openings.[3]

In a world in which everyone now knows they are being watched and in which, over more than half a century since World War II, a series of inadequately explained sociohistorical traumas—from the JFK, Martin Luther King Jr., and RFK assassinations to the crashes of TWA Flight 800 and EgyptAir Flight 990—have inspired widespread tension resulting from explanations given and public suspicions. Paranoia in such a context becomes "a way of knowing" and "a mode of perception," noting the connections between things declared by official authorities as unconnected.[4] Such cultural paranoia, more than just an indicator of madness, can also be a *method*, providing a way of seeing multiple, interconnected—though officially denied—stratifications of reality. The post–World War II period in the United States gave rise to novels, films, and television series that collectively constitute a minority discourse on cultural paranoia, bringing together contiguous forces—political, economic, epistemological, ethical—to create an artistic reality, a "structure of feeling," that seeks to illuminate hidden dimensions of history.[5]

This cultural paranoia is also evident in the novels of Thomas Pynchon and such popular literature as John Grisham's novel *The Firm* or Don DeLillo's *Libra* and *Underworld*. What in the past was usually dismissed as anecdotal now confirms the conspiratorial; what was accident becomes evidence of a larger design. Under such conditions, paranoia is increasingly a binding force for the whole nation. From below it is a popular movement within a population sensing it is being manipulated and controlled; from above it is a mind-set encouraged by national political leadership and the mass media. In the United States, first in the cold war and then in the 1980s and '90s and into the current century, a nation allegedly besieged by terrorists became, in the minds of a significant segment of the public, a society watched over by helicopters and "men-in-black." Ultimately, what brings people together in such a society is the sense that they are "wary participants in an unfolding historical plot over which they have no control."[6] Paranoia becomes for them a reflection of their perceived powerlessness, a way of coming to terms with a reality too complex to fathom or occluded by the immense size and intricacy of the revealed (or unrevealed) plots and envisioned conspiracies.

Much of the twentieth century in the United States was a period defined by political paranoia—especially suspicion of foreign enemies and their alleged domestic agents. There was the long-term fear of Communist attack or subversion in the cold war era, beginning as early as the first domestic Red Scare of 1919–20 and lasting up until the fall of the Soviet Union in 1991. A later source was the fear of third world "terrorist" states and movements—which often arose out of conditions the United States helped create—beginning with Fidel Castro's revolution in Cuba in 1959. The trend continued through the media-hyped hostilities toward Iran's revolutionary Islamic regime after the seizure of hostages at the U.S. Embassy there in 1979. This attitude was later displaced onto Col. Muammar al-Qaddafi of Libya—whose agents supposedly had infiltrated the United States in the early 1980s seeking to assassinate former president Ronald Reagan.[7] Similarly, the Sandinista revolutionary government of Nicaragua and the leftist rebels in El Salvador in the same period were both presented by the Reagan administration as threatening the southern border of the United States. This image was reflected in the widely seen but critically despised film *Red Dawn* (1984, John Milius), reportedly a text repeatedly viewed by right-wing militia members-in-training. The hysteria continued and was next projected onto Iraq's Saddam Hussein in 1990–91 and after in order to justify the continued bombing of Iraq; to Saudi terrorist Osama bin-Laden and his alleged agents in 1998 and 1999; to Yugoslav Serbian strongman Slobodan Milosević in 1999; and on and on. Fear and suspicion of these and other assorted heavily hyped alien threats characterized appeals to and manipulation of domestic U.S. public opinion by national executives throughout much of the cold war era, progressing from presidents Carter to Reagan to Bush to Clinton—even as the cold war dissipated as a result of the disintegration of the "Soviet Threat."[8]

## IDENTITY POLITICS AND GENDER PARANOIA

Rising "identity" politics in the last third of the twentieth century added further dimensions of suspicion and threat to the discourse of cultural paranoia: women became openly expressive of fears of exploitative treatment, harassment, emotional and physical abuse, and various forms of sexual predation. Developing significant cultural and political movements of support and resistance, they pursued and—with the help of concerned males—established widespread networks of regulation and legal protection so successful that many now see them as capable of being abused as instruments of reverse discrimination and expressions of overt hatred of men, which in Daphne Patai's revelatory critical study is termed "heterophobia."[9] Patai's account demonstrates how in three short decades the concept of "sexual harassment" became all-pervasive and the ideological climate of antimale hysteria and paranoia it generated led to profound, unintended consequences resulting from well-intentioned social policy. Modern sexual harassment laws and regulations now place the liability burden on employers rather than harassers. This creates economic incentives for the restriction of a lot more speech and behavior than the law actually forbids in order to avoid expensive lawsuits and judgments. Indeed, as another student of the field suggests, "prudent companies have little choice but to restrict a great deal of sexual expression that no jury would ultimately condemn. The law has transformed inquisitions into the emotional lives of employees into an ordinary matter of corporate self-interest."[10]

The evidence is growing that males can be charged with sexual "harassment" on the smallest shred of evidence, simply because the accusation has been raised. One can lose one's job, or worse, for doing something within the ever-expanding category of offenses not precisely illegal but which—in terms of existing policies and practices in large organizations, businesses, and universities—can be judged "harassment" simply because the charge has been made.[11]

## RACIAL PARANOIA

Judging from all available evidence, reports of paranoia among African-Americans, originating in their treatment during the slave period and continuing up to the present, seem well founded and based on actual treatment, policies, practices, and attitudes of significant portions of the larger white society. With justification in real historical events, African-Americans are much more willing to entertain notions of conspiratorial intent by the larger, white structures of power. Interestingly, empirical studies have demonstrated that "African-Americans who believe in conspiracy theories are better educated than those who do not believe," and, moreover, are more active politically, more in touch with problems of their communities, and "closer than are skeptics to the front line of both inter-ethnic conflict and cooperation."[12]

From the days of slavery through covert FBI operations against civil rights workers and allegations of CIA complicity with crack cocaine dealers in the 1980s, educated African-Americans have maintained or gained an awareness of numerous, increasingly well-documented conspiratorial operations carried out against them by non–African-Americans. Where such "concerted and secretly planned social action is an everyday accomplishment of industries and government agencies,"[13] it would be irrational to treat such conspiracy theories as unrealistic manifestations of "paranoid" thinking rather than as evidence of harmful, racist, conspiratorial designs against out-groups carried out through larger structures of power—processes evident in such films as *Devil in a Blue Dress* (1995, Carl Franklin) and *Rosewood* (1997, John Singleton).

## THE PARANOID STYLE

Hysterical public construction of enemies, suspicion of out-groups, and general paranoia have been distinctive elements of American politics since the early 1800s. Richard Hofstadter wrote his essay "The Paranoid Style in American Politics" back in 1965,[14] but in more recent years a number of trends have come together to produce a renewed popular cultural manifestation of belief in plots and conspiracies, often denigrated as a manifestation of "paranoid" thinking. Others have dismissed the adoption of similar conceptions by both right- and left-wing movements as "fusion paranoia," suggesting that both varieties had gone to such extremes that they met one another, fusing in a circle of irrational fear and suspicion of repressive conspiracies by agencies of the state or even an emerging "new world order."[15]

Paranoia, in the most general sense, is the belief by an individual, or among a group, that it is being conspired against with the intention of inflicting harm. Increasingly widespread at the end of the twentieth century was the related but more specific belief in conspiracy originating within sectors or agencies of the U.S. government. This, too, is a reflection of fundamental, historically well documented aspects of the American political system and the larger society.

From a sociological perspective, there is evidence that those who are at lower status and relatively powerless positions—and thus vulnerable to victimization and exploitation—such as the poor, women, and members of minority ethnic groups, are more likely to be mistrustful of others and to believe in external control of their lives. This may be an accurate and objective assessment of their situation.[16] Increasingly this feeling seems evident among close to a majority of the citizens of the United States who do not vote and do not consider themselves an affiliate of one of the two mainstream political parties.

Feelings of powerlessness reached an all-time high in 1990, as evidenced by the large numbers of Americans surveyed who said they felt politically powerless. National opinion surveys in the United States during the period showed significant portions of the population agreeing "completely" or "mostly" with the following statement: "People like me don't have any say about what the government does." In May 1990 57 percent agreed; in July 1994 54 percent agreed; and in November 1997 46 percent "mostly" or "completely" agreed.[17] This question (one of a commonly asked series designed to elicit feelings of political powerlessness) has been asked on national surveys in the United States at least since 1956, when the proportion in agreement was only 28 percent, rising to 30 percent in 1960, 36 percent in 1966, 41 percent in 1968, declining to 36 percent in 1970, and ranging from 40 percent in 1972, to 42 percent in 1976, to 46 percent in 1978, to 40 percent in 1980.[18] Such data from national surveys provides substantial evidence of a trend toward increasing degrees of public perceptions of powerlessness, which is particularly in evidence since the assassination of John F. Kennedy in 1963 and the onset of the Vietnam War. In a survey of the meanings of public perceptions about the assassination of John F. Kennedy, political scientist Sheldon Appleton suggested that the widespread belief—consistently 75 to 80 percent—that there was a conspiracy in JFK's death actually reflected more fundamental public feelings of powerlessness, itself a precursor of paranoia.[19]

## CLINICAL PARANOIA

While references to "paranoia" abound in popular discussions of conspiracy, there are no studies of the occurrence of actual clinically diagnosable paranoid character in the general population. The American Psychiatric Association's *Diagnostic and Statistical Manual* (commonly known as DSM I, II, III, or IV)[20] distinguishes between "Paranoid Personality," "Paranoid Personality Disorder," "Delusional (Paranoid) Disorder," and "Paranoid Schizophrenia." Those with paranoid personality disorder may function in society even though they experience continual mistrust, see the world as a threatening place, and are hyperalert. The delusional (paranoid) disorder is characterized by a "persistent, non-bizarre delusion." The most common delusion is that of persecution, that is suspecting others of harboring plots to hurt or injure them. Other delusional themes noted in clinical studies include: extreme romantic jealousy; erotic delusions (the belief that one is loved by another); grandiose delusions (the belief that one has special powers); and somatic delusions (the belief that something is very wrong with one's body, that it might emit foul odors or have bugs crawling all over it).[21] That all Americans are obviously encouraged in some of these feelings by the advertising culture probably does not help the situation.

The delusional paranoid disorder is not as severe as the form of schizophrenia called "paranoid schizophrenia," a condition commonly manifested by extremely bizarre delusions or hallucinations. Some individuals, for example, might hear voices that others cannot hear, or believe their thoughts are controlled from elsewhere. One male student believed women were shooting poisoned webs at him when he walked across the campus.[22] (This is potentially interesting material for a screenplay.) While important gradations characterize each of these conditions, all contain the overwhelming fear of being persecuted and conspired against. Precise data on the distribution of such psychological conditions in the general population is not available, though clinical diagnosis of classic paranoid schizophrenia is a very rare phenomenon, affecting less than half of 1 percent of the total population. In a sample of five hundred people, for example, it would be extremely unlikely to find a case, though more general types of schizophrenia might occur among 1 percent of the population.[23]

Important and suggestive insights into the long-term tendencies concerning trust, efficacy, and political cynicism—all factors at some distance from outright paranoia but suggesting the movement of public thinking in that direction—are provided by the National Election Studies (NES), available since 1952, which supplement the data previously noted.[24]

## DECLINING LEVELS OF TRUST

Beyond indications in surveys of widespread feelings of powerlessness, the most striking trend in public opinion is the thirty-year decline in "Trust of the Federal Government" from 76 percent in 1964—who said that you can trust the federal government "most of the time" or "just about always"—to an all-time low of only 21 percent in 1994. This rose to 34 percent in 1998.

This striking downward secular trend line roughly conforms to the dates of U.S. involvement in the Vietnam War (1963–73) and the outpouring of published criticism (beginning in 1968) of the Warren Report's findings concerning the assassination of former president John F. Kennedy to Oliver Stone's popular and highly controversial film *JFK* (1991) covering the same event. Stone's film, commonly thought to be both a significant *cause* of the emergence of conspiracy thinking in the 1990s, is probably a better *indicator* because it actually did not alter preexisting widespread views among the public of the conspiratorial origins of JFK's assassination.[25] It didn't have to since there were plenty of other forces engendering cultural paranoia.

## PERCEIVED POWERLESSNESS

In a study of paranoia and powerlessness, sociologists John Mirowsky and Catherine Ross pointed out:

> Sociological theory indicates the prolonged and regular experience of failure and lack of control are inherent in conditions of powerlessness, structural inconsistency, and alienated labor. Each of these objective social conditions tends to elicit an awareness or world view that is its subjective image, providing a continuing stream of experience from which to infer external control.

If powerlessness is the inability to achieve one's ends, belief in external control of aspects of one's life, that "outcomes are determined by forces external to one's self . . . often represents an awareness of objective conditions."[26] Other sociological theories view the belief in external control as synonymous with an awareness of such objective powerlessness, as their subjective image.

This is a realistic assessment for many subgroups within the U.S. population—particularly those of lower economic status, minority ethnics, many women, the aged, and the unemployed—in earlier historical periods marked by high unemployment. But the anxieties over loss of control of the conditions of one's employment are much more widespread in American society. Despite the economic prosperity in the United States in the late 1990s and into the new century, virtually everyone in the United States has been conditioned to feel that no job is certain or secure, to accept job loss through "downsizing" as a routine fact of economic life, and to acknowledge the necessity of multiple occupational choices throughout one's life. Setting aside the question of whether to react with extreme suspicion of employers as a general principle or to expect the worst from those in control of one's economic security, it is not an irrational orientation for many, given the fluctuating history of minority employment and unemployment.

Justifiable underlying suspicion and skepticism among the disadvantaged groups noted are also symptoms. Through a ladderlike process, beginning with basic mistrust, it can lead to an outlook usually termed paranoid but actually a profound form of social alienation. To believe one has enemies conspiring to do one harm reflects more than a sense of detachment from others; it reveals a feeling of antagonism and hostility. Whether correct or a delusion, it has self-fulfilling tendencies. In either case, the perception has a reality, representing a deep sense of alienation from society. Such generalized paranoia, while a reasonable reaction and a "rational" response to conditions of objective powerlessness, is not a particularly adaptive one for most individuals simply trying to survive and function in this society.

To abstract from this level of analysis to systemic cultural generalizations might seem questionable, but the sociological data suggests directions for analysis and hypotheses about the genesis of paranoid modes of thinking. A population that feels itself to be powerless—as approximately half or more of national samples of U.S. citizens repeatedly indicated in the 1990s—is a society with widespread potential for paranoid thinking.

If there are real enemies and one truly is powerless, some form of paranoia may be considered "rational," justifying the old saying that "even paranoids have enemies." A "mental state" has a reality if held consciously (or unconsciously), especially if it affects behavior. If it is a subjective reflection of objective conditions, it becomes even more "real"; Freud suggested that paranoia always contains a "kernel of truth." In his discussion of the celebrated and classic early-twentieth-century case of Daniel Paul Schreber, Freud acknowleded there might be "more truth in Schreber's delusion than other people are as yet prepared to believe."[27]

The Schreber case (and Schreber's own account of his illness, originally published in 1903) is the point of origin of all studies of paranoia in psychiatric and psychoanalytic literature. Eric L. Santer's study of the Schreber case[28] has expanded our understanding of the larger political implications of the Schreber material—particularly its relevance in prefiguring or anticipating the rise of Nazism—though several earlier writers found in Schreber's memoir and case material on it "a storehouse of protofascist fantasies and fantasy structures."[29] Santner reaches the conclusion that, based upon the

> profound connections between the Schreber material and the social and political fantasies at work in Nazism, fantasies endowing Nazism with the status of a perverse political religion, the series of crises within the delusional medium of what I call his "own private Germany" were largely the same crises of modernity for which the Nazis would elaborate their own series of radical and ostensibly "final" solutions.

The Schreber case thus can be seen as providing profound insight "into the deepest structural layers of the historical impasses and conflicts that would provisionally culminate in the Nazi catastrophe."[30]

The growing popularity of a case at the turn of the last century that prefigured the rise of fascism anticipates and coincides with similar phenomena at the end of the twentieth century and developments anticipating the recent millennial change. It is increasingly common to note disturbing new expressions of paranoia in the United States and elsewhere, with new geopolitical arrangements, ideological formations, and shifting populations and capitals coinciding with the end of the cold war.[31] One need not adopt such views as Santner's hyperbolic "Where there is a culture of paranoia, fascism of one kind or another may not be far behind"[32] to appreciate the new forms of paranoia in the present era.

Earlier insights into manifestations of paranoia in the contemporary period have stressed its endemic nature in the culture of American capitalism. If the case of Daniel Paul Schreber provided insights early in the twentieth century concerning the subsequent rise of fascism in Europe, Philip K. Dick's science fiction provided unique insights into the post–World War II period in the United States. Dick's science fiction stories often contained situations and themes that were among the most paranoid of late-twentieth-century popular fiction. His paranoia reflected a distinctive mental pattern characteristic of late capitalist culture and society in the United States. Given the operating economic principles of such a society, Dick's paranoid literary images might be an accurate and quite appropriate reflection of what many experience—in the era of "downsizing"—as crushingly inhuman, instrumental treatment.[33] The massive demonstrations against corporate "globalization" in Seattle, Washington at the end of 1999 and renewed demonstrations in Washington, D.C., in April 2000 suggested the emergence of new movements against such practices.

For true paranoiacs, every detail has meaning. Nothing can be left uninterpreted or taken for granted. Their conceptions of meaning, both totalizing and hermeneutic, make them the most rigorous of all metaphysicians. The paranoid outlook can be internally logical, never trivializing, and capable of explaining any or all observed phenomena as aspects of larger, symmetrical totalities. Indeed, as Carl Freedman has argued, "no particular of empirical reality is so contingent or heterogeneous that the paranoiac cannot, by a straightforward process of point-for-point correspondence, interpret its meaning within the framework of his or her own grand system."[34]

Of Dick's voluminous literary creations, the most famous is the novella *Do Androids Dream of Electric Sheep?* (1968). With major transformations, it served as the basis for the screenplay of Ridley Scott's bleak future sci-fi film masterpiece *Blade Runner* (1982).[35] Dick's residence in northern California during the drug culture years of the 1960s and after—his own apparent use of some stimulants, such as amphetamines, aided his intense literary productivity and generated an immense number of novels and short stories—heightened his awareness of, and sensitivity to, drug-induced paranoia and the distinctive attitudinal states and behaviors of paranoia. In Dick's novel *Clans of the Alphane Moons* (originally published in 1964),[36] a small moon is inhabited by a society of psychopaths, an insane asylum where the patients have formed clans based on their respective psychoses. In this society whole political tendencies have grown up around such diagnosed mental conditions. The elaborate narrative notes the utility to the larger society of behaviors and orientations consistent with paranoia, as well as other psychoses usually regarded as incapacitating illnesses in the societies back on Earth.

*Clans of the Alphane Moons* answers the old question as to what would happen if the inmates ran the asylum—in this case the remote moon of the Alphane system, which bears a remarkable resemblance to the officially "sane" planet Earth. Basic to the society described in Dick's novel is a functional system made up of the psychotic inmates of a lunar hospital organized according to a clinical caste system. As Norman Spinrad characterized the novel, "partly it is parody, but it is also a description of how divergent and even crippled individual consciousnesses can synergize into a functional whole. It could be Dick's bedrock paradigm for the human condition."[37]

## PARANOIA, INFANTILIZATION, AND THE DEMISE OF CITIZENSHIP

Paranoia can also be viewed as a realistic and reasonable cultural method and strategy of analysis in the face of the "infantilization" of U.S. citizens during the cold war era and after.[38] Basic to the notion of infantilization is the view that U.S. citizens have been treated as less than adults, denied full information, deceived, controlled, manipulated, spied on, and lied to for much of the century. Indeed, a variety of cultural myths and narratives, serving to reaffirm elements of national ideology, also reenact rituals in which essentially naïve citizens travel to Washington to learn that the system "really does work." Oliver Stone's movie narratives intersect with such cultural mythology—in ways that contest it—showing characters observing and witnessing the operation of diverse aspects of "the system." In *Salvador* (1986) Richard Boyle (James Woods) witnesses and then flees from the system of horror and political terror created in that country with the aid of U.S. advisers. In *Platoon* (1986) in the film's climactic moment the character named Chris (Charlie Sheen) kills Sgt. Barnes (Tom Berenger), one of the archetypal operatives of the dominant system of power, who boasts, "I am reality." In effect having killed the lethal, toxic, dark side represented by Barnes, Chris escapes by flying back to the States. In *Wall Street* (1987) Sheen again plays a similar everyman character witnessing the depredations of the philosophy "greed is good," in the person of Gordon Gekko (Michael Douglas), who wants to dismember the company employing Sheen's father (played by his real-life father, Martin Sheen). In *JFK* (1991) the idealized, Capraesque version of "Jim Garrison" (Kevin Costner) goes to Washington, and is informed by "Mr X" (Fletcher Prouty, played by Donald Sutherland) that the system "works" through a gigantic murderous civilian-military cabal/plot/conspiracy that murdered the president, who supposedly sought to challenge it. One need not accept all, or much, of the specifics of the latter explanation in the film—hammered into the listening and viewing audience represented in the person of the idealized "Garrison"—to appreciate the structure of the narrative and the metonymic use of the naïve observer in such narratives. In Stone's *Nixon* (1995) even the Lear-like "President Nixon" (Anthony Hopkins) is shown as something of a tragic, though in some ways also innocent, figure in fear of what "they"—the secret operatives of the invisible state—can do even to him. Such naïve innocents appear not only in Stone's films but in popular films going back to Capra's *Mr. Smith Goes to Washington* (1939), finding a recent incarnation in the Fox television network's adult cartoon series *The Simpsons,* where young "Lisa Simpson" goes to Washington.[39] The process continued in the 1999 comedy film *Dick,* in which two naïve teenagers, like Rosenkrantz and Guildenstern in Tom Stoppard's drama, witness and become the sources for Woodward and Bernstein's deconstruction of the Nixon White House.

During the past half century of U.S. popular film, rarely—and usually only metaphorically in wholly fictional narratives—has there been any representation of or concern regarding the nature and operation of the clandestine U.S. national security state and its motivations. This remained the case until the "men-in-black" references began to appear in the 1980s and '90s.[40] Extremely rarely, as in Costa-Gavras' *Missing* (1982) and his earlier *State of Siege* (1973), does one encounter specific, literal analysis of the operations of the U.S. national security state. Only the first of these could be considered an American film. Given the deceitfulness of U.S. officials in Chile, as portrayed in *Missing*, and the harrowing narrative in Thomas Hauser's book *The Execution of Charles Horman*, on which the film is based,[41] both qualify as some of the best representations of the infantilization strategy of those in power. In the film *Missing* it is evident when Charles Horman's father (Jack Lemmon) and his wife (Sissy Spacek) are systematically lied to—and treated almost as if they were children uncovering parental secrets—as they try to find out what happened to Charles Horman in the aftermath of the 1973 Chilean coup, in which the United States played a significant though officially denied role.[42] (This film is discussed at length in Chapter 5.)

In Marita Sturken's discussion of Oliver Stone's "docudramas"—one of the strongest, most revelatory cases made for the power and value of the total body of Stone's work as a positive act of engaged, concerned citizenship—it is suggested that Stone's perspectives should be seen as "an essential component of the experience of citizenship" in the recent history of the United States, rather than demeaned, as they often are, as "conspiratorial."[43] Unacknowledged, often hidden, frequently denied dimensions of the national security state should lead Americans to be generally skeptical of government explanations of policies and past events. Given the intricate and elaborate dimensions of systematic, widespread surveillance and domestic covert action against a diverse variety of political movements outside (and often within) the major parties—including left wing, post–New Deal Democrats in the cold war, and later opponents and critics of the Vietnam War and Central American policy in several later administrations—this process will inevitably be reflected in film and television narratives during the period, a dynamic this study attempts to describe.

More than an aspect of individual psychology, paranoia can be used as a method of social and historical practice: "At a simple level, paranoia is the belief that some kind of threat is both ongoing and imminent, and that the truth is being hidden from view. Yet, paranoia is also about understanding the world in terms of connectedness, indeed, perceiving it to be organized beneath the surface."[44] Paranoia thus becomes a reasonable kind of social practice as a response to unreasonable, manipulative, deceitful political power, demanding a responsive strategy not simply of skepticism or the attenuated attention which characterizes cynicism but a more total orientation toward power, one by which often powerless citizens can mediate their perceived relation to structures of power that do, indeed, threaten them in a variety of ways. Such a social practice of fantasied representations for the powerless is evident in the body of films and television programs discussed in the following chapters.

Suspicion of authority in the population, as manifested in related images in U.S. popular culture—especially in the examples of visionary cultural paranoia I am discussing here—reflects on the way government agencies and their enthusiastic media agents and cheerleaders address citizens.[45] Given the fact that most Americans know that the U.S. government, represented by its officials or specific agencies, routinely lies,[46] there are related dimensions of public complicity and denial involved in the governing process. Since, at one level, the public is complicit in being lied to, a sector of the U.S. population literally and willingly refuses the status of responsible adult citizenship, acquiescing in being "infantilized"—finding satisfaction and security in an illusory political process—and exulting in an alleged democratic system that is more a representation of democracy than a representative system.

## THE MASS MEDIA, DENIAL, AND INFANTILIZATION

The mass media, especially television, facilitates public denial and repression of the unpleasant and can easily be manipulated, thereby contributing to the infantilization of the public. Numerous observers, particularly in books and articles in the closing years of the Reagan administration (see chapter 6), noted the emergence in recent decades of a vast, increasingly homogeneous global common communications network, a new form of collective community united by the common participation in widely shared—and highly constructed—television images satirized in such films as *Wag the Dog* (1998, Barry Levinson). Joshua Meyrowitz has pointed to the special quality of television in creating a uniquely new kind of "shared arena."[47] In contrast to print media—which might serve specific needs related to personal identity—television is used for a wide variety of generalized needs, including companionship, escaping boredom, and passing the time. Where book reading might be used to enhance and crystallize one's internal reality, television is often used for "keeping in touch with main events in the world . . . as a means of monitoring external reality"[48]—or maintaining the illusion one is doing so.

Television seems to confirm the "reality" of events, which do not seem to have occurred unless shown on television. Thus, by maintaining control over what is "on" television, the public sense of reality is manipulated. In a widely discussed work, media critic Gerry Mander suggested that the whole system of relations between viewer and what is viewed approximates classic conditions of autocracy.[49] The content is selected by anonymous individuals from a large and unknown subset of information, according to principles which the audience remain unaware of.

A direct connection between heavy television watching and various other forms of addiction has been suggested. Empirical studies connect obesity and watching television, a sedentary activity that interferes with physical exercise. Hypothesizing a direct encouragement of addiction through television, Stanton Peele has suggested that it occurs "because it is a passive, consumer-oriented form of entertainment [that] depletes the . . . resources for direct experience and interaction with the environment in favor of vicarious experiences and involvements."[50]

Such conditions were never more evident than in early 1991, in the opening weeks of the Persian Gulf War. As reported on PBS's NewsHour at the time, the Times-Mirror survey indicated that 81 percent of those surveyed literally "could not pull themselves away" from the war coverage on television. What they saw was a combination of video-game and cheerleading anchor persons feeding censored, "reviewed" information to waiting millions in the viewing audience while retired military "hired experts" and former Reagan administration officials or CIA officers were asked to explain what it all meant.[51]

Yet, for all the illusion of participation in "reality" conveyed by television, its content is comprised of a highly constructed or selected series of situations and images that also function to create a sense of distance from what happens. The greater the distance, the easier it is to deny or ignore real pain, suffering, deprivation, and violence. Paradoxically, the further the audience is from events, the more dependent it becomes on the constructed images presented via television to know anything about the "events" or—in the curiously twisted lexicon of televisual society—"nonevents"—set up for television, such as most presidential appearances.[52] This situation facilitates what used to be called "lying."

## "GOVERNMENTS ARE RUN BY LIARS"

I. F. Stone—the independent Washington journalist active from the 1950s to the 1980s, whose *I. F. Stone's Weekly* was one of the few consistently critical and objective sources available during the darkest days of the cold war and the Vietnam era—once remarked in an interview that the good reporter must adopt as a strategy of reporting the assumption that "governments are run by liars."[53] Who in the United States does not feel he or she knows that government has lied in the past and continues to do so? Because the public accepts the fact that agencies of the U.S. government have the "right"—perhaps even the duty—to lie to protect national security, and that citizens are socialized to believe that even though they vote and pay taxes to support it, they do not have the right to know all the government's secrets, one's whole personal strategy of political alignment might well depend on whether one thinks the government lies "in our interest" or "for our own good."[54]

The critical alternative visions of film and television discussed in the following chapters represent ways minority discourses are recognized in terms of potential markets, yet they are also represented as "fantasy bribes."[55] While such cultural images help create and maintain further subcultures of paranoid discourse, cultural paranoia is also a rational response to infantilization and symbiotic public denial. Genuine citizenship, however, requires the ability to break through any complicit relationship with this dysfunctional system of government lies and public acceptance. Here the logic of paranoia as mediating response becomes problematic in that it can be self-defeating and self-deluding. Common opinions about government lying are not conclusive demonstrations of reality, though they create a kind of reality consisting of "attitudes"—predispositions as to how to behave or react toward persons, institutions, or issues. The extensive dimensions of government lying have been conclusively and repeatedly established in recent decades. Deception and denial, while endemic to the American system (as well as most others), paradoxically are also regarded as essential techniques in effective political leadership—a fact political observers as early as Plato noted breeding a kind of political schizophrenia.

## REAL CONSPIRACY: J. EDGAR HOOVER, THE FBI, AND THE CLANDESTINE HISTORY OF POLITICAL REPRESSION

The 1990s were called the "Conspiracy Decade" in the United States, but the label might well have been applied to the whole century. Conspiracy involves two or more people planning and acting together secretly for an unlawful, evil project, scheme, or plot. In part, the phenomenon of increasingly widespread cultural projection of plots and conspiracies might be seen as a fad or fashion, like horror movies at drive-ins. But it can also have deeper significance, reflecting profound problems with our political culture that cannot be blamed on Oliver Stone movies or Internet websites. More Americans than ever before in the history of public-opinion polling felt powerless. They did not trust—and even feared—their government; for many the pattern persists in the first decade of the new century. The growth and development of these opinion trends originated with practices of agencies of the U.S. government early in the twentieth century.

What has been known as "McCarthyism" since the 1950s might more appropriately have been called "Hooverism" after the man who rose to power based on the information contained in his immense card files on radicals, begun in 1919 and continued beyond his death in 1972. John Edgar Hoover ushered in what Frank J. Donner has called "The Age of Surveillance," in which the primary but unstated goal of surveillance and political-intelligence gathering by state agencies such as the FBI and domestic operations of the various services' military intelligence—at least until 1970—was not simply the collection of evidence of illegal activity for potential criminal prosecutions but literal repression and punishment of critics of the status quo in order to undermine and destroy social-change movements.[56]

In film culture, vague, paranoiac sensibilities—of things ominous and threatening—were repeatedly expressed during the same period and after.[57] While they underlay much of film noir in the 1940–58 period, they were also evident in science-fiction films and television.[58] Such themes continued into the 1960s in the striking paranoia films directed by John Frankenheimer: *The Manchurian Candidate* (1962), *Seven Days in May* (1964) and *Seconds* (1966). (I discuss these films in chapter 4).

With the waning years of the Vietnam War and the Watergate scandals in the mid-1970s, a new wave of conspiracy texts much more explicit than the oblique leftism previously seen in film noir emerged, suggesting secret forces at work behind the scenes in ways so complex that no investigator could effectively understand their importance, dimension, or extent. In such films as *Klute* (1971, Alan J. Pakula); *The Parallax View* (1974, Alan J. Pakula); *Chinatown* (1974, Roman Polanski); *The Conversation* (1974, Francis Ford Coppola); *Three Days of the Condor* (1975, Sydney Pollack); *All the President's Men* (1976, Alan J. Pakula); *Capricorn One* (1978, Peter Hyams); *The China Syndrome* (1979, James Bridges); *Blow Out* (1981, Brian DiPalma); *Silkwood* (1983, Mike Nichols), and in *Winter Kills* (1979,William Richert; re-edited 1983), the odd, darkly comedic parody of the JFK assassination based on a Richard Condon novel of the same title, such themes appear and reappear as visionary reflections of an underlying artistic/political consciousness that recognized the market for such film texts among the American public.

By the mid-1980s, warring conspiracies of the Left and Right were evident in such films as *Missing* (1982, Costa Gavras), *First Blood* (1982, Ted Kotcheff) and *Rambo: First Blood Part II* (1985, George Cosmatos) and its successors. The latter films usually portrayed loyal soldiers like Rambo (an organic vegetarian; an unbelievably skillful killer who has merged with nature to the point of invisibility, virtually impervious to bullets or the law of gravity, rising out of the mud and slaying hundreds of the faceless, evil "enemy") as being sold out by government bureaucrats, who had their own agendas and wouldn't let them win, who couldn't be bothered by a few troops left behind in some godforsaken prison camp or jungle.[59] A cultural subtheme of guilt effectively manipulated by the national executive in the Gulf War of 1991 was reflected in such films as *Clear and Present Danger* (1994, Phillip Noyce).

During the period, one can see manifestations of the "political unconscious" and visionary paranoia in public opinion and popular cultural reactions to what is perceived as nothing less than "state conspiracy"—the covert, repressive activities of the expanding national security state. Looking back at its hidden and often forgotten history in relation to popular culture, one can retrospectively conclude that conspiracy was not new. It had been standard operating procedure, a recurring preoccupation of the national government, military intelligence services, hundreds of local and state red squads and antisubversive units, and hundreds of thousands of members of such groups as early as the American Protective League during and after World War I.[60] From the Palmer Raids of 1919–20, through the attack by government agencies and agents against the Branch Davidian compound at Waco, Texas, and the 1996 "antiterrorism" act—enthusiastically endorsed by the Democratic Party's president—complex and largely secret programs of surveillance and domestic covert action against perceived "national security" threats to whatever the existing order valued have been almost continuous. In the past, these have included massive actions against the opponents of World War I and radical labor movements such as the Industrial Workers of the World (IWW). In the World War I era and after, of crucial significance to government activities was the involvement of the American Protective League, a private voluntary surveillance network consisting of hundreds of thousands of self-appointed guardians of order associated—as private "secret agents"—with the forerunner agency of the FBI, the Justice Department's General Intelligence Division (GID).[61] This volunteer program involved at least three hundred thousand men and women—possibly attaining a million members at its peak in 1919, including those lower-level company informers who were not aware of the overall shape of the organization but played crucial roles as informants.

As historian Joan M. Jensen has made clear,[62] the extent and competence of the American Protective League in supplying information to the GID led IWW leaders to believe their organization had been thoroughly infiltrated, though it actually hadn't. Utilizing its own operatives and other patriotic vigilante groups, the government similarly collected immense amounts of data on the American Socialist Party, emerging communist groups, anarchists, attorneys representing these groups, and journalists who criticized such repressive policies. It may possibly even have instigated campaigns to destroy Socialist Party and local newspaper offices and printing presses, hounding organizers and radical opponents of government polices to death—sometimes literally—in a period of what outwardly appeared to be "indigenous" vigilante terror against both the Socialists and the IWW.

The contours of such government and military surveillance and state conspiracy were traced, over a period of nearly seventy-five years, in two detailed surveys: Frank Donner's study *The Age of Surveillance* and Robert Justin Goldstein's *Political Repression in Modern America.* Especially revealing throughout this historical period was the use of military-intelligence agents against the domestic civilian Left from 1917 to 1970.[63] The first revelations of such long-term programs of massive military surveillance of civilians were made in 1970 by ex-Captain Christopher H. Pyle, a former Army intelligence officer who had been a political science graduate student at Columbia. Pyle published two articles in *Washington Monthly* that caused a firestorm of congressional criticism, formal hearings, and purportedly the total destruction of the twenty million files in the name-and-data archive at Fort Holabird, Maryland.[64] If history is any guide, such destruction is doubtful. In Donner's view, "copies of the Army collections have [probably] been secretly retained by intelligence agents and added to other file holdings. . . . [J]udging from the past, the Army files have surely been acquired by private agencies to augment collections originally built through the same process of clandestine acquisition."[65] While the observation might be true, the potential future utility of any such historical data is rather questionable, based as it was on such variable criteria as individual judgments of agents and hearsay testimony.

The period of military surveillance of civilians up to 1941, with some brief references to the post–World War II to Watergate eras, has been surveyed by Roy Talbert Jr.[66] A former military intelligence officer while attached to the Pentagon in the early 1970s, Talbert compiled a comprehensive (and "classified") study of dimensions of military surveillance of civilians after 1957. It has never been declassified, nor, according to Talbert, has it ever been located by scholars. Whether it still exists or was destroyed when the Army allegedly destroyed much of its post–World War II surveillance data after Senator Sam Ervin's Constitutional Rights Subcommittee hearings remains unclear. It now seems certain that Donner's misgivings had some justification—reports of use of military-intelligence agents to carry out surveillance of demonstrators against the World Trade Organization meetings in Washington, D.C., in April 2000 circulated at several Internet sites.[67] All this historical surveillance and its ramifications are further described by both its victims and practitioners, whose descriptions help to delineate the immensity of the extent of FBI surveillance after 1939.[68]

Coextensive government/private conspiracies may have existed, for example, against Democratic Congressman Marion Zionchek, who had criticized the FBI in speeches in the House in the first two terms of the New Deal. Zionchek, known as "The Wild Man from Washington," described himself as a "radical" and friend of the labor movement. In a dramatic moment in April 1936, he made an impassioned speech on the floor of the U.S. House of Representatives in which he denounced J. Edgar Hoover himself. Shortly after this speech, Representative Zionchek was kidnapped, forcibly institutionalized, held incommunicado in D.C.-area mental clinics, and was worked on by some of the leading psychiatric professionals of the day. A few weeks later, after returning to Seattle, he fell (or, some suggest, was pushed) to his death from the window of his fifth-floor office in the Arctic Building in downtown Seattle. According to contemporary newspaper accounts, this occurred after he was released from his forced imprisonment and intensive treatment—for an undisclosed illness—in D.C.-area mental institutions.

In a case not immediately connected to this one, Frances Farmer, liberal Hollywood actress and supporter of progressive causes—like Zionchek also originally from Seattle—was permanently politically demobilized through similar confinement in mental hospitals, where, sometime in the late 1940s, she was eventually lobotomized. In researching a book on Frances Farmer, reporter William Arnold uncovered several informants, including a man claiming to be Congressman Zionchek's former bodyguard, who alleged that Zionchek had been "murdered" as a result of a conspiracy that involved the FBI and a shadowy group known as the Patriotic Vigilantes of Washington, who had later also targeted Frances Farmer. (Farmer's case and the popular film based on her life is discussed in chapter 6.)[69]

That such surveillance and covert action continued—and came to be a common experience—for thousands of leftists in the United States from the late 1930s through the 1950s, has been described, for example, by Griffin Fariello, Joel Kovel, and David Caute. According to Caute's biography of blacklisted director Joseph Losey, the latter left the United States for England to be able to continue his directing career.[70] Losey's example, plus the Zionchek and Farmer cases—a body of literature known largely to older leftists and a few historians—suggest the relentless complexity and vast extent of the FBI network of observers/informers and other surveillance and information-gathering activities against designated leftists, beginning in the late 1930s and continuing throughout the cold war years. (The political context of the intense repression of the 1940s and 1950s is discussed in chapter 3).

In the 1960s and '70s, in addition to FBI efforts, the CIA operated a domestic-surveillance program of infiltration and covert action described by Angus Mackenzie in his 1997 book *Secrets.*[71] Surveillance of pop musician-composer John Lennon is related by Jon Weiner,[72] whose research and publications on Lennon and related cases and issues continues.

In the 1980s extensive repressive surveillance of opponents of the Reagan administration's Central American policies was undertaken by the FBI.[73] One is also reminded here—to cite a related and continuing example of bipartisan collusion and cover-ups—of the failure of the Clinton administration to admit the extent of U.S. covert military involvement in the El Salvador civil war of 1979–92. That was a period in which U.S. troops were officially *not* involved in the war—only fifty-five actual U.S. advisers supposedly being present in El Salvador—though any observer who has carefully studied the situation knows the United States was paying virtually the total financial cost of the antiguerilla war and domestic terror campaign, including the salaries of probably hundreds of "private" contracted agents and advisers, mostly former or "retired" U.S. military and other operatives.[74] A CBS *60 Minutes* segment (May 26, 1996, hosted by Ed Bradley) ostensibly dealt with the failure of U.S. military veterans to get combat medals for flying huge C-130 gun platform planes over El Salvador during the Reagan and Bush administrations (1981–92); even conservative Republican Robert Dornan was interviewed in support of the men getting combat medals. But there was an interesting subtext to the segment in that it retrospectively confirmed long-denied dimensions of secret but overwhelming direct U.S. combat involvement. In numerous night missions, U.S. planes and active duty personnel, flying out of Panama, inflicted massive, devastating losses on the leftist guerrilla forces, killing hundreds—perhaps thousands—who were literally shredded to bits by the intense waves of firepower. While never acknowledged by the U.S. government nor by major U.S. media at the time, it was all carried out by, and under the direct control of, U.S. active duty personnel, whose involvement and decisive role in deciding the outcome in the conflict had not, over a decade later, been admitted by the opposing party's administration. President Clinton's cautious apology to Guatemala, while on a visit there in 1999, for decades of support of repressive regimes in that country—going back to the coup the CIA engineered in 1954—was really a grudging and belated admission of decades of denial by eight U.S. national executives.[75]

Further examples might include the government's handling of the standoff against the Branch Davidian complex at Waco, Texas, in 1992–93, which has been documented in several studies and films—in particular the profoundly disturbing *Waco: The Rules of Engagement*—and was the subject of a follow-up investigation by special prosecutor former senator John Danforth.

Throughout the 1990s, conspiratorial right-wing militia movements grew; some were victims of government repression, while others were victims of their own delusions.[76] U.S. government treatment of opponents at Ruby Ridge, Idaho—the assassination of the wife of separatist Randy Weaver remains a defining event for many rightist anti-government activists—and the events at Waco—demonstrated how ruthlessly violent federal agents could be when their rigid, self-imposed secret agendas and deadlines—known only to themselves—were carried out.[77]

In these and thousands of other cases, one could easily conclude that paranoia concerning perceived conspiracy by government agencies was not delusional but logical, given the actual experiences of victims and documented lies and deceptions of the government. Such deceptions—perhaps endemic to centralized government—will continue to breed suspicion, contempt of authority, and, ultimately, a popular paranoia that, while commonly deprecated, is in many ways an understandable response to government deceit and secrecy. This routine practice, though denied, over half a century of U.S. national administrations and programs, is reflected in and represented by the substantial body of films discussed in succeeding chapters.

# Film Politics

*It is not as mirrors reflect us but rather as our dreams do that movies most truly reveal the times.*

—*Barbara Deming,* Running Away from Myself

Exploring the film politics here described as visionary paranoia involves an examination of how movie images attempt to make political statements, have political consequences, or are experienced and used by viewers to construct political meaning.

Anyone who has ever seen the film *Thelma and Louise* (1991, Ridley Scott), can identify with the efforts of the two central characters to free themselves from the past, which is crucial to the film's narrative. The audience reacts profoundly to the scene outside the country music bar, where Louise (Susan Sarandon) impulsively pulls a gun from her bag and shoots the drunken cowboy pawing—apparently trying to rape—her friend Thelma (Geena Davis). While of shocking impact for the ordinary viewer, for those who strongly identify with the long, painful struggle of women for sexual and personal autonomy the act is, though violent, also an exhilarating moment of exultation, where a crude form of justice is finally restored. In this sense it is one of the most emotionally cathartic images in any film of recent decades. The shooting can be seen as a "political" act, as can the audience response. The act can also be seen in terms of sexual politics, that is, as an example of *gender paranoia.* Louise's experience of a violent rape in the past shaped her view of all males, justifying for her the use of a gun as a means of self-defense and of retributive violence. She provides a "substitute" image for members of the audience, vicariously expressing what some of them might wish they had the courage to do—acting politically—through her image.

As an exploration of such political meanings, uses, and functions of cultural images and narratives in film, this study confronts two important and quite basic questions: How do films represent such political themes? How do such films and their images influence politics? Among film critics, Robin Wood views movies "as at once the personal dreams of their makers and the collective dreams of their audiences, the fusion made possible by the shared structures of a common ideology."[1] In this sense, the films representing conspiracy and paranoia can be interpreted as "collective nightmares." In Wood's sense, as expressed in his acclaimed essay on the horror film," the conditions under which a dream becomes a nightmare are that the repressed wish is, from the point of view of consciousness, so terrible that it must be repudiated as loathsome, and that it is so strong and powerful as to constitute a serious threat." More broadly, he has suggested that writing about movies from a political standpoint means demonstrating how the films under analysis reflect and "dramatize, as they inevitably must, the conflicts that characterize our culture: conflicts centered on class/wealth, gender, race, [and] sexual orientation.[2] Such insights carry forward perspectives traceable back to not only Marx but especially to psychological perspectives of Freud and Jung.

Bertolt Brecht once said that "if art reflects life, it does so with special mirrors."[3] Historically American movies have represented political themes through a variety of very special mirrors. During Brecht's stay in Hollywood from 1942 to 1947, he observed that the hundreds of European émigré filmmakers and screenwriters in the movie capital were somehow expected to decipher the hidden needs of the mass audience of American filmgoers (when the movies truly were the mass media of the day), and, through the imagery presented in the movies, to discover or devise for them—at least symbolically—ways of fulfilling those needs and unacknowledged desires. Brecht described this as the screenwriter's task of "delivering the goods" in what he perceived to be a network of "buyer and seller, master and servant," surrounded by hierarchies of "experts and agents."[4]

Before he fled the United States—after being hauled before the House Committee on Un-American Activities (HUAC) on the morning of October 30, 1947—Brecht, the ultimate outsider, was, like scores of other members of what was dubbed the "club for discontented Europeans," simply trying to make a living in Hollywood but failing to achieve financial success or even subsistence. One of his "Hollywood Elegies" expressed the view that no really *serious* artist would work in Hollywood for any reason but money:

> Every day to earn my daily bread
> I go to the market, where lies are bought,
> Hopefully
> I take up my place among the sellers.[5]

While Brecht didn't "make it" in Hollywood, many others—including some of his close associates in Hollywood—did effectively fulfill the demands (according to Brecht's vision) of an insane system of executives screaming at writers and directors to "deliver the goods," to divine the public's secret desires and imagistically fulfill their needs in the dream factories. They did so, Fredric Jameson has argued, by tapping into "the political unconscious," every film text being, in Jameson's view, at its most fundamental level a kind of political fantasy, a deep psychological manifestation of human hopes and repressed fears, articulating the actual and potential social relations that constitute individuals in this society.[6]

Oliver Stone's version of the Kennedy assassination certainly did not create nor even affect the skeptical views of a majority of the American public about "official" explanations of the JFK killing. In fact, 80 percent of those responding to variants of the question "Do you feel Lee Harvey Oswald had accomplices, or did he do it [shoot President Kennedy] alone?" believed it was a conspiracy (ABC News/*Washington Post* public opinion survey, November 1983). Only 13 percent of the national sample felt Oswald did it alone. Stone's film was only seen by 9 percent of national samples in 1992 surveys, and those respondents indicated that their opinions had not changed a great deal after seeing the film. Clearly, Stone's film was *projected into* a market already predisposed to believe in its imagery of conspiracy, one that viewed the particular event and its aftermath as part of a more basic cynicism about the relation of the government to its citizens.[7]

Expressing or attributing political meaning in movies is a problematic and contested process. Films are political in two senses, as Stuart Samuels has pointed out. They may *reflect* as well as *produce* ideology: They "reflect, embody, reveal, mirror, symbolize" through "reproducing (consciously or unconsciously) the myths, ideas, concepts, beliefs, images of an historical period."[8] This may be evident either in themes and content or through the techniques or forms of the text. The production of ideology emerges through the creation of a unique expression of reality, a portrait of a reality that arrests the attention of viewers and remains in their minds.

Any film can function in political ways even though its primary intention may be to entertain. Precisely why and how does a film entertain an audience? How does it arrest the attention of viewers, thereby entertaining them? On one level, all films are "determined" by the ideology of its creators—not simply the particular "director" or "producer" but all those whose creative talents, ideas, and perspectives are "encoded" or incorporated into the complex process that results in a so-called Hollywood product. In recent decades "stars" have come to play such a major role that they consider themselves the "auteur" of any given production.[9]

## Reception and Reaction

To speak only of the production side says little about the way the political content of any film is received by viewers: whether its particular political or ideological meanings and messages are recognized, accepted, modified, or rejected by the audience.[10] At the level of action or behavior, what do the viewers/readers do with, or how do they act upon, the messages perceived? Specifically, if characters and roles are seen as prototypes of social roles and attitudes at a particular historical moment, does the film present them in a manner that reinforces or critiques them? What wider social norms are evident or represented in a film? How is the representation perceived by the audience? What is the role of historical context?

### *INVASION OF THE BODY SNATCHERS*

Three separate film versions based on Jack Finney's novel *The Body Snatchers* (1954), spanning over nearly forty years, provide remarkable insights into the ways such texts both mirror and represent cultural trends and issues, as well as contribute images and thematic material to a reservoir of cultural resources continually being tapped and recycled.[11] Comparing the three historical film versions (1956, 1978, and 1994), of Finney's novel (as I have done in my classes for several years) effectively illustrates for students many of these issues. Samuels' revelatory essay on the first version, supplemented by J. Hoberman's discussion of all three, demonstrates some of these issues and their complexity. Each version—especially viewed retrospectively—provides insights into the era in which it was created, carrying images that could only come from a particular historical moment.

*1956*

The original version, directed by Don Siegel and based on Daniel Mainwaring's screenplay, was presented in wide-screen SuperScope, though it was not reissued that way on video and was not evident in repeated television presentations, thereby affecting the way the mass audience has subsequently encountered it. Some interpretations (Samuels) seem to be based on the smaller-screen version, particularly with reference to the film's sense of being enclosed and contained.

The 1956 film is conventionally interpreted in a cold war context, with the pod people/body snatchers seen as a metaphor for the "communist threat." This view is insightful, given public opinion at the time, but also wrong in several important respects. Senator Joe McCarthy was preceded by the Truman administration's loyalty checks and red-baiting of Henry Wallace supporters in 1948—all part of cold war liberal anticommunism antedating McCarthy's taking up the issue in 1950. A study by Harvard professor Samuel Stauffer, published in 1955, uncovered some terrifying national trends. According to Stauffer, 52 percent of a national sample polled favored imprisoning all communists, while 80 percent wanted to strip them of their citizenship.[12] Another poll conducted in 1952 had shown 77 percent of respondents agreeing that all communists should be banned from the radio. Hostility to minority views was not confined to communists: 45 percent would not allow socialists to publish a newspaper and 42 percent wanted to deny the press the right to criticize the "American form of government.[13] The 1956 version provides remarkable glimpses into pressures and issues of the time. Conformity, red scares, conspiracy, and paranoia are all represented, but so is the fear of loss of individuality in a mass society and in the emerging big corporations. Seen retrospectively, the images of authority in the 1956 film are hilariously naïve: the FBI is asked to stop an epidemic whereby people are being transformed into alien beings who are their exact duplicates, hatched from gigantic seedpods. The process is somehow initiated when seeds, "floating though space," descend to earth, germinate, and take root "in a farmer's field."

Gender politics of the 1950s are also evident in the film, striking present-day audiences as virtually medieval, almost literally from another planet. Men order women about—it doesn't matter whether they are human or pod people—illustrating how gender stereotypes transcend the solar system and alternate life forms. The women seem to have no occupations at all, except for one nurse and a woman who wipes the car windows at her husband's gas station. Women are presented as physically weak, overemotional, and with no apparent volition except to serve their men—or pod men. There are no minority ethnic groups in the little community of "Santa Mira," located in Northern California; everybody in the cast is a WASP. What the film *does* effectively capture is the pressure on individuals of the era to conform—or suffer the consequences. This overwhelming pressure to conform was also evident in C. Wright Mills' sociological classic *White Collar,* the paperback edition of which was published the same year as the film.[14]

*1978*

The 1978 remake, directed by Philip Kaufman with a screenplay by W. D. Richter, reflects the profound transformation in sex roles in society during the intervening twenty-two years. Women are shown playing much more central and productive occupational roles in the San Francisco of 1978. They run the family business in the case of the writer Jack Bellicec (Jeff Goldblum) and his wife, Nancy (Veronica Cartwright), who manages the bathhouse. In the 1956 film version, Jack Bellicec (King Donovan) was a mystery writer, while his wife Teddy, or Theodora (Carolyn Jones), mainly screamed and acted distraught. Elizabeth Driscoll (Brooke Adams) is now not a divorcée at loose ends but a health department technician only slightly below her boss, Matthew Bennell (Donald Sutherland), who has experienced an upgrade in status from small-town general practitioner to public employee in a major city. The rich ethnic diversity of the city is also evident. Political authority seems more remote, though still, in the case of the police, in the hands of the pods. Generalized paranoia is represented in all crowd shots as people stare blankly at the camera and at other characters. An added amusing aspect is the recognition of the hypnotic effect of television over the decades; Elizabeth Driscoll's partner, Geoffrey, is just as podlike while watching TV prior to his transformation as after. The hip, touchy-feely pop psychology of the 1970s is effectively evoked in lines like, "What are you feeling, right now," spoken by Doctor Kibner (Leonard Nimoy), as well as in enforced hugs between a not-yet-snatched woman and her podified husband at a Kibner book signing. Don Siegel and Kevin McCarthy, both involved in the 1956 version, appear in cameos.

*1994*

With the arrival of the third version, *Body Snatchers* (Abel Ferrara), now set on a Southern military base in the aftermath of the Gulf War, several important new dimensions were added, reflecting the concerns of the era. One sees further evidence of changes in American society reflected in the transformation of the family, with the film's "blended" family consisting of Dr. Malone (Terry Kinney) and his second wife (Meg Tilly), with their step-daughter, Marti (Gabrielle Anwar), replacing Miles (Kevin McCarthy) and Matthew Bennell (Donald Sutherland) as the central character. The cast is still largely white, though African-American Forest Whitaker is added as the camp psychiatrist, and many black military personnel appear. The growth of the youth market is reflected in the choice of Anwar as the main character; she must be all of sixteen if one reads the plot correctly, but she looks even younger. She is involved romantically—and rather implausibly—with a veteran helicopter pilot who must be in his mid- to late twenties. The film is a teenage paranoia vehicle, with every adult and even her preschool half brother being a suspect. The conformity theme, so strong in the 1956 version, is reasserted in a striking classroom scene where the little brother encounters homogeneous pod children who all produce identical finger paintings. The podification of the base commander's acutely alcoholic wife—first seen passed out on the couch—is marked by her sudden sobriety and her wish to join "the girls" for a game of bridge, a game her punk daughter says she doesn't even know how to play. The screenplay astutely plays on the similarities between military discipline and podification by raising the question of how difficult it would be to discern whether highly disciplined troops were actually "snatched." The pod people here are linked to some kind of environmental toxicity. Doctor Malone, a government environmental scientist, comes to the base to assess toxic waste buildup. The coconutlike pods, seemingly connected to toxicity in a swamp, are harvested by the podified troops and placed near their victims, who are entered with long tendrils that snake into bodily orifices and then leave a husk that disintegrates in marvelous special effects. The podification conspiracy here is linked to the whole military establishment, utilizing its bases as steppingstones and its networks as ways to spread the pod disease throughout the country. J. Hoberman has suggested that in its references the film even exceeds Oliver Stone's vision in *JFK,* with a systemwide conspiracy of aliens so immense one cannot tell where it ends.

While all three versions play off the universal fear of losing one's identity, central to all three—and the defining aspect of the plot—is the continued use of the Capgras delusion, the fear that one's closest associates and relatives are not who they appear to be, that they have been taken over by somebody or some*thing* else. This notion is a particularly arresting theme in several sci-fi features of the 1950s, such as *Invaders from Mars* (1953, William Cameron Menzies) and *I Married a Monster from Outer Space* (1958, Gene Fowler Jr.). All three evoke the potent paranoid terror of common networks of urban and government services—the gas and telephone companies, sanitation, and, above all, the police and the military—that are no longer trustworthy, having been taken over by aliens.

Each of these films provides useful and instructive examples of what Douglas Kellner has described as *diagnostic* and *relational* criticism: using film to diagnose social issues and conflicts, and using historical contexts to view or enhance the subtexts elements of each film.

## Politics and Popular Media Culture: The Personal and the Political

In the chapters that follow I will explore how popular films (and selected television programs) consumed by Americans, especially through their use of what I term "substitute imagery,"[15] serve as an important way in which individuals and the wider public identify, name, and satisfy some of their deepest psychological needs and desires, as well as their anxieties and their hopes.

Psychological categories are frequently employed because they have essentially become *political* categories, though they can also be used to demean, "psychologize," and consequently reduce genuinely political impulses to issues of medical or emotional health and mental illness. This is the case with the uses of the term "paranoia." For the last half century traditional distinctions between individual psychology, on the one hand, and political and social philosophy on the other, have become obsolete. As Herbert Marcuse once remarked, "Formerly autonomous and identifiable psychical processes are being absorbed by the function of the individual in the state—by . . . public existence." Thus issues that once might have been seen in psychological terms become political problems: "Private disorder reflects more directly than before the disorder of the whole, and the cure of personal disorder depends more directly than before on the cure of the general disorder."[16] This is markedly the case with respect to visionary paranoia.

Film can also function in many important ways as a type of political behavior. Film involves both "purposive" and "effective" dimensions of political behavior.[17] Purposive dimensions involve a sense of explicit intention, an instrumental usage by means of which one or more people somehow influence or attempt to influence the ideas or behavior of others. Given the structure of the film industry, unless the financial backers or creative team of the film have a "message" they want to convey, explicitly political films have not been common, though many significant political films have been made recently, including *Bob Roberts* (1992, Tim Robbins), *Wag the Dog* (1997, Barry Levinson), *Enemy of the State* (1998, Tony Scott), *Primary Colors* (1998, Mike Nichols), *Bulworth* (1998, Warren Beatty), *Erin Brockovich* (2000, Steven Soderbergh), *The Insider* (1999, Michael Mann), and Stone's *Salvador* (1986), *JFK* (1991), and *Nixon* (1995).

During World War II, as Clayton Koppes and Gregory Black point out, in the United States there was a collective concern over supporting the war effort and a strong political will in Washington, enforced by programs and policies of the Office of War Information, all of which combined to enhance the common belief that "movies had extraordinary power to mobilize public opinion for war."[18] Paradoxically, as the same critics make clear, there was also extreme industry-imposed censorship in the very period movies reached their all-time peak in popularity. These dimensions are not accurately charted in film history since the literature and criticism is often confined to film texts and their reception. In contrast to the World War II experience, many critics noted the absence of films explicitly about the Vietnam War while it was underway.[19] As the war began to grow, one had to look to such films as *The Sand Pebbles* (1966, Robert Wise), which was set in a much earlier historical period in China, as an analogue to events in Vietnam, even though that film did contain oblique, though pointed, critiques of U.S. imperialism. Aside from such notorious rightist texts as *The Green Berets* (1968, John Wayne, Ray Kellogg), it was only *after* the war—when public opinion overwhelmingly held the view that U.S. involvement had been a mistake—that big, well-financed film productions were undertaken, including *The Deer Hunter* (1978, Michael Cimino), *Apocalypse Now* (1979, Francis Ford Coppola), *Platoon* (1986, Oliver Stone), and *Born on the Fourth of July* (1989, Oliver Stone).[20]

There is commonly perceived to be a unique quality of movies (also true of some types of music) to "create" a kind of spontaneous collective identity or to facilitate the investment of people's psychological energies. In this way movies might be considered a form of "effective" political behavior. Effective political behavior, in contrast to purposive behavior, exerts an influence, intended or otherwise. While not a specifically political example, Alfred Hitchcock's *Psycho* (1960) instilled in millions of viewers a fear of taking showers while alone in a house. Janet Leigh, the victim in the famous shower scene, has said that ever since appearing in the film, she has made certain the doors were locked when taking a bath.

At some point in the 1980s, characters—usually men—dressed in black began to be utilized in movies to represent repressive governmental power and the ability to get away with virtually anything. One of the first examples I can recall occurs in a relatively obscure film entitled *Flashpoint* (1984, William Tannen), the story of two Border Patrol agents, played by Kris Kristofferson and Treat Williams, who find a jeep with 1963 Texas plates, a skeleton, a Mannlicher-Carcano rifle and scope, and eight hundred thousand dollars buried in a riverbank near the border between Texas and Mexico. Their secret inquiries bring several men-in-black from Washington, current representatives of the secret group within the U.S. government that supposedly carried out the 1963 assassination of JFK.[21] Recurring images of such individuals in film and television made them part of everyone's consciousness by the 1990s.

Any popular film or TV show, as well as any aspect of popular culture, may serve a multiplicity of uses. Once a film or program is created, it is "set free" for use by anyone, including a psychotic Charles Manson, who took a song by the Beatles and perversely twisted its meaning to carry out his cultish 1969 murder of several people.[22] During the 1980s, Ronald Reagan's speechwriters tried to appropriate the songs of Bruce Springsteen, such as "Born in the U.S.A." Perhaps even more incomprehensible was the scene in a 1987 election-eve rally when Britain's Conservative prime minister Margaret Thatcher stood before several thousand Conservative youths, who joined together to sing a rewritten text of John Lennon's "Imagine," which had previously been considered a kind of anthem of (perhaps naïve) utopian visionaries.[23] Oliver Stone was unjustly charged throughout the 1990s with *introducing* through his films—particularly *JFK* and *Nixon*—what numerous critics said was unjustified fear, suspicion, and even paranoid delusions about U.S. government agencies. (These issues are considered in depth in chapter 10.)

## Unconscious Political Uses and Influences

Political themes in films may be openly expressed or felt unconsciously. Films, television programs, and news events are used by audiences, for example, in ways that mark points in the development of their own identities or group boundaries. Historically, in the 1950s, an emerging youth culture reversed the intentions of the ostensible anti-"delinquency" images in several 1950s films by identifying positively with the then youthful (and much slimmer) motorcycle hood, played by Marlon Brando, in *The Wild One* (1954, Laslo Benedek); or by identifying with anxiety-ridden and confused James Dean in *Rebel Without a Cause* (1955, Nicholas Ray); or by identifying with the mindlessly violent and destructive orientation of the high school hoods who smash their teacher's jazz records in *Blackboard Jungle* (1955, Richard Brooks). By the 1960s, of course, a full-fledged youth culture had emerged, contributing to the cultural resistance that characterized that decade. (This era is considered at length in chapter 4.)

In 1976 the young John Hinckley moved to Los Angeles. He wrote to his parents: "I live about three blocks away from the famous Hollywood & Vine corner and two blocks away from Sunset Strip." He went to the movies all the time. During its run at the Egyptian Theater, he said he saw the film *Taxi Driver* (1976, Martin Scorsese) fifteen times, even finding the book on which the screenplay was based and buying the record of the soundtrack. Like Travis Bickle in the film, Hinckley bought guns. If Bickle was making himself into what Gary Wills has called "some kind of Oswald," Hinckley wanted to impress a different public image: film actress Jodie Foster. Eventually he would shoot Ronald Reagan. Did the repeated viewing of *Taxi Driver* create in him the desire to kill the then president of the United States, "causing" him to shoot Ronald Reagan?[24] Millions have probably seen the film over the past quarter century, yet they all recognized in the Travis Bickle character the psychotic assassin-in-formation Robert De Niro's portrayal made him out to be. Hinckley's reaction was one in a million, yet it's still difficult to conclude the film "made him" shoot President Reagan outside the Washington, D.C., Hilton Hotel in 1981.

After the April 20, 1999, shootings by two students of several high school students at Columbine High School in Littleton, Colorado, it was noted in media reports that the killers had repeatedly played violent video games and (possibly) watched the images of killing in *The Basketball Diaries* (1995, Scott Kalvert). In that film—in a fleeting, almost subliminal, dream sequence—Leonardo DiCaprio portrayed a young man in a long, dark coat who killed classmates with a shotgun. It was suggested by several television commentators and other "authorities" on youth violence that the film influenced the behavior of Eric Harris, eighteen, and Dylan Klebold, seventeen, who killed twelve fellow students, a teacher, and then themselves. The film also supposedly provided models of dress for possible high school terrorists—conceivably creating the "trench coat mafia"—and even "caused" the Colorado events, it was suggested, through a process of modeling or conditioning. This was the argument of a former army Ranger and paratrooper, Lt. Col. Dave Grossman, who once taught psychology at West Point and was the author of a book on the psychology of killing.[25] While in the military, his task was to train men to be more effective killers. On a segment of CBS-TV's *60 Minutes* program that aired three days after the Colorado high school killings, Grossman suggested that video games had literally "trained" the two young men in Colorado to kill. Yet millions of teenagers play such games and do not kill or engage in violence external to the image context of the video games.

It has long been a matter of debate whether the intentions expressed or "encoded" in any popular cultural text are received by its audience. The ways any text actually functions politically is a complex matter of analysis and attribution growing out of the essentially *interactional* character of text and audience. The meaning of any movie or text in popular culture is determined by the multiplicity of uses it receives. Aside from the two youths who shot classmates in their Colorado high school, none who saw the film in theaters or on home video killed anyone with a shotgun. Among forty-five students surveyed by the present writer, seventeen had seen the film prior to the Colorado killings but only two could confirm that they even recalled the dream sequence enacting the shooting. (Many millions subsequently saw the film clips on news and magazine accounts of the events in Colorado.) The images in the film are horrifying, but what they mean, and what the effects of viewing them might be, are open to debate.

Images in popular films and television programs speak to wider publics that may experience the information, feelings, and situations in them as their own; may accept only part of what they see and hear; or may reject or reinterpret them in accordance with their own belief systems. Such images of media culture—termed "substitute imagery"—help people to define themselves, to establish an identity and a style.[26] Popular films may be so used in creating a self-identity, a particular place in society, but the process is complex and difficult to chart.

Media images also provide the viewers with ways of managing their overlapping public and private emotional lives and in this way may also take on personal political implications. In the same way that most popular music consists of love songs, most films contain love scenes and relationships (now less universally heterosexual or only between members of the same racial group than in the past) that relate to intended "markets" and the shared experiences of people who view them. Most significantly, the love scenes and love interests of major characters relate to one of the most important functions of popular films (and popular music): the ability to give shape and voice to emotions that ordinary people have but find difficult to express with coherence and without embarrassment. As such, popular film assumes wider significance through the interrelation of individual and social situations, with personal categories becoming political categories. Because of this property—shared by other forms of popular culture—any film might also potentially serve significant critical and even radically transformative functions. Later in this study (see chapter 3) I suggest that the investigative narrative in detective fiction and films, especially in film noir and "neo"-noir, might serve as an analogue to radical social critique and analysis.[27] But the degree to which it does so significantly depends on the dynamic interaction between the work itself and the way it is received. This is especially the case with a film such as Stone's *JFK,* which uses the central character's investigative quest as a way to unmask the national security state. Or take the film *L.A. Confidential* (1997, Curtis Hanson), which, though set in the 1950s and seemingly a critique of police corruption in that era, might easily be taken to be a comment on the LAPD today or the American political system as presently constituted. Whether this was a conscious intention on the part of its creators—novelist James Ellroy, screenwriter Brian Helgeland, and director Curtis Hanson—is open to debate. Yet in this and many similar examples, the original intention may be less significant than what the audience gleans from it. That the film (discussed at length in chapter 9) speaks to the broader and more timeless issues of racism, police corruption, and public deception seems obvious. Its images certainly fall within Ellroy's definition of "noir" (in a *Salon* online interview) as "bad white men doing bad things in the name of authority."

There is in such popular-culture texts what Stuart Hall once termed a "double-stake," or dialectic. On the one hand, there is an effort by its creators to "contain" the interpretation of meanings to those encoded into any text. On the other, there is equal effort by those receiving it to invest that text with a meaning that may "resist" the one encoded by its creators.[28] The implication is that there probably is no authentically autonomous "popular" culture as such. It is all "mediated" and might better be termed "media culture."[29] This is not to suggest that popular and media culture is simply imposed upon the public by powerful media and culture industries. While cultural domination and cultural imperialism do exist and have real effects, there are important points and moments of resistance—even overcoming the intentions of culture industries and government propagandists. Defining the "popular" requires the search within any period for "forms and activities which have their roots in the social and material conditions of particular classes" of real people and, more significantly, express a "continuing tension (relationship, influence and antagonism) to the dominant culture."[30] In other words, popular and media culture is an *interactional process* within which tensions and conflict exist over what is preferred and what is to be transformed. This may range from themes that outwardly appear purely personal to broader conceptions of society. Both are evident in all types of popular films. The observer is here confronted with the problem of film "signification"—the appropriate methods by which to determine the meanings attributed to and the ways people use movies, especially in a political sense. Analysis becomes especially complex when one considers the multiplicity of ways popular films are mediated. First, what, precisely, is the "message"? Second, does the audience "get" the message? Does it understand the meaning attributed by the film's creators (to the extent it can be said there is explicit attribution)? Third, how does the audience "use" it? Fourth, how is the initial message structured or inflected by the systems of production and transmission or diffusion?

Popular films are, of course, only one among a variety of cultural commodities (in both senses of "use" and "exchange" values that Marx distinguished). People use such cultural commodities to define both their identities and a particular subculture or personal style. This common procedure involves subverting and transforming elements of popular culture from their given meaning and use to other meanings and uses. Movies can be so utilized because, among other things, they are commodities. Aside from the few films supported by public funding through grants, films would probably not be made if someone did not think people would pay to view them, thus making more money for somebody. Popular films serve as items of exchange, yet they also serve their audience through a multiplicity of their own real and potential functions, especially in their ability to contain the investment of a range of interpretations and assignments of meanings.

This process is not without built-in inequities that might seem to favor large corporations and mass media industries. But even they must operate within the constraints of "market" forces, though they exercise tremendous market power through products and advertising. Films that deal with the Vietnam War or the assassination of JFK are excellent examples. Anti–Vietnam War films were released after the war ended, when public opinion overwhelmingly felt that the United States should never have gotten involved.[31]

How are popular films a valid indicator of social attitudes or behavior? Unlike popular music, where explicitly stated intentions are significant indicators of the artists' or songwriters' intended meanings,[32] movies are the collective products of a complex production team, so the notion of any authorial "intention" or "auteur" function is more difficult to determine, though it is a common convention in film criticism to note the director and year of release after mentioning a title. People may frequent movie theaters or rent videos, but whether they are truly "reading" the film text, understanding what the filmic representations are "saying," or acting on those messages is another matter. Content should never be confused with effect.

Yet filmmaking and film viewing does, in many ways, function as political behavior. One of the most effective theoretical discussions of the political nature of film is that by Michael Ryan and Douglas Kellner.[33] Central to their argument is the recognition that movies and television have significant political stakes, given their potential role in "cultural representation." The latter can be understood as a kind of system of interrelationships operating to create "psychological dispositions," or attitudes, that result in particular constructions of social reality. Simply put, the images in movies and television simultaneously contribute to our understanding of what social reality is and to the universal conception of what the world is like—or *ought to be* like. In this sense, cultural representations or images might be said to sustain or undermine social institutions. Even such generalities embody a significant amount of social science of the past century and encompass diverse, often conflicting, perspectives.

Hollywood films contain "representational conventions" of form and subject matter that can serve ideological functions. How the conventional Hollywood product functions remains open to wide interpretation. Formal conventions, as noted by Ryan and Kellner, include such aspects as "narrative closure"—movies are expected to present a story that ends—and "image continuity"—things and people look roughly the same, or their ambiguities or transformations have a purpose—which can be terrifying, as in Roman Polanski's *Rosemary's Baby* (1968) or John Carpenter's remake of *The Thing* (1982). Viewers have also come to expect a "non-reflexive camera"—they see as all the characters see, through shot/reverse/shot editing. The reflexive, or "point-of-view" camera is used only briefly, for effect. Robert Montgomery's *Lady in the Lake* (1946) employs this mode throughout the whole film, to the point where it becomes an absurd, almost laughable exercise. A more effective use occurs in Delmer Daves' *Dark Passage* (1947), where the Humphrey Bogart character's face is not revealed until nearly midway into the film. When he is first seen looking into a mirror while contemplating the handiwork of the plastic surgeon, it is to considerable effect and with great impact on the viewer, who already knows and recognizes the Bogart film persona, but we can only hear his voice and see other characters looking at him for nearly half of the film. In Roman Polanski's *Macbeth* (1971) the reflexive camera is used to striking, quite bizarre effect, suggesting the faces of MacDuff's troops through the eyes of Macbeth's severed head. Martin Scorsese's *GoodFellas* (1990) begins with an extended point-of-view shot of a character moving through a nightclub hangout popular with the mob.

Further conventions with ideological potential include "character identification," whereby viewers see who the central characters are, identify with them, and—at least as the films are constructed—see things as they do. While the viewer might identify with the characters, it is often through "voyeuristic objectification"; for example, it is rare to stare openly at people engaged in lovemaking, but in a darkened theater all the audience members become voyeurs, observing people in ways they would not ordinarily do outside a movie theater or while watching a video at home. (This is not to ignore the appeal and use of the financially lucrative genre of erotic and pornographic films and videos, a subject beyond the scope of this study).

To create a "realist intelligibility," several filmic conventions may be used. One is sequential editing, which leads viewers to expect things to follow from what precedes, even when crosscutting to simultaneous action or using flashbacks. This was violated in *Pulp Fiction* (1994, Quentin Tarantino) when John Travolta's character dies and then is shown later—or earlier—without identifying the image as a flashback. Additional conventions include causal logic (the expectation of events happening "because of" something else); dramatic motivation (why things happen or why characters act in a certain way); and shot centering and frame balance (the refitting of the wide-screen image to TV-picture size—the latter being the way a large portion of viewers have come to know the films discussed in this book).

Such conventions, as Ryan and Kellner argue, may be combined to make rhetorical arguments that "project" rather than "reflect" particular worlds. In a sense, then, a film might be said to "construct" an apparent reality, seeking to impose on the viewing audience—which can, of course, accept or reject it—political positions and points of view that are masked through the skillful elimination of all signs of artificiality.

In any given film, certain "thematic" conventions are evident, including gender-role stereotypes, heroic male adventures, romantic quests, women's melodramas, the redemptive use of violence, racial or criminal stereotypes (which are often related). These thematic as well as formal conventions may be utilized in very different ways, depending upon the particular historical moment.

In *Media Culture* Douglas Kellner describes the technique of the "diagnostic" and "relational" critique: using history to read film texts and, conversely, using film texts to explore history. Historically this technique might be said to run the risk of what some critics describe as the fallacies of implied homology. For example, in terms of this study, paranoia in some movies can be taken to mean the whole society is paranoid—which is not my intention—though there are extensive indications of near-paranoia in public opinion. Another risk is encountered in overly simplistic varieties of "zeitgeist" criticism. For example, film noir might be described as demonstrating the social malaise of post–World War II America rather than a critical or oppositional minority discourse about direction of policy and political developments during that period.

In his classic work *From Caligari to Hitler* (1947) Siegfried Kracauer suggested that German films produced between the wars evidenced a fear of emergent chaos as well as a mass disposition to submit to authority, thus reflecting and engendering the passivity and antidemocratic attitudes associated with Nazism. There is certainly some basic truth in Kracauer's suggestion that internal psychological dynamics and conflicts might somehow be projected onto the movie screen, but the analogies and homologies presented as evidence are much more complex and less direct than he suggests. Take, for example, his comments regarding *The Blue Angel* (1930, Josef von Sternberg): "It is as if the film implied a warning, for these screen figures anticipate what will happen in real life a few years later. . . . Their silent resignation foreshadows the passivity of many people under totalitarian rule."[34]

In his own analysis, Douglas Kellner suggests a greater complexity in the relationship between film and social developments, finding neither mirror images or exact analogues of the other. Instead, he sees a dynamic in which "films take the raw material of social history and of social discourses and process them into products which are themselves historical events and social forces."[35] He further suggests that although films can provide information concerning the "psychology" of an era—its tensions, conflicts, anxieties, hopes—"they do so not as a simple representation or mirroring of an extra-cinematic social reality. Rather, films refract social discourses and content into specifically cinematic forms which engage audiences in an active process of constructing meaning."[36]

## Discursive Transcoding

Central to the postulated relationship of film and social history in both *Camera Politics* and *Media Culture* is the process of "discursive transcoding," whereby images in films and television are viewed as becoming part of the wider cultural system that "constructs" social reality. An earlier, simplified version of this argument applied to all forms of popular art appeared in Alan Gowans' *Learning to See,* which suggested that popular culture "works" for the audience by providing "substitute imagery" of characters and situations with which the audience can identify.[37]

Yet the whole process of deriving meaning from movies remains largely interactional, a battle over contested terrain. Some viewers may take images provided by film creators as their own, while others may not. There is no clear-cut empirically verifiable relationship or connection between a single film, or series of films, "about" a particular topic, nor is there any clear connection between films evidencing aspects of politics, such as paranoia, or involving larger social attitudes or political movements. The fact that there might be an increase in films of what is loosely termed "paranoia" does not say much about the actual distribution of diagnosable paranoid schizophrenia in the general population nor, conversely, about the relation of that psychological phenomenon to the products of the culture industries, though the public-opinion data and cultural examples presented in this study are certainly suggestive. The whole process of deriving meaning from movies is much more indefinite.

The process of discursive transcoding arguably involves the internalization of discourses. Social life can be conceived of in terms of discourses that both represent the visions of cultural creators yet also shape the substance and form of human existence. Popular and media culture, considered as a type of discourse, is composed of a variety of "constructs—involving all forms of human relations and possibilities—gleaned from the broader culture and presented and re-presented in the popular media. These representations literally become part of the mental "reality" of a culture, providing, in a phrase coined by Walter Lippmann, "pictures of the world" on which people act.[38]

## "Visionary" Cultural Paranoia and the "Political Unconscious"

While they may prove entertaining to general audiences, the films discussed in this study can also be viewed as efforts to "see" connections—and an order—in what might outwardly appear to be chaotic, random social situations where events "just happen." Retrospectively imposing a category on what might seem a diverse body of films is hazardous. As an organizing concept, Fredric Jameson's notion of a "political unconscious" informs the present discussion largely in terms of the general notion that cultural texts present fantasies reflecting a "repressed and buried" underlying reality.[39] Jameson's approach suggests that through a society's dominant ideology, unresolved conflicts and internal contradictions arising out of the pursuit of the grand narrative of human liberation are *repressed.* Yet a careful study of literary and film texts—much like the psychoanalyst's study of a patient's dreams—permits an exploration and assessment of what might be described as the ideological coping mechanisms of the larger culture and society. Literary and film texts may be seen as *symbolic acts,* utopian dreams through which individuals might, in subtle ways, experience the contradictions and conflicts of society. The film text may not always provide an explicit commentary on social circumstances, but it must *represent* such circumstances enough to engage the audience. In this way, mass-culture texts, such as films, can be seen as "transformational work on social and political anxieties and fantasies, which must have then some effective presence in the mass cultural text in order subsequently to be 'managed' or repressed."[40] As Jameson has observed, "There is nothing that is not social and historical. . . . [E]verything is 'in the last analysis' political. The assertion of a political unconscious proposes that we take just such a final analysis and explore the multiple paths that lead to the unmasking of cultural artifacts as socially symbolic acts."[41]

The "visionary" notion used here, linked with paranoia in a largely rhetorical sense, originated in Carl Jung's distinction between "the psychological" and "the visionary" in literature. The psychological dimension is seen as representing the pathology of ordinary life, daily experience, and human feelings—which undeniably comprise the main content of popular media culture. Here one finds the usual interpersonal dramas and melodramas of love, sex, loss, and longing; most popular music is similarly preoccupied with such topics. The visionary dimension goes beyond such phenomena to represent, express, or reveal political dimensions not previously seen, known, or understood. While Jung's original context described a realm of religious and mystical experience, the emphasis here is on revelatory *political* qualities in works of popular culture. Hidden aspects of American politics; secret or denied events in the history of American life; fantasized, sometimes delusional, visions—all may be discerned in film and television images and narratives. In Jung's terms, such examples transcend the bounds of conventional "psychological intelligibility,"[42] illuminating dimensions previously unrecognized. In Jung's view, the function of such visionary works is to permit glimpses into the previously unfathomed.

While such visionary artistic revelations might be dismissed as illusory or delusional—the products of disturbed mental states—there is, Jung suggested, even in "the mental output of psychotic persons a wealth of meaning." The often frightening revelations in such visionary artistic creations are not merely symptoms; they can have a "*psychic* reality" no less real than physical reality. Such works arise out of the intuitions of their creators, which "point to things . . . unknown and hidden—that by their very nature are secret." What appears in such visionary artistic works, Jung and his interpreters suggest, is the *collective unconscious,* "a certain psychic disposition . . . compensatory to the conscious attitude [that] can bring a one-sided, abnormal, or dangerous state of consciousness into equilibrium in an apparently purposive way. In *dreams* we can see this process very clearly."[43] The examples of visionary paranoia in media culture explored in this study might be said to reflect, in the broadest sense, a *collective political unconscious.* They are representative glimpses of a repressed cultural counterportrait to the establishment's celebration of American society. Ultimately it is a story of denied realities, "dirty truths"[44] reflected in the media culture's films and television programs.

In an essay on the continuing mysteries of the JFK assassination—the beginning point of much modern conspiracy theorizing—Carl Oglesby described this particular variety of paranoia as a way of discerning the outlines of plots and of uncovering parapolitical relationships.[45] Embodying meticulous knowledge and skepticism, paranoia becomes a reasonable analytical strategy in a political system and culture that denies secrecy, plots, lying, disinformation—even assassination—carried out covertly by, or in the name of, "an invisible state."[46]

The "visionary" perspective on paranoia described here retrospectively seeks to illuminate images in film culture of aspects of this complex political/social system—dimensions forgotten, unknown, or hidden from the general population but widely known among a minority of historians, intellectuals, and participants in non-mainstream political movements, who possess, in Foucault's terminology, "subjugated knowledge" of its secret operations.[47] Such knowledge concerns political phenomena falling within the categories of surveillance, repression, covert action, and assassination, historically associated with less-than-visible operations of both public and private concentrations of repressive power. While the literature on such phenomena is extensive, it is not widely known among the general public and is often ignored or dismissed by mainstream news media as well as many academics. With the passage of time, a process of historical forgetting has created a political amnesia about the repressive policies of the past. Some familiarity with such practices is essential if one is to comprehend the cultural paranoia reflected in the films described in this study.[48]

# The Dark Vision of Film Noir

An exploration of visionary paranoia in American movies might begin with the body of films known as *film noir,* a collective style or mood in which urban America is depicted as a dangerous, dark, and insecure place—usually photographed in black and white—characterized by paranoia, menace, violence, personal betrayal, greed, lust, and the corrosive effects of a society based on the pursuit of money. Film noir virtually exploded in 1946 and 1947 with scores of films—that nobody at the time called "noir." Among all the various cinematic categories, it alone is an ex post facto rubric. Nobody knew they were making "film noir" when they started. The extracinematic history of the 1940s is largely responsible for the emergence of film noir. For many of its creators, it functioned as an oppositional, expressive politics; a kind of countercinema to the optimistic Hollywood product of the time. For others, including the audience, the style may have served unconscious functions. For still others it might have been simply a marketable fad—crime movies, mysteries, detective stories manufactured for the mass audience of the 1940s. The same qualities that proved entertaining to the masses might make the identical films appear as a dark, bleak comment on humans and human nature. Such complex and ambiguous uses account, in part, for the continued fascination of this distinctive American film style. There *is* something there, but what is it? If it is a film "discourse," it still remains—after more than half a century—also a contested, ambiguous aesthetic.[1]

As has often been mentioned in the literature, French critics defined the American product, but the process was largely accidental. In 1946 French audiences were presented with a group of exported American films following the lifting of wartime trade restrictions: *Double Indemnity* (1944, Billy Wilder); *The Maltese Falcon* (1941, John Houston); *Laura* (1944, Otto Preminger), *Murder, My Sweet* (remade as *Farewell, My Lovely* in 1975) (1944, Edward Dmytryk); and *The Woman in the Window* (1945, Fritz Lang). These films, seen by the French public—particularly Parisian critics—prompted their naming and subsequent theorizing about a new popular cultural phenomenon: *film noir,* literally, "black film."[2] The noir canon or myth—anticipated in France by domestic crime films and translations of American novels in the *série noire*—begins with these films and their bleakly critical view of American society, especially its women, its families, its decadent or corrupt upper classes, and its general take on human nature. Though all noir films do not necessarily exhibit these same characteristics, retrospectively it is easy to see a shared general sense of enclosure, suspicion, distrust, and outright paranoia—all wrapped up in an investigative narrative.

At its peak classic film noir mirrored the fear and paranoia of the Hollywood red scare era, first created as a result of the House Committee on Un-American Activities (HUAC) hearings on the film industry in 1947 and 1951. Hearings conducted by Senator Joseph McCarthy's Permanent Subcommittee on Investigations utilized characteristic name-calling, browbeating, vilification of witnesses, threats, and eventual blacklisting—all now commonly known as "McCarthyism."[3] Theoretical explanations and empirical exploration of this often-noted confluence is still inadequate. Taking as one's starting point a conception of radical and critical political implications of noir discourse, and viewing the style as a countermovement among a minority of filmmakers to the "American celebration" of the post–World War II period and, even more explicitly, as a cultural expression of resistance to the political and artistic repression experienced in those years, the way film noir cycle mirrored the red scare era can be more effectively traced. The precise mechanisms by which such social trends are reflected in film remain a matter of considerable dispute and discussion.[4] Douglas Kellner's suggestion that "films take the raw material of social history and of social discourses and process them into products which are themselves historical events and social forces"[5] might well apply to the cultural significance of film noir.

Richard Maltby once suggested that many writers on film noir "have identified a noir sensibility, traced it across a body of films, and then sought to attach it to a general America cultural condition of 'postwar malaise.'"[6] The problem with such an approach—a "*zeitgeist*" theory of film as cultural history—is that it is based less on the precise location of films according to the situations that led to their creation or consumption than on ingenuity in the interpretation of texts. According to Billy Wilder, nobody in the 1940s knew they were making "films noirs," nor had ever heard the term at the time. The category was first developed by critics *after* the creation of the first two dozen or so examples—and, with the burgeoning critical literature, projected back into the past. Amazingly, the first film actually initially marketed and advertised from the start as a film noir was Dennis Hopper's *The Hot Spot* (1990).[7] To admit such ambiguities—Mike Davis has described the Los Angeles roots of noir in *City of Quartz* as the "ideologically ambiguous aesthetic" of film noir—is not to deny there is a less easy to define "something" described by the term. That indescribable element is captured in Raymond Chandler's "streets dark with something more than night" yet it is also not simply "a process of historical distortion which comes about from the practice of generic identification, and has the effect of imposing an artificial ideological homogeneity on Hollywood production."[8] But what is the relationship between film context and film content? To what extent can one—following Douglas Kellner's suggestion describing the technique of diagnostic and relational criticism—use history to "read" films and read history from films, such as films noirs?[9] The answers to these questions demand a careful reading of actual, historical politics against film politics.

## The Noir Revival and Its Political Meanings

That the classic period of film noir (1940–59) continues to fascinate is obvious from numerous publications and video reissues.[10] As images and narratives of these films are continually recycled, and long-forgotten "B" pictures have achieved cult status, their meanings are also subjected to exponentially widening varieties of critical perspectives and comment. One can find in this body of films many examples of the distinctive American expressive use of popular culture as political commentary. Given the absence of continuing organized parties outside the traditionally sanctioned, largely pro-business Republicans and Democrats, such cultural politics has over time been the most consistent and recurring form of radical expression in the political culture of the United States. It has produced an enduring body of literature, film, and popular music that in many ways constitutes an alternative political tradition—although in a society in which one of the most definitive put-downs is "you're history," it may take significant education or reeducation to remind people of such aspects of their own culture.[11]

Discussing whether noir is a tendency, movement, cycle, style, mood, or genre, or (dismissively) "a slick new variety of packaging, faddish at the time and subsequently much prized by connoisseurs: a nexus of fashions in hair, fashions in lighting, fashions in interior decoration, fashions in repartee, fashions in motivation"[12] is a needless, increasingly tiresome exercise, given the extensive literature on the subject.

In order to discuss the political influences that may have shaped the style—and to reflect on its "politics" and political uses—a brief review of its historical periods and central qualities is in order. In its classic, or primary, period of expression in the United States—many French films of the 1930s and German films beginning in 1919 would fit the category, as several critics have noted[13]—

American film noir roughly extends from Orson Welles' *Citizen Kane* (1941), John Huston's film of Dashiell Hammett's *The Maltese Falcon* (1941), and, a year earlier, Boris Ingster's miraculous and lesser-known *The Stranger on the Third Floor* (1940) to Orson Welles' striking *Touch of Evil,* first released in 1958 and reconstructed in 1998. This first period perhaps ends with Robert Wise's *Odds Against Tomorrow* (1959)—one of the ultimate "caper" films.

Subsequent homages or pastiches based on classic film noir continued to be made, though now in color, including *Chinatown* (1974, Roman Polonski), *Night Moves* (1975, Arthur Penn), and *Farewell, My Lovely* (1975, Dick Richards). Each in very different ways represents some of the best films of the 1970s—and among the best of the "neo-noir" period. The 1980s and 1990s saw an explosive proliferation of films that can also be seen as "neo-noir,"such as David Lynch's *Blue Velvet* (1986) and Curtis Hanson's *L.A. Confidential* (1997). Ridley Scott's *Blade Runner* (1982) initiated the category of "future noir," continuing into the stunning images of Alex Proyas' *Dark City* (1998), one of the most remarkable-looking films of recent years.

## Visual Style

Noir may best be defined visually, though there are important narrative elements to the style. The noir "look" is frequently emulated, especially in television commercials, whose images are noir visual clichés and parodies. One of the distinctive aspects of film noir visual motifs is the *setting*—the underside of post-war urban America, often shot on location in identifiable cities such as New York, Chicago, Detroit, San Francisco, or Los Angeles—in run-down hotels, boarding houses, seedy lunch rooms and cafés, or back room hideouts in warehouse districts. A typical film noir might also include several of the following: low-key, high-contrast lighting; low or odd camera angles; use of wide-angle lenses and deep-focus techniques; nighttime shots on rainy, wet streets; use of windows and doorways or alleys and passageways as frames; extreme closeups of faces, often partly in shadow; fragmentation of images by intersecting shadows from venetian blinds, multiple panes of glass, or broken mirrors; flashing neon signs photographed through windows, alternately illuminating or darkening rooms or faces;[14] clothing might include fedora hats on well-dressed men, police detectives, private investigators (PIs), bad guys, news reporters; half-shaven men in wool topcoats or grimy (though occasionally clean and pressed) well-worn double-breasted, belted raincoats; women stylishly attired beyond their means, always in high heels, photographed holding cigarettes and often positioned provocatively while talking "tough." There are sometimes surrealistic dream sequences. Dreary settings were often contrasted with ritzy nightclubs, luxurious apartments, and the palatial homes of the rich, decadent upperclasses and the swank lifestyles of the criminal elites, who, if one reads between the lines, often manipulate the police and the political system.

This stylistic "look" of noir films was taken up in a variety of film categories, including the western (*Pursued* [1947, Raoul Walsh] and *Blood on the Moon* [1948, Robert Wise]) and the musical *(Love Me or Leave Me* [1955, Charles Vidor] and *Pete Kelly's Blues* [1955, Jack Webb]). The visual style of film noir, Alain Silver and Elizabeth Ward argue, "rooted as it may be in other movements and however much it may borrow from various genres, is essentially a translation of both character emotions and narrative concepts into a pattern of visual usage."[15]

Not all films categorized as "noir" share a common visual style. Such films as *Laura* (1945, Otto Preminger) and *The Postman Always Rings Twice* (1946, Tay Garnett, remade in 1981, directed by Bob Rafelson), for example, are so brightly lit and photographed in such a conventional style as to seem quite different in overall appearance from such darkly photographed noir features as *T-Men* (1947, Anthony Mann, with photography by John Alton), *He Walked by Night* (Alfred Werker and Anthony Mann, 1949, photography by John Alton), or *Touch of Evil* (1958, Orson Welles, photography by Russell Metty). Such other aspects as theme, mood, narrative—or simply conventions of categorization—may characterize them as film noir.

## Narrative Style

In terms of their narrative patterns and conventions, almost all the noir films have an investigative narrative that, like the narrative of Welles' *Citizen Kane,* creates a space for what Laura Mulvey has described as "the voyeurism of curiosity,"inviting the viewer into the solving of some kind of puzzle or mystery.[16] In addition, narratives in noir films of the classic era attempt to evoke the following: a sense of alienation and unease; a "dark," deeply pessimistic tone or mood; suspicion of authority; and a sense of people being enclosed, trapped, or enmeshed in a web of forces perhaps of their own making but now fated and beyond their control—all components of the commonly understood definition of paranoia.[17] These are magnified by the strategic use or threat of violence, which became increasingly evident as the style evolved in the 1950s and exploded in the neo-noir features of the 1990s directed by African-Americans, such as *Deep Cover* (1992, Bill Duke) and *One False Move* (1992,

Carl Franklin). Especially important for the potential political uses of the style is a narrative sense of *mystery*, of the influence of "something" buried in the past that can either grip or enclose like fate, or serve as the object of a quest for exposure or revelation. Of course, one can always find a noir film that doesn't exhibit all of these qualities—as in some of the semidocumentary crime films of the late 1940s and '50s—though the majority of films that comprise the central canon (three hundred to five hundred films) share several such attributes.

## VOICE-OVER AND FLASHBACK

Freudian psychology and the notion of the unconscious are key influences in film noir. The filmic narrative device of the flashback is crucial to film noir classics such as *Out of the Past* (1947, Jacques Tourneur) or *Murder, My Sweet* (1944, Edward Dmytryk) or *The Killers* (1946, Robert Siodmak). Though there are many noirs that lack them, the flashback and the related voice-over, usually spoken by the central character, are central elements of many noir features.[18]

The flashback can been viewed as a kind of visual representation of the unconscious. If the mind absorbs all sorts of information, becoming a kind of archive from which the entire history of each individual can be recalled, as it were, out of the past to elucidate or advance plot development, the flashback is its visual equivalent, able to represent or express feelings of guilt, regret, hurt, rage, or envy—and even to describe, from the point of view of the central character, the psychopathology of noir's pantheon of femmes fatales and some of its weird, twisted villains and antiheros. Most commonly the flashback is used to provide an explanation in the present by flashing back to events that occurred somewhere in the past. It is often a clarifying device, seemingly a way for the main character to explore with the audience something he or she still does not quite understand and wants the viewer to review one more time. This is the purpose of Robert Mitchum's voice of a dead man in *Out of the Past* or Joe Morse's voice-over in *Force of Evil* (1948, Abraham Polonsky). Notable voice-overs by women include Claire Trevor's character in *Raw Deal* (1948, Anthony Mann) and Joan Bennett's in *Secret Beyond the Door* (1948, Fritz Lang). Later, notable neo-noir voice-overs include Lawrence Fishburne's magnetic commentary in *Deep Cover* (Bill Duke) and Denzel Washington's in *Devil in a Blue Dress* (1995, Carl Franklin). (I discuss both films in chapter 9.)

## GENDER STEREOTYPES AND SEXUAL IMAGES

Noir films also contain striking gender stereotypes and sexual images, often presenting a binary view of women as either childless embodiments of sensual pleasures, "bad," even profoundly evil—the classic *femme fatale*—or, as "redeemers" who are nurturing, blandly attractive, but often rather conventional "good" women, possible marriage partners who look forward to creating "a family"—possibly with the central male character.[19] (These distinctive representations of women are discussed in greater detail in chapters 7 and 8.)[20]

Noir protagonists are usually single men emotionally burdened with betrayals or losses suffered somewhere in the past, often psychologically flawed or wounded and sometimes almost fatally incapacitated. Where, as detectives, they appear morally ambiguous or compromised, they still might attempt to do the right thing, adhering to some personal code. In the classic post–World War II period, they are often depicted as war veterans. Prototypically—at least through *Kiss Me Deadly* (1955, Robert Aldrich)—the central protagonists are private investigators who were once cops, best represented by film portrayals of Dashiell Hammett's Sam Spade and Raymond Chandler's Philip Marlowe. Chandler's character always demonstrated what seemed a chivalrous moral code in the novels,[20] appearing more ambiguous on film due to the diversity of screenwriters, directors, and actors involved in portraying him over nearly forty years. Later writers, such as "neo–hard-boiled" James Ellroy, argued that for the males in works by Chandler and his successors "the basic subtext is always *male self-pity*—I find the self-pity so thick that you could cut it with a gigantic bread knife."[21]

Among other noir private eyes, Robert Mitchum's portrayal of the doomed, fatalistic private detective Jeff Markham in *Out of the Past* remains among the most memorable. (I discuss the film in detail in chapter 7.) Humphrey Bogart's portrayal of both the Spade and Marlowe characters—in John Huston's 1941 version of *The Maltese Falcon* and in Howard Hawks' 1946 version of *The Big Sleep*—remain distinctive reference points for subsequent noir "private eyes," though the performance of Ricardo Cortez in the 1931 version of *The Maltese Falcon* (directed by Roy Del Ruth) is sometimes more engaging in its provocative sarcasm, seeming closer to Jake Gittes (played by Jack Nicholson) than Bogart.

Some form of cynicism—even fatalism—and hard-bitten wisecracking is universal among these PIs, as is their aura of compromised, world-weary morality. In the 1941 film version of *The Maltese Falcon* Spade/Bogart is not very surprised when he receives the late-night phone call informing him of the shooting death of his partner Miles Archer, coldly showing no interest at all in viewing Miles' body at the murder scene, and is even reluctant to acknowledge that Miles might have had some good points. Despite Production Code restrictions on such topics,[22] viewers might easily conclude that Spade had had an affair with Archer's wife. In the pre-Code 1931 version Spade/Cortez is even more sexually active, a real playboy, hustling women in and out of his apartment and openly discussing his sexual affair with Archer's wife with her while Archer secretly listens in on another line.

### THE INVESTIGATIVE-DECONSTRUCTIVE NARRATIVE

A key element of the political appeal of classic film noir is that the "investigators"—usually detectives, but also war buddies (*Dead Reckoning* [1947, John Cromwell], *Fallen Sparrow* [1943, Richard Wallace]) or a brother (*Force of Evil* [1948, Abraham Polonsky])—are on a crime-related mission to uncover what lies behind—to deconstruct—some implausible explanation provided to them to explain certain past events. These might involve the disappearance of persons, money, or valuable objects—and even deaths. While easily traced as far back as Edgar Allan Poe's stories of the mid-1800s, this aspect of the crime novel of the 1920s and '30s—significantly influenced by Dashiell Hammett's early Continental Op—became virtually paradigmatic in crime novels and films noirs of the 1940s and '50s. It was further developed in the 1970s neo-noir and conspiracy films (see my discussion in chapter 5), continuing into the 1980s and '90s with the darkly allusive films of David Lynch (*Blue Velvet* [1986] and *Twin Peaks* [1992]). Even Oliver Stone's *JFK* represents a continuation of this tradition, both politically and narratively, as his almost Capraesque version of Garrison tries to track down the assassins of the president. Moreover, *JFK* has significant traces of noir visuals in the use of flashbacks; the rainstorm; the dingy office in which the private investigator, right-wing former FBI agent Guy Bannister (Ed Asner) and his associate, Jack Martin (Jack Lemmon), appear; and the nightmarish murder scene in the apartment of David Ferrie (Joe Pesci), presented in almost subliminal flashbacks after his death.

This investigative-deconstructive element was especially evident in Hammett's creation, in his early pulp fiction, of the investigator and, by extension, public servants such as police detectives, district attorneys, or investigators on their staffs and, finally, reporters, whose task, as Steven Marcus has noted, is "to deconstruct, decompose, deplot, and defictionalize" the initial "reality" which is "a construction, a fabrication, a fiction, a faked and alternate reality."[23] This distinctive narrative quality of film noir appealed to leftist social critics as a potentially radical political form of expression, though it might also fuel paranoid or conspiratorial delusions. In the postmodern era of media fragmentation of images, the appeal of the conspiracy became an elusive search for political coherence and closure that was perhaps impossible to achieve.

Through often convoluted narratives, investigators continue on their quest—though for what is not always clear. *The Big Sleep* and *Out of the Past* are paradigmatic examples from the classic period of film noir, still puzzling viewers and critics a half century later. *Kiss Me Deadly* (1955) continued this trend, followed by the neo-noir *L.A. Confidential* (1997). The investigation might involve dark, complex, often hidden forces and conspiracies—revealing depths of corruption most of the audience would probably rather deny—which would result in scandals if publicized. While this process sometimes forced protagonists to recognize repressed and hidden aspects of their own pasts, it could also implicate higher levels of society—a quality that proved appealing to muckraking leftists, attracting later generations of left- and conspiracy-minded cineasts and subsequent generations of filmmakers. These qualities have been described by philosopher Dan Flory as the distinctive "epistemology" of film noir.[24] (This dimension is also explored in chapter 9, in relation to the "bad cop" cycle.)

Dashiell Hammett's central narrative theme, as Steven Marcus characterized it, dealt with "the ethical irrationality of existence, the ethical unintelligibility of the world. . . . [L]ife is inscrutable, opaque, irresponsible, and arbitrary."[25] Yet, most people live as if life somehow has an order and rationality to it. These investigators evolved throughout the twentieth century. First it was Hammett's Continental Op, followed by his Sam Spade; then came Bogart in 1941 on film and Howard Duff on radio; then Chandler's Marlowe in novels, radio, television, and many films; concluding with all the "private eyes" of the 1940s and '50s and their nostalgic recreations in later decades. In the post–World War II era it was often a public employee such as a police detective or a government agent. Or it might be an undercover agent, such as the double character played by Laurence Fishburne in *Deep Cover.* All these investigators begin by tracing out what happened, but as their initial impressions begin to unravel, they are forced "to construct or reconstruct out of it [the fabricated reality] an account of what really happened."[26] The narrative thus provides for viewers or readers what can be described as an "alternative system of knowing" and a "parallel universe of experience."[27] In the psychotherapeutic discourse of the late twentieth century, others might see it as breaking through "denial."

On one level of noir discourse, the audience is told things it does not know and perhaps would rather not know. But at a deeper level the protagonists themselves are represented as first having to trace out, discover, and then experience for themselves the nature of the largely unknown or inadequately understood systemic forces that either wish to contain or—more terrifying and exciting for the audience—eliminate them. An excellent example of this is the following exchange between Noah Cross (John Huston) and J. J. Gittes (Jack Nicholson) in *Chinatown:* "You may *think* you know what's going on here, Mr. Gittes, but believe me, you don't."

As Dan Flory has pointed out, the act of "acquiring, having, or withholding knowledge characteristically drives noir narratives."[28] This dynamic is evident, for example, in the sparring between Spade and Gutman over the meaning of "the black bird" in *The Maltese Falcon;* in Jake Gittes' obsession with past events in the "Chinatown" of the past in *Chinatown;* in Harry Moseby's insatiable quest in *Night Moves;* and in the meaning of "Rollo Tomasi" for Ed Exley, Bud White, Jack Vincennes, and Dudley Smith in *L.A. Confidential.*

Such hidden and withheld knowledge those in power might wish left unknown—yet becomes the object of radical and revelatory exposure—might, as Flory suggests, be broken up into several categories.

*The sort of information that lies at the base of so-called family life.* This might include incest, rape, family violence, and murder (often representing still more profound derangements in the social-political order), as evidenced in such films as *Shadow of a Doubt* (1943, Alfred Hitchcock), *Chinatown, Blue Velvet, The Hot Spot, Internal Affairs* (1990, Mike Figgis), and *Twilight* (1998, Robert Benton).

*Activities or relationships that must be kept hidden from the law.* These may snowball, expanding into complex, often disastrous, plots. Some film examples might include *Detour* (1945, Edgar Ulmer), *Quicksand* (1950, Irving Pichel), *The Big Heat* (1953, Fritz Lang), *Rogue Cop* (1954, Roy Rowland), and such later films as *Internal Affairs* and *Deep Cover.*

*Knowledge that endangers those who have it.* Some film examples here might include *Out of the Past, Desperate* (1947, Anthony Mann), *Night Moves, Chinatown, Kill Me Again* (1989, John Dahl), and *Red Rock West* (1993, John Dahl). This type of knowledge can lead directly to radical criticism, potentially subversive of dominant social, political, or economic structures and systems.

*Knowledge revealed, effectively shattering the "foundations of knowledge itself."* This potentially even more radical dimension of noir discourse may force characters in the narrative—and the audience through character identification—to change the way they see the world. *Force of Evil* and *Chinatown* are two of the best examples of this knowledge-shattering effect, though one can easily trace it back to Hitchcock's *Shadow of a Doubt* (1943)—or even earlier to his *Foreign Correspondent* (1940) and *Rebecca* (1940)—to Welles' *Citizen Kane,* and certainly to their predecessors in Weimar German cinema, who greatly influenced hundreds of European expatriates who came to Hollywood in the 1930s and '40s.[29] Among the films that provide examples of such knowledge one should mention *Crossfire* (1947, Edward Dmytryk), *In a Lonely Place* (1950,

Nicholas Ray), *The Stranger* (1946, Orson Welles), and even *Keeper of the Flame* (1942, George Cukor). The narrative elements—essentially "bits of subversive knowledge," to use Flory's terms—challenge viewers "to examine and reconstitute their own epistemologies, to fundamentally change their standard ways of knowing the world and how they live it."[30]

## Literary Sources

Dashiell Hammett, the father of hard-boiled fiction and the creator of the Thin Man and Sam Spade, was openly a member of the U.S. Communist Party, signing statements, donating money, and appearing for various progressive causes from the 1930s through the 1950s. Late in his career, while a trustee of a fund supporting the civil rights of radicals, he was hauled before the House Un-American Activities Committee in 1951 and was subsequently jailed for contempt after refusing to divulge what seemed to him confidential information about contributors to the fund. While Hammett published no novels for the last two decades of his life, he still pursued an exceptionally active career in the 1930s and '40s both as a screenwriter for others and in adapting his characters for screen and radio. One could even argue that his literary career continued in his role as the instigator and chief critic and editor—some say even coauthor—of the plays of his sometime companion Lillian Hellman. After his period in jail, his ill health—caused by acute alcoholism and exposure to poison gas during World War I—made him an invalid. He never wrote again, though his alcoholism was probably a much greater contributor to his subsequent silence than anticommunist political repression, which he consistently fought for over two decades.[31]

Raymond Chandler—another acutely alcoholic novelist who contributed to film noir—had an even bleaker view of human deceitfulness than Hammett, possessing a profoundly skeptical, cynical, even nihilistic outlook on social institutions. As Tom Hiney points out in his biography of Chandler, "all institutions were to be instinctively distrusted, all witness accounts doubted, and everything straightforward ignored. In the majority of Chandler tales, the story to the detective by the person who hires him turns out to be deceitful. . . . Ultimately, the only person the detective can trust to be telling the truth is himself. . . ."[32]

In addition to the usual "hard-boiled" writers such as Hammett and Chandler, Cornell Woolrich contributed bizarre, grotesque twist-of-fate elements to the style.[33] Among the Woolrich stories that were made into films noirs are

*Phantom Lady, Street of Chance, Deadline at Dawn, Black Angel, The Window, The Night Has a Thousand Eyes,* and *Rear Window.* Scores of novels, short stories, radio scripts, and screenplays poured out of Woolrich in the 1930s and '40s. Woolrich, an alcoholic and a reclusive bisexual, was so prolific that he also wrote under the pseudonyms of "William Irish" and "George Hopley," both based on his middle names. Dubbed the "Poe of the twentieth century and the poet of its shadows" by his biographer,[34] of Woolrich's over two hundred short stories and twenty-two novels, more were made into film noir features than any other single writer.

"Ellery Queen," one of the deans of mystery fiction, said of Woolrich that he "projects a powerful atmosphere of fear, shock and violence, and usually his stories end with a whiplash of surprise."[35] In the Woolrich/Irish/Hopley books and stories, there are bizarre, fatalistic occurrences and grotesque twists of fate over which ordinary mortals have neither prescience nor control. Many other films used plots similar to his, among them *The Wrong Man* (1956, Alfred Hitchcock with a screenplay by Maxwell Anderson and Angus MacPhail based on Anderson's book). As late as 1968, François Truffaut directed a striking French color version of Woolrich's *The Bride Wore Black.* Woolrich narratives and plot devices survived the author's death and were continually recycled without attribution. Numerous *Twilight Zone* and *Alfred Hitchcock Presents* episodes and other teleplays of the 1950s and '60s borrowed liberally from Woolrich. While it is difficult to find most of his books, many of which are out of print, they remain important influences on later screen- and television writers.[36]

The "structured sensibility"[37] of film noir—expressing a profound sense of unease, foreboding, dread, and paranoia—is usually linked to the hard-boiled detective tradition, but the Woolrichian tales of weird and grotesque coincidences are especially arresting, haunting the memory years after being exposed to their images, situations, and settings. It is probably no coincidence that these narrative threads also intersect with descriptions of alcoholic "blackouts," given the fact Woolrich, Hammett, and Chandler were often incapacitated by alcoholic addiction and experienced alcoholic amnesia.[38]

In addition to Hammett, Chandler, and Woolrich, several other literary sources might be mentioned, especially James M. Cain's novels *Double Indemnity, Mildred Pierce,* and *The Postman Always Rings Twice,* all of which became notable examples of film noir, in which adulterous marriages and the early deconstruction of the "happy family" ideology were portrayed. Foster Hirsh profiles such other novelists who contributed to the film noir style as David Goodis, Dorothy Hughes, and Patricia Highsmith.[39]

### FRANZ KAFKA

Franz Kafka's representation of and contribution to the paranoia that is the central psychological dynamic characteristic of film noir should not be underestimated. Kafka's fiction, which emerged in the United States in the 1940s and attained cult status among the cognoscenti by the end of the 1950s, left its mark on the consciousness of vast numbers of readers. His stunning images of tribunals, trials, and mazes of bureaucracy became passwords to the twentieth century. According to George Steiner, Kafka foresaw,

> in an act of clairvoyance more telling than explicit prophecy or political argument, the world of the death camps; he heard the knock of the faceless policeman on the night door; he saw human beings transmuted to vermin and swept into garbage. . . . No actual narrative of the Stalinist purges is more authentic than *The Trial.* No record of Auschwitz conveys so much of the obscene intimacies of torture and victim as does *The Penal Colony.* It is in Kafka even more than in Marx that we find the controlling insight of our historical epoch—the absolute extension to man of logic of mass production, the transformation of politics with their potential of anarchic challenge into the inertial, self-perpetrating motion of technology.[40]

## From Unter den Linden to Hollywood Boulevard: The Role of Expatriates

In the 1930s and '40s Los Angeles became the preferred destination of hundreds of European intellectuals and artists who were fleeing the terrors of Nazism and the coming war.[41] There was, of course, also the attraction of the mediterranean climate and the burgeoning film industry. German refugees enjoyed a success in Hollywood unmatched in any other area of American life. Their contribution was crucial in fashioning what came to be known as film noir. Indeed, the examples of film noir first noted by the French were largely the products of three émigré directors: Otto Preminger, Billy Wilder, and especially Fritz Lang. (Several other German and European expatriates should also be noted, such as Robert Siodmak, Edgar Ulmer, Curtis Bernhardt, Michael Curtiz, Jacques Tourneur, Fred Zinneman, Max Ophuls, and Douglas Sirk.) Each produced striking examples of what retrospectively has been characterized as the noir sensibility. By combining visual motifs—derived from German expressionist films with which they were identified or had created[42]—with American materials (screenplays and novels, locations, actors), they were able to "see" aspects of American life and illuminate them for American audiences in ways that would fundamentally affect the future of the American film industry.

As Brecht once observed, "Émigré film-makers—although the demand was not limited to Hollywood—were expected to decipher the Americans' hidden needs and discover for them a means of fulfilling them: this was called 'delivering the goods.'"[43] In delivering them, they presented what the audience thought were quintessentially American images but were actually critical representations of social reality lost on the majority. They contributed to film noir an enduring repository of images. For those who were able to decipher the often encoded meanings, they presented penetrating, even devastating, critiques of capitalist culture and society in America.

## FRITZ LANG

Fritz Lang was one of the greatest expatriate contributors to film noir in the post–World War II period of red-hunting in Hollywood.[44] Creator of *Metropolis* (1926), one of the visual masterpieces of world cinema, the German *Mabuse* series (1922, 1933), and the paranoid masterpiece *M* (1931), with Peter Lorre as the doomed child murderer—all were important forerunners of film noir. In the twenty years stretching from *Fury* (1936), which marked Lang's American debut, to *Beyond a Reasonable Doubt* (1956), Lang created—despite the limitations of the studio system—and using mainly American settings, actors, and screenplays—a stunning series of films[45] presenting a portraits of paranoia in a ravaged society where, as Andrew Sarris once put it, "man grapples with his personal destiny and invariably loses." A pattern of paranoia runs through Lang's films, beginning in Germany with *Mabuse* (1922), *Metropolis* (1926), *M* (1931), and *The Testament of Dr. Mabuse* (1933); and persisting thoughout the best of his Hollywood films: *Fury* (1936), *The Woman in the Window* (1944), *Scarlet Street* (1945), *Secret Beyond the Door* (1948), *House by the River* (1950) (discussed in greater detail in chapter 8), *Clash by Night* (1952), *The Big Heat* (1953), *The Blue Gardenia* (1953), *Human Desire* (1954), and *While the City Sleeps* (1956). Ironically, for a director supposedly serving a film industry dishing out dreams, Lang was far more likely to represent the nightmares of the mass audience. Through his studied construction of clinical and corrosive imagery (to quote Sarris again) Lang was singularly impressive in his "undercutting audience expectations of a moral balance regained."[46]

Flames and burning are prevailing images in many of Lang's U.S. films. Spencer Tracy, the hero of *Fury*, is nearly burned to death by a mob. In the gothic thriller *Secret Behind the Door* a woman avoids murder at the hands of her psychotic husband through psychological detection, only to have them both nearly engulfed in flames. In *The Big Heat* the wife (Jocelyn Brando) of detective Dave Bannion (Glenn Ford) is blown up by a car bomb when she turns on the ignition of the family car, though in the most memorable sequence of the film a gangster's girlfriend (Gloria Grahame) has her face horribly burned by boiling coffee thrown by a brutal killer (Lee Marvin), who is paid back by her with the same treatment. (This film is discussed at greater length in chapter 9.)

In his early study of the auteur's American period, Peter Bogdanovich concluded that "as a creator of nightmares Lang has few peers."[47] His corrosive perspective on society helped create a critical edge that stretched from his German creations through his American films. Geoffrey O'Brien has suggested that Lang made the same movie over and over, communicating "the same numbed unease from a murder, an embrace, or a moment of dead time in which someone looks out the window . . . with the methodical determination of someone compelled to re-enact a crime; or, perhaps, of a warden keeping his prisoners under close surveillance."[48]

For a brief period (1951–52) Lang believed he was a victim of the blacklist that others, such as Billy Wilder and Otto Preminger, had successfully avoided. Preminger's strong sense of public responsibility, learned early in his career in Germany, contributed to his hiring of a blacklisted writer (Dalton Trumbo) to provide the screenplay for *Exodus* (1959). Preminger's *The Moon Is Blue* (1953), distributed without Production Code approval, contributed to the latter's demise.[49]

The ironies of political fashion and the extreme shifts in the political environment in Hollywood from the 1930s through World War II were acutely evident to this expatriate antifascist German. As Lang put it in a 1969 interview,

> I was never a Communist. I was never a member of the Communist Party. I had many, many Communist friends. It was very chic during the Roosevelt time to belong to the party. When I came to this country, the Big Powers—England, France too—tried to appease Hitler, and what actually happened? No one really gave a damn about what was going on in Germany. Some of us saw it coming, but the only ones who were really opposed (we thought they were the only ones) were the Communists. That was one of the reasons why so many people here in Hollywood turned to the Communists—because they believed that the Communist Party was the only group really fighting the Nazis.
>
> During the McCarthy times many of us were accused of being Communists, which wasn't true; we were liberals. We were very shocked. . . . I knew [many of my friends] were Communists, but who cared in those days? The

most important thing was the defeat of the Nazis. That is why I made so many anti-Nazi pictures; it was, so to speak, my contribution.[50]

The case of Lang and numerous other expatriate directors who infused their films with visual motifs and elements drawn from German expressionism of the 1920s indicates how much of what is called "American" popular culture was a product of the intervention of external viewers, who genuinely "saw"—or even helped construct—aspects of its psychology. Their role, as Brecht noted, was to decipher our hidden needs and to provide ways to gratify them on the screen through substitute imagery—film representations in which the American public could recognize itself, perhaps subconsciously, and discern elements of its own complex hidden neuroses and repressed desires.

Such examples fused with developments in American society, becoming part of an emergent discourse of Americans experiencing the aftershock of the terrors of the era: World War II showed mass killings on a scale of tens of millions. After the war, the dislocation of nearly sixteen million U.S. men and women in uniform—the result of millions of women being rapidly mobilized into the war effort and then just as rapidly forcibly demobilized—created widespread social disorientation, which was reflected in the popular media culture.[51]

Beyond these developments, the death of President Roosevelt in 1945 was like the loss of a parent or grandfather for those who had elected him four times. The atomic bomb and nuclear energy brought completely new technological and military anxieties, associated with the emerging cold war. Although a significant political minority on the left felt manipulated by often cynical elites, most political centrists and conservatives opted to experience the promise and opportunity of the era. With the rise of cold war anticommunism and domestic red-baiting, however, many liberals and leftists missed the sense of political agency and possibility that had characterized the 1930s and '40s New Deal era and the popular front. In American culture there was now a general consensus on the desirability of raising a family, moving to the suburbs, and consuming new cars, houses, TVs. Eating steak for dinner was the single most commonly accepted indicator of prosperity in the era. (A Gallup poll conducted in 1948 revealed that a steak dinner with a baked potato was the first choice of most Americans.) In Lang's *The Big Heat* such elements reflecting the popular culture of the day are prominent: the main scene at the home of the detective (Glenn Ford) features him cutting and eating a huge chunk of blackened, broiled beefsteak prepared by his wife (Jocelyn Brando). The two main female characters stage a crucial confrontation, with both dressed in mink coats—the status symbol and sign of prosperity for many women in the 1950s.

More significantly, a new Red Scare—the first had been in 1919—was underway soon after the end of World War II. FBI surveillance of alleged Communists was stepped up, though it had already been active since about 1939; Hollywood leftists had found themselves the objects of detailed surveillance, which increased after 1945.[52] The experiences of such leftist contributors to film noir in later years were arguably infused in diverse ways into films, often communicating a sense of anxiety, enclosure, menace, and generalized paranoia. Artistically such paranoia—clearly evident in the films of the 1940s and early '50s featuring John Garfield—had its roots in German expressionist films and literature, such as Kafka's stories and novels, which had reached cult status by the end of the 1950s. The immense exodus of cultural innovators from Europe included writers, philosophers, and film directors who might be Jews, democratic leftists, or former Communists. They settled in New York and Los Angeles in the 1930s. Their personal experiences, which infused their cultural insights, had taught them that they had good reason to fear that people were conspiring against them.[53]

## Noir Ideology?

Under the arresting title, "From the Nightmare Factory: HUAC and the Politics of Noir" Philip Kemp has sketched themes and provided film examples, focusing on tendencies in what might be called a noir counterideology to the postwar American celebration.[54] Some Hollywood practitioners seemed almost to subscribe to these tendencies while making their films even if they did not explicitly or openly avow them.

Among the thematic categories mentioned by Kemp is the all-pervasive and corrosive power of money, which corrupts everything in American society, a theme evident in virtually every film in the noir canon, but most notable in *Double Indemnity* (1994, Billy Wilder), *Out of the Past* (1947, Jacques Taurneur), *The Asphalt Jungle* (1950, John Huston), *Body and Soul* (1947, Robert Rossen), and *Force of Evil* (1948, Abraham Polonsky).

Second, the theme of social class is presented as purely oppressive and not as a reasonable outcome of diverse levels of enterprise and initiative. It was a central element in popular capitalist ideology and is even evident in such films as *Red River* (1948, Howard Hawks), a western, which is both an expression of the glories of free enterprise and entrepreneurship and a treatise on the new postwar labor climate, suggesting—through the lessons learned by Tom Dunson (John Wayne)—the importance of a new managerial ethic in relation to labor.[55] Instead of approaching with humor aspects of the class system—as was done in many 1930s films—by the mid-1940s class was no longer funny. This is quite evident in the portrayals of wealth in *Murder, My Sweet* (1944) and *The Big Sleep* (1946). Social relations were seen as predatory and rapacious. U.S. society is a dog-eat-dog world, tempered only by class loyalties—recall here the cabdrivers who aid John Garfield in *The Fallen Sparrow* (1943, Richard Wallace), help Robert Mitchum in *Out of the Past,* or assist Humphrey Bogart in *Dark Passage* (1947, Delmer Daves); or the lunch-counter operator (James Whitmore) who helps "Dix" Hanley (Sterling Hayden) in *The Asphalt Jungle.*

## The Political Basis of Noir Paranoia

### FRUSTRATED EXPECTATIONS

In hindsight it is important to recall how political expectations had been raised in the 1930s and early '40s—by visions of social and economic democracy inspired by FDR and the New Deal as well as by Communist and Socialist minorities in various indigenous, rapidly organizing industrial-union movements, who naïvely believed that a formula for social renewal could be found in the experience of the Soviet Union. A variety of local progressive movements, such as Upton Sinclair's End Poverty in California (EPIC) campaign; sharecroppers unions in the South; and, on a nationwide basis, supporters and members of the Townsend Plan committees (early advocates of a form of Social Security) all fueled this optimism.

It is in the post–World War II frustration of many of these movements that one can trace, at least in part, the roots of much of the politically relevant and socially critical themes of film noir. The latter might well be viewed as a kind of "return" in media culture of what, in the Truman and McCarthy period (1946–54), was being repressed politically. The bewilderment, indignation, and humanism of older Communists, or nonparty member leftists, in Communist Party–sponsored organizations and unions of the 1930s and early '40s, was best expressed in the emotional testimonies of those interviewed for the 1983 documentary *Seeing Red: Stories of American Communists* (directed by Julia Reichert and James Klein).[56]

Earlier expectations of American leftists and progressives, made more acute at the end of the 1930s thanks to anxiety over the rise of fascism and Nazism, had been hyped by wartime platitudes and declarations such as the "Four Freedoms," which blended with the visceral patriotism of wartime. These were further multiplied as a result of the U.S. alliance with the Soviet Union, one result of which was Soviet dictator Joseph Stalin's image on the cover of *Time* as "Man of the Year" for 1943. Many Communist Party members in the United

States experienced a sense of bewilderment at the buildup and then ebb of favorable images of the Soviet Union and its leader throughout this period.

Contrary to common impressions of a Red Scare hatched in Washington and unleashed in Hollywood, the first investigations of HUAC into alleged Communist influence in the film industry were initially the product of antilabor, anti-Roosevelt, archconservative, pro-studio management groups in Hollywood. HUAC was literally *invited* to Hollywood as early as 1944 by the Motion Picture Alliance for the Preservation of American Ideals (MPA), a management-led, antiunion organization headed by conservative director Sam Wood, a crony of anti–New Deal publisher William Randolph Hearst.[57] It included Walt Disney—later a secret operative and informant for Hoover's FBI—as a vice president.[58] Wood—who became so virulently anticommunist that his heirs had to swear they were "not now, nor ever have been" communists in order to receive their share of his estate[59]—set about denouncing as a "communist" anyone too pro-Roosevelt during the war years or who supported the growing Conference of Studio Unions (CSU), a democratic, militantly progressive union that had made major inroads among studio workers.[60] The MPA played an important role in getting the cold war under way in Hollywood. Arriving in 1944, the invited HUAC investigators found a number of people ready and eager—largely for reasons connected with the local industry labor battles—to denounce alleged and actual "Reds" in Hollywood and to testify to their supposed insidious influence. With the release of the film *Citizen Kane,* Hearst publications had already denounced Orson Welles for alleged "communist" tendencies. An extensive FBI file was developed on Welles, with entries going back as early as 1941.[61] Welles was never a Communist party member, though some of his associates were. Welles, who championed FDR in the 1944 campaign and introduced him at campaign rallies, was even mentioned as a possible running mate with Henry A. Wallace on a future Democratic Party ticket.[62] Welles' active support of Roosevelt allegedly created such a bond between the two that FDR personally called Welles' then wife Rita Hayworth—who was expecting a child and resented her husband's absence—to assure her that Welles was doing important political work. Ironically, Welles was also secretly meeting another woman in New York.[63]

## THE INFLUENCE OF THE COMMUNIST-ORIENTED LEFT IN HOLLYWOOD

The Hollywood Screen Writers Guild numbered among its members several influential Communists—John Howard Lawson, Albert Maltz, and Dalton Trumbo—who essentially controlled the organization. They were also successful in the industry, though little evidence of their direct influence on film content has ever been demonstrated.[64] They were simply adept at writing generally politically liberal, patriotic wartime scripts. Seen another way, such apparent lack of influence on content might also be a reflection of the type of content analysis conducted. While explicit elements of Communist Party ideology might not be evident, the more subtle evidence of a broader, structured sensibility—that "complex of . . . conscious assumptions and taken-for-granted, half-articulated assumptions about art and politics which a number of people held in common"[65]—is everywhere, though it might better be described as socially liberal in that it defended basic liberties against fascism in the 1930s and '40s.

The point here is not retrospectively to imply that there was a need for more thorough censorship of film content at the time but rather to suggest that there are many ways in which political content and secret messages could be encoded and read. In his early discussion of film noir, Paul Schrader noted that "the theme is hidden in the style and bogus themes are often flaunted."[66] In the movies generally, and in much of the noir cycle, middle-class, Production Code–era values were ritualistically invoked as "best," whereas the real focus of the narrative was to present a more obliquely critical statement about society and those who run it.

### THE APPEAL OF NOIR DISCOURSE

Given the anti-Red, antiunion situation unfolding in Hollywood, Left-leaning screenwriters and directors might well have been drawn to the often stark realism and sense of suspicion, enclosure, and paranoia evident in the types of films we now call film noir, the emerging elements of style arguably providing potential weapons for instilling a sense of profound sickness, evil, and wrong in American society. Paradoxically, many of those same "leftists" also worked on a wide variety of mainstream, apolitical film products as well. In the emerging political climate of the cold war, film noir provided ways to hint obliquely at inequality and corruption, utilizing what Mike Davis has described as a "transformational grammar" instead of attacking outright corporate capitalism, though some now-celebrated films—such as Abraham Polonsky's (then largely unknown) *Force of Evil*—provided images of striking impact, suggesting the similarity of crime to the larger system of capitalism.[67]

### LEFTIST OPINION AS POLITICAL-CULTURAL AUDIENCE

The beginning years of the cold war—especially the repression of the U.S. Communist Party and its thousands of members—clearly produced a climate of fear and paranoia among segments of an American Left that earlier had favored the continuation and expansion of Roosevelt's New Deal policies in the post–World War II period. In Hollywood the fear was especially strongly felt after actions by influential studio leaders helped create a search for Communists, which led to congressional hearings and a formal declaration of studio executives—the Waldorf Statement of November 1947—to collaborate in running "Reds" out of the business. Among the Hollywood intelligentsia, especially screenwriters, there were a significant number of leftists, including left-liberals, social-liberals, European social democrats, and actual Communist Party members. Nationally, the Left included not just the Earl Browder faction in the American Communist Party,[68] which sought to continue the broad-based coalition politics of liberals and leftists typical of the war years as well as earlier aspects of the Popular Front of the 1930s, and the William Z. Foster period that followed, with its reaffirmation of class conflict.

Recent studies of American Communists have focused on elite organizational orientations and alleged "instructions" from Moscow, singling out the willingness of a few hundred individuals to gather classified "information" and pass it to the Soviets.[69] In fact, hundreds of thousands of ordinary rank-and-file Communists, "fellow travelers," and left-liberal, or social-liberal New Dealers, most likely did *not even know about* such internal organizational struggles among the Communist Party hierarchy. Large numbers felt a surge of loyalty toward FDR's former vice president, Henry A. Wallace, who on September 20, 1946, was fired from his cabinet post as secretary of commerce by his successor, Harry S. Truman.[70] Wallace had been an immensely popular figure among rank-and-file Democrats.[71] But what a difference four years of history made.

From the substantial sector of social-liberals and left-liberals—most of whom had voted for Roosevelt—literally millions expressed some initial support for Henry A. Wallace in what became the ill-fated Progressive Party campaign for the presidency. Given Harry Truman's lack of popularity, which had dropped as low as 36 percent in polls at one point, even such an astute observer as former Roosevelt adviser James A. Farley predicted in 1947 that if Wallace ran an independent candidacy in 1948, he could take ten million votes away from Truman.[72] The initial expressions of the "Wallace for President" phenomenon—irrespective of the merits of Wallace's projected programs and policies—are indicative of a broad, though minority, tendency in American political opinion in the early post–World War II period.

Such a body of support could also be taken as one indicator of the political context of the first wave of film noir. At one point in 1947—the peak year of the explosive output of film noir—prior to the campaign in which he would run on the Progressive third-party ticket (derisively dubbed by opponents as well as supporters "Gideon's Army"), support for an independent Wallace candidacy against Truman stood as high as 27 percent, eventually dropping to 8 percent in February 1948, and then to about 4 percent in response to strategic, well-coordinated red-baiting from the Truman forces, who were in control of the Democratic Party. In the end, Wallace's candidacy gained only slightly more than 1.1 million votes, incredibly even less than Dixiecrat presidential nominee Strom Thurmond.[73]

Initially positive views of Wallace in polls must have come from millions of disenchanted New Dealers and progressives—people who missed the presence of Roosevelt, and really did not like Harry Truman very much. By election day 1948, however, many progressive, potentially pro-Wallace former New Dealers were demoralized, disaffected, or even fearful of such governmental sanctions as the loss of employment, the Waldorf Statement of Hollywood studio administrators, and the first wave of HUAC investigations of Hollywood, which ended in November 1947.

## THE EMERGENCE OF THE COLD WAR

Among the factors shaping opinion throughout this period was the onset of international tension in the form of the emerging cold war between Russia and the United States; the enunciation by President Truman on March 12, 1947, of the Truman Doctrine in the Middle East; the enunciation by Secretary of State George Marshall on June 5, 1947 of the Marshall Plan for the economic recovery of Europe, and the consequent Soviet rejection of it and formation of an alternative eight-nation bloc in the countries occupied by the Soviet Union; the Berlin blockade and airlift; and the 1948 Communist coup in Czechoslovakia, including the apparent "defenestration" murder of the (non-Communist) Czech cabinet minister, Jan Masaryk. Any of these developments might have been enough to sway the loyalties of a politically attentive person, though each was interpreted through diverse ideological prisms.

Nationally, in the elections of 1946 the Republican Party regained control of the U.S. Congress for the first time since 1930. Richard M. Nixon was one of the first to use the "Communist" label to defeat liberal Democratic Congressman Jerry Voorhis in California and gain the House seat that would later allow him to propel himself to national notice as the discoverer of the alleged espionage of New Dealer and influential U.N. founder Alger Hiss. Joseph McCarthy was elected to the U.S. Senate from Wisconsin in the same election, earlier defeating Robert M. LaFollette Jr.—namesake of the legendary early twentieth century Progressive—in the Republican primary. But McCarthy still had to be shown—in part by the Democrats as they went after Wallace and the leftist

Progressives—the potency of the Communist issue, not making himself known as a red-baiter until late 1949 and only expressing his sentiments openly in speeches delivered in early 1950.[74]

### TRUMAN-McCARTHYISM VERSUS GIDEON'S ARMY

Truman supporters were worried that a large third-party vote for Wallace could throw the election to the Republicans. An onslaught of media and red-baiting Democratic Party vilification—initially planned by Truman adviser and strategist Clark Clifford[75]—contributed to reducing actual Wallace votes to a pitifully small total either by reducing turnout or by bringing defection-minded, potential third-party voters back to Truman. In 1947 Clifford wrote a forty-three page memorandum on strategy for Truman—coincidently while HUAC was completing its first round of hearings on alleged Communist influence in Hollywood—urging a liberal campaign program for 1948, partly to outflank a projected Wallace independent candidacy. In the memo, Clifford argued that

> every effort must be made now jointly and at one and the same time—although by different groups—to dissuade him [Wallace] from leading a third party and to isolate him in the public mind with the Communists. . . . [T]he Administration must persuade prominent liberals and progressives—and no one else—to move publicly into the fray. They must point out that the core of Wallace's backing is made up of Communists and fellow travelers.[76]

As if playing a role orchestrated by the U.S government, the U.S. Communist Party, increasingly feeling and reflecting emerging cold war paranoia—was itself experiencing internal leadership struggles, in which the Popular Front–period leader Earl Browder was defeated in challenges by William Z. Foster and Eugene Dennis. In 1946 Dennis called for the formation of a third party. Following this, the party's New York–based national paper *The Daily Worker* began to praise Henry Wallace as a potential "peace" candidate for 1948.[77]

The strategy (suggested in Clifford's memo) of focusing on Wallace as a "tool" of the Communists to discourage potential Truman voters from supporting FDR's former vice president proved effective, especially given the party's central role in Wallace's campaign. Assessing the precise impact of Democratic red-baiting is difficult, given the absence of national preelection or exit-poll data directly bearing on voter choice. One thing seems clear: the content of pro-Truman rhetoric, both from the president and his supporters, directed at Wallace constituted a powerful, early demonstration of what later came to be called "McCarthyism," or, as Robert Justin Goldstein more accurately termed it, "Truman-McCarthyism"—over two years *before* the Wisconsin senator engaged in it.[78] In the face of these tactics, many left-liberals who might have favored Wallace at some point simply did not vote in 1948, either because they did not want to "waste" their votes or in response to the targeted anti-Communist appeals.

## THE HOLLYWOOD LEFT PERSPECTIVE

From the perspective of the Hollywood Left, this immediate postwar climate—from the 1948 campaign through the peak years of McCarthyism—was recalled by director Joseph Losey, who in this period directed *The Boy with Green Hair* (1948), *The Lawless* (1950), *The Big Night* (1951), and *The Prowler* (1951). Losey was a victim of the second wave of HUAC-inspired blacklisting in the 1950s. He had to leave the country to continue his career, directing some of his finest work from Britain. Here is how he characterized his take on the earlier era: "The conflicts and optimism of the 1930s made it difficult to accept the brutality and degradation of the end of the 1940s. . . . But after Hiroshima, after the death of Roosevelt, after the [HUAC and McCarthy] investigations, only then did one begin to understand the complete unreality of the American dream."[79] Such a sense of the unreality of the promise of American life—indeed, of any kind of a planned version of a better society—is reflected in the sensibility informing much of what is now called film noir.

Direct economic interest of the Hollywood movie corporations, combined with cynical, calculated political tactics designed to win the 1948 election, also contributed to the emerging and well-orchestrated Red Scare, nationally, but especially in Hollywood, as a weapon to destroy the aggressive, expanding efforts at unionization. At the national level, after making wage concessions during the war and facing reduced opportunities for family income in the peacetime economy—with its constant threat of unemployment and rising prices—workers and unions sought wage increases and greater economic security. Thus began a great postwar series of strikes, both sanctioned by unions and on a wildcat basis, including some especially bitter ones against Hollywood studios. The wave of strikes in 1945–46 was the largest in American history, estimated to have cost 107,475,000 lost person-days of work. Influential segments of the public, of course, were horrified and outraged at the disruption of the formerly peaceful wartime labor/management relations.[80]

This growing climate of anticommunism of the early postwar period led to an intense atmosphere of fear within the Hollywood Left. HUAC had just completed its first public hearings in the fall of 1947, and studio executives had agreed, after the Waldorf-Astoria meetings held November 23 and 24 that same year, to weed out suspected Communists and ensure that they were not employed in the future. Against this very complex social-political background, film noir virtually exploded in popular movie culture. Scores of classics came out in 1946 and 1947[81]—including *Dead Reckoning* (1947, John Cromwell), *The Big Sleep, The Killers* (1946, Robert Siodmak), *Out of the Past, Brute Force* (1947, Jules Dassin), *Body and Soul,* and *Dark Passage*—among over fifty films now classified as noirs that were released in those two years.

## Didactic-Realist Left-Wing Noir

Following their indirect strategy of social criticism, most noir films left as their distinctive message, as one critic put it, a "darkling vision of the world, a view from the underside, born of fundamental disillusionment perhaps, but also . . . of a confrontation with nihilism."[82] Whereas some of these films presented a pessimistic view of human nature rather than directly attacking the system, others took a different direction. A minority of writers and directors—particularly those in the U.S. Communist Party—used the style in very direct ways to make powerful, explicit, even didactic social-political statements in films such as *Crossfire* (1947, Dmytryk) and *Try and Get Me/Sound of Fury* (1951, Cyril Endfield). Most of these individuals were either excluded from Hollywood productions in the period of the blacklist, or were forced to "name names," recant, and apologize for their former left-wing affiliations in order to keep their careers.

In his pathbreaking analysis of the blacklist era in American cinema, Thom Andersen has described a noir subcategory of relentlessly bleak, socially conscious, critical films—including virtually all films in which John Garfield appeared—such as *The Fallen Sparrow* (1943, Richard Wallace), *Body and Soul* (1947, Robert Rossen), *Force of Evil* (1948, Polonsky), *The Breaking Point* (1950, Michael Curtiz), and *He Ran All the Way* (1951, John Berry).[83] Of the last three, *The Breaking Point* and *He Ran All the Way* were virtually lost from view during the blacklist years. Only *Force of Evil* has developed an intense cult following, thanks to its director, Abe Polonsky. Lionized by succeeding generations, Polonsky remained to the end of his life a perceptive commentator on movie aesthetics and politics, holding true to his earlier progressive convictions. He died in his Hollywood home on October 26 1999, nearly eighty-nine years old.

### *FORCE OF EVIL* (ABRAHAM POLONSKY)

Polonsky's film, one of the darker takes on crime, the economy, and—at first viewing—human nature in the entire noir canon, was the only film the now-celebrated radical writer-director made on his own before being blacklisted after his courageous facedown with HUAC in 1951. Based on Ira Wolfert's 1943 novel *Tucker's People*, and working in close consultation with the author, Polonsky streamlined and extensively rewrote the author's first effort at a screenplay.[84] The film describes the effort ("the enterprise") to take over the "numbers" betting racket in New York City. The numbers was a diversion played by millions of poor and working-class people in prelottery days who poured their hard-earned money into the system, only to be systematically exploited by it.

In the movie, 1940s film icon John Garfield plays Joe Morse, a lawyer for a crime syndicate bent on bringing all the other small numbers operators—including Joe's brother, Leo (Thomas Gomez)—under control, essentially "legalizing" the racket, which is apparently under police and paid political protection, though this aspect is underdeveloped in the screenplay. The plan was to rig the three-digit number that came up on July 4 so that it would be "776"—1776 being the date of the Declaration of Independence—commonly bet on the holiday. As a result, there would be so many winners that most of the smaller banks would go bankrupt, opening the way for "Tucker's people"—gangster Ben Tucker (played by Roy Roberts)—to take control of all of them.

The vision of the film presents the numbers racket as a "surrogate reality"[85] symbolizing the whole system of capitalism. "It's business" is a recurring line in this film, anticipating by a quarter century the phrase used throughout *The Godfather* series. Garfield, as the lawyer driven only by thoughts of making money, experiences a crisis of conscience by the film's end, seeking to break free of "the system"—the economic environment that shapes both brothers and, by extension, everyone in society. This system ultimately puts out a contract on and then kills his brother, Leo Morse. Both the economic and legal system, including the police, are represented in the film as "a kind of mirror image of the racket—as impersonal (using the telephone to assert itself), as threatening, and probably as corrupt."[86] This dimension is essential for understanding the radical vision of the film and why—in contrast to the dark visions of many of Fritz Lang's American films, where people in general tend to do bad things if given an opportunity—its approach was not meant to imply that innate moral deficiency governs the behavior of the protagonists.

Joe Morse's crisis of conscience emerges as he sees the pain Tucker's syndicate inflicts on his brother Leo, on Leo's employees, and on his beautiful young secretary Doris (Beatrice Pearson), with whom he is falling in love, though he tells her it is "too early" to verbalize it. Doris is the only bright spot in his life and the only cheerful element in the film, transforming scenes merely by her presence. She represents everything Joe's world is not, the possibility of a future beyond the rackets. It takes most of the film for Joe Morse to realize that making piles of illegal money destroys other people's lives and inevitably must take its toll on him. He sees his older brother's little numbers scam systematically crushed by Tucker's violent enforced takeover—with death threats for those who want to quit—followed by repeated police busts instigated first by Joe himself in order to make Leo comply and then, under mob threats, by Leo's chief bookkeeper, Freddy Bauer, a weasley, balding, nervous, little man in glasses (very effectively portrayed here by Howland Chamberlin). David Raksin's score underlines events with almost hymn-like transfiguration motifs, as the terrified Freddy is shot at point-blank range, shattering his glasses—one of the film's most striking visual images—while Leo, convulsed with acute angina and on the verge of a fatal heart attack, is dragged away by the thugs.

Despite all the evidence before him, it still takes his brother's abduction and death to make Joe Morse face up to the kind of system in which he is enmeshed. Even Doris, who finds Joe so attractive, fears being marked by his crime ties. Facing a mob rubout by Tucker and his cohort, Morse summons all his energy and faces them down in a pitch-black shoot-out in Tucker's office. When it's over, Joe Morse survives, while Tucker and his crony lie dead on the carpet.

At the conclusion of the film, Garfield's character appears to become an informer, his voice-over saying that if the syndicate could do this to his brother, maybe it was time to talk to the task force of crime investigators and its faceless special prosecutor. According to Polonsky, this was only done to get a Production Code seal of approval. As he recalled thirty years later, "What he was doing was cooperating with what was suppressed in his own nature and in the society in which he found himself. . . . For me, it was the law of history he meant. Naturally, I had no practical suggestions in the film for political organizations, since even now as we search, we still don't find."[87]

Based on a novel once described as an "autopsy" on capitalism, seen retrospectively *Force of Evil* constitutes one of the best examples of a radical body of American film that attempted to be profoundly political through its critical images of "the system." Conventionally viewed as offering alternatives to that system only indirectly—by portraying intolerable conditions through its stark and powerful images—there is actually a great deal more to the film, which fuses existential and socioeconomic issues. The crisis of conscience of Joe

Morse is meant as an inspirational example. Joe discovers, as Polonsky put it, "what was suppressed in his own nature and in the society in which he found himself."[88]

Garfield, here at the peak of his career, was as big a figure in films of this era as Bogart.[89] He had an immensely attractive film persona, combining an emotional and physical aura that made audiences easily identify with him in diverse roles and situations. Here is how Polonsky described part of his appeal: "Garfield was the darling of romantic rebels—beautiful, enthusiastic, rich with the know-how of street intelligence. He had passion and a lyrical sadness that was the essence of the role he created as it was created for him."[90]

### *Visual Style*

Polonsky wanted his film to look like the paintings of Edward Hopper, as he explained in an interview: "Third Avenue, cafeterias, all that backlight, and those empty streets. Even when people are there, you don't see them, somehow the environments dominate the people."[91] Polonsky's direction and George Barnes' photography achieve this in numerous ways, especially in the effective use of available New York City locales. The film is dark in appearance and tone, with most of the scenes taking place at night. Aside from the opening shots of exteriors and the concluding scenes, much of the film's action occurs in small, bleak interiors. The film uses the biblical Cain and Abel tale as a model for its portrayal of the two brothers; at one point Leo says to Joe, "All that Cain did to Abel was murder him," implying that what Joe was doing was even worse.

Opening with an establishing shot of the Wall Street financial district, the film later features a visually striking scene showing Joe's early-morning stroll across the same locale, where he is a tiny figure surrounded by huge buildings. In the film's visually most impressive closing minutes—there is the vérité immediacy of a kind of solemn processional—accompanied on the soundtrack by an elegiac, voice-over by Garfield—as Joe descends a long series of stairs to the East River—with the huge Williamsburg bridge looming in the background—to find his brother's lifeless body half submerged at the river's edge. These impressive images and starkly evocative urban settings create a kind of visual poetry that, over fifty years later, still provide a spareness and immediacy to the film, lingering in the viewer's mind long after it ends.[92]

### *Audience and Message*

*Force of Evil* took many years to find its intellectual audience. It was first released in December 1948 and was distributed by MGM. Originally advertised as just another gangster flick, it soon disappeared from theater screens and was given little publicity. It reappeared on television in the 1950s and became a cult item in succeeding decades. Once an "underground classic," it now regularly appears on cable television.

The film was decades ahead of its time. On first viewing one might find it puzzling, brief, obscure, and schematic. Arguably leaving viewers suspended between the conditions exposed and their own desire for solutions, it creates a longing for answers. The film's devoted viewers may themselves carry repressed visions of the possibility of utopian alternatives to counter the bleak and negative systemic images. The film's original intended "message" is difficult to express, given the passage of time and the obliteration of past ideologies. The retrospectively naïve optimism of American Communists of the 1930s and '40s was undoubtedly a contributing factor. Whether Polonsky's membership in the Communist Party influenced the film's content is contested. The director has suggested in interviews that he underwent other influences on the set, including the photographer, Garfield's magnetic presence as well as that of the other strong cast members, and even the actual sets of New York City's financial district and other locales.

While few alive can recall it—or might wish to deny it in this post–cold war era celebrating the globalization of capitalism—the American Communist vision was animated by a great ideal of community. As onetime party member Joseph Starobin put it, it was "a political party which they tried to make into a fraternity of comrades, animated by the great ideal of human brotherhood . . . a community that went beyond national boundaries and differences of race and creed." Driven by the certainty that the human sojourn on earth could be happier if only "social relations were transformed from competition to cooperation, these Americans were sure that a universal strategy for creating a new society had been found in the experience of Russia and China."[93] This new naïve view undoubtedly hovered in the background of Polonsky's film, but there was a great deal more to Polonsky's vision, as he himself stated in several interviews in later years.[94]

Today the film's appeal certainly lies neither in the then misguided, deluded idealization of the Soviet Union nor in the confused ideology of the Henry Wallace Progressives of 1948.[95] *Force of Evil*—its vision of crime as capitalism and capitalism as crime anticipating the epic vision of social evil in Francis Ford Coppola's *The Godfather Parts I* and *II* and its situation and characters serving as a model for Oliver Stone's *Wall Street* (1987)—still delivers a powerful moral message. Now widely celebrated and proclaimed by Andrew Sarris in 1968 as "one of the great films of the modern American cinema,"[96] the film today appears anomalous in its evocation of the evils of capitalism. But, as later films and events have suggested, its totalistic image of an "evil" system might more appropriately be applied to the extensive crimes of the CIA or perhaps certain sectors of local law enforcement.

*Garfield's Obliteration*

John Garfield had his reputation destroyed in the blacklist period to the point where hardly anyone who was not an avid filmgoer in the 1940s even knows his name.[98] Michael Curtiz's film *The Breaking Point* (1950), starring Garfield and Patricia Neal, is an impressive—even riveting—and truer adaptation of Hemingway's *To Have and Have Not* than the more celebrated version with Bogart and Bacall (1944, Hawks), though Garfield and Neal lacked the extracinematic romance of Bogie and Bacall and the pointed dialogue added to the Hawks version by William Faulkner and Jules Furthman.[98]

Garfield was one of the most familiar—almost archetypal—figures in World War II–era films (*Air Force* [1943, Howard Hawks], *Destination Tokyo* [1943, Delmer Daves], *Pride of the Marines* [1945, Delmer Daves]) and the quintessential anguished protagonist in such noir features as *The Postman Always Rings Twice* (1946, Tay Garnett), *Nobody Lives Forever* (1946, Jean Negulesco), *Humoresque* (1946, Negulesco), *Gentleman's Agreement* (1947, Elia Kazan), *Body and Soul* (1947, Robert Rossen), *Force of Evil,* and *He Ran All the Way* (1951, John Berry). He was literally hounded by FBI surveillance up to and just after his subpoenaed appearance before HUAC on April 23, 1951. To the dismay of the red-baiters, although seemingly cooperative, Garfield refused to name names.[99] Pursued by his FBI shadows, lacking film work for eighteen months, and under enormous pressure from HUAC to "rat" on friends and associates, Garfield—like Joe Morse in *Force of Evil* and Nick Robey in *He Ran All the Way*—found himself backed into a psychological corner from which there was no escape. He died of a heart attack on May 21, 1952—hastened by extreme anxiety and stress, combined with suicidally heavy drinking and chain-smoking.

## Other Examples of Left-Wing Noir

It is often noted that many noir films involved writers, directors, and producers who had either been members of the original Hollywood Ten—jailed and blacklisted after hostile face-offs with HUAC in 1947—or other blacklistees from the second, post-1951 round of hearings, such as Polonsky, Cyril "Cy" Endfield, and Jules Dassin.[100] Dassin's *Thieves' Highway* (1949), *Night and the City* (1950), and his French film *Rififi* (1954); Nicholas Ray's *They Live by Night* (1949) and *Knock on Any Door* (1949); John Huston's *The Asphalt Jungle* (1950); Joseph Losey's *The Lawless* (1950) and *The Prowler* (1951); and the last three films in which John Garfield starred are all characterized by intense psychological and social realism.

### *DESPERATE* (ANTHONY MANN)

This list might well be expanded by the addition of the noir films of Anthony Mann.[101] Thanks, in part, to the camera work of the great Hungarian émigré John Alton, several of Mann's noir features—now increasingly well known and almost cult items—provide striking narrative and visual examples of the gritty social realist style, including *Desperate* (1947), *Railroaded!* (1947), *T-Men* (1947), *Raw Deal* (1948), *Border Incident* (1949), and *Side Street* (1949). He also partially directed *He Walked by Night* (1949).[102]

Mann's first noir, *Desperate,* though a B picture like Tourneur's classic *Out of the Past* the same year (discussed at length in chapter 7), is typical of an era in which the social order was commonly viewed as unable to protect ordinary people. In this film a young couple, played by Steve Brody and Audrey Long, are victimized and pursued by a gang, led by Raymond Burr, the gang's savagely cruel chief, who is photographed throughout from low angles to enhance his menacing appearance. Indeed, the paranoia of the film becomes all-pervasive as they are pursued by Burr's minions from L.A. to a Minnesota farm, ultimately realizing there is literally no place for them to hide. Narratively speaking, one wishes the character played by Brody would not be so obsessively resistant to seeking police help. His failure to enlist the aid of the law perhaps reflects a working-class fear—and knowledge—that bringing in the police means more "trouble." (The police, in this case, meant the now-feared LAPD.) As a result, events snowball as the two flee across the country.

There are strikingly photographed images and scenes featuring Burr and the other criminals, thanks in part to Mann's direction and George Diskant's remarkable camera work. Though not as celebrated as John Alton's work on subsequent Mann films, there are several quite striking noirish visual sequences in this first of the director's noir features. The criminals in their hideout are visually presented as quintessentially evil, especially the villainous and physically immense Burr, whose face is alternately illuminated and cast in shadow by an overhead swinging light, while his thugs sadistically inflict a beating on a suspected informer. In a later scene Burr's character is injured and recovering in bed, while a light outside his window goes on and off, suggesting his unstable character and the violent fluctuations of his mood. A final stairway shoot-out sequence is one of the best in any noir feature, featuring high and low dramatic angles, with shadows from the banister falling across the characters.

By contrast, the ordinariness of the couple in their Los Angeles apartment before their involvement in the events precipitating their flight is captured in bright, high-key light that makes their existence seem empty and one-dimensional, like the spare settings of Glenn Ford and Jocelyn Brando's little tract house in Fritz Lang's *The Big Heat* (1953).

Virtually all the noir directors mentioned—except Mann, who shifted to making westerns, which proved to be his greatest commercial successes—were subject to the blacklist and had to leave the United States in order to work. The massive surveillance system of the FBI and other agencies was no paranoid delusion. From the late 1930s onward, a staggering amount of material was collected on alleged and actual Communists in the film industry and elsewhere.[103] The number of agents required—many blacklistees recall being followed around the clock for months or even years by two assigned agents—and the cost to administer such a program of surveillance must have been financially exorbitant, though for Hoover's FBI nothing was more important than the war on the "malignant disease" of Communism. The costs in shattered lives and interrupted careers as a result of such obsessive repressive surveillance are almost beyond computation.

Despite close to five hundred examples reflecting the classic-era noir sensibility, it remained a countermovement, most often represented in "B-"pictures, to a larger body of bright, optimistic Hollywood ("A") products.[104] Viewed as bleak by former leftists and disaffected social liberals from the New Deal era, for most the years from 1946 into the mid-1950s were nonetheless the period many genuinely remember as "The Best Years"—the partial title of the box-office hit of 1946–47 and of a popular history of the period.[105] Some film historians have suggested that the emergence of film noir in this period largely served to highlight the basic optimism of this postwar era,[106] noting that many films were simply "derivations" of the tough detective novels popular at the time. They further suggest that whatever genuine directorial sensibilities were involved, the particular look or visual style was more important than the narrative content: "Film noir's evocation of evil may have served only as a delicious contrast: making the ultimate victory of goodness and justice that much more glorious. Thus, though film noir did introduce the American audience to the darker side of the human spirit, that initiation was one that was more of form than of content, and one that hardly ruffled the basic self-confidence of the era."[107]

Such a reading obscures one important way in which popular culture has political significance: its appeal is not always based on overt, clearly understood statements and responses to intended or encoded messages, nor on conscious and rational choices on the part of consumers. Because it arises out of barely articulated, often repressed longings, or is directed toward some of the potential audience's worst fears, it can be made to "work" for them and to provide much-needed gratification of their (unconscious) needs.

## Repressed Negativity in Noir-Era Films of Affirmation

Another aspect of these films commonly included in the classic noir cycle is that the confidence of the immediate postwar period carried a built-in element of doubt, of narrowly averted calamity. Such subtexts are evident in three major non-noir, "affirmative" features all released in 1946—*The Best Years of Our Lives, It's a Wonderful Life,* and *Till the End of Time*—each of which illustrates important narrative themes at the start of the classic film noir period.

### *THE BEST YEARS OF OUR LIVES* (WILLIAM WYLER)

In 1946 contrasting but critical representations of American society could be noted in popular films. Mainstream "A" features presented, on balance, a more positive view that celebrated American free-enterprise, culture, and its institutions. In contrast, film noir presented a more somber and critical portrait. Practically everyone who saw a movie in 1946 saw William Wyler's *The Best Years of Our Lives,* which was astutely promoted by producer Samuel Goldwyn to become the number one box-office and Academy Awards (it won seven Oscars) hit of 1946–47.[108]

Wyler's film relates the experiences of three returning vets: Dana Andrews plays Fred Derry, a former soda jerk now an Air Force officer and a hero with no job prospects, who is married to a beautiful, but two-timing Virginia Mayo. Frederic March plays Al Stephenson, a married, middle-aged banker who served as an army sergeant and now returns to banking. He measures the inequalities of peacetime "credit worthiness" against the sense of collective loyalty and egalitarian sentiments of war. His wife is played by Myrna Loy. Like the other "good" women of the film, she is all-knowing, exceptionally resourceful, and totally loyal. She has a grown daughter, played by Teresa Wright, who displays similar virtues and maturity and provides the love interest (carefully within Production Code guidelines) for the disillusioned Andrews. Harold Russell, a nonactor and navy vet, plays Homer, who has lost his hands and is fitted with prosthetic hooks. Initially Homer feels useless and is filled with self-loathing, afraid to resume his relationship with Wilma, the young woman next door, played with appealing strength and insight by Kathie O'Donnell. Homer's character—through indirection and avoidance of questions of what they all were really fighting for—is meant to illustrate the "real" (but worthwhile) costs of war, as opposed to those who are merely afflicted with feelings of inferiority and a loss of sense of place as they struggle to readjust to the peacetime economy.

Despite winning seven Oscars and being widely praised, the film was blasted by such noted critics of the day as James Agee and Robert Warshow. Writing in *The Nation,* Agee described the film as "a long pious piece of deceit and self-deceit embarrassed by hot flashes of talent, conscience, truthfulness and dignity."[109] Warshow was even more critical. Writing for the elite, left-of-center *Partisan Review,* he noted that although the film presented

> an optimistic picture of American life, and of postwar America in particular, making suitable reference to such accepted symbols as democracy, the American character . . . making [the viewer] . . . feel a certain confidence that the problems of modern life . . . can be solved by the operation of 'simple' and 'American' virtues . . . [these ideas] accepted readily enough as public symbols . . . will not bear serious examination and they cannot be made to emerge forcefully from any true presentation of reality.[110]

Since the aim of the film was to create a positive representation of the more complex reality of the time, such optimism, embodying a fundamental denial of the profound inequalities of American life, remains for later generations to analyze. Thus, the problem of the monopoly of capital, as Warshow saw at the time, "is reduced to the question of the morals of banks: if bankers are good men, then they will grant small loans (not large loans, apparently) to deserving veterans (those who are willing to work hard) without demanding collateral. . . . [T]he small loan is apparently conceived to be some kind of solution to the economic difficulties of capitalism—cf. *It's a Wonderful Life.*"[111]

### *IT'S A WONDERFUL LIFE* (FRANK CAPRA)

The effort at affirmation was also evident—though expressed with some ambiguity, given the starkly negative vision in the twenty-five-minute dream sequence preceding it—in the brief "happy" ending of *It's a Wonderful Life* (1946) Frank Capra's most successful and personal favorite. (Although still a Christmas season fixture, it was used in the film *Menace II Society* [1993, Allen and Albert Hughes] to represent the utter irrelevance of its message to the hellish lives of African-Americans in the Watts area of Los Angeles.) The film's quick narrative switch back to "transcendent reaffirmation" at the end leaves the viewer with a sense of regret and overwhelming loss as a result of the disturbing and complex counterimages in the final dream sequence. Here, as Dana Polan has noted, "only the presence of George Bailey [the central character, played by James Stewart] prevents a fall into chaos—not a very optimistic vision of human value: here, the film's ostensible populism shades into fascism and the suggestion that the masses are a rabble saved only by a strong individual."[112] Moreover, as Robert Ray put it, the positive or happy outcome of the film "depended utterly on George's vision, provided by Clarence [the guardian angel character]: the chance to see what Bedford Falls would have been like if he had never been born. . . . Without it the film would have been unbearably bleak. . . . Without him, Bedford Falls had become Pottersville, a film noir landscape of human wrecks and neon signs."[113] Because of its stark juxtapositions, the film could not—in common with the other two postwar "positive" films discussed here—hope to completely allay the anxieties invoked. The Scrooge like Mr. Potter is never called to account. As Ray has suggested, this is "a serious weakness in the displacement mechanism—as if *Casablanca*'s Major Strasser had avoided Rick's retribution."[114] For a film seeking to express the nobility of ordinary people's lives, *It's a Wonderful Life* implicitly served to discredit every ordinary person except George. Without him people became drunks, hookers, brutal bullies, went crazy, never married, or ended up as bitter old ladies. Finally, the expressed aim of the film—to show how money is inferior to close personal relationships—ends, somewhat ironically, in a scene suggesting that the quality of personal relationships could be gauged most accurately by money.

Perhaps the most pessimistic aspect of the film plays right into the central film noir narrative convention, which claims that our most cherished relationships and institutions rest on "the thinnest tissue of sustaining faith that could be torn by the most random of accidents."[115] This is a view that could have come directly from one of the quintessential noir novels and stories of Cornell Woolrich. Indeed, such an insight into the ultimate illusory quality of American life links *It's a Wonderful Life* and Arthur Miller's play *Death of a Salesman* (1948–49). The guardian angel tells George Bailey "no man is a failure who has friends," whereas Miller's Willy Loman was supposedly "well-liked." The film's effort to affirm traditional sorts of reconciliation made it only superficially optimistic. The fact that everybody was in tears at the end suggests how close things came to disaster and how tenuous was the faith in solutions dictated by an exiting ideology.[116]

In both *The Best Years* and *It's a Wonderful Life* there is a conscious effort to carry forward the nationalist ideology and affirmational discourse of World War II films[117] and, through the more problematic aspects of the narratives, to establish a link with returning veterans and their families in readjusting to a peacetime economy. The basic message of finding purpose and meaning in civilian work and in the newly reaffirmed traditional family in reality resulted both in the baby boom and in feelings of depression and longing for careers established as a result of the massive employment of women in World War II.[118] (Betty Friedan effectively cataloged these issues for a mass readership in *The Feminine Mystique* of 1963.) To achieve any positive hold in the minds of viewers, such images had to be linked to the more complex and conflicted realities of the era that were represented in the films.

### *TILL THE END OF TIME* (EDWARD DMYTRYK)

Similar tendencies, though with perhaps greater disillusionment, are evident in another film of returning veterans directed by Edward Dmytryk.[119] *Till the End of Time* remains one of the most significant films of the period, both in its portrayal of the protracted and painful struggle of three vets to find their rightful place in the postwar world and in its affirmation of working-class solidarity.[120] It is especially noteworthy for its depiction, in the opening section, of the egalitarian nature of the armed services at the end of World War II and in the very positive efforts of the military to work for the readjustment of veterans to the peacetime economy. It presents one of the few genuinely positive portrayals in popular films since *The Grapes of Wrath* (1940, John Ford). This positive portrayal of a government program is consistent with the Dymtryk's explanation, in later years, of his decision to join the Communist Party in 1944, as a result of their excellent and extensive support programs for families of servicemen.[121]

*Till the End of Time* presents a series of individual choices. An ambiguous love relationship develops between a deeply disillusioned war widow, played by Dorothy McGuire, and the central male character, played by Guy Madison, who spends most of the film trying to find his place in the new postwar world. Robert Mitchum, in his first major role, plays a wounded vet who loses all his money while gambling and then is nearly beaten to death in a bar brawl with some racist, cryptofascist veterans. This fight also involves another vet, a former boxer now without the use of his legs, who manages to shake off his depression enough to make his way to the bar on crutches in time to reaffirm the egalitarian solidarity of the war years by joining his other two buddies in the fight and thrashing the (apparently) fascist bad guys. While this scene is an important reaffirmation of proclaimed American World War II ideals, by the end of the film there remains little sense of the possibility of solidarity and community beyond such individual loyalties. It is difficult to see how the Production Code would have permitted it, given the fact that it would have developed within the context of struggle and opposition to dominant institutions the code (and the whole ethos of Hollywood) expressly sought to uphold.[122] At the film's conclusion, the promise of a future relationship between the McGuire and Madison characters, the uneasy satisfactions of his job, nostalgic recollections of the past, and solidarity with his war buddies are all that remain. Much of the prewar environment has been transformed and recollections of it seem tinged with regret at its passing.

Even in these three major celebratory filmic portraits of postwar America, there is a continuing undertone of profound personal alienation, identity confusion, malaise, uncertainty, and a genuine questioning of the American Dream—all of which were also central qualities of film noir. Even though each of these films has a happy ending, the sense of loss and the possibility that things might end badly shifts attention to the larger picture as an accumulation of negative outcomes that must be faced realistically.[123] Hundreds of film noir features in succeeding years did precisely that.

Still bleaker judgments of the underlying, subtextual messages in supposedly affirmational narratives of 1940s films could be made. In an excellent but not widely known work, Barbara Deming has examined a large number of popular "A" films representing a variety of genres. In recollecting them she discloses an underlying hopelessness. As Deming put it, "The figures I have presented seem together to form a hopeless circle. The hero who sees nothing to fight for; the hero who despairs of making a life for himself; the hero who achieves success but finds it empty; and the malcontent who breaks with life to find himself nowhere—each mourns a vision of happiness that eludes him."[124] What were these particular visions of happiness? Their implications were far-reaching, calling into question the operation of important social institutions and related attitudes. In the case of male attitudes toward women, this was not always an essentially "progressive" or "politically correct" vision, though, as I shall argue, one can discern an alternative vision through subtextual and against-the-grain readings of specific examples.[125]

## Original Audience Reception of Noir Features

It should come as no surprise that few noir films of the 1940s and '50s reached the top ten or twenty in box-office receipts, given that they were a low-budget "B" medium meant to play on the bottom of double features.[126] Of some 298 films listed in the *Motion Picture Herald* as the top moneymakers between 1944 and 1956 (the peak years of film noir production), only 9 could be considered "consensus" noirs,[127] even though a substantial audience saw the films. They always generated a profit, even at flat-rate rentals rather than the percentage basis of "A" features, requiring far less rental return to their distributors than higher-budget films. They made money, in part, because they were often very cheaply produced. Initially this was the case because of wartime government-imposed production regulations, which indirectly resulted in some of the visual stylistic characteristics so central to the noir canon:[128] night scenes and low-key lighting (which made the cheap sets less visible); use of available urban locations or existing sets rather than expensive new sets; short shooting schedules (due to limited amounts of film stock); and the use of lesser-known actors and little-known though often highly skilled directors who could work within a limited budget and time constraints. Later such stylistic elements were emulated because they had a certain box-office appeal. Originally conceived as mystery thrillers, with an investigative narrative, at the most basic level people watched simply because they wanted to see how the story turned out. Whether or not they absorbed any aspects of what is retrospectively evident as the critical noir zeitgeist is a matter of conjecture. Frequent filmgoers in the years of the classic noir cycle were rarely if ever attracted to, or even saw elements of, a radically critical political perspective in such films.[129] Though the precise makeup of the original viewing audience for most noir features is uncertain, total film rental receipts reached an all-time high in the United States in 1946[130] with an estimated audience of as many as ninety million regular weekly moviegoers. This was the peak of theater-based movie viewing, just prior to the introduction of television. Movie attendance subsequently began to decline—actually starting before television became a major factor since the viewing audience was home "creating" and then babysitting for the "baby boomers"—from which it did not recover as the primary viewing venue for movies.[131]

Real tendencies, trends, and conflicts in U.S. domestic politics in the years of peak film noir production were all obviously directly correlated—the postwar emergence of film noir as a minority voice and countermovement mirroring the political paranoia engendered by the emerging Red Scare and HUAC investigations. Film noir seems—in complex, sometimes ambiguous, ways—rooted in the concrete realities of the era of the blacklist and the broader tendencies of repressive red-baiting usually labeled "McCarthyism." It began with the Democratic Party's Truman administration, particularly its strategic, focused attacks on Henry Wallace's independent peace candidacy as the head of a Progressive

Party heavily supported by the U.S. Communist Party, antedating McCarthy's own discovery of the communism issue in late 1949 and early 1950 and continuing long after McCarthy's censure by the Senate on December 2, 1954, and his death in 1957.[132] There may be some ironic retribution in the sense that the repression of the domestic Left helped create the political paranoia that was a necessary condition and cultural resource critical screenwriters and filmmakers drew upon and used, integrating sometimes diverse visual and narrative elements in a then fashionable manner into what, retrospectively, could be described as virtually a film movement—film noir—linked in complex ways to larger, longer-term historical and cross-cultural literary "noir" discursive practices.[133]

# The Culture of Resistance in Films of the 1960s

An ambush execution shot in agonizing slow motion, with hundreds of bullets tearing the flesh of Clyde Barrow (Warren Beatty) and Bonnie Parker (Faye Dunaway) at the conclusion of *Bonnie and Clyde* (1967, Arthur Penn). Fatal shotgun blasts from the rednecks' pickup that blow away Wyatt/"Captain America" (Peter Fonda) and Billy (Dennis Hopper), sending sections of their bike tumbling into the ditch at the end of *Easy Rider* (1969, Dennis Hopper). Each of these horrifying, violent, bloody cataclysms represents some of the bleakest projections in movies of anxieties arising out of the culture and resistance movements associated with the 1960s. These films—as well as others, such as *Cool Hand Luke* (1967, Stuart Rosenberg)—express the darkest, grimmest varieties of visionary paranoia, an almost hopeless pessimism, and the most terrifying possibilities—of literal personal obliteration—in confronting or challenging "the system." Yet many other films of the era—and a great deal of the popular music—embodied a searching scrutiny of all institutions and mores, explosively critical insights, uplifting expressions of hope, and boundless, even revolutionary, optimism.

The 1960s was a time of *both* hope and despair, rising expectations and profound frustrations. Challenges to the very foundations of the social order were accompanied by a secret history of domestic covert action and extensive surveillance by the FBI, the CIA, and even internal surveillance by military intelligence agencies.[1] The popular culture of visionary paranoia in the 1960s reflected this climate, reinforcing what has been termed an emergent "adversary" or "resistance" culture[2]—a moral protest of revulsion against the dominant cold war liberal consensus of the post-1946 era and the society it had produced. Beginning with the first inchoate glimpses of a distinct youth culture at the end of the 1950s—evident in the public's identification with movie gangs and such conflicted images as those of James Dean in *Rebel Without a Cause* (1955, Nicholas Ray)—the concurrent rise of the civil rights movement, and the emergence of a domestic peace movement after the Cuban Missile Crisis of

1962, all these strands converged to create a culture of political opposition, which became a massive movement of resistance by the close of the decade and played a significant role in ending U.S. participation in the Vietnam War. Leaving suspicion of corporate and government power as a cultural residue, it also contributed to what has derisively been termed the "fusion paranoia"[3] of the closing years of the twentieth century, perhaps adding fuel to the horrifying tragedy of Waco in 1993 and inspiring the kind of irrational fury evident in the Oklahoma City bombing in 1995. Several films and much popular music of the 1960s played a crucial role in the growth of this resistance culture, while other films served as important retrospective indicators of changing attitudes and values.

## Cold War Hysteria and the Rise of Resistance

In the early 1960s, in the midst of the cold war, Americans experienced the continuing threat of nuclear warfare, peaking in the October 1962 Cuban Missile Crisis, which made terribly real a long-repressed war anxiety. The Cuban Missile Crisis, combined with the endemic secrecy of the national security state, had grown to immense proportions, and this led to the creation of a number of films having fear, suspicion, and paranoia as their major themes. From the early 1960s, there had been a growing subculture of opposition to the postwar cold war consensus. Evident particularly after the nuclear war scare of the 1962, first among educated whites and eventually among all economic levels of blacks, it came to have a profound, long-term effect on public opinion, popular culture, and politics.[4]

Disillusionment with the war in Vietnam proved to be a major accelerator for the growth of this resistance subculture, but it had really begun in the civil rights movement's enlisting of white students earlier in the decade. By the end of the 1960s, the nation seemed to be coming apart; majority opinion in several polls viewed being involved in Vietnam as "a mistake," yet Washington, first under LBJ and then under Nixon, persisted in the war.

Over the years Vietnam has become emblematic of the "bad" war, "profoundly subversive, undermining a rich and powerful set of expectations concerning the nature of heroism, patriotic virtue and the sorts of actions that create and sustain them."[5] While this supposedly set the Vietnam conflict apart from most of American history, from an opposite perspective the war was deeply rooted in American history and culture.[6] Whatever the case, never before in U.S. history had dissension over a war been dealt with so profoundly in popular culture. This was especially the case with popular music, which continued unabated as the war went on. Only after American involvement had ended did movies explicitly represent aspects of the fighting and its aftermath, thereby contributing to a cultural reservoir of distrust and suspicion of central, "higher" authority, both political and corporate.[7]

## FOLK MUSIC AND RESISTANCE

Emerging opposition among college students and left-liberal groups is reflected in what were then called "folk songs," such as those of Pete Seeger, Bob Dylan, and Phil Ochs. Seeger's "Waist Deep in the Big Muddy," first written in 1963, was revised for the recording issued on the Columbia label in 1966 to reflect the speeches of President Lyndon Baines Johnson. Widely remembered for its striking metaphor for the Vietnam experience, it actually had little actual airplay, due both to Seeger's earlier blacklisting and the song's lyrical use of statements by Johnson, with a refrain ridiculing LBJ's exhortations to hold the course. Johnson soon became fair game for everybody during the era.

Most striking were the grimly relentless indictments in many songs by Bob Dylan. His inspirational "Blowin' in the Wind" proved a big hit and was sung by over sixty artists, reaching number two on the singles charts in 1963 in the version by Peter, Paul and Mary. His "Masters of War," "A Hard Rain's Gonna Fall," and "With God on Our Side" from the 1962–63 period were something else again. While critical minorities on the Left might have given voice to similar sentiments, most Americans had never heard on commercial recordings anything approaching such bitter comments on aspects of their nation's history and wars. Though none made it to the top of the popular music charts, they were released on Columbia records, which was available everywhere. Sales figures vastly underplay the input of such recordings, which were listened to repeatedly.

Oppositional subcultures growing among whites and blacks were fueled by feelings of indignation over perceived contradictions between proclaimed American values and revelations of flagrant incongruities in actual policy.[8] The civil rights movement began it, but many events in the Vietnam War era were especially significant: the systematic bombing of North Vietnam in early 1965 by "peace" president LBJ; conflicts between members of the Senate Foreign Relations Committee and arrogantly dismissive administration spokesmen in hearings aired on national television; TV images of the Tet offensive of January-February 1968 (including Walter Cronkite's remark, "I thought we were supposed to be winning"); Martin Luther King's assassination in April 1968; Robert Kennedy's assassination in June 1968; demonstrations and police riots at the Chicago Democratic National Convention in August 1968; public admission, in late 1969, of the 1968 My Lai massacre; the U.S. invasion of Cambodia in May 1970; and the Kent State killings of student demonstrators. Also significant was the worldwide student movement, with mass demonstrations in Mexico City, Prague, and Paris—the latter 1968 May revolt being one of the most portentous developments of the period. The result in the United States was an increasing sense of empowerment combined with indignant rage, fueling the further growth of long-gestating cultural resistance. As early as October 1962, the Cuban Missile Crisis made many feel that their lives were in the hands of a bunch of men who thought they could play God and "manage" any crisis. Dylan's songs expressed this frustration, but some of the most influential events of the early 1960s, at least in retrospect, were most vividly expressed by the publication of a novel.

## *CATCH-22* (JOSEPH HELLER)

Joseph Heller's complex 1961 novel was in wide circulation in the early 1960s. It's title has become part of everyday speech, although very few individuals today have actually read the novel or seen the less successful film. Together with Stanley Kubrick's film, *Dr. Strangelove* (1964), Heller's *Catch-22* was an essential text in the emergent oppositional culture at the beginning of the Vietnam War. The book was also required reading in the early 1960s, when college students actually read novels. Starting as a cult item among the intelligentsia, it eventually sold more than ten million copies in the United States alone. Its impact was cumulative and gradual, but the surreal portrait of the military it contained was unforgettable, raising the consciousness of a whole generation.[9] The novel, based on Heller's experience as an Army Air Corps bombadier who flew sixty combat missions over Italy, is especially remarkable as a prefiguration (it is set in World War II) of the surreal horror and madness of the Vietnam War.

The novel's protagonist, Capt. John Yossarian, is a bombadier who tries to have himself declared crazy so he won't have to fly more missions. However, according to an examining psychiatrist, "Anyone who wants to get out of combat duty isn't really crazy." This bind was called "Catch-22." Other memorable characters included an elusive major, who only permitted visitors to his office when he was not there, and a remarkably inventive and manipulative wheeler-dealer named Milo Minderbinder.

Novelist E. L. Doctorow, interviewed on the occasion of Heller's death in December 1999, said that "When *Catch-22* came out people were saying, 'Well, World War II wasn't like this.' But when we got tangled up in Vietnam, it became a sort of text for the consciousness of that time. They say fiction can't change anything, but [it] can certainly organize a generations' consciousness."[10]

*Catch-22* was released in 1970 as a less successful film directed by Mike Nichols. The film now seems labored and sinks under the weight of a large cast of stars (including Jon Voight, Alan Arkin, and Orson Welles), whose obvious enthusiasm paradoxically almost brought it off. Heller's novel and Kubrick's film, it was thought at the time, changed the way elite popular culture would subsequently regard the military—but the Persian Gulf War demonstrated otherwise. The Vietnam War, and the experience of millions of veterans, completed the deconstruction, until the carefully reconstructed military images of the Gulf War appeared in 1990–91. It was not until the end of the 1990s that the hype and manipulation of Operation Desert Storm was recognized in film, with *Wag the Dog* (1997, Barry Levinson) and *Three Kings* (1999, Spike Jonze).

## *THE MANCHURIAN CANDIDATE* (JOHN FRANKENHEIMER)

This film, with one of the most striking, bizarre plots of any film, remains a distinctive artifact of the media culture of the 1960s. A film with prefigurative insight, it anticipated actual historical events, such as political assassinations, with an eerie prophetic realism and touches of black humor. Political assassination has figured in countless films in the course of the twentieth century,[11] including Alfred Hitchcock's first version of *The Man Who Knew Too Much* (1934; remade in 1956 with James Stewart and Doris Day), his *Foreign Correspondent* (1940) and *Saboteur* (1942); Robert De Niro's portrayal of a psychotic Vietnam vet and assassin-in-training in Martin Scorsese's *Taxi Driver* (1976); and the many analogues of the JFK assassination in film.[12] One can discern certain common elements in most of them: the calculated murder of an important political figure; the generation of suspense through a combination of psychological melodrama and semidocumentary techniques; an approximation of real historical events; and the suggestion of a conspiracy at work that may or may not be uncovered by the film's end.[13] Such films simultaneously distance viewers from the reality of events, and yet increase uneasiness through parallels with real-life events, echoing them or (in this case) anticipating them.

Frankenheimer's film is in many ways the modern prototype of such political-assassination thrillers. Its screenplay by George Axelrod was based on Richard Condon's popular novel of the same title, which was reported a personal favorite of John F. Kennedy (who urged its filming, even speculating on the ideal cast). Because it was released in 1962, a year before JFK's death in Dallas, it has always seemed especially chilling in retrospect, given its apparently prophetic realism and its anticipation of the revelations of CIA activity and other mind-control efforts in later years. While the central character in the narrative, unlike the alleged political assassins of the 1960s, is not an obscure loner, the film inevitably raises questions about who alleged assassins Lee Harvey Oswald, Sirhan Sirhan, James Earl Ray, and Arthur Bremmer really were.

The film concerns a supposed Korean War hero, Medal of Honor winner Raymond Shaw (played by Laurence Harvey) who, along with other members of his military unit in Korea, had been captured by North Korean and Chinese troops, brainwashed and conditioned by a team of Russians and Chinese while in their custody, and somehow programmed to become a political assassin by responding to present commands after a specific set of links have been activated. In this case the catalyst is, "Why don't you pass the time by playing a game of solitaire." The subject then begins to deal the cards. When the queen of diamonds appears, he snaps into a trance-like state, ready for his instructions from his "American operator," who happens to be his own mother (Angela Lansbury), a covert agent for the Soviet Union. Mother has remarried, this time to a dim-witted but intensely vocal ultraconservative, right-wing senator John Isselin. (If the couple prefigured Ronald and Nancy Reagan over twenty-five years later, it was completely coincidental—or fortuitous—for liberal and left critics of Reagan in later years.)

Suspense increases as Shaw's commanding officer in Korea, Major Bennett Marco (played by Frank Sinatra in one of his best roles)—whose testimony played a major role in his winning the Medal of Honor—uncovers the plot and rushes to head off the apparent planned assassination of a presidential nominee during a national party convention designed to put Isselin, the vice-presidential candidate, at the head of the ticket, and his wife (a Soviet agent) at his side.

While critic Pauline Kael saw subtextual elements of political satire in the film, categorizing it as an early "black" or "nightmare" comedy—though recognized as such only years later—director John Frankenheimer clearly meant the film as an attack on the lingering influence of McCarthyism. Through the use of so-called brainwashing techniques actually applied to American prisoners in the Korean War[14] the director was commenting on larger developments within American society: "We believed that we lived in a society that was brainwashed. And I wanted to do something about it. I think our society is brainwashed by television commercials, by advertising, by politicians, by a censored press (which exists in the country whether you want to admit it or not) with its biased reporting. More and more I think that our society is becoming manipulated and controlled."[15]

The fact that John F. Kennedy died at the hands of an assassin (or assassins) less than a year later not only boosted the reputation of the film but made frighteningly real the narrative point that the impossible could become reality.

In the film, the assassination-thriller formula is followed as viewers watch Sinatra, suffering from recurrent nightmares, first become aware of his own brainwashing and then, with the aid of government psychologists and intelligence agents, trace the larger, more diabolical dimensions of the conspiracy as he races against time to head off Shaw (Harvey), the programmed assassin.

What really makes the film stick in the mind is the director's (and editor's and cinematographer's) ingenious handling of the brainwashing episodes. The film's basic plot depends on Major Marco gradually shedding implanted, false, or "screen" memories and recovering—through flashbacks during his nightmares—his memories of what happened in the Chinese prison where he and Shaw were brainwashed.

The actual process of working on Shaw is never shown. Viewers experience not the actual brainwashing but the scene after it has occurred, as the men are exhibited by their captors. There is intercutting, almost surrealistic in effect, between what are supposed actual scenes of American prisoners on a stage, under the influence of a sinister, sardonic, supposedly Soviet controller, Yen Lo (played by Khigh Deigh, who was often cast as an all-purpose Asiatic villain), with other Russian, Chinese, and North Korean officials in the audience. These images are juxtaposed and confused with conditioning-induced, implanted, false or "screen" memories of small-town New Jersey women (depending on who is dreaming, either African-American or white). Three completely separate versions of the scenes were filmed and then intercut, with different images inserted with each 360-degree pan from the stage to the audience, creating a three-way tension as multiple realities of what really happened are contrasted with events unfolding in the present of the film's narrative in the United States.

In the film's bizarre combination of Communist brainwashing, anachronistic though still relevant red-baiting in Washington, D.C., and the possible assassination of a future president of the United States by a psychologically programmed assassin, Frankenheimer's film probes deeper than Hollywood had ever done before. As Kael remarked, "Although it's a thriller, it may [also] be the most sophisticated political satire ever to come out of Hollywood."[16]

With a script sometimes stretching credulity (particularly the strange sequence in which Janet Leigh encounters Sinatra on a train) and often bordering on black comedy, the film takes on an eerie prefigurative power, anticipating the assassinations of so many major political figures in the years to follow. As later studies have suggested,[17] it might not be as absurd a premise as it initially appeared. Ironically, John Frankenheimer, a personal friend and supporter of Senator Robert F. Kennedy, drove him to the Ambassador Hotel in Los Angeles in June 1968 after his victory in the California presidential primary. Frankenheimer had originally intended to stand next to Kennedy during his victory speech but stepped aside to view the proceedings on television monitors, somewhat in the manner of events in one section of *The Manchurian Candidate.* A moment after leaving the stage, RFK was shot. Frankenheimer even believes he brushed up against Sirhan Sirhan, the alleged assassin of RFK; by some accounts he was a brainwashed, programmed assassin and was even dubbed a "Manchurian Candidate."[18] By recirculating and giving an almost hyperreal quality to (and thus ridiculing and critiquing) the most extreme 1950s paranoia about enemies within the nation, *The Manchurian Candidate,* through its mood of paranoia and suspense as well as its dark, ominous, sometimes even comedic images, made a significant early contribution to an emerging oppositional, resistance subculture of the 1960s.

## *SEVEN DAYS IN MAY:* THE NOVEL AND THE FILM

Prior to *Dr. Strangelove,* a remarkable political novel and a film based on it conjured up a riveting vision of political conspiracy. A direct follow-up of *The Manchurian Candidate,* this taut political thriller is less an "auteur" creation by a director who had become known for such types of movies than the collective product of a creative team. Frankenheimer was hired to direct an already written screenplay and a previously selected cast. The film project was based on a 1962 novel of the same name by Fletcher Knebel and Charles W. Bailey that dealt with a hypothetical military coup.[19] Kirk Douglas, one of the two major stars of the film—the other being Burt Lancaster—recalls being at a White House reception and overhearing someone behind him asking, "Do you intend to make a movie out of *Seven Days in May?*" It turned out to be John F. Kennedy, who spent the next twenty minutes explaining to Douglas why the popular novel would make a great movie. Douglas, who had already read the novel, had been warned that the subject of a potential military coup might be too hot to handle effectively in a major Hollywood production. Convinced by JFK, however, he decided to buy the rights for his company, Joel Productions. The novel's authors were skeptical that their intentions would be carried through, hoping it would not be just another "typical Hollywood movie."[20] With so many films to his credit at this point—including *Spartacus* (1960, Stanley Kubrick), *Lonely Are the Brave* (1962, David Miller), and *Paths of Glory* (1957, Stanley Kubrick)—Douglas was resentful of the authors' skeptical attitude. He was certain it could be done—and done the right way.

Rod Serling was hired to do the screenplay. Mainly known as the creator and host of *The Twilight Zone* television series (1959–63), Serling was reportedly eager to do the film because it dealt with two of his favorite subjects, the power of the military and nuclear disarmament.[21] In creating what was probably his finest screenplay, he helped make the film one of the most significant political documents of popular culture of the mid-1960s. Frankenheimer's skill at interweaving timely political themes, Serling's eloquent screenplay, and the outstanding cast entranced U.S. audiences with what was then a new and unfamiliar world of military-political conspiracy.

The actual film features veteran actor Fredric March, then sixty-seven, effectively portraying the besieged liberal president Jordan Lyman, in ill health and with low poll ratings, who pushes an arms-limitation treaty with the Soviet Union through the Senate. He is opposed by all but one member of the Joint Chiefs of Staff (Admiral Barnhart, played by John Houseman). The villain is General James Matoon Scott (Lancaster), the right-wing chairman of the Joint Chiefs, who is portrayed with low-key, self-assured menace. The plot involves Scott's coordination of a secret conspiratorial network within the military, hidden even from his own chief of staff, Col. "Jiggs" Casey (Douglas). The latter comes across evidence of a large, top-secret, privately financed base in the Texas desert (anticipating Iran-Contra by twenty-five years), with an elite force of nearly four thousand men who are being trained to seize all major national communication networks on Sunday, May 18, the date of the running of the Preakness horserace. A detailed description of the conspiracy must be assembled in a few days to enable the president to prevail in a public confrontation with Scott and his fellow conspirators.

In some of his finest work for films, Serling here penned strikingly persuasive lines for Lancaster as General Scott, who at one point says, "There's not a single piece of paper in history that's ever served as a deterrent to a Pearl Harbor. Every twenty years or so we pick ourselves up bleeding off the floor and forget that. Mistakes which are delivered to us C.O.D. by peace-loving men and bought and paid for by peace-loving men—men in uniform." Even more moving lines were written for the politically beset, well-meaning president, which March delivers with utter naturalism. His belief in democratic principles and the peaceful resolution of international conflicts comes through in the climactic showdown with Lancaster. The final confrontation of Lancaster and Douglas is also priceless. General Scott, mustering his cool, subdued air of menace, says to Casey, whom he clearly regards as a traitor for revealing his plot to the president, "Do you know who Judas was?," to which the latter replies, "Yes. He's a man I worked for . . . until he disgraced the stars on his uniform."

In retrospect, the film's scenario becomes even more believable when one examines recent revelations of conflicts within the Kennedy administration over nuclear preparedness. JFK had campaigned using what now seems extremely hawkish and aggressive rhetoric involving a "missile gap," the need for a modernized military, and greater preparedness in the arms race. Moreover, he inherited the disastrous CIA Cuban exile invasion plan, begun in the Eisenhower administration, now known by the site of its failure, the Bay of Pigs. It is now clear that Kennedy was grossly misled by the CIA concerning the probability of its success.[22]

Still more fascinating was Kennedy's desire to have a film made of *Seven Days in May.* Earlier, it will be recalled, he had supported a film version of Richard Condon's novel *The Manchurian Candidate.* He now offered the White House for filming, believing, according to former White House insider Arthur Schlesinger Jr., that it could serve as "a warning to the nation."[23] According to a fascinating article, the Joint Chiefs, the director of the CIA, and others told Kennedy at a July 20, 1961, secret meeting of the National Security Council that a "window of opportunity" would exist in late 1963 permitting the United States to launch a preemptive strike that would almost completely destroy the nuclear capacity of the Soviet Union.[24] According to various reports, Kennedy, apparently angered, ordered absolute secrecy, insisting "that no member in attendance disclose even the subject of the meeting." Profoundly disturbed at even the hypothetical discussion of a first strike, Kennedy disgustedly remarked to Secretary of State Dean Rusk after the briefing, "And we call ourselves the human race."[25]

In his investigation of the complex political background leading up to JFK's assassination, Anthony Summers explores the possibility that the assassination might have been the first step in a planned military takeover, or an excuse to exploit this projected "window of opportunity" to launch a first strike against the Soviet Union. This, Summers suggests, might explain an extensive and problematic body of alleged "intelligence" linking accused assassin Lee Harvey Oswald to Soviet or Cuban intelligence operations; a supposed Army Intelligence "file" on him; and even a very brief period when president Johnson lacked nuclear weapons codes.[26]

In defeating the cold, silent menace of General Scott and his coterie of high-level plotters, President Lyman expresses his faith in constitutional government and the power of a people acting together to effect their destiny. His reaffirmation of civilian control of the military was expressed just prior to the precipitous drop in public trust and confidence as a result of the Vietnam War and Watergate. With a conviction that still inspires the viewer, Lyman claims that the real cause of the move to overthrow the Constitution is not the lust for power of one man but a concentration of fear and anxiety that are the product of the nuclear age: "It happens to have killed man's faith in his ability to influence what happens to him." This final statement remains a high point in one of the distinctive popular cultural texts of the 1960s.

## *DR. STRANGELOVE:* A REVELATION OF "BACK REGION" BEHAVIOR

Stanley Kubrick's "nightmare" comedy played widely across the nation, especially in theaters near college campuses.[27] It remains the most important American political film made between *Birth of a Nation* (1915) and *JFK* (1991) and one of the most significant political statements of the 1960s.[28] In terms of *radical* documents, it is arguably as important as Martin Luther King Jr.'s "I Have a Dream" speech, Malcolm X's *Autobiography* (written with Alex Haley), the SDS "Port Huron Statement," Herbert Marcuse's *One-Dimensional Man,* or the songs of Bob Dylan. No single cultural artifact better represents the disintegration of the American consensus in the early and mid-1960s and the new cultural forces challenging it.[29] It is the quintessential parodic portrait of cold war anti-Communist paranoia, visionary in its moral critique of the arrogance of power and presumptive conceit of military planners who seemed certain that an accidental nuclear war could never occur.

In the film, the all-male members of the ruling class are represented as either incompetents or sex-obsessed near-psychotics. Mid-level and lower-ranking military and other officials appear as affectless, loyal, efficient near-robots who follow orders. The opening voice-over explains that the Soviet Union has built a "Doomsday Device" that will detonate automatically if a nuclear weapon explodes anywhere within its territory. This is deterrence carried to absurd, suicidal lengths. Meanwhile, a hard-line, clinically paranoid ultra-Right Air Force general has sealed off his base and ordered a bomber wing of B-52s to attack their Russian targets. (He is unaware, along with the rest of the world, of the existence of the Soviet Doomsday Device). When the U.S. president discovers the attack orders, he finds the planes cannot be recalled because only the general knows the recall codes, whereupon he orders the base attacked and the general arrested. The general shoots himself prior to his capture. After a hilariously inept phone conversation between the Soviet and American leaders, the United States agrees to assist the Russian air defense in destroying the U.S. planes, but one gets through, dropping its bombs and setting off the Russian device. The film concludes with the image of a nuclear apocalypse.

Joshua Meyrowitz has described the notion of a "back region" of behavior by public persons, referring to those aspects of life not ordinarily evident to the general population.[30] Back region activity is anything public figures do when not acting in their official capacities. Examples of back region activities might include the intimate, family life of presidents (FDR's behind-the-scenes preparations, necessitated by polio, prior to giving a speech); toilet and bath habits (reported "farting" by President LBJ); and sleep practices (Ronald Reagan's frequent napping). Even more fascinating are "deep back region behavior, such as JFK's apparent use of stimulants to counter adrenal insufficiency (Addison's disease) and to maintain his high level of energy; or his sexual affairs with Marilyn Monroe, Judith Campbell, and many others.

In Meyrowitz's formulation, the revolution of mass communication creates a new kind of public arena or community, one in which, because of the universality of television, the visual image becomes privileged. It registers the triumph of the visual as fundamental to the grammar of politics of the late-twentieth and early-twenty-first centuries. Often noted by later observers (see the account in chapter 6 of the Reagan White House), and expressed cogently in films such as *Wag the Dog*, this phenomena creates immense opportunities for the distortion of reality and an overpowering of reasoned discourse about public policy, which can lead to mass manipulation of public opinion through image construction.

*Dr. Strangelove* provides a powerful instance of a wholly fictional yet believable representation of such back region behavior of public figures: what they might do when not in uniform; what they really say in phone conversations or in candid exchanges with subordinates. What the Joint Chiefs or the president might do in extreme situations, when not in the public view, is the subject of *Dr. Strangelove.* The film can be seen as part of an emergent trend to reveal more of the private lives of public individuals and hold them up to public scrutiny. In the film, it is as if hidden cameras were present in the hotel room of an Air Force commanding general, "Buck" Turgidson (George C. Scott) who is supposed to be "going over some paperwork" with his secretary, Miss Scott, but is actually having a sexual encounter. Most striking—and the central metaphorical device of the whole film—is the aide—Group Captain Mandrake (Peter Sellers), who essentially serves as the audience—overhearing the paranoid ravings in the inner office of the outwardly sane but increasingly lunatic base commander Jack D. Ripper (brilliantly portrayed by Sterling Hayden), who—worried about the way supposed "communist"-inspired fluoridation of water is sapping his "precious bodily fluids," is clearly (from the hindsight of four decades) *clinically insane,* though it was not noticed in an era in which his rhetoric mirrored that of a significant section of the national leadership—has just ordered a bomb wing to bomb Russia, initiating a world nuclear cataclysm. Every key scene of the film similarly exposes fictional back region behavior, including shouted recriminations at a meeting of the National Security Council in the War Room of the Pentagon, or bizarre "cowboy" heroics aboard a B-52 just receiving what appear to be authentic orders to drop nuclear weapons on the Soviet Union.

*Dr. Strangelove* is part of a larger trend of the media rooting around for stories, which reached an absurd end point in the Clinton-Lewinsky scandal of 1998–99. Though containing completely fictional images, the film expressed a profound moral truth in its condemnation of higher circles of power. It also prefigured and anticipated the shattering of public confidence in leading political figures and a declining faith in public institutions.

Prior to *Dr. Strangelove,* the military had—with the exception of such films as *The Caine Mutiny* (1954, Edward Dmytryk) and *Paths of Glory* (1957, Stanley Kubrick)—almost always received the most positive images in the movies. Since 1964, there have been numerous filmic portraits of incompetent or insane military officers and sleazy, corrupt, devious, incompetent government officials—though often the likes of Sylvester Stallone, Chuck Norris, Steve McQueen, or Clint Eastwood might be present to represent the "true" interests of the audience. In *Dr. Strangelove,* by contrast, virtually everyone is either crazy, power hungry, delusional, or victimized. There had never been anything quite like these mad images before, and few films have approached them since, as a direct comparison with the later, highly applauded satirical film *Wag the Dog* easily demonstrates.

Director Stanley Kubrick began his screenplay for *Dr. Strangelove* with the idea of a serious military suspense thriller built around a scenario of possible accidental nuclear war, taking off from Peter George's *Red Alert.* As Kubrick later recalled in an interview, "As I kept trying to imagine the way in which things would really happen, ideas kept coming to me which I would discard because they were so ludicrous. I kept saying to myself: 'I can't do this. People will laugh.' . . . I began to realize that all the things I was throwing out were the things which were most truthful."[31] Eventually Kubrick decided he could only resolve his dilemma by moving in a completely different direction: "The only way to tell the story was as a black comedy, or better, a nightmare comedy, where the things you laugh at most are really the heart of the paradoxical postures that make a nuclear war possible."[32] When Terry Southern, one of the "black humor" writers of the era, was hired to work on the screenplay, a link was established with one of the defining literary movements of the 1960s. Black humor has been described memorably by Morris Dickstein as "the breaking point where moral anguish explodes into a mixture of comedy and terror, where things are so bad you might as well laugh."[33]

The phrase "the banality of evil" was then in wide circulation among campus intellectuals following the publication of Hannah Arendt's *New Yorker* series (in February and March 1963) on the Eichmann trial in Israel and the book that followed.[34] Here, in an amazing artifact of black humor, a trailblazing and explosive "nightmare comedy," was a darkly humorous example of the phenomenon.

The crew uses all its initiative and American ingenuity to keep the damaged bomber on course, while flight commander Col. "King" Kong (Slim Pickens) uses handyman heroics to open the bomb bay doors. Only the audience knows that the absurd heroics of completing their mission will result in the Soviet "Doomsday Device" eventually destroying all human life.

Part of the paranoia stimulated by *Dr. Strangelove* arises from the recognition by attentive viewers of the irony that they, too, are trapped by a defining aspect of American culture so terrifying one has no choice but to laugh. If people began to feel increasingly paranoid about their leaders after seeing *Dr. Strangelove,* it was because they recognized they were part of a culture trapped in its military technology, unable to recognize the enormous horrific possibilities posed by nuclear weapons and strategies, and full of illusions about the ability of humans to control them.[35]

Stanley Kubrick's film remains one of the greatest—if not the greatest—political films, still madly disconcerting and terrifying for its "back region" images of a national military and civilian leadership totally out of touch with the horrific realities of nuclear war and yet utterly believable despite the insane anachronisms of Major "King" Kong (Pickens); Gen. Jack D. Ripper (Hayden), who could launch a nuclear war because he feared fluoridation of water; Gen. Buck Turgidson (Scott), who equated a possible twenty million American dead as getting "our hair mussed"; or even the engaging minor presence of Col. "Bat" Guano (Keenan Wynn), who is fearful of "deviated preverts" and so mindful of the value of private property that he reminds Group Captain Lionel Mandrake that if he shoots open a vending machine to get change to make a phone call that might prevent nuclear apocalypse, "You'll have to answer to the Coca-Cola Company!" These characters are held together by the remarkable performance of Peter Sellers, playing three crucial characters: Gen. Ripper's aide Group Captain Mandrake; President Merkin Muffley (in bald wig obviously referencing liberal Democrat Adlai Stevenson); and Dr. Strangelove (physically resembling Henry Kissinger but obviously referencing Herman Kahn, Dr. Edward Teller, Werner von Braun, and other foreign-born military/defense intellectuals). While an overt assault on the previous cold war military consensus, the sexual associations evoked by the names of these and other characters (Ambassador "DeSadesky" and Premier "Kissov") added an additional level of comedy to what was effectively a revolutionary critique of the higher immorality and insanity of a national defense policy based on nuclear deterrence.

*Dr. Strangelove* put such expressions as "deviated prevert," "precious bodily fluids," and lines such as, "Gentlemen, you can't fight here, this is the War Room!" into wide circulation as insider codes used by a generation that increasingly regarded its national leaders as manipulative liars following insane policies. Images and characterizations in *Dr. Strangelove* resonated with a generation that increasingly could see—to quote the opening words and title of a later song by the Jefferson Airplane—that when the truth is found to be lies, "Don't You Need Somebody to Love?"

Another point of these filmic examples—*Catch 22*, *Dr. Strangelove*, and, to a lesser extent, *Seven Days in May*—is that the very appeals that traditionally might have been used to motivate one segment of the population to display patriotic fervor were, from the early days of Vietnam involvement, increasingly regarded with skepticism—even cynicism—by a smaller but growing segment as wrong, misguided, ludicrous, and laughable (though the humor was of a dark, sardonic sort), and ultimately insane and profoundly immoral. The *Dr. Strangelove*-loving, college-educated, early baby-boomers saw the whole military enterprise of the cold war and nuclear deterrence as "crackpot realism," utterly and profoundly crazy.

## Anti-industrial Paranoia and the Anti-Western

Several other films spoke to aspects of the political crisis of the 1960s, reflecting the disorientation, suspicion, fear, paranoia, and intimations of conspiracy that would characterize mass cultural images of politics and society by the mid-1970s. These films were often outgrowths of literary works and reflected broader, longer-term sensibilities. One significant impulse was evident in several westerns at the end of the 1950s and early '60s, reflecting both the closure of the Old West and the beginnings of an environmental consciousness.[36]

Early in the 1960s several post- or anti-westerns expressed the frustration of individuals faced with the capitalist industrial culture's destruction of nature. Among these were *The Misfits* (1961, John Huston), with a screenplay by Arthur Miller; *The Man Who Shot Liberty Valance* (1962, John Ford); *Ride the High Country* (1962, Sam Peckinpah); *Hud* (1963, Martin Ritt); and *Lonely Are the Brave* (1962, David Miller).[37]

### *LONELY ARE THE BRAVE*

This film opens with a lone cowboy named John W. "Jack" Burns (Kirk Douglas) reclining peacefully in his saddle while looking up at clear sky over a vast New Mexico semidesert. Three jet vapor trails leave streaks overhead and their roar is heard on the soundtrack, marking the first of several images suggesting the violent intrusion of the modern world into his life. Burns' horse, a spirited mare named "Whiskey," has a will of her own, picking the blanket off her back whenever he tries to put on the saddle. They are next seen confronting a barbed-wire fence and posted range. Producing a set of wire cutters, Burns calmly and methodically cuts through the fence and continues his ride until he reaches a noisy modern highway. The huge trucks and an endless stream of cars roaring by (emphasizing the horrific din of what we call "civilization") spooks the horse, which rears up on its hind legs and wheels about on the centerline, in the middle of traffic. When the latter clears, they proceed to the opposite side, arriving at a gigantic stack of wrecked cars that towers above the horse and rider—a monument to our throwaway society. Burns calmly talks to the horse, explaining that she has to be more responsive when told to "hup." The apparently relaxed, free-spirited cowboy and his horse, on a visit to a friend and his wife, proceed into a residential area at the edge of town as calmly as if driving a car or pickup like the rest of the residents.

*Lonely Are the Brave* is a penetrating, sentimental, often starkly cruel representation of the conflict between culture and nature in the modern American West. The screenplay by Dalton Trumbo is a sensitive translation of Edward Abbey's novel *Brave Cowboy.* Abbey later said that the screenplay significantly improved on his book, especially the spoken dialogue. One of the central voices in the environmental movement of the 1960s and '70s, he later wrote the popular eco-sabotage cult classic *The Monkey Wrench Gang*—thereby coining the tactical movement and technique of "monkey wrenching"—as well as several remarkable books of environmental essays, such as *Desert Solitaire* (1968).

Burns, a genuinely free person who knows who he is, is played by Douglas as if it were his own life story (it was his all-time favorite role) as he confronts the social system that is trying to make him (and everyone else) conform. As Douglas described its message, "If you are different, they will try to crush you."[38]

Trying to see his idealistic friend Paul Bondi, who has been jailed for aiding illegal immigrants (in the novel he is a noncooperative conscientious objector jailed for draft resistance), Burns gets himself jailed after a bar brawl with a one-armed man.[39]

Finding his friend Paul, Jack fails to get him to agree to an escape plan. Paul, now married to "Jerri" (Gena Rolands), a woman Burns is still in love with, also has a young boy. He appears to have grown less wild and reckless in the years since the two friends last saw each other. In the novel, Paul, as a principled anarchist, is shocked that Burns would urge him to try to escape the repressive power of the state, preferring to serve as a living example of the evils of the system. In the film, Paul, like Thoreau and anticipating Martin Luther King Jr.'s "Letter from Birmingham Jail," also proudly says he knows he has to pay for doing what he knew to be the right thing.

Burns antagonizes the jailer, Gutierrez, played with malevolent, menacing enthusiasm by George Kennedy. Called out of his cell in the middle of the night by Gutierrez, Burns receives a vicious beating. Using two hacksaw blades hidden in his boot, he spends the rest of the night sawing through a bar (aided by several other prisoners, including two Native Americans). After a farewell to Paul, Burns squeezes through the hole and escapes through a second-floor window. Returning to his friend's house to get his horse, Burns tries to escape over the mountains to Mexico before the police find him.

Meanwhile, in a subplot, a trucker (played by Carroll O'Connor) is shown driving a large tractor-trailer loaded with toilets. Earlier he has been glimpsed several times on the road, starting in Joplin, Mo., on old U.S. Route 66, holding his gut, popping Tums and Rolaids, suffering indigestion from the greasy highway café food. He and Burns are destined to meet. The anonymous trucker, inexorably moving his giant tractor-trailer across the country, embodies one of the forces of modern civilization closing in on Jack Burns.

The other is embodied by Sheriff Johnson (played by Walter Matthau), who is somewhat bemused by the Burns character and displays a growing admiration for the resourceful cowboy-fugitive, whom he has never met.

At one point, trapped inside the closing ring of the posse, Burns gets the drop on Gutierrez, the man who viciously beat him. Gutierrez begs Burns not to shoot him. It is not in Burns' character to kill. Instead, he deftly administers the butt of his rifle stock, knocking the bully unconscious. Burns is no killer, he just wants to get away, to get out of this place. He also acts in accord with author Abbey's code of the eco-warrior, summed up in his final novel, *Hayduke Lives:* "Rule Number One is: Nobody Gets Hurt, not even yourself."[40] In this case the second half of the rule proves impossible to enforce.

One of the brave cowboy's tragic failings is his refusal to abandon his horse. Through binoculars, the sheriff spots him—horse in tow—heading up the mountainside. Later, as darkness falls, the now wounded Burns tries to make a run for it. Burns and his horse still have to cross a busy two-lane highway in a driving rain. The destined rendezvous with the trucker finally occurs. The horse—again spooked by the headlights, the driving rain, and peals of thunder, spinning in terror in the middle of the rain-slicked highway, with car and truck headlights coming from all directions,—is hit by the truck. Burns, perhaps fatally injured, lies in pain at the edge of the pavement. Sheriff Johnson and his deputy drive up. The deputy shoots the badly wounded, writhing animal as the camera focuses on Burns—lying disabled and bleeding under a blanket in the downpour—as he recoils at the sound of the shot. The sheriff watches as Burns is lifted into an ambulance, feeling Burns' pain at his horse's untimely death.

The film is initially quite engaging—almost humorous—in its portrayal of the fiercely individualistic Jack Burns, a character apparently closely modeled on Abbey. But it gradually becomes an inspiring struggle of determined hope against increasing odds and the grim advance of the whole "machine"—as Abbey described it—of capitalist industrial society and its relentless legal system. (Abbey is quoted as saying that "growth is the ideology of a cancer cell.")[41] The film's conclusion hits from the viewer's blind side with an emotional impact very much like Burns' fate. This is a world in which those who crave freedom are crushed or go to jail and those who love them pay the price and try to survive after them.

*Lonely Are the Brave,* a product of Douglas' production company, was abysmally handled upon its original release by Universal Studios, being abruptly withdrawn from circulation just as it was gaining a word-of-mouth reputation and garnering very positive reviews in New York and London. Over the years it has developed a cult following.

The film haunts the memories of those, like the present writer, who view it repeatedly in hope that somehow Jack Burns and his horse will make it over that mountain to that refuge in Mexico Burns muses about.

Since Burns is the embodiment of freedom, Abbey couldn't let him go. In the film it's not clear what ultimately happens to him. The sheriff apparently can't identify the badly injured Burns since he has never seen him up close. Burns reappears in *The Monkey Wrench Gang* as the "mysterious stranger" who assists in sabotaging bulldozers and giant dragline earthmovers. Increasingly decrepit, he reappears in *Good News* and, finally, in Abbey's last novel *Hayduke Lives!*

Kirk Douglas continued to regard *Lonely Are the Brave* as his favorite among the over seventy-five films he made. He wrote a touching tribute to Abbey following the latter's obituary ("Thoreau of the American West"), in which he said,

> I never met Mr. Abbey, but we wrote to each other several times. . . . In the opening scene, I played Jack Burns (Edward Abbey), who rides across a wide plain and comes up to a large wire fence. I get off my horse, taking a pair of pliers, cut the fence and ride on. In your article you quote Abbey: "I am the one who loved un-fenced countries." In the more than [seventy-five] films that I've made, this is my favorite. I am very pleased when I get a letter, or someone comes up to me saying it is also their favorite.[42]

*Lonely Are the Brave* is one of most moving evocations of the death of individual liberty as the West is swallowed up by developers. Edward Abbey described this new kind of western aristocracy as

> car dealers, tract-slum builders, and *Book of Mormon* financiers . . . overgrazers, clear-cutters, strip-miners, widespread operations [employing] a

corps of flunky journalists, who manage the regional TV stations and newspapers, and a regiment of Quisling politicians. This process is called "growth." Our Mafia aristocracy is indifferent to the fate of our children and grandchildren, for short-term profit is all that matters. To reverse this would require something like a political revolution in the Southwest, indeed, national politics.[43]

Jack Burns remains part of the advance guard of that revolution.

### *SECONDS* (JOHN FRANKENHEIMER)

No director contributed more to the discourse of visionary paranoia in movies during this period than John Frankenheimer and his "paranoia trilogy"—*The Manchurian Candidate* (1962), *Seven Days in May* (1964), and *Seconds* (1966)—though the original source novels obviously played a major, if not crucial, role in all three.

*Seconds* is the story of a middle-aged banker, Arthur Hamilton (effectively played by former blacklistee John Randolph in its first section), who experiences the emptiness of middle age and feels smothered in his present life; he is used up and played out—almost dying. Contacted by a former friend who supposedly had died, he is told of a secret organization, The Company, that promises a new life for a huge fee. It fakes one's death, provides a facsimile corpse, arranges for plastic surgery, and supplies all the trappings of a completely new identity.

After almost forty minutes into *Seconds,* following real scenes of actual plastic surgery, the bandages come off and John Randolph is transformed into Rock Hudson, who delivers one of the finest performances of his career. Now a wealthy Malibu artist named Antiochus "Tony" Wilson, the transformed Randolph is supplied with faked paintings and given painting lessons and the outlines of a style. But he struggles with his new identity, not knowing what he wants to do with his new life and unable to forget his former life even though it was at a dead end. Tony (Hudson) fails to adjust to his new life, getting drunk at a party of new friends (themselves all "Seconds"), blubbering about his former life and dissatisfaction with his changed existence. (The director actually had Hudson drink before the scene, which was done in one take. It apparently became for him a moment of emotional release about his own personal anxieties—then publicly unadmitted—over his repressed homosexuality.)

Pretending to be a friend of her "dead" husband, Tony visits his wife, who doesn't really seem to miss him. Asking for another chance, he is taken to a kind of testing center where he encounters other men in a similar lapsed state. The Company demands that Tony name another candidate for them, but he refuses, asking for new surgery as soon as possible. There he meets Charlie, the "deceased" friend who first called him, who also wants another chance.

The shocking realization dawns that they are to be used as corpses by the procurement section. One night Tony is awakened, strapped to a gurney, gagged, and read the last rites. Heavily sedated, he dreams—in a kind of "Rosebud" sequence—of a man on a beach with a child on his shoulder (something he missed in his life) just moments before a drill bores into his skull, permanently extinguishing all memories and hopes of another life.

Aside from the existential questions raised by the quest for a new life, *Seconds* was striking and poignant in its echoes of the reported eighty-thousand men in the United States who each year abandon their families and former lives.[44] The notion of a top-secret organization resonates through subsequent movie history in the form of The Parallax Corporation in *The Parallax View* (1974, Alan J. Pakula) and, more hollowly, in the Consumer Recreations Services of *The Game* (1997, David Fincher). Most recently, in Stanley Kubrick's *Eyes Wide Shut* (1999) another super-secret society, made up of people who will stop at nothing to have their way, stages elaborate sex orgies that lead to the sacrifice of human life.

### *BLOW-UP* (MICHELAGELO ANTONIONI)

When it was first released in 1966, Michelangelo Antonioni's *Blow-Up* was greeted with tremendous enthusiasm, becoming an immediate cult film. It was the era's "art film for the masses"—a hip, timely, mysterious, and visually intoxicating "foreign" film that addressed larger philosophical questions of illusion and reality and—at a more concrete level—the nature of film and photographic images.

*Blow-Up* is set in what was then seen as the swinging, "mod" London of the Beatles and the Yardbirds (who appear in the film). The central character is a fashion photographer (David Hemings) who, in retrospect, displays a cynically manipulative and arrogant attitude toward women, especially his models, which can be interpreted as a broader statement on constructed reality. He basically uses his camera as an instrument of seduction and then coldly shoos his models out of the studio. It's a frivolous, fantasy-filled existence and it will take a major event to change his outlook on what is "real" and what is illusory, what is trivial and what is significant.

One day, while shooting nature scenes in a park for a book to which he is to contribute a number of starkly *serious*, black-and-white real-life pictures—we see him discussing with an editor several photos of poor people, naked prisoners, industrial workers—he photographs a woman (Vanessa Redgrave) and an older, distinguished gray-haired man. She asks for the film, but he refuses. Later she comes to his studio to plead for the photos. He attempts to seduce her—they both remove half their clothing—but she has to leave, so he gives her a roll of exposed film that does not contain the shots taken at the park. He becomes suspicious that something important happened in the park. In a sequence that at the time positively riveted audiences, he develops the film and makes successively larger "blow-ups," creating huge, almost life-size sheets that he pins to his studio wall and scrutinizes with a magnifying lens. Anticipating a generation of JFK assassination-photo analysts[45] and several later films, he discovers what he believes to be a man holding a gun standing in the bushes. A blow-up of another photo suggests an image of what could be a body lying on the grass, partially concealed by bushes.

That night Hemmings returns to the park—significantly *without* his camera—and finds the body of the man he had seen with the Redgrave character. Unable to decide what to do, he returns home. At daybreak—now *with* his camera—he returns to the park, but the body he saw is not there. Returning to his studio, he finds that his blow-ups as well as the negatives have been stolen. There is thus no proof that what he saw was "real." Did he think he saw something because he wanted to? He must now question the reality he thinks he knows. Without the photographic evidence, he has only his personal recollections of what he thought he saw. The point seems to be that the introduction of a camera itself distorts reality; moreover, since each individual has unique sensibilities, no single person can see any absolute "truth."

Thirty-five years later, *Blow-Up* appears somewhat pretentious. The sexism and sexual politics offend our postmillennial sense of political correctness. But the revelatory darkroom sequences remain absorbing, clearly anticipating and serving as models for Francis Ford Coppola's *The Conversation* (1974)—where Gene Hackman works with audiotapes to reveal a murder—and Brian De Palma's *Blow-Out* (1981)—in which soundman John Travolta works with both audiotapes and a series of photographs to reveal an assassination. *Blow-Up* today seems far longer than its 111 minutes. Still, the final sequence—where Hemmings, observing a group of mimes simulating a tennis game, joins in by retrieving and tossing an imaginary tennis ball—remains one of the most unforgettable moments in film history.[46]

### *BULLITT* (PETER YATES)

The atmosphere of America in the Vietnam years is present, though one feels it almost indirectly, knowing that anyone connected with the film or viewing it will supply the sense of conflicted suspicion of authority it depends upon. Directed by Peter Yates in his first U.S. film, the screenplay for *Bullitt,* based on Robert L. Pike's novel *Mute Witness,* was written by Alan Trustman and Harry Kleiner. (The latter wrote the screenplays for the film noir features *Fallen Angel* [1946, Otto Preminger], *House of Bamboo* [1955, Samuel Fuller], and *The Garment Jungle* [1957, Robert Aldrich and Vincent Sherman].) Steve McQueen plays loner homicide detective "Frank Bullitt" in this crime drama with a complex deconstructive narrative that anticipates conspiracy/paranoia conventions of the 1970s and—especially in McQueen's portrayal of the central character—serves as an interesting counterportrait to Clint Eastwood's later San Francisco-based "Dirty Harry." The character also prefigures Harrison Ford's role in Ridley Scott's future noir *Blade Runner* (1982); some scenes (and Harrison Ford's general appearance throughout in a turtleneck sweater and shoulder holster) seem directly influenced—or at least prefigured by—McQueen's image here. Bullitt demonstrates real investigative expertise—McQueen's performance communicates genuine personal integrity—but the emotional distance he must necessarily assume while investigating the brutal murders that are part of his job increasingly exacts an emotional toll, a kind of psychic numbing, that turns off his chic commercial artist girlfriend (Jacqueline Bisset).

The complex narrative has Bullitt providing security for Chicago mobster Johnny Ross, who is to be sprung as a surprise witness at crime hearings being held by a publicity-hungry, manipulative, and opportunistic senator, Walter Chalmers (played with a venomous yet subdued intensity by Robert Vaughn), with subtle threats and gratuitous hurtfulness.

Combining a police procedural with an investigative narrative, the film maintains an air of mystery, including a quite bizarre twist early on when the witness being guarded by Bullitt is killed by professional hit men. The witness is the exact double of another character—the viewer is not certain until the end whether or not it's the same person—though they are played by two different actors. Reasonably enough in a year that saw the assassinations of Dr. Martin Luther King Jr. and Senator Robert Kennedy, as well as the domestic political crisis over Vietnam, there are intimations of some kind of wider conspiracy involving Senator Chalmers, though its dimensions are not clear until the very end of the film.

The shotgun killing in a small hotel room, though very brief, remains a stark, color enactment of noirish realism. In striking scenes in a dingy hotel on Embarcadero Road next to a freeway, where the witness—supposedly the Chicago mob figure Ross, who is ready to testify before Chalmers' committee the next week—is held under Bullitt's protection, viewers see the witness being guarded actually unlock the door of the seedy hotel room to permit two men to enter. To everyone's surprise, they aim a quick blast to the legs of the detective guarding Ross, upending him and leaving him bleeding in agony on the floor. They turn to the witness. Genuinely surprised, he recoils, backing onto the bed in horrified disbelief as a single explosive burst from the shotgun throws him against the wall, his blood splattering everywhere. The shotgun blasts are delivered by one number of a pair of aging professional killers. The shooter, gray—almost white-haired—holds a Winchester pump shotgun that he stashes in special pockets inside his light raincoat. The other, the driver and backup, wears dark, horn-rimmed, Cary Grant–style glasses. (The same actor would later play a very similar role in *Hickey and Boggs* [1972, Robert Culp].)

While not as bloody as those in later films, this scene is brief, methodical, and—because it comes as such a surprise—of shattering impact. The killers are like old-time butchers behind the display case of a local meat market, quickly and efficiently trimming and wrapping a meat purchase—only they do it with a shotgun.

Bullitt knows it's a professional hit. He suspects some sort of conspiracy when he is told that the door was unlocked by the victim.

There follow tense, almost silent, scenes in which the killer returns to the hospital to finish off the witness, is discovered and tracked by Bullitt to the basement, and escapes. The witness—thought to be Ross—dies of his original wounds, whereupon Bullitt hides all records of the death and spirits away the body from the senator, who appears several times at the hospital with his entourage of aides, reporters, and police allies. Senator Chalmers at one point lavishly commends the black emergency room surgeon who worked on the badly shot witness, then duplicitously asks a superviser to replace the man he just commended with a higher-ranking person. Bullitt and the surgeon, who are within earshot, exchange knowing looks that register their disgust. The hospital interior pursuit scenes, shot in low light, are deftly staged. The killer, pursued by Bullitt, escapes from darkness into bright sunshine, later returning with his driver to stalk Bullitt as the latter begins his investigation by touring San Francisco's downtown.

Although *Bullitt* was immensely popular and widely seen during its original release in late 1968 and throughout 1969 (it was number three among the top twenty in revenues for 1969), the film has never been given the attention it deserves by critics. It gained and maintains a word-of-mouth notoriety for its extended car chase through San Francisco (with McQueen, coached by a professional driving his own Highland Green 390 Shelby-Mustang, especially prepared by veteran auto racer and car builder Max Balchowski). Thanks to Yates' tight direction, William Fraker's photography, and Oscar-winning film editing by Frank Keller, the chase remains one of the best in move history; it preceded by several years the more celebrated but contrived New York City chase scene in *The French Connection* (1971, William Friedkin) and was not equaled until the remarkable chase sequences in *Ronin* thirty years later (1998, John Frankenheimer).

In a larger context, *Bullitt* can be read as a comment on what Marshall Berman would later call the tragedy of development.[47] It critiques the sense of alienation, depersonalization, and emerging hyperurbanization of a once intimate city, the place Hitchcock—surveying the city for *Vertigo* in 1955—called the "Paris" of North America. Bullitt lives in a neighborhood that looks pleasant enough and might have housed Hammett's San Francisco–based Sam Spade thirty years earlier (it looks very much like Hammett's old apartment building). By showing freeway scenes of massive traffic congestion and the on-foot pursuit of the witness by Bullitt across airport runways, the film speaks to the diminishing significance of humans in an era of massive technology (and machinelike organizations.

There is a memorable scene just before the film ends where Bullitt's girlfriend drives him to a deluxe San Mateo motel on a supposedly routine check of a possible connection to the case, which turns out to be a murder scene involving the strangled body of a woman. Bullitt quickly moves into her line of vision to spare her the horror of the scene. After they leave, she reveals her feelings about the horrors of his world (which she has just witnessed). The scene resonates both as a comment on her sense of disintegration of all her illusions about her little personal world and, in a larger sense, expresses—through the urban industrial image that surround them—the tragedy of development of the San Francisco region. She says to Bullitt, "I thought I knew you, but I'm not so sure anymore. . . . Do you ever feel anything—really? Or are you so used to it you don't care? You're living in a sewer, Frank. . . . With you, living with violence is a way of life. How can you be a part of it without becoming more and more callous. . . . What will happen to us in time?" All Frank can say in reply is that the violence is out there but that what happens between them is all that matters now.

As played by McQueen in what has to be the finest performance of his career, Bullitt in many ways adopts the conventions of the middle-class cop/investigator in the tradition of Sam Spade and Philip Marlowe. Unlike these earlier hard-boiled PIs, however, the central character is still part of the official police organization and he's younger. (McQueen was thirty-eight when the film was made, while Bogart was forty-one as Spade in *The Maltese Falcon* and forty-six as Marlowe in *The Big Sleep*. Moreover, at the time of the film's release viewers had witnessed McQueen's repeated stints in solitary confinement, with his baseball and glove, in *The Great Escape* (1963, John Sturges)—anticipating

Paul Newman's stints in "the box" four years later in *Coolhand Luke*—his bravura performance fleeing his Nazi captors on a motorcycle in the same film, and his extracinematic reputation as a race car driver and motorcyclist, giving him unique skills and an action persona that the earlier film investigators lacked.

These aspects aside, there is still an overcontrolled, cool, yet edgy quality to Bullitt's manner as McQueen plays him. He shows a resigned realism before the constant manipulations of the chain of command, represented by Senator Chalmers. This can be read as a weary, almost burnt-out tenseness, combined with an unflagging commitment to do his job no matter what. When he arrives at his girlfriend's apartment at the end of a particularly bloody day, before he joins her in bed he looks into a mirror and, one senses, doesn't particularly like what he sees. It's as if he knows that his integrity will never make up for the price the job exacts. He remains a more believable, realistic alternative to the vengeful neuroticism of Eastwood's Dirty Harry Callahan.

While in many ways representative of its time, *Bullitt* evokes, in the manner of classic film noir, the sense of a menacing society and—through the character of the senator—a corrupt political system. It presents arresting and enduring images of the tragedy of urban overdevelopment, of alienation, of individuals subject to forces beyond their control, with early intimations of paranoia and wider systemic corruption of politicians (though the senator's criminality is never conclusively proven). In all these aspects it anticipates films of the '70s, whose images reveal investigators facing more than meets the eye but—unlike Bullitt—less and less able to deconstruct the plot and doubting if it will make any difference if they do.

Images of the 1960s are constantly being reconstructed in film culture. The choice of films discussed in this chapter is idiosyncratic and personal in the case of *Lonely Are the Brave, Seconds*, and *Bullitt*, but, by critical and box-office standards, *The Manchurian Candidate* and *Dr. Strangelove* remain two of the most significant cultural documents of the era and are still eminently viewable four decades later.

The visionary and prefigurative power of paranoia in *The Manchurian Candidate* was recaptured in such films of the 1990s as *JFK* and the less successful, though engaging, *Conspiracy Theory* (1997, Richard Donner), with its subtext of CIA brainwashing and the construction of a programmed assassin. *Dr. Strangelove* remains perhaps the best political satire of any era; its wonderfully bizarre scenario is still utterly horrifying. The novel *Catch-22* remains a permanent part of the vocabulary of every literate adult, capturing some of the surreal insanities of World War II military life, prefiguring the more bizarre events of Vietnam, and anticipating a world of centralized bureaucracy and globalized capitalism. As director Mike Nichols once remarked, "We *all* work for the same six guys."[48] Lastly, *Lonely Are the Brave* remains a fitting memorial to author Edward Abbey, who died in 1989.

All the films discussed in this chapter reflect the growth of oppositional politics—either at a personal or wider cultural level—throughout the 1960s. One finds in them flashes of visionary paranoia concerning conspiracies, secret organizations, and corrupt officials, though none (except for *Lonely Are the Brave, Dr. Strangelove,* and the novel *Catch-22*) ever approached the intensity and almost nihilistic anarcho-terrorism of extreme factors of the New Left, or the generalized and naïve cultural identification with third world Marxism-Leninism. Such critically acclaimed blockbusters as *Bonnie and Clyde* and *Easy Rider* came close, with their nihilistic, total paranoia and bloody climaxes serving as horrifying dystopian end points, obliterating a generational search for new social possibilities. Only twenty years later, in Oliver Stone's *Born on the Fourth of July* (1989), does one finally find an effective filmic expression of the profound *personal* transformations and intense spirit of radical leftism of late 1960s and early '70s.[49] Many late 1960s films—particularly Arthur Penn's *Bonnie and Clyde*—were analogues "to what we were doing in Vietnam," but, as he himself suggested, "given what was coming out of Vietnam at this point, how could a fictional *movie* generate such controversy?"[50] The film expressed the totality of systemic violence American society and its war machinery could produce on a massive scale in Vietnam—a process now largely forgotten by film audiences mostly too young to even remember except through post-Vietnam war films. Such films were anticipated by and, in retrospect, perhaps even surpassed by some of the smaller yet still striking examples discussed here.

# "You May Think You Know What's Going On Here"

## From Neo-Noir Cynicism to Conspiratorial Paranoia

The 1970s saw widespread and deepening cynicism about American political and corporate elites, stimulated by domestic crises surrounding Watergate, the collapse of the U.S. effort in Vietnam, and related inquiries into the repressive role of the CIA, FBI, and military intelligence in domestic politics. That was the view at the end of the decade, as summarized by Thomas Powers in his study of Richard Helms and the CIA,[1] to be followed almost two decades later by Kathryn Olmsted's study, which reached similar conclusions.[2] Both works demonstrated the failure of the news media and Congress to acknowledge the operations of the secret government.

Just months after Richard Nixon's 1974 resignation, *New York Times* reporter Seymour Hersh unearthed information of the CIA's Orwellian domestic spying on dissidents opposed to the Vietnam War, which was followed by congressional efforts to probe the scandal over CIA-plotted assassinations of foreign leaders, as well as far-reaching FBI harassment of civil rights and student groups. Yet, as Olmsted's study demonstrated, little had changed. Reports of the coming demise—or fundamental transformation—of these agencies were greatly exaggerated. All investigations by diverse committees of the House and Senate clearly "kept the secrets." In the Senate, the Select Committee to Study Governmental Operations With Respect to Intelligence—known as the Church Committee after its chair, Democratic Senator Frank Church—clearly cooperated with the agencies being investigated, even submitting its findings to the agency prior to publication in order to ascertain what the CIA wanted disclosed. In the House of Representatives, the House Intelligence Committee—known as the Pike Committee after its chair, Democrat Otis Pike—did not agree to submit its reports to the CIA and FBI prior to publication. Responding to agency pressure and Executive Branch concerns for security, the whole House voted to keep the report secret. CBS reporter Daniel Schorr managed to leak a draft of the Pike report to *The Village Voice,* but it did not appear in the *New York Times, The Washington Post,* or other major national papers, thus making it available only to a very small group of people. As a result of the leak, Schorr was suspended by CBS.[3] The whole affair suggested an instance of cozy cooperation between major mass media outlets and government in the area of alleged "national security." In its final report, the House Intelligence Committee concluded that "if this Committee's recent experience is any test, intelligence agencies that are to be controlled by Congressional lawmaking are, today, beyond the lawmakers' scrutiny."[4] As Howard Zinn suggested in his popular critical history of the era, everything was clearly "under control."[5] Ironically, the ultimate effect seems to have been public cynicism, magnified by the media and Republican criticism of the Carter administration (discussed in chapter 6), and the election of Ronald Reagan at the end of the decade.

Strikingly pessimistic, negative visions of American society appeared in the films of the 1970s. Some of the greatest American political films were produced during this period. Many simultaneously resurrected earlier socially critical noir conventions while transforming them into quintessential neo-noir portraits of a sick, perverted society. Francis Ford Coppola's *Godfather* films summed up a view of organized crime, as Pauline Kael puts it in her *New Yorker* commentary on *Godfather I,* "as an obscene symbolic extension of free enterprise and government policy, an extension of the worst in America—its feudal ruthlessness. Organized crime is not a rejection of Americanism, it's what we fear Americanism to be. It's our nightmare of the American system."[6]

## *CHINATOWN* (ROMAN POLANSKI) AND NEO-NOIR

Whereas the figure of the resourceful, tough, often heroic private detective actively pursuing justice through harsh and morally ambiguous urban cityscapes defined American popular culture during the classic period (1940–59) of film noir, almost becoming a mythical element of that culture, the central figures in many of the visionary political films of the 1970s often seemed bewildered by what they discovered, increasing the sense of paranoia that is a by-product of powerlessness. Like all myths, the earlier image of the deconstructive investigator evolved and adapted, reflecting changes in the society and the diminishing power of investigators to "solve" mysteries, affect outcomes, or even discern the real beneficiaries of many government decisions or public policies. Douglas Kellner has suggested that such films "ultimately helped advance the conservative cause . . . and played into the hands of the conservative Reaganite argument that government was the source of much existing evil."[7]

But *Chinatown* stands out from several other examples in its focus on the evils of those usually seen as the builders of twentieth-century America.

This 1974 film, directed by Roman Polanski and based on a Robert Towne screenplay, occupies a crucial point in the evolution of the noir cycle and the myth of the private eye. Using color photography yet mobilizing traditional forms, the film is set in a Los Angeles of 1938 that functions as a kind of indefinable, distant past. Filled with subtextual elements and extracinematic aspects—such as the history of water politics, capitalism, ecology, incest, and urban development—the film functions both as an homage and a pastiche, summing up a specific time and a style. It is distinguished from many other neo-noir films of the 1970s in its essentially Rooseveltian liberal perspective on the evils of a class of businessmen and developers, driven by greed, who seek control of the future itself. Jack Nicholson—who was part of the production and development of the film from the very beginning and who was also a close friend of the author—plays J. J. Gittes, a private detective. Unlike earlier PIs in fiction or film, he is a well-established businessman. Where Philip Marlowe operated alone, Gittes has two "operatives" in addition to his secretary. Yet, for all his fine suits, Gittes is still a bit uncouth, laughing too loudly at jokes, repeating unsavory stories before women, unable to avoid profanity when speaking.

Very much like Peter Falk's Lieutenant Columbo—who first appeared in the role on network television six years before this film—Gittes literally seems to be trying to get on people's nerves. Cocky, insulting, provocative, often aggressive to the point of provoking a violent response, he is still a shrewd investigator with a nose for sniffing out underlying connections—so good he gets it sliced open. He recognizes that he doesn't always know what is going on, a cautious posture learned years earlier while walking a beat in Chinatown. Something happened there involving a woman, and it still haunts him. Now that he is in business for himself, Gittes can follow his instinct for underlying and hidden connections, but one suspects he often acts without considering all the consequences. Gittes has strong professional ethics and he might even be the most moral man in the world in which he operates. Intrigued at finding corruption moving from the darker recesses of Chinatown into the larger city and about to spread to the purer country of orange groves and the "northwest valley," his fascination grows the more he uncovers.

Seeking to find the killer of Water Commissioner Hollis Mulwray, Gittes uncovers a monumentally complex swindle involving massive land speculation, illegal water diversions, and a fake drought—all aimed at getting voters to approve a bond issue that would make millions of dollars for the schemers. He begins to trace the immense dimensions of the conspiracy after being hired, under false pretenses, by a woman (Diane Ladd) in the pay of the conspirators.

Impersonating the real Mrs. Mulwray (Faye Dunaway), she asks Gittes to find out about an alleged affair her husband has been having. (He was actually visiting his adopted daughter.) Mulwray's real wife, Evelyn, married him as a face-saving cover for the child born out of her incestuous relationship with her father, Noah Cross (John Huston), Mulwray's former business associate and the boundlessly corrupt, manipulative character at the center of the complex plot, who will stop at nothing to get his way—even if it involves murder.

Evelyn Cross Mulwray, married in name only to Hollis, indulges in brief compulsive sexual promiscuity. Gittes finds himself in her employ and in bed with her less than forty-eight hours after her husband is found drowned. Gittes ultimately uncovers the story of Mulwray's death at the hands of Cross' henchmen, which includes Roman Polanski playing the knife-wielding, Elisha Cooke–type minion who slices Gittes' nose. It turns out Mulwray was killed to silence him, covering up the dimensions of the gigantic land-and-water grab. But finding out and knowing the truth is easier than proving it.

Trying to help Evelyn and her daughter/sister escape the quintessentially evil Cross, Gittes finds himself under arrest by the police. They think Evelyn killed her husband and hired Gittes to help cover it up, yet Gittes is certain Noah Cross ordered it. Gittes' theory is confirmed in a chilling late-evening face-off with Cross and his thug at the Mulwray house.

The film climaxes—with all the principals assembled on a main street in Chinatown—in a horrendous, tragic series of misunderstandings. Gittes, protesting to the police that Noah Cross killed Mulwray, is handcuffed as an accessory to murder, while Evelyn (who the police believe is the murderer) grabs her daughter at gunpoint and shoots her father in the shoulder and tries to flee. Evelyn is shot in the back of the head, one of her eyes blown out as the bullet exits her skull. She is dead, her body slumped over the wheel as the horn continues to drone like an eerie wail of sorrow and grief. Her shrieking daughter/sister is enfolded by the arms of her father/grandfather, with all the implications of more incest to come.

Unable to protect Evelyn and her daughter or to pin the murder or conspiracy on Cross, Gittes is finally released by the police. The camera pulls up and back in a high crane shot, leaving them all to their fate. This downbeat ending, involving the death of Evelyn Mulwray, was added to Towne's story by Polanski—over Towne's protests—though most critics agree it simply had to be that way. Polanski later said, "I know that if *Chinatown* was to be special, not just another thriller where the good guys triumph in the final reel, Evelyn had to die. Its dramatic impact would be lost unless audiences left their seats with a sense of outrage at the injustice of it all."[8] As Polanski described it, *Chinatown*, "a film about the '30s seen through the camera eye of the '70s," is an homage to the detectives of the 1930s and '40s, indirectly referencing Chandler but informing the story with an oblique Marxism in its critique of mystified economic power that owes much to Hammett. There are touches of Chandleresque chivalry in its central protagonist despite his explicit preoccupation ("I do matrimonial work; it's my métier"), which Marlowe loathed. Gittes is not a down-at-the-heel imitation of Marlowe. Rather, as Polanski described his impression of Towne's screenplay image of him, he is "a glamorous, successful operator, a snappy dresser with a coolly insolent manner—a new, archetypal detective figure."[9] He resembles the 1931 version of Sam Spade played by Ricardo Cortez in the first film version of *The Maltese Falcon* (also known as *Dangerous Female)* directed by Roy Del Ruth.

*Chinatown,* a pastiche of times, places, and situations drawn from Los Angeles politics early in the century (roughly 1904 to 1913), transplants them to the more immediate pre–World War II milieu in order to draw obvious parallels with an epically corrupt America at the end of the Vietnam War, experiencing the multiple political scandals and revelations called Watergate. Whether this reflects an imaginative stroke of genius or a failure of imagination and political courage, as Fredric Jameson has suggested,[10] is open to debate.

Much has been said and written about *Chinatown* for over three decades. Like coming to *Citizen Kane* once again, one is predisposed to be blown away by its expected revelatory power, but the effect, in the case of *Chinatown,* is more subtle. The film remains a central pivot point, a milestone. James Naremore summed up its place in film history as "a metaphor for the whole of Richard Nixon's America . . . a critique of the American past."[11]

*Chinatown* can be viewed as a metaphor for much more than a corrupt past or the Nixon/Watergate scandals. Throughout the early decades of the twentieth century, "Chinese" meant that which was foreign, unknown, distant, inscrutable. The notion of a Chinatown contains all that and more: the mysterious Orient in the Sax Rohmer Fu Manchu mysteries; Charlie Chan; references to "Chinese" puzzles and boxes; uncomprehending traditional jazz musicians in the 1940s describing the then new bebop of Charlie Parker and Dizzy Gillespie as "Chinese music." Orson Welles made his own contribution by setting the climax of his *Lady from Shanghai* (1948) in San Francisco's Chinatown, moving from an incomprehensible Chinese opera there directly into the acclaimed funhouse mirrors sequence, thereby adding a further dimension of inscrutability.

Pauline Kael's reviews of Francis Ford Coppola's *Godfather* films of the same era saw in them the embodiment of the corruption of American life and politics of the early 1970s. Such themes of corruption, personal greed, and incest—Noah Cross' rape of his own child and figurative rape of nature—in

*Chinatown* seem almost banal by comparison with what is now known of the dimensions of human evil. Yet in its underlying critique of the mystifications of power, it continued the deconstructions of lies seen in Hammett's detective fiction decades earlier.[12] Noah Cross' oft-quoted line—"You may think you know what is going on here, Mr. Gittes, but believe me, you don't" captures the spirit of the post-Vietnam, post-Watergate era.

Noah Cross' dark conception of human nature ("At the right place and the right time people are capable of *anything*") could well sum up the whole twentieth century. If Noah Cross really had existed in 1938, how prescient a comment that would now seem, given the history that was to come. Nearly thirty years after the first appearance of the film, it still elicits a terrible, profound weariness in the viewer, like the mood of despair and exhaustion in the songs written at the very end of the 1960s. The soap-operatic sexual and financial corruption of the Clinton presidency is one thing, but how can one even begin to understand the larger issues raised by NAFTA, the deindustrialization of the United States, and the continuing globalization of capitalism?[13]

To embody or personify corruption in one person, Noah Cross, as the screenplay of *Chinatown* does, makes him an easy mark as a villain. But one does not just hate him. Like Gittes, one is puzzled and mystified, wondering "why" he does it. His aim is more boundlessly, arrogantly evil than mere financial greed: he wishes to shape the future itself according to his designs. Today his aims are carried out by developers, outwardly "nice" people who adhere to "good" business practices.

*Chinatown* remains a landmark of 1970s American film, incorporating a retro look at genres, locales, and actual history and synthesizing it all into a statement about American life, ethics, and the capacity for corruption and evil. In an interview for the 1996 PBS series *Cadillac Desert,* based on Marc Reisner's book of that title,[14] Robert Towne, discussing the origin of Cross in the character of William Mulholland—father of the grand thefts of California lands and rivers needed to build the Los Angeles water system—pointed to the film's central moral insight: "Some crimes are so monstrous they can't figure out how to punish them. They actually sort of *reward* them. . . . Muholland's name is on the scenic route of the city. . . . Criminal's names are on plaques—as city founders, rather than in jail, where they belong." All the so-called great builders are also destroyers of many "little worlds" as Marshall Berman argued.[15]

*Chinatown* mobilized the established narrative of the private eye working on the fringes of official institutions of justice, who encounters interconnected criminal acts. The American detective now finds a society so corrupt that its leading figures—wealthy, respectable, or politically influential—are themselves criminals or linked to criminals. The whole system of law enforcement is

*Peter Lorre's doomed protagonist in Fritz Lang's* M *is the embodiment of film paranoia. (Museum of Modern Art Film Archive)*

*"Beautiful and lethal" femme fatale Kathie Moffett (Jane Greer) just before she commits murder in Jacques Tourneur's* Out of the Past. *(Museum of Modern Art Film Archive)*

*Mob thugs execute the bookkeeper in Abraham Polonsky's* Force of Evil. *(Photofest)*

*Quintessential film noir star John Garfield is fatally shot in John Berry's* He Ran All the Way, *Garfield's last film. (Museum of Modern Art Film Archive)*

*Dana Wynter and Kevin McCarthy running for their lives in Don Siegel's film classic* Invasion of the Body Snatchers. *(Photofest)*

*Frank Sinatra interrogates the brainwashed assassin (Lawrence Harvey) in John Frankenheimer's* The Manchurian Candidate. *(Photofest)*

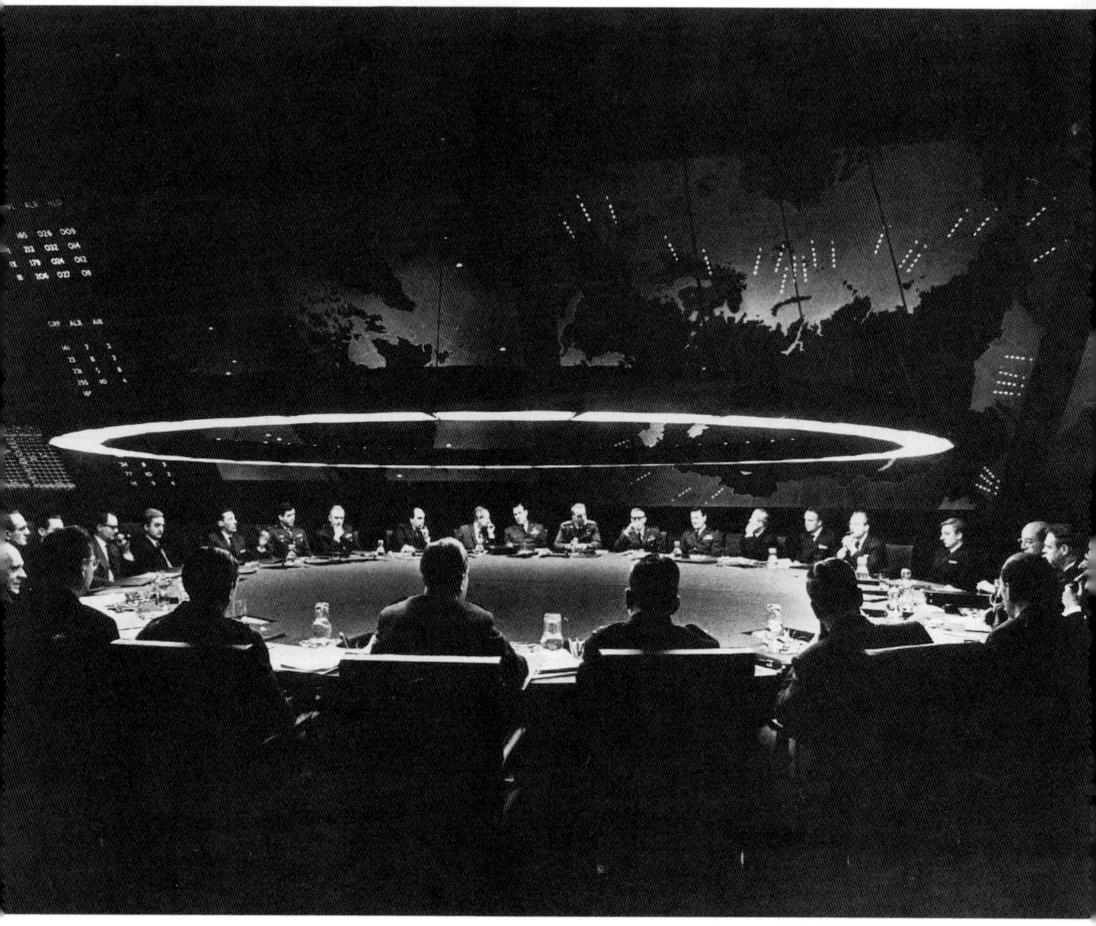

*The president and his advisers confer after Colonel Jack D. Ripper orders an unauthorized nuclear attack against the Soviet Union in Stanley Kubrick's* Dr. Strangelove. *(Photofest)*

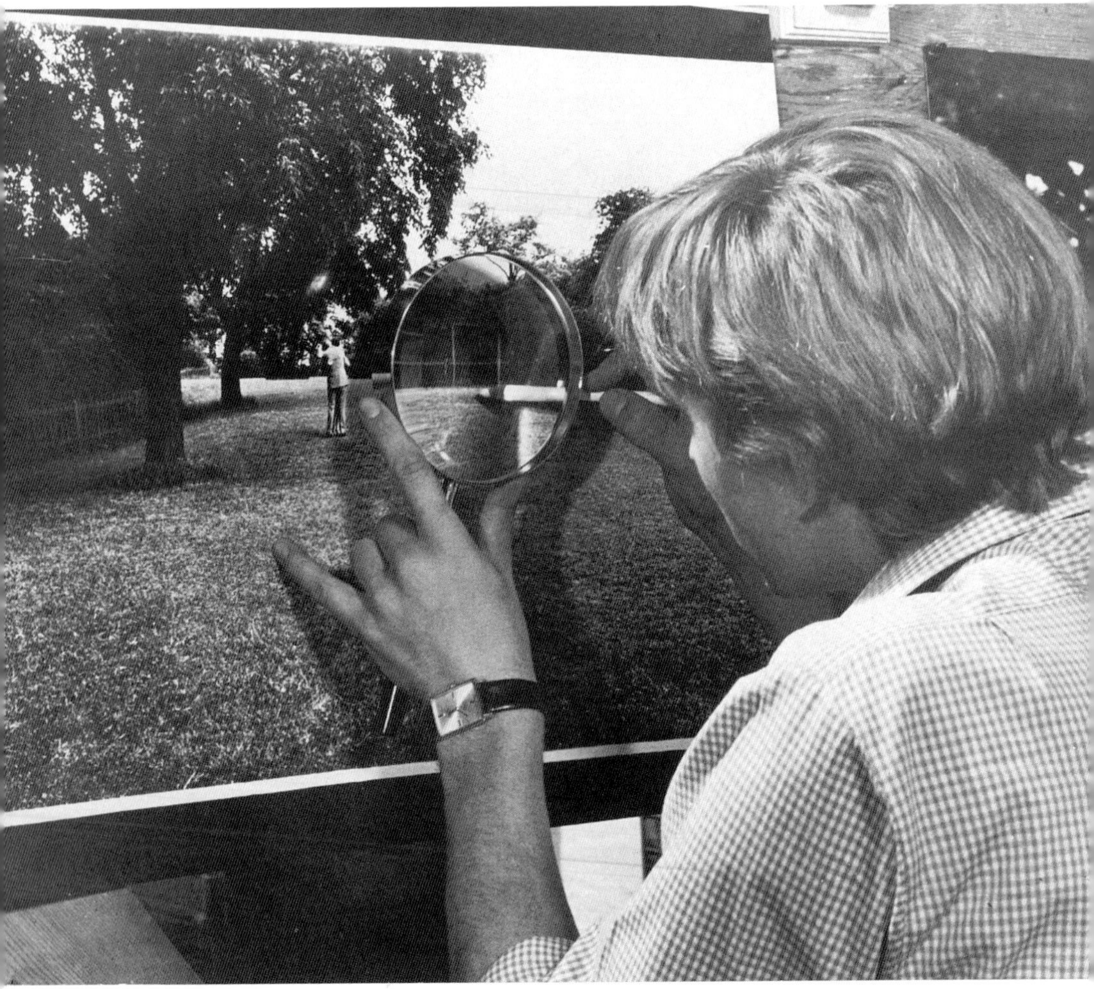

*In Michelangelo Antonioni's* Blowup, *David Hemmings thinks he's photographed something much more ominous than a mere idyllic tryst. (Photofest)*

*A pregnant and paranoid wife (Mia Farrow) explains her theory to her skeptical and unsympathetic husband (John Cassavetes) in Roman Polanski's* Rosemary's Baby. *(Photofest)*

*Detective Bullitt (Steve McQueen) taking a call while his partner and their star witness listen in Peter Yates'* Bullitt. *(Photofest)*

*Corporate executive, family man, and psychokiller Peter Cable (Charles Cioffi) struggles with prostitute Bree Daniels (Jane Fonda) in Alan J. Pakula's* Klute. *(Museum of Modern Art Film Archive)*

*Detective J. J. Gittes (Jack Nicholson) about to get his nose slashed in Roman Polanski's neo-noir classic* Chinatown. *(Museum of Modern Art Film Archive)*

*Evelyn Mulwray (Faye Dunaway) tries to escape her fate in* Chinatown. *(Museum of Modern Art Film Archive)*

*Professional wiretapper and loner Harry Caul (Gene Hackman) thinks he's uncovered a murder plot in Francis Ford Coppola's* The Conversation. *(Museum of Modern Art Film Archive)*

*Investigative reporter Joseph Frady (Warren Beatty) finds himself trapped in the catwalks in Alan J. Pakula's* The Parallax View. *(Museum of Modern Art Film Archive)*

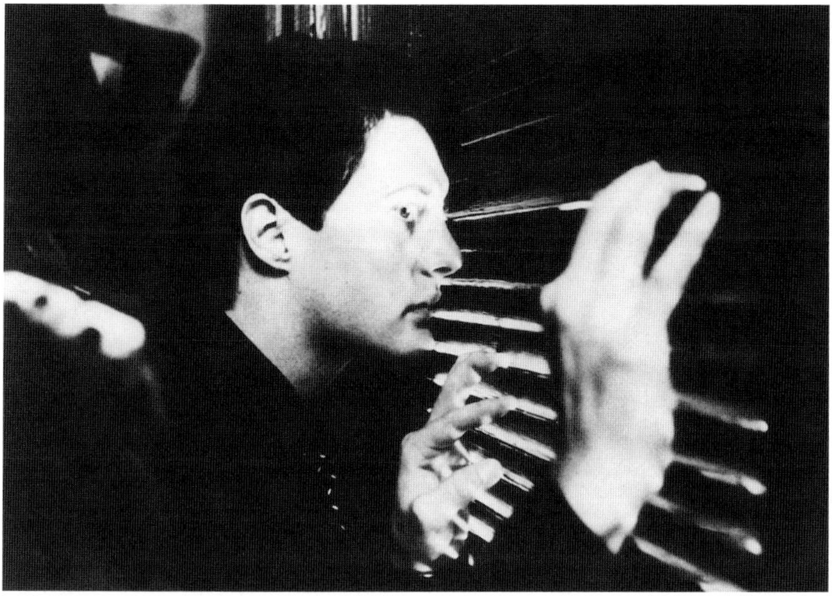

*Family Secrets: Jeffrey Beaumont (Kyle MacLachlan) discovers a very strange nocturnal world in David Lynch's* Blue Velvet. *(Photofest)*

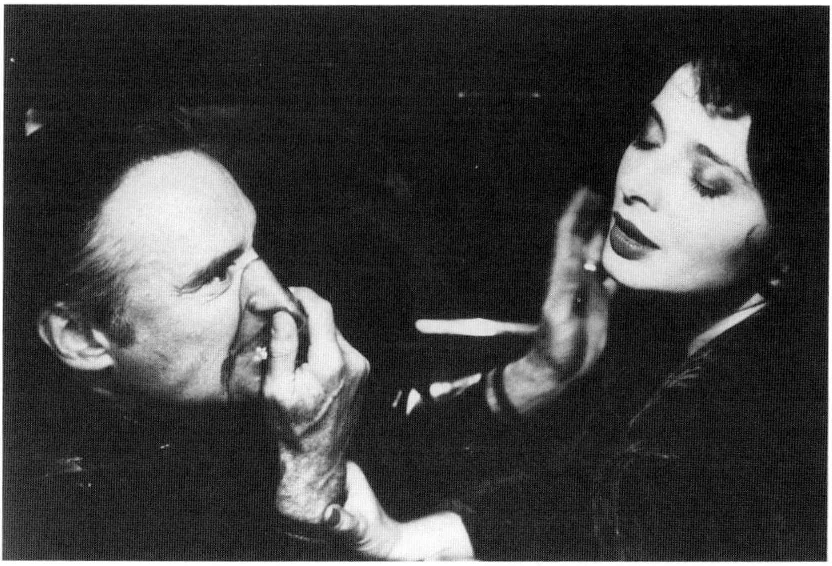

*Family values? "Daddy" Frank Booth (Dennis Hopper) sucks laughing gas before abusing captive "Mommy" Dorothy Valena (Isabella Rosselini) in* Blue Velvet. *(Museum of Modern Art Film Archive)*

*Alex Forrest (Glenn Close) won't take no for an answer as she pursues an errant husband (Michael Douglas) in Adrian Lyne's* Fatal Attraction. *(Photofest)*

*Oliver Stone recreates a president's assassination in his controversial, conspiracy-minded film* JFK. *(Photofest)*

*A bad cop (James Cromwell, left) and his unsuspecting "lads" (Guy Pearce, Russell Crowe, and Kevin Spacey) in Curtis Hanson's* L.A. Confidential. *(Museum of Modern Art Film Archive)*

*William B. Davis stars as the world-weary "Cigarette-Smoking Man" in* The X-Files *television series. (William B. Davis)*

revealed to be itself corrupt or ineffectual at rendering any ultimate justice.[16] In contrast to earlier British English detective fiction, which usually involves corrupt individuals, the American PI increasingly faces a much more complex system of incompetence, political manipulation, and outright evil.

Morever, because of the ambiguities of the world in which he or she is immersed, the private eye must also decide whether personally to restore justice. This is often achieved by arranging some accident or "blowing away" the villains if the legal system won't do it. Such a model of behavior is evident in much of the best-selling male crime/detective fiction of the 1980s and 1990s, especially the works of Elmore Leonard, James Lee Burke, James Ellroy, and several others classified as "neo" hard-boiled. But in *Chinatown* and several other films of the 1970s, once heroic detectives are now tragically diminished and transformed. However, in *Chinatown* Gittes seems to embody the last gasp of the radically democratic Rooseveltian New Deal. Set in 1938, the view of the ruling economic class in *Chinatown*—personified by Noah Cross—prompts in Jake Gittes that sense of democratic skepticism and suspicion of economic power typical of FDR's speeches a few years earlier. However, by the film's conclusion he is brought to the (then) historical present—to the disillusionment characteristic of the Watergate and post-Vietnam era.

## *THE LONG GOODBYE* (ROBERT ALTMAN)

Not only in *Chinatown* were such developments evident. They appeared in several other features of the period, markedly so in Robert Altman's deconstruction of Marlowe in *The Long Goodbye* (1973), which was released a year earlier. Initially dismissed by most reviewers (except Pauline Kael)[17] as a cavalier, even outrageous send-up or destruction of Chandler's character, the story is certainly changed in veteran Leigh Brackett's screenplay, which alters the conclusion of Chandler's novel. It was primarily Elliott Gould's offhand, seemingly improvised performance that contributed to the initial feeling of trivial dismissal of the Marlowe icon. The casting of a New York City Jewish actor as Marlowe mystified and even offended many. Bogart and Dick Powell were notable early film Marlowes, but Anglophile Chandler thought Cary Grant would be ideal. James Garner preceded Gould, in *Marlowe* (1969, Paul Bogart). Moreover, having Marlowe drive around 1973 Los Angeles in a 1948 Lincoln Continental at first seemed ludicrous. Retrospectively, both choices were brilliant, illustrating how much of an anachronism the 1930s and '40s private investigator had become in the Los Angeles of 1973. The change in the ending of the novel also was for the better, with Marlowe transformed from an easily manipulated "born loser" to a man who refuses be used.

The original Chandler novel, dating from the early 1950s, presented a wistful, nostalgic backward glance at a Los Angeles receding into the past. Brackett's updating of the tale to 1970s L.A. creates a world where there is no clear sense of moral values, where only money and violence matter. The smog and garish lighting of twenty-four-hour markets are there. The police seem less ominous than the "owned" cops of earlier—and later—films. (See the discussion of "bad cops" in chapter 9.) Here they are just trying to do their jobs. Unlike earlier incarnations who spend time in police custody, Marlowe actually spends three days in a jail cell.

Marlowe's problems begin when he agrees to help his friend Terry Lennox (Jim Bouton), who arrives in the middle of the night, his face scratched in a fight with his wife—whom he has murdered, although at this point he does not confess to it. Lennox needs a ride to Tijuana. Marlowe obliges—in the 1948 Lincoln Continental—leaving Lennox's car parked in L.A. at Marlowe's apartment. Marlowe conspicuously stops the old Lincoln just this side of the complex border crossing, leaving Lennox to walk through. The next day two detectives question Marlowe about the brutal death of Sylvia Lennox, assuming Terry killed her. Marlowe is held for three days—until word comes from Mexico that Terry is dead, supposedly a suicide, with a note confessing to killing his wife. The police consider the case closed and Marlowe is released. But the mystery has just begun.

About fifty minutes into the film, gangster "Marty Augustine" (played by director Mark Rydell), his girlfriend, and several thugs appear at Marlowe's apartment. This scene marks a crucial development as Marlowe is threatened with violence. Augustine—looking like a dissolute, slightly puffy-eyed Paul Anka or Eddie Fisher[18]—takes an empty soda bottle, smashes it, and mutilates his girlfriend's face. This is done to terrorize Marlowe into revealing the whereabouts of Lennox—who has a large sum of the mobster's cash. One of the most brutal, shocking moments of graphic violence in movie history, it reveals the tensions and seething anger beneath the surface of the story, as well as the indifference of virtually everybody in the film.

After going to Mexico, conferring with the coroner who pronounced Terry Lennox dead, Marlowe returns to L.A., where he is invited to a party at the house of Eileen Wade (Nina Van Pallandt), who had earlier hired him to find and retrieve her alcoholic husband, Roger (Sterling Hayden). Eileen suggests Roger might have killed Sylvia Lennox, so Marlowe asks the L.A.P.D. to reopen the Lennox murder case, but they refuse, so Marlowe returns to Mexico, bribes officials to reveal the supposedly dead Lennox's location, and finds him in a hammock, blithely unconcerned, by a pool. Enraged at Terry's manipulation of their friendship, Marlowe pulls out his gun and shoots him, blowing him backward into the pool, which turns red with blood. As he leaves, in a moment referencing the final moments of *The Third Man* (1949, Carol Reed), Marlowe passes Eileen Wade, confirming his suspicions that she lied about her relationship with Lennox. Marlowe simply ignores her, takes out a harmonica, and instead of playing the theme song "The Long Goodbye"—which is played throughout the film by a dozen pianists, singers, mariachi bands, and even a door chime—begins to play "Hooray for Hollywood," dancing away into the distance as in some Charlie Chaplin film.

This version of Chandler's celebrated private eye finds him lost in a world he barely comprehends. Alienation and violence are everywhere, as are references to seeing and voyeurism. Many scenes are shot through windows or utilize reflections. People are often shown passively observing a scene without being involved in it. What Altman seems to be conveying is the utter indifference of society to what goes on around us and the illusory nature of it all. The only kind of corruption in Altman's film images is of an overwhelmed public bureaucracy. In this culture nobody cares about anyone else. If Marlowe seems to care about friendship and loyalty, it is purely out of self-respect. When he discovers that Terry Lennox lied to him and violated his trust, he is so disillusioned that he shoots him—which is totally out of character and unlike any previous film version.

This bleakly ironic perspective seems to be a foreshadowing of Altman's film *The Player* (1992, screenplay by Michael Tolkin). In both films the Hollywood—and, by extension, American—ethos is "anything goes; as long as you can get away with it." Marlowe tries to take a stand, asserting meaning in a meaningless situation, restoring a kind of "justice" through an act of violence. Yet this personal solution has no effect on society, which is apparently beyond remedy through human intervention. Not even the once resourceful PI can do anything. Individual action appears increasingly futile. Such feelings of powerlessness are potent precursors of paranoia.

### *FAREWELL, MY LOVELY* (DICK RICHARDS)

Marlowe's last, best film incarnation in the 1970s was in *Farewell, My Lovely* (1975), Dick Richards' neo-noir homage and evocation of 1940s Chandler-era Los Angeles, featuring as Marlowe the world-weary, heavy-lidded, noir star Robert Mitchum. An evocative look back on Mitchum's earlier work, it actually surpasses some of it while conveying a darker-than-noir despair. Mitchum and John Ireland, as Detective Nulty, are like two old wrecks somnolently moving through an embalmed Los Angeles, beautifully photographed by John Alonzo just a year after his remarkable work in Chinatown. Mitchum later appeared in

Michael Winner's much less successful attempt at a remake of *The Big Sleep* (1978). While truer to the novel than the 1946 Hawks film with Bogart, and contemporary rather than campy, it is incomprehensibly set in London. Despite a fine cast, it does not come off. James Stewart is miscast as General Sternwood. Sara Miles as Vivien is no Bacall. Mitchum seems merely there. What is worthy about the production—and definitely worth seeing for that alone—is its attempt to convey the breadth and complexity of Chandler's story.

### *NIGHT MOVES* (ARTHUR PENN)

Penn's *Night Moves* (1975) revisits classic noir themes, with Gene Hackman as L.A. detective Harry Moseby. Moseby, a onetime professional football player, is now merely a watcher. He watches people for money. He views his marriage disintegrating as his wife (Susan Clark) carries on an affair with a more intellectual man, who has a physical disability. The story involves Moseby being hired by an alcoholic former film actress and leading lady, Arlene Iverson (Janet Ward) to travel to Florida to retrieve her young, sexually hyperactive daughter Delly (Melanie Griffith) from her stepfather Tom Iverson (John Crawford). Unlike many of the investigative films of earlier eras, which were geographically confined to the Los Angeles area, *Night Moves* takes on a transcontinental flavor as Moseby travels from Los Angeles, to New Mexico, to the Florida Keys in his search for and the destructively promiscuous nymphet.

*Night Moves* retains elements of the world of Bogart updated to the (then present day) 1970s. The convoluted plot typical of late Chandler and related films are still there, though they are now more complex and confusing. Moseby has been described as a "figure of contemporary anxiety."[19] Placed in a situation with all the complexities of *The Big Sleep* of the 1940s, this PI questions his own sense of who he is, what he knows, and what he can accomplish. Like traditional detectives of earlier decades, he seems driven by a need to know, to find out things, even though it usually makes him unhappy.

Existential uncertainty pervades every aspect of Harry's life, including his competence as a private eye. His basic impotence as a detective is mirrored in his personal life. Sex is used as a kind of weapon throughout the film, especially in Harry's deteriorating marriage. At one point early in the film his wife's lover taunts Harry to hit him, "like Sam Spade" might have, ridiculing Moseby's profession and pointing to the absurd conceit that finding out things, especially for money, is worth anything, a belief Harry's wife seconds.

While searching for Delly, Harry meets an attractive yet compromised woman named Paula (Jennifer Warren), who has joined with Delly's stepfather and others in a complex smuggling operation involving pre-Columbian artifacts. Several deaths—probable murders—appear related to the operation, which encompasses a growing circle of Harry's acquaintances—possibly even his own wife, who works in an antiques store.

Sex in such an environment weighs heavily on each character; aside from its use as sheer manipulation, it is ultimately a depressing activity that leads to betrayals and increasing anxiety.[20] Moral corruption—especially among of the upper class—was often evident in the work of Chandler and his generation, but one rarely encountered the kind of emotional paralysis one sees embodied in Harry Moseby and the weary, joyless amorality evident in most of the other characters. There is a parallel established in *Night Moves* between the complex past and present emotions the characters experience and the labyrinthine plot Harry uncovers in Florida with links back to L.A. Everybody begins to die. While diving, Delly finds a plane containing the body of one of her former lovers. Horrified, she agrees to return to her mother, which Harry counts as a victory.

While performing a bit part in a film, Delly is killed in what is purported to be an accident. Checking in with his old friend Ziegler (Edward Binns), who was in charge of and suffered injuries in the same stunt, Harry is once again assured it could only have been an accident. However, after reviewing films of the event, Harry begins to suspect otherwise. An explicit reference to newsreel footage of the RFK assassination—looking as if it were "filmed underwater"—provides a subtle subtextual link to wider political conspiracies of the preceding decade.

Harry returns to Florida, where he discovers Tom Iverson and Paula, his sometime mistress, more deeply involved in a crime ring than he initially believed. After a brutal fight sequence that leaves Iverson disabled and unconscious, Paula agrees to assist Moseby in uncovering the full plot. She asks him why he can't be satisfied since he "solved the case." Harry replies, "No I didn't, everything just fell in on me." She joins him on the ironically named getaway boat *Point of View*—the irony being that Harry tragically seems to have none—and they proceed to a buoy marking the site. While Paula is diving to retrieve the smuggled contraband a seaplane appears, piloted by Ziegler, Harry's movie stuntman friend. He shoots at Harry, wounding him in the leg, and his pontoon hits Paula in the head, killing her. As the plane crashes into the boat and sinks, Harry looks down, seeing Ziegler dimly through a window in the floor of the boat. The film closes with Moseby, stranded and helpless, a captive of the *Point of View* as it moves aimlessly in ever-wider circles.

Harry Moseby was a sharp investigator, but, like J. J. Gittes, he was not smart enough. His knowledge was not empowering. At the end of the film, everyone

Moseby is associated with is either compromised or dead. His marriage lies in ruins. Alone and badly wounded, he has nothing left—certainly not "the truth." *Night Moves* seems to argue that perhaps there is no ultimate truth, only that murky newsreel footage.

Each of the films discussed in this section are usually seen as reflecting a sense of withdrawal from the kind of engagement with events usually identified with the activism of the 1960s, sometimes shading into an incapacity to control or even to understand history.[21] Yet they also reflect a sober, more realistic examination and reassessment of the history of their time. To effect political outcomes would have required a knowledge and competences far beyond that available to the older PIs.

## Paranoia Thrillers

As the myth of the private detective diminished, a new, rapidly expanding genre of paranoia thrillers developed. A decline in political trust was reflected in post-Vietnam and post-Watergate public opinion polls, yet this lack of trust had a self-limiting aspect. From other opinion data and the testimony of journalists and members of Congress, the public were willing to hear "bad" things about their nation only up to a point. As congressional investigations proceeded and as investigatory journalists such as Seymour Hersh and Daniel Schorr continued to uncover the deeper layers of secrecy, public confidence in the investigators themselves also began to erode. According to reporter Anthony Lewis, constituents simply did not want to know the full dimensions of government abuses in the preceding decade. As Representative Otis Pike, chair of the House Intelligence Committee surveying the abuses of the CIA and FBI, put it, as a result of Watergate the American people were asked to believe "their President had been a bad person. In this situation [investigation of CIA and FBI abuses] they are asked much more; they are asked to believe that their country has been evil. And nobody wants to believe that."[22]

But that is precisely what many observers *did* conclude. Vietnam and the cumulative abuses of military intelligence, the CIA, the FBI, and other agencies resulted in the darkest views of American institutions in the nation's history. Such bleak perspectives inevitably found their way into novels, screenplays, and a body of film that raised questions about all our public institutions. Here was cultural paranoia at one of its peak periods—and occasionally its most visionary moments.

## *THE CONVERSATION* (FRANCIS FORD COPPOLA)

In *The Conversation* (1974), Gene Hackman plays Harry Caul, a sound technician implicated in a murder conspiracy. One of the most insightful films of the 1970s, it deals with the alienation and increasing isolation of Harry Caul, a master electronic eavesdropper operating as a private "consultant." For enough money he just "delivers the tapes," as he says at one point. The only problem with such an ethic, Caul begins to realize, is that he has no control over the use of what is on the tapes. The information could lead to someone being killed.

From the very start of the film the viewer's attention is focused on Caul and associates methodically pursuing a young couple in San Francisco's Union Square via an intriguing variety of microphone techniques. Like the revelations of murder that emerge before the eyes of the photographer in Antonioni's *Blow-Up* (1966), Harry Caul's tapes begin to intimate a conspiracy—in this case involving murder.

The film was released in the midst of the Watergate crisis, though the director said it was planned before these events. Watergate seems to intersect with and inform the narrative, themes, and central character of this film—Harry even resembles and dresses like Watergate figure and ex-CIA agent James McCord. The allusions to Watergate and conspiracy are at first presented somewhat obliquely. One wonders why these two people in Union Square are being surveilled by so many men. Are these the "Plumbers" on a West Coast operation? The film begins to intimate some kind of conspiracy, but the "higher circles" from which it emerges are here vaguely, anonymously represented.

In a manner almost out of Kafka, the surveillance is initiated and paid for by a figure known only as the "Director" (played in a cameo by Robert Duvall). All arrangements and payments are made by his personal assistant, Martin Stett (played by a young Harrison Ford), giving off a kind of assured competence untroubled by any sense of conscience. As the narrative develops, he appears quite amused at Harry Caul's clumsily expressed pangs of emerging—then anguished—conscience.

Obsessed with his own privacy—perhaps because of his own skill at surveillance—Caul could be described as "paranoid" if informed and politically savvy viewers were not also aware of the events of the preceding decade involving domestic spying by U.S. government agencies.[23] But *The Conversation* is about more than justified paranoia. It is also about an emerging crisis of what used to be called "conscience." The film portrays, in Caul's moral/existential crisis, the growing awareness of someone who formerly never weighed the implications of what he did now beginning to think about personal responsibility and becoming emotionally involved. He is gradually losing his ruthless, unfeeling attitude that for years had given him an edge over his competitors. While his voice still expresses excitement as he explains a particularly challenging engineering problem, increasingly he feels responsible.

In the past a bugging assignment once led to the deaths of three people. The memory still plagues Harry. He doesn't want it to happen again, yet he does not know how to become more responsible. He tries not delivering the tapes, but he is manipulated by an aging blond trade-show hostess, who seduces him and makes off with the tapes. Harry later realizes she was acting as an agent for Stett and, indirectly, for the Director.

The ease with which Harry was seduced, deceived, and robbed confirms his vague feelings of menace, now grown palpable and real. He feels he can't trust anyone. His isolation and alienation degenerate into an anguished helplessness as he begins to come apart emotionally. Up to this point the film seems to be a study of the devastating emotional consequences of cold-blooded professionalism. But now the plot takes a grotesque twist. Harry had initially feared that the young couple—revealed as the very young wife of the Director and her lover—would be killed. He follows them to a hotel they mentioned in the conversation he taped. Listening through the wall, he assumes they have been murdered by the Director or his men, a fear that is confirmed when he later enters the room and flushes the toilet which overflows—with blood. Harry deduces that the couple were executed and their bodies somehow destroyed in the room.

Driven by anguish, he goes to the Director's headquarters, where he is astonished to find a news conference under way, the young wife (alive), Martin Stett presiding over the scene, and members of the press asking questions and getting information about a purported automobile accident wherein the Director was killed. The plot is inverted and the conspiracy appears more diabolical than Harry had dreamed. What the couple actually said in the hotel room—with emphasis added now for clarification—was "He'd kill *us* if *he* had the chance." The wife and lover had killed the Director in the hotel while Harry was in the next room with his listening devices. Now he knows what actually happened—and *they* know he knows—but he can't do anything about it. He is hopelessly compromised and implicated. Returning to his apartment, he gets a phone call on his supposedly unlisted phone. The voice (apparently that of Martin Stett) says, "We know you know. We'll be listening to you." The film ends in an exercise of desperate, methodical, paranoia as Harry completely demolishes his apartment, in a fruitless attempt to find the bug. He is trapped, as is the audience, which initially felt morally superior but end up feeling just as deeply implicated and vulnerable as Harry Caul.

Timothy Corrigan has suggested that in its representation of a "conversation through technology," concluding with the complete collapse of an individual who was a devout Catholic yet also a very tortured soul, *The Conversation* might well describe Francis Ford Coppola's own career. The latter once described Harry Caul as "a man who has dedicated his existence to a certain kind of activity, to technology, and who in a part of his life experiences regrets and realizes that the weapon he uses for others in a certain fashion is destroying the man himself. . . . [T]he single reason for which he is destroyed is perhaps that he has started to question all that."[24]

*The Conversation* expressed the mood of cynicism and powerlessness of the country better than most of the political rhetoric of the mid-1970s. What remains startling nearly thirty years after the events is the personal anguish that comes through in Harry Caul, the central character. The film's vision is despairing, tormented; the world it reveals is utterly without faith. Whether or not it is intended as an autobiographical statement, Coppola captured what it felt like to be living through that period of disillusionment and social disintegration. Offering little or no consolation, *The Conversation* remains one of the darkest, most disturbing films ever made about this or any period in American history.[25]

### *THE PARALLAX VIEW* (ALAN J. PAKULA)

Before the appearance of Oliver Stone's *JFK* (1991), *The Parallax View* (1974) was considered the definitive, most complete expression of political paranoia. It provided a film blueprint of how an assassination of a major political figure could be carried out by a secret network specializing in political killings and then covered up by leaving a patsy, a "loony loner" to take the rap. Unlike Pakula's later film *All the President's Men* (1976), which optimistically portrayed the role of the investigator in influencing the political process, *The Parallax View* presents a dark, well-crafted conspiratorial vision of almost total paranoia.[26]

The film opens on a sunny day in Seattle. During a campaign appearance by a well-burnished senatorial candidate named Carroll (Bill Joyce)—a sequence that might reference the June 5, 1968, RFK assassination in Los Angeles—one glimpses disheveled, long-haired reporter Joe Frady (Warren Beatty) off to one side, while manic TV reporter Lee Carter (Paula Prentiss) interviews the candidate and his wife. A few moments later the candidate is shot in the restaurant atop the Space Needle. While security men chase the supposed assassin, a waiter named Thomas Richard Lindern, a second "waiter"(Bill McKinney) whose shot actually killed the senator slips away. (He reappears several times in the film as a silent messenger of death.) A Warren-type commission reports that Lindern alone shot the senator.

A few years pass. A distraught Lee Carter visits former boyfriend Joe Frady, now a reporter in Oregon, and recount the mysterious deaths of those present at the earlier assassination who thought they saw a second gunman. Frady thinks she's paranoid—until she is also found dead of a supposed drug overdose, which he feels certain was not accidental. He begins to follow up her stories of the various deaths, finding much more than he ever expected.

A trip to the site of the death of one the witnesses leads to a violent bar fight with a sheriff's deputy, then the sheriff unexpectedly offers to take Frady to the dam where the witness subsequently drowned. He tries to kill Frady at the dam, but is drowned during their struggle. Frady flees to the sheriff's house—where he finds puzzling recruitment materials from something called "The Parallax Corporation"—and steals a patrol car, leading to an obligatory chase (one of the few weak moments in an otherwise tautly written screenplay.)

Frady's editor Rintels (Hume Cronyn) refuses to see anything in these developments but mere coincidences. According to Pakula, unlike Frady, who sees the world as "full of alienated people wandering around in totally alienated worlds with a seeming absence of continuing relationships," Rintels represents "certain nineteenth-century American humanist values: tradition, rootedness, responsibility, optimistic belief in the perfectability of man and that we live in the best of all possible worlds in the most enlightened society so far created . . . a kind of old-fashioned decency and optimism."[27] Anachronistically, he still embodies hope.

Frady searches for the assassinated Senator Carroll's chief of staff, Austin Tucker (William Daniels), who has gone into hiding. He finally makes contact and interviews Tucker on a yacht. While they look at pictures of a second unidentified gunman, the yacht is suddenly blown up, killing Tucker and his bodyguard. Frady somehow escapes death, but his death notice is published, and he decides to go undercover.

After getting advice from an ex-FBI agent friend, Frady tries to infiltrate The Parallax Corporation by getting a convicted mental patient and murderer to fill out its questionnaire, passing himself off as Richard Paley while he operates under his new assumed identity of Richard Parton. Soon contacted by a representative of Parallax, Jack Younger (convincingly played by veteran character actor Walter McGinn), he is told that even though they know his real identity, his "aggressive" qualities make him ideal for their kind of "security" work (which Frady deduces is killing by contract). Frady then submits to an interview/test designed either to elicit deep psychological processes or to further brainwash him. What Frady—and the audience—don't know is that they test not only for killers but also for likely candidates on whom to place the blame. Frady is destined to be the next patsy, the next Oswald or James Earl Ray.

Glimpsing the assassin/waiter from Tucker's earlier photo on his visit to the Parallax building, Frady follows him to the airport and sees him check a bag (containing a bomb). After an interminable delay aboard the plane—the slowest section of the film—Frady manages to pass a note to a stewardess, warning that a bomb is on board. The plane returns to the airport, is evacuated, and explodes (a prominent senator had been aboard).

Frady's editor is next shown listening to a tape of Joe's conversation with Younger, the Parallax rep. The Parallax assassin, disguised as a deli delivery man, reappears and delivers a lunch order. The editor dies as soon as he drinks his (poisoned) coffee. Any hope of a rational, optimistic, outcome to Frady's quest dies with him.

Meanwhile, Frady follows the assassin to a large exhibition hall where a prominent candidate named Senator Hammond is rehearsing his speech. (In its overhead catwalks and side galleries it resembles the Trade Mart in Dallas where JFK was to deliver his last speech.) Frady, up in the catwalks following the assassin he thinks will shoot Hammond, finds a rifle, probably leaving his fingerprints on it. But the senator is suddenly shot dead by a supposed security man who is in reality a Parallax assassin. Frady, now hiding in darkness on the catwalk, is spotted and surrounded by security staff. Spotting an open door, he tries to run but is fatally shot by the second assassin/security man. A few months later a Warren Commission-style panel concludes that Frady, obsessed with the earlier Carroll assassination, blamed Hammond for it and, acting alone, shot him dead.

*The Parallax View* effectively links its story to other assassinations of the previous decade. Everything resonates with public misgivings about the Warren Commission's report on Oswald, JFK's alleged assassin, as well as James Earl Ray, who at first pled guilty to the Martin Luther King Jr. shooting and then recanted. Even Sirhan Sirhan, the convicted RFK assassin, was in front of and not behind Kennedy, the location from which the coroner, Thomas Noguchi, said the fatal shots were fired at close range.[28] Though none of these alleged assassins were investigative journalists, like Joe Frady, all were "weird loners." It is now known that Oswald had connections to the CIA, naval intelligence, and the parapolitical underworld. He vehemently insisted on national television that he was only "a patsy." *The Parallax View* raises the question of whether a secret agency like the Parallax Corporation could exist. The answer now seems obvious, given what is known of CIA proprietary agencies and revelations after the events of Iran-Contra. The CIA managed a major assassination operation, the Phoenix Project, throughout much of the Vietnam War. Although much of the killing was carried out by surrogates, reportedly U.S. operatives were present.[29] That Central and South American death squads—some prepared by U.S. police programs—trained operatives, selected victims, and carried out hundreds of assassinations is suggested or implied in several films, including Costa-Garvas' *Z* (1969), *State of Siege* (1973), and *Missing* (1982); *Under Fire* (1983, Roger Spottiswoode), *Salvador* (1986, Oliver Stone), and *Romero* (1989, John Duigan).[30] The final step—a private or proprietary "security" agency that is contracted to kill people for commercial or political reasons—seems a logical and realistic extension of what is already virtually common knowledge and certainly a reasonable and logical conclusion based on available documentation. It is no paranoid fantasy to conceive of an operation like Oliver North's massive apparatus—uncovered in the Iran-Contra scandal and investigation—remaining completely undetected.

If any assassinations were carried out the way *The Parallax View* suggests, the film might explain a lot of history. If they didn't, the film still remains a most effective representation of a "perfect" paranoid vision. The film itself is a "positive feedback" version of paranoia in that all the known information leads to one conclusion and the information left out helps to consolidate it; everything the central character does feeds into the case that will be brought against him. Here anything can be a clue. There are no such things as accidents in this story. No stranger means well. Chance meetings not only are not to be trusted, they simply don't happen without a reason linked to the larger conspiratorial design.

As Pakula later stated in an interview, the film

> represents my view of what's happening in the world. [It says] the individual will be destroyed; it's Kafkaesque that way. Central European. The irony of the film lies in the contrast of all the pop-art American motifs, indicating the innocent, open society; you get the feeling we used to associate with Central Europe—of the individual destroyed in a secret maze by forces of which he has no knowledge.[31]

With the release of *All the President's Men* in 1976, Joe Frady was resurrected in the persons of Woodward and Bernstein.[32]

### ***THREE DAYS OF THE CONDOR*** **(SYDNEY POLLACK)**

In this 1975 paranoia spy thriller, adapted from James Grady's novel *Six Days of the Condor* by Lorenzo Semple Jr. and David Rayfiel, Robert Redford plays Joe Turner, a New York City–based CIA book reader, who leaves his quiet office complex for lunch and escapes being wiped out by a meticulously planned assassination of everyone in his office by killers dressed as U.S. Postal Service employees. Just why the killing occurred and who was behind it is not clear.

Turner and his associates seem to have discovered something in his reading and translations that threatened the existence of a secret conspiratorial network inside the CIA. As the sole survivor of the massacre, he is suspected by everybody in the agency, including both the "official" CIA and the secret, "rogue" group. *Three Days of the Condor* is an unrelenting exercise in paranoia in which virtually nobody can be trusted—especially the mailman.

Cliff Robertson and John Houseman, playing high "official" CIA coordinators, seem trustworthy, though the audience is never quite certain. Max von Sydow is menacing as a gracious, elegant European assassin in the employ of the secret network, though Robertson's character is more threatening and unnerving precisely because he seems so very friendly and open.

Perhaps the key climactic moment—which still leaves the viewer puzzled and in doubt a quarter century later—occurs when Redford, at a prearranged meeting on the street, tells Robertson that he has sent to the *New York Times* his written account of both the covert conspiracy and massacre and the "official" agency counteractions to suppress the plot. Robertson, with a smile of relief, asks Redford "How do you know they'll print it?" Here the film anticipates the official media's widespread suppression of the Pike Committee report on intelligence abuses.[33] It also presciently hints at Carl Bernstein's explosive allegations-to-come of significant CIA connections to major television and print media. In an extensive and controversial *Rolling Stone* article, Bernstein described how more than four hundred American journalists secretly carried out assignments for the CIA from the 1950s to the mid-1970s. Indeed, Bernstein even suggested that the *New York Times* itself provided cover for ten CIA agents from 1950 to 1966.[34]

### *ALL THE PRESIDENT'S MEN* (ALAN J. PAKULA)

This film, based on Bob Woodward and Carl Bernstein's best-selling memoir of the Watergate incident, has a screenplay by William Goldman. This is the third in Pakula's "paranoia trilogy" (the others being *Klute* and *The Parallax View*). Pakula was actually brought in to direct by producer Robert Redford after the screenplay was complete and he (playing Woodward) and Dustin Hoffman (Bernstein) had been cast as the leads. The public already knew—or thought they knew—the background to the story. As Pakula himself acknowledged, "There's never been a film I know of that has depended so much on the basic knowledge the audience has and that uses that, takes it for granted."[35] Thanks to Pakula's brilliant direction, the film contains often riveting moments of paranoia, achieved through extreme close-ups of phone conversations or through face-to-face interviews. Noir lighting techniques are evident in Woodward's nocturnal meetings with Deep Throat in darkened parking garages, with faces obscured by shadow. All these directorial touches convey a mounting sense of menace—yet nothing violent ever occurs. The audience is strung along through a combination of astute directorial manipulation and Gordon Willis' camerawork. Instead it gets a civics lesson in why freedom of the press is so important to American democracy, a system that really "works."

There are outstanding lead performances—by Robert Redford as Woodward, Dustin Hoffman as Bernstein, Jason Robards as *Washington Post* editor Ben Bradlee, and Hal Holbrook as Deep Throat. In addition there are great character performances, such as Jane Alexander's portrayal of an anguished Republican insider. Despite these fine performances, the film conveys the most conventional, mainstream ideas about the operation of American politics and never gets beneath the surface of Watergate. There is no suggestion at all that there were far deeper, even more shocking secrets never uncovered. To some degree this was inherent in the Woodward and Bernstein story, which "resurrects" the hero myth. Indeed, as Pakula suggested, this film is totally unlike *The Parallax View,* which

> leads you to the bottom of society, the people who do not live like everybody else, the people who have not made it, the people whose lives have been destroyed. All the President's Men is the opposite of that. If it's a detective story, it's a middle-class, establishment one [about] establishment corruption.[36]

In *All the President's Men* there is no searching inquiry into the secret state or the clandestine dimensions of the U.S. government: the shadowy world of the CIA; the intelligence services of the various branches of the military; the penetration and control of both parties by the national security establishment; and the even murkier world of double agents and contract agents obviously involved in the Watergate break-in. Yet critical studies of the era by Olmsted and Powers and personal recollections by Daniel Schorr and others suggest far deeper dimensions of the Watergate events. Moreover, two books—Jim Hougan's *Secret Agenda* and Len Colodny and Robert Gettlin's *Silent Coup*—published long after the Watergate events have raised explosive new questions concerning the deeper dimensions of the multiple conspiracies, the latter making Watergate seem like a surface event.[37]

Hougan's book posits a fascinating subtext in which the CIA played an important—even central—role. Hougan attacks the official version of Watergate constructed and endlessly reinforced and mythified by Woodward and Bernstein as well as a number of other journalists, government prosecutors, and the congressional investigators working for the Senate Watergate Committee.

He sees it as a "counterfeit history" in which, for example, E. Howard Hunt and James McCord were secretly working for the CIA while using the White House as a cover for domestic intelligence operations, and (in Hunt's case) spying on the very administration it was supposedly serving. Hougan concludes that "the covert operations of the White House and the CIA overlapped and, finally, collided." Those of the White House clearly took second place.

Colodny and Gettlin's *Silent Coup,* although clearly utilizing many of Hougan's revelations, fleshes them out in rich, well-documented, often excruciating detail, including the fact that Bob Woodward, while a naval officer and briefer (1969–70), had become friendly with Alexander Haig, who provided much of the information Woodward identified as coming from "Deep Throat," whom he met in parking garages. They further suggest that in reality "Deep Throat was a dramatic device meant to throw everyone off the trail of the Woodward-Haig relationship formed those 1969–70 briefings in the White House basement. Clearly Haig was Woodward's secret White House source. . . ."[37] They also suggest that John Dean knew a great deal more than he revealed in public testimony, arguing that he lied to the president, Congress, and the public partly seeking to cover up his wife's friendship with a woman who was part of a call-girl ring that was the real object of the original Watergate break-in. Both books leave the strong impression that Nixon was toppled at the instigation of a secret national security party involving members of both the Republican and Democratic parties, of which there is not a hint in *All the President's Men.* Indeed, in the postscript to the paperback edition of their book Colodny and Gettlin argue that the establishment press—particularly Bob Woodward and *The Washington Post*—is still more interested, after a quarter century, in maintaining the cultural myth of Watergate as the public knows it than in exploring the dimensions of the secret national security party and national security state as it operated in the Nixon era and, as Roger Morris has suggested, as it was again evident during and after the Gulf War, "with some of the same techniques and mouthpieces . . . foisting off a fresh mythology of personality and power."[38]

### *CAPRICORN ONE* (PETER HYAMS)

A film that effectively plays off the increasing recognition of the mediation of all political knowledge through television, *Capricorn One* (1978) belongs on any list of the most devious and conspiratorial scenarios ever foisted on an unsuspecting public. The film, based on the widely circulated legend that the original 1969 moon landing was a hoax—one is reminded of Ron Howard's remarkable

1995 movie simulation of the Apollo 13 mission—examines the question of reality and fiction in space travel, with a movie version's simulation appearing more "real" than the original documentary footage.

*Capricorn One* concerns a fictional NASA Mars mission that failed. According to the film narrative, because the agency knows in advance the mission will fail, the Mars crew (James Brolin as Charles Brubaker, Sam Waterson as Peter Willis, and O. J. Simpson as John Walker) is removed from their space capsule shortly before liftoff and flown to an old military base somewhere in the Southwest that has been converted into an elaborate sound stage—where the mission will simply be "simulated" and fed to the television networks.

Hal Holbrook, playing the director of the Mars mission, explains to the crew that while this particular mission isn't possible, someday it might work—if it agrees to cooperate in creating appropriate images to feed to an unsuspecting Congress and taxpayers in order to keep up funding for the agency's programs. Their careers are indirectly threatened, and the welfare of their families are at stake, so they dutifully simulate their time in the capsule and during reentry. Unforseen by the planners of the conspiracy, the actual unmanned capsule on which the whole plot hinges burns up during reentry, leaving those in charge of the elaborate charade with three astronauts who are very much alive. Those within the agency in charge of the plot decide the three crew members have to be eliminated to make the conspiracy credible. Guessing its probable fate, the crew flees across the desert, pursued by government assassins in an extended and imaginative chase sequence containing some of the first "black helicopters" of the conspiracy era. Meanwhile, an investigative reporter named Robert Caulfield (Elliott Gould) begins his own investigation, himself becoming a target for elimination when he gets too close to the truth. Tension is generally sustained, but the film ends—rather abruptly—with the astronauts' appearance in public at their own funeral, the audience left to speculate on further developments.

*Capricorn One* contains some pointed and witty dialogue, with wildly imaginative flashes of insight on the public's naïve receptivity and captivity to television images.

## Anti-"Nuke" Paranoia and the Menace of the Nuclear Industry

Long-term fears over nuclear war and radiation fallout reached a crescendo in the early years of the Reagan administration. *The Day After* (1983, Nicholas Meyer), a grimly realistic postnuclear apocalypse film portraying the aftereffects of an atomic attack in Lawrence, Kansas, generated one of the largest audiences for a made-for-television film and created a considerable amount of controversy. The same year saw Mike Nichols' film *Silkwood*, with Meryl Streep playing the ill-fated nuclear worker and union activist Karen Silkwood, who died under mysterious circumstances in 1974. The film effectively utilized anti-nuclear industry suspicions and the public's belief in the government's involvement in some sort of cover-up to generate an atmosphere of apprehension and implied threat.[39]

### *THE CHINA SYNDROME* (JAMES BRIDGES)

The coincidental release of *The China Syndrome* on March 16, 1979, and the near meltdown at the Three Mile Island nuclear power plant near Harrisburg, Pennsylvania, on March 28—just twelve days later—is one of the most remarkable events in film history. The film, a gripping political thriller, portrays the experiences of a television news crew accidentally witnessing a control-room crisis at a fictional "Ventana" California nuclear energy plant, with the crew's photographer actually shooting the event. The film created justifiable paranoia over the possibility that energy industry contractors, driven by the desire for higher profits, could omit x-rays of all the welded joints in a nuclear power station's water pumps, creating the potential for catastrophic failure in an extreme situation—such as the earth tremor portrayed in the film. Even more frightening than the question of what might happen if contaminated water reached the environment is the possibility that faulty instruments could indicate reactor power rods are being cooled when they are, in fact, exposed and generating uncontrollable heat, with the nuclear material burning right through the thick underlying level of concrete "all the way to China"—hence the title.

*The China Syndrome* is also a commentary on the growing power of the media to shape public awareness. As the film opens, viewers see Kimberly Wells (Jane Fonda) as the Channel Three news reporter, while disembodied voices of station directors are heard controlling the actual newscast. Unseen individuals effectively decide what the viewers see. When Wells complains, "Hey, is anybody listening to me?," her question is meant to highlight audience dependence on highly controlled and constructed (edited) television news images in addition to what this ostensibly political film seeks to say about the nuclear power industry itself.

The story involves television news reporter Wells (Fonda) and her cameraman Richard Adams (Michael Douglas), who visit the power plant to do a routine feature. During their visit an earth tremor triggers an emergency alert in the plant's control room. Adams films the events through the glass observation window separating visitors, management, and clerical staff from the main control room. After he and Wells arrive back at their television station, management refuses to air the footage. He is furious, suspecting a cover-up involving the station and executives at the Ventana plant.

Following the event, there is a swift, apparently thorough investigation into the incident, and the briefly shut down plant is restored to full operation. However, Jack Godell (Jack Lemmon), a veteran middle-management figure who loves the plant (and the industry), noticed a secondary shudder during the earth tremor, which the camera captured, signaling that Lemmon will be the crucial figure who decides what course of action is taken. Godell must weigh the overwhelming economic pressures to immediately put the plant back in operation against the fact that catastrophic possibilities were overlooked, which drives Lemmon into a crisis of conscience.

*The China Syndrome* is also a dramatic study of media responsibility, television artifice, and the public's right to know. After Adams lets his camera roll during the accident inside the plant, his station manager won't broadcast the film because he claims the story is "unconfirmed." It would, in his view, be an irresponsible use of the power of the media were he to screen it, and would, moreover, invite lawsuits from the industry. Adams views this as cowardice, perhaps even collusion. The phrase "no accident" recurs through the film, with all the semantic associations it evokes. The ominous threat posed by corporate power is effectively represented by shots of the chairman of the board looking down on Wells and Godell. (Associations of nuclear industry involvement in the death of Karen Silkwood, possibly resulting from actions by industry security agents, are here effectively evoked by surveillance tails on Wells and Godell.)

The story is no fantasy. The first draft of the 1974 screenplay by Mike Gray was based on a real event at the Dresden II reactor near Chicago in 1970, the result of a stuck needle on a water-level gauge. Another event involving a fire at the Browns Ferry reactor in Alabama in 1975 was incorporated in a second draft. An engineer by profession, Gray understood the technology and used actual terminology to make the screenplay vividly real. Photographs of the control room of the General Electric Trojan nuclear plant near Portland, Oregon, were used to construct the set for the film's fictional Ventana plant. The literature on nuclear accidents—and the subsequent events at Three Mile Island and the catastrophe at Chernobyl in 1986—make it clear that the scenario of *The China Syndrome* was no paranoid delusion but a powerful and potentially real possibility.[40]

## Vietnam Veterans and the Dark Side of American Society

### *WHO'LL STOP THE RAIN* (KAREL REISZ)

Robert Stone's *Dog Soldiers* (1974) is one of several novels in which the protagonists attempt to free themselves of the myths that drew the nation into the Vietnam War. One of the three most praised literary works to emerge after the war's end (the others being Michael Herr's *Dispatches* [1977] and Tim O'Brien's *Going after Cacciato* [1978]),[41] it served as the basis of the film *Who'll Stop the Rain* (1978). Stone did two versions of the screenplay, which was completed by Judith Rascoe, who streamlined significant elements in the novel, especially the section in Vietnam.[42] The film, starring Nick Nolte, Michael Moriarity, and Tuesday Weld, was to bear the novel's title, but was then retitled by the distributors, who preferred the Creedence Clearwater Revival song, composed by John Fogerty, that is heard to powerfully evocative effect on the soundtrack. In the words of one critic, Reisz's film remains "a remarkably faithful and astute adaptation of a strong novel."[43]

Stone's novel is a horrific allegorical paranoia thriller that describes the corrosive effects of the Vietnam War on American society and culture, as well as an exploration of the psychic and moral consequences on its participants. These qualities are effectively presented in the screenplay and film, though the novel is even more sordid and violent.

The novel and film open with Converse (Michael Moriarity), a burned-out, disillusioned, once liberal writer, who is traumatized by the grotesque absurdities he has witnessed in Vietnam and consequently thinks only of himself. He enlists his former buddy Ray Hicks (Nick Nolte), another burned-out but physically fit Vietnam combat veteran, in a plan to smuggle three kilos of high-grade heroin into the country, for which he would get 10 percent of the twenty-five thousand dollars supposedly to be paid to Converse. The latter acquires the heroin from a woman, Charmian (Gail Strickland), his sometime lover and the beautiful daughter of a former Southern governor, who feeds off a sea of corruption and high connections in Saigon and stateside. The deal, however, turns out to be an elaborate setup and double-cross, with a crooked federal narc, Antheil (played with repellant zeal by Anthony Zerbe), alerted to its delivery. Back in California, Converse's wife Marge (Tuesday Weld, in a brittle, human portrayal) is supposed to hand off the dope to what Converse believes to be corrupt CIA agents. When Hicks delivers the dope, Marge (an addict and an alcoholic) does not have his portion and may not even be aware that it is heroin her husband is trying to smuggle in.

Meanwhile, Antheil has sent two hireling thugs to watch the house: wisecracking, explosively brutal Danskin (Richard Masur) and his associate (Ray Sharkey). The two hirelings, while brutal, are no match for Hicks, a kind of zen warrior/ "returned hero,"[44] who is appalled by the moral degeneration he finds in American society. Nolte's impressive performance galvanizes the film, creating one of the most memorable filmic anti-heroes. Hicks subdues Antheil's two thugs and flees south with Marge (with whom he has become sexually involved) and the dope. When the cynical, weak Converse returns to Berkeley, the thugs threaten him, gaining his abject cooperation in their pursuit of Hicks.

Both the narrative and the film versions contain one of the greatest chase sequences as the characters move from Vietnam to Berkeley-Oakland, then to Los Angeles, and on to the California desert in an attempt to unload a kind of "anti-grail"—three kilos of the highest grade heroin ("you could cut this stuff to infinity") smuggled in from Asia.

Nobody is in the right here and everyone *is* compromised—with the exception of Marge Converse's bookstore-owning Old Left father (David Opatashu), who puts down his son-in-law's dope smuggling with the devastating comment that "a sense of unreality is not a legal defense." Converse himself (though perhaps too sleazy and spineless in Michael Moriarity's characterization) might represent the kind of sleepwalking, crisis-managing intellectuals who helped create the initial climate for the Vietnam War and then, disillusioned and horrified at the catastrophic outcome, retreated to academic refuges. His wife, though once supposedly an antiwar activist, is almost totally lost to her addiction in the novel but (thanks to the revised screenplay and Weld's performance) comes across as more sympathetic in the film.

Nolte, as the central character Hicks, displays the physical attributes later associated with a Rambo, but he has more spiritual and philosophical depth—Nietzsche and Zen are repeatedly referenced—despite the fact that he has no real cause to champion. He might stand for the legions of brave and competent ordinary men who willingly fight wars, paying the dues for all the follies of the Converses, who don't get caught and escape the obvious physical costs—yet even they pay a psychological price.

The mood of *Who'll Stop the Rain* is one of pervasive apprehension verging on paranoia. Once Hicks comes into possession of the heroin, no place is safe; there are no sanctuaries. There is no place for Hicks in this society, nor any way out. Yet the screenplay and Reisz's direction provide him with multiple, extended exits. His elaborate arming and preparation for the final struggle with Antheil and his crooked local agents generates hope that he will somehow find a way out. His final, agonized trek along miles of railroad tracks winding through the hellish inferno of salt flats is one of the memorable final acts in film history. A samurai warrior with no war to fight, Hicks, in "fighting an enemy identified with the machine," has become the Viet Cong he fought.[45] Fatally wounded and exhausted beyond measure due to the desert heat, he finally drops dead on the tracks with his rifle and the heroin. Found there by Converse and Marge, they surrender what is left of the heroin to the pursuing Antheil who, in a surprising plot twist, scrambles for the drugs in the dirt, only to have them taken from him by persons unknown. The Converses are left with nothing but their wasted, debased lives. While their survival might suggest new possibilities, there is no optimism possible in this story of a Vietnam War veteran's savage journey into an American hell.[46]

### *CUTTER'S WAY* (IVAN PASSER)

This 1981 film, another allegorical paranoia crime thriller with a Vietnam veteran as its central character, is based on Newton Thornburg's 1977 novel *Cutter and Bone* (the film's original title). The narrative unfolds in the post-counterculture twilight zone lingering in Santa Barbara in the aftermath of the Vietnam War. (The deceptively beautiful California location is given a menacing inflection by the director and the cinematographer, Jordan Cronewith.)

John Heard plays Alex Cutter, a badly disfigured and maimed Vietnam vet. He has a vicious satirical wit that never lets up—even when it threatens to elicit violent reaction from those he verbally abuses. His iconoclastic commentary at first fascinates and then challenges the listener. While waiting for someone to ignore his war hero status and simply punch him out, one begins to recognize that he possesses a unique, sometimes revelatory degree of insight. His best friend, Richard Bone (Jeff Bridges) is a sleek, tanned yacht salesman who rarely sells anything and mainly supports himself as a stud. When not sleeping with older women, he hangs out with the Cutters at their small Santa Barbara house. Bone, like most of the males of his generation, assiduously avoided getting into Vietnam. Cutter never lets him forget it, reminding him of his evasion and seeking a way to make him commit to something—anything—to pay what he regards as Bone's "generational dues." They are both obviously in love with Cutter's loyal and long-suffering wife Mo (Lisa Eichhorn), who exists in what appears to be a terminal state of exhaustion from Cutter's continuing verbal abuse, and somewhat narcotized—whether from dope, medication, or the glass of alcohol always in her hand is unclear.

On his way to visit the Cutters one night, Bone's car stalls in the rain and he witnesses someone dumping something into a trash can. (It turns out to be the body of a young woman.) When he's questioned by the police, he can't positively identify the car or the driver—it was raining, dark, and the other car sped away after disposing of the body—but the impression lingers. While watching the annual "frontier days" parade with the Cutters in old downtown Santa Barbara, Bone stares at the grand marshal, an oil corporation executive named J. J. Cord (Stephen Elliott). Bone suddenly says to himself, "It's him, it's him!" Cutter, hearing his friend's comment, wants him to act on his realization that Cord was the probable murderer of the young woman.

Instead of going to the police, Cutter takes matters into his own hands by fashioning an elaborate blackmail plot involving the dead girl's sister. He sends letters to Cord's corporate headquarters and then recklessly appears at the offices and alleges knowledge of Cord's involvement. Bone regards this behavior as insanely dangerous, given Cord's power and resources, but Cutter seems to exult in it, claiming that it's like being back in combat in Vietnam.

As Cutter grows more obnoxious and reckless, his wife orders him out of the house. Bone finally gets Mo into bed. Sometime that night—after Bone had left—the house is blown up. In the resulting fire Mo is killed and her body burned almost beyond recognition. Cutter (and the viewer) must surmise it was a message from Cord, an attempt by his security men to kill Bone. Cutter resolves to kill Cord.

At one level Cord—like Peter Cable in *Klute* and Noah Cross in *Chinatown*—becomes "a vague, clichéd personification of untouchable power-wielding 'evil.'"[47] The novel's bleak and hopeless outcome—Cutter goes completely insane and is institutionalized, while Bone is ambushed and killed by security men—is completely recast in the film, with a different conclusion invented by the director and screenwriter Jeffrey Alan Fiskin, an ending extolled by the film's devotees.[48]

The film's conclusion introduces a powerful new subtext as Cutter forces Bone to put his life on the line. Invading an elaborate garden reception at Cord's estate, Cutter steals a white horse from the stable, leaps across a pool, and smashes through a window. Fatally injured, he is confronted by Cord and his security men, who have already captured Bone. Bone accuses Cord of being the man who killed the young woman (undoubtedly not the first time he so disposed of one of his sexual playthings). Cord disdainfully sniffs, "What if I were?" In response, Bone shoots Cord, thereby accepting "Cutter's Way."

## *MISSING* (CONSTANTIN COSTA-GAVRAS)

On September 17, 1973, six days after the military coup that overthrew the democratically elected government of socialist president Salvador Allende, Charles Horman, thirty-one, a citizen of the United States, was arrested by agents of the Chilean military. One month later his fingerprints were matched to a body found in the Santiago morgue. With Frank Terrugi, his was one of two confirmed American deaths in the Chilean coup. Horman was among the thousands seized, tortured, and murdered in the days after the U.S.-backed coup that killed nearly thirty-two hundred, drove tens of thousands into exile, and left another thousand "disappeared" during the military regime of Augusto Pinochet. These events constitute the background to and provide the basic material for Costa-Gavras' film *Missing* (1982).

In the first chapter of his book on the Horman incident,[49] Thomas Hauser uses the film to illustrate the technique and dynamic of government "infantilization" of citizens. Reading his poignant, often agonizing account of the search for Charles Horman by his father and wife in post-coup Chile, I was reminded of my own stay there. In 1967 and again in 1969 I spent several months in Chile doing background research for a doctoral dissertation and additional research for subsequent academic publications.[50] The lifestyles of young American social science academics at the end of the 1960s in Chile were very much like those portrayed in *Missing,* though the intense political polarization of the Allende period (1970–73) had not yet developed. What did seem to exist then was the sense of the country as a rich political laboratory with a complex democratic and vigorous left-wing political tradition, with European-style mass membership parties linked to trade unions, including a viable Communist Party with a long tradition of effective participation in electoral politics and a significant base of voter support.

The film by Costa-Gavras, based on the Thomas Hauser book, was a visionary window back in time. Jack Lemmon's portrayal of Ed Horman, Charles' father, his efforts to find his son (in the company of Joyce, Charles' wife, played by Sissy Spacek), and his personal transformation along the way cannot fail to leave a lasting impression. *Missing* ranks with Coppola's *Apocalypse Now* and Stone's *Salvador* for the revelatory power of the central character's journey of discovery through the labyrinthine world of deception by U.S. diplomatic and security officials. It is a kind of reverse *Heart of Darkness* journey[51] for the Hormans as they gradually become aware of the dimensions of American involvement. The film and its background have been analyzed in great detail in John Michalzyck's study of the films of Costa-Gavras.[52]

Over the years, other researchers have shed additional light on the mysterious disappearance and death of Charles Horman. A series of documents concerning the complicity of the United States in the whole affair have been released under the Freedom of Information Act. Among these, there is a telegram dated February 11, 1974, from then U.S. ambassador David Popper to Secretary of State Henry Kissinger reporting on a meeting between Assistant Secretary of State Jack Kubisch and then Chilean foreign minister General

Huerta designed to deal with the controversy surrounding the execution of the two Americans. In it Kubisch said he is raising the issue "in the context of the need to be careful to keep relatively small issues in our relationship from making cooperation more difficult."[53]

Such "relatively small issues" as the life of Charles Horman became the basis of the film. It now appears that Horman became one of many thousands of leftist activists and intellectuals named on death lists drawn up with the assistance of U.S. intelligence operatives—in Horman's case because he apparently "knew too much."

As the film effectively shows, on the day the Allende government was overthrown (September 11, 1973) Charles happened to be visiting Vina del Mar, a coastal resort near Valparaiso, which apparently served as the base from which—as the screenplay by Costa-Gavras and Donald Stewart implies—American military and intelligence forces coordinated the coup and bloodbath. Charles Horman ran into undercover American active-duty and covert intelligence operatives in Valparaiso as they were exulting over the success of their operation. Horman's careful notation of his conversations with various U.S. military officers—as well as those individuals he suspected were covert intelligence operatives—enabled him to put together a systematic portrait of the U.S. role in coordinating the coup. After returning to Santiago, on September 16 his apartment was systematically searched and ransacked and he was taken to the national stadium, probably tortured, dying on September 19, 1973.

Later accounts, such as the Church Committee report, stated that "the CIA received intelligence reports on the coup planning . . . throughout the months of July, August, and September 1973."[54] William Blum provides a detailed summary of events leading up to the coup in his history of CIA interventions. According to him, the American role was substantial but often hidden. Beginning in Valparaiso, Chilean naval troops were dispatched to Santiago, while

> U.S. Navy ships were present offshore, ostensibly to participate in joint maneuvers with the Chilean Navy. The American ships stayed outside of Chilean waters, but remained on the alert. A United States WB-575 plane—an airborne communications control system—piloted by U.S. Air Force officers, cruised in the Chilean sky. At the same time, thirty-two American observation and fighter planes were landing at the U.S. air base in Mendoza, Argentina, not far from the Chilean border.[55]

That the United States played a central role in coordination of the coup seems an inescapable conclusion.

Although the Horman family sued the United States for their son's wrongful death, because the CIA refused to release relevant files the case was dismissed.

The senior U.S. Military Group officer in Chile during the coup, Ray Davis (Captain Ray Tower [Charles Cioffi] in the film) filed a sixty million-dollar libel suit against the director and Universal Studios, but it was dismissed in 1987 on summary judgment.

More recent revelations—based on State Department documents declassified in October 1999—include a letter, dated August 25, 1976, which admits that CIA agents were at least partially responsible for the death of Charles Horman. According to several press reports directly quoting passages from the document, it stated that "there was circumstantial evidence to suggest that U.S. intelligence may have played an unfortunate part in Horman's death." Regarding the role of the CIA, it stated that "at best [the CIA] was limited to providing or confirming information that helped motivate his murder by the government of Chile. . . . At worst, U.S. intelligence was aware the government of Chile [the junta that was in the process of seizing power] saw Horman in a rather serious light and U.S. officials did nothing to discourage the logical outcome of the paranoia."[56] Reading from the document at a Washington, D.C., news conference, an emotional Joyce Horman, widow of Charles, said, "I think this is close to the smoking pistol here." A CIA spokesman denied that the agency was involved in Horman's death but said the agency was examining its own files on operations in Chile and might declassify some of them in the future.[57]

Over time, the visionary revelations of *Missing* are gradually being confirmed as a grim and horrifying reality; if it is paranoia, it is reasoned, fact-based, and visionary, not delusional.[58] The U.S. officials in the film, usually described by establishment reviewers as "cardboard cutouts," are now acknowledged as accurately drawn portraits of government operatives carrying out the counterinsurgency tasks of the "country team."[59]

In all these films—from the end of the 1960s into the 1980s—the central characters find themselves in a state of agonizing uncertainty. The traditional private eye, often succeeded by the investigative reporter, has become diminished, ineffectual, irrelevant. Towne and Polanski's J. J. Gittes, Altman's Marlowe, Penn's Harry Moseby, Richards' Marlowe, and especially Pakula's Joe Frady are all increasingly positioned within a worldview that—anticipating Lynch's *Blue Velvet* (1986) and culminating in Stone's *JFK* (1991)—is filled with more evil, more corruption, and more enigmas than anyone but the most paranoid had previously dreamed. The conventional private eyes, investigative reporters, or efficacious and involved citizens have become, if not victims of their arrogance, then at best witnesses to events.

By contrast, in *Missing*, the patient efforts of generations of investigators gradually confirmed the revelatory and visionary paranoia of the film. While

Charles Horman—the "investigator" in this particular case—died, he never truly disappeared, living on in Thomas Hauser's excruciating study and in Costa-Gavras' memorable film, energizing a continuing inquiry into human rights violations that finally managed to place one of the architects of genocide, General Pinochet, under arrest twenty-five years after the events described in the film.[60] Others—like the American military, diplomatic, and intelligence personnel—fall into the "banality of evil" category consisting of those who were just "doing one's job." Still others, like former secretary of state Henry Kissinger[61]—in many ways the author of the Chilean coup and the last phase of the Vietnam War—became, in Robert Towne's apt phrase, criminals so great they were honored rather than jailed.

CHAPTER SIX

# Family Values?

## The View from Ronald Reagan's Closet

"Family Values" became a slogan in the Reagan era of the 1980s, but the term represented contested ideological terrain. The political faction of the emergent New Right joined a growing cadre of moral crusaders championing a renewed religious Right. As Rosalind Petchesky suggested in a perceptive analysis early in Reagan's first term, these two dimensions were fused around interlocking themes:

> The first, the antifeminist backlash, aimed initially at abortion but extended from abortion to all aspects of sexual freedom and alternatives to traditional (patriarchal) family life. The second, an antisocial welfare backlash, aimed at the principle (given a certain amount of legitimacy during the New Deal and the 1960s) that the state has an obligation to provide for economic and social needs through positive government-sponsored programs.[1]

The antifeminist backlash, chronicled in Susan Faludi's book on the subject,[2] was embodied in a campaign for family values from a most unlikely source, given the actual realities of the Reagans' family life. As Michael Rogin perceptively pointed out, "The split between what Ronald Reagan represents and who he is . . . reassures Americans who are also confronted with difficulties in living out traditional family values but who preserve them in the realm of the signifier."[3]

Beyond the elaborately constructed image of its "leader," which has been analyzed in a large body of literature,[4] in many ways "Reaganism," a short-term ideology that permanently shaped American political culture, initially represented the effective mobilization of white males—who exhibited a kind of paranoia of status-threatened members of the patriarchy—into a supranational political coalition. Domestically it was centered around issues of antifeminism, covert racism, class privilege, conservative religion, and traditional values and lifestyles. Internationally the agenda included remilitarization, a reanimated and intensified cold war, and the assertion of traditional U.S. power and imperialist politics in the Caribbean and Central America. *Denial*—seemingly a defining attribute of Reagan's personality—became an operant principle, with "It's Morning in America" theme in the 1984 campaign.

In a study of films of the era, Stephen Prince suggested that

> certain key films of the 1980s, such as *Back to the Future* (1985, Robert Zemekis) and *Field of Dreams* (1989, Phil Alden Robinson), seem to be intimately connected with the *zeitgeist* of the decade, particularly with the nostalgic myths incarnated by the Reagan-era political culture and the desire for retrieval of and reconciliation with a past conceived in idealized and romanticized terms.[5]

In the first of these immensely popular movies, Michael J. Fox literally returns to the past, while in the other, Kevin Costner somehow recreates the past in an Iowa cornfield. Central among Reagan's contributions to the America of the 1980s was a childlike desire never to grow up, blending nostalgia and history, and shifting easily between reality and movie image.[6] The biggest money-making films of the 1980s, including those of Steven Spielberg[7] and George Lucas—the latter's *Star Wars* series contributing "evil empire" and other catch-phrases to the political vocabulary of the era—also reinforced the simplistic manichaean political discourse of good versus evil utilized by Reagan's speech-writers with telling effect among his supporters.[8]

Speechwriters and handlers of Reagan, Bush, and Quayle worked over and manipulated the notion of family, idealizing a nonexistent past. The public was presented with utopian images of family life and a small town, "Greenfield Village on the Potomac"[9] and Disneyland version of an America that existed only in the movies.[10] It apparently tapped the public's need and desire for a positive, supportive closeness (identified with the concept of the family), which had increasingly been eroded by our modern consumer society. The discourse begun in the Reagan years continued in the Bush administration—with vice president Dan Quayle castigating a television character (Murphy Brown) for single motherhood in 1992—and into the 1996 presidential conventions, where rival parties disputed whether it takes a "family" (Republicans) or a "village" (Democrats) to raise a child effectively.

## The "Family" as an Ideological Project

Weighed down with such emotional and ideological baggage, "family" as a kind of normative concept, as one anthropologist has argued, is "a socially necessary illusion" in that it both "expresses and masks recruitment to relations of production, reproduction, and consumption—relations that condition different kinds of household resource bases in different class sectors."[11] The family thus becomes an "ideological project." As Jimmie L. Reeves and Richard Campbell pointed out in their study of the Reagan-era "drug wars": "The Modern Family works as a major consciousness-producing instrument and a powerful vision of social control in the political economy."[12] The alleged crisis in the family, peaking in Reagan-era discussions, served as a coded critique of the failure of social control in preceding years, echoing earlier Nixon and Agnew campaign denunciations, in 1968 and 1972, of permissiveness and loose morality as somehow linked to earlier antiwar protests, as well as support for the ill-fated presidential candidacy of Senator George McGovern in 1972.

Women (coded as "mothers") were what much of this discourse over family involved. They simply refused to stay "at home"—where they supposedly "belonged." This view neglected the long involvement of significant percentages of women in the labor force.[13] A high level of male and female anxiety and resentment over transformations in role expectations existed during the Reagan years. This was not a new development. In the 1960s Betty Friedan had pointed out that "the mother could be blamed for everything. In every case history of the troubled child [or] alcoholic, suicidal, schizophrenic psychopathic, neurotic adult [there was] a rejecting, overprotecting, dominating mother."[14]

In the Reagan years, women were charged, as mothers, with a profound range of duties ranging from breeding to the formation of politically correct subjectivity. Feminist efforts to free women from a traditional division of labor were viewed as attempts to undermine the social order. As one psychiatrist has indicated,

> Perceived or real defects in the emotional environment of the family or the child's psychological development have usually been attributed to some failure in the mother rather than in the father. . . . The mother is seen as responsible for the family environment, for the psychological well-being of her children, and for the emotional atmosphere in the home. To whatever extent we have believed that mothers do something special for their children, we have been more willing to believe that failures in mothering do something devastating to children.[15]

This is a remarkable example of attempted projection onto women of social problems, and, more fundamentally, a denial of basic social, economic, and media cultural influences.

The family was once considered a refuge from the public sphere, but in the Reagan era its meaning changed. While some, like Fredric Jameson, saw a utopian dimension surrounding the family at the beginning of the Reagan years,[16] by the middle of the 1980s the concept had largely become commodified, though its meaning was still being contested. Family became something to "have" in order to validate one's place in the public sphere.[17] In the political campaign of 1988, Bush, Dukakis, and Jesse Jackson all claimed they had the best families. The point, apparently, was that each could be admitted to political life and the public sphere because they had "real" families. In this era, Terry Eagleton suggested, there was a kind of displacement of the family by mass culture. Where the institution might once have functioned as a site or arena for the negotiation of desires and needs, it was now overwhelmed by the dynamics of mass culture. One had to have "it," though what that was remained unclear.[18]

## Dystopian Families in Movie Culture

Over the past half century, family values rhetoric has had its "shadow" side in American life, particularly in the visionary paranoia evident in several films directed by Alfred Hitchcock. Perhaps the most powerful critiques of efforts to constitute some kind of happy family ideology in the 1980s are evident in David Lynch's film *Blue Velvet* (1986), as well as such lesser-known films as *The Stepfather* (1987, Joseph Ruben) and *River's Edge* (1986, Tim Hunter).

Lynch's *Blue Velvet* had many precursors. One could see early elements in Hitchcock's *Shadow of a Doubt* (1943, with a screenplay cowritten by Thornton Wilder, author of the celebrated play *Our Town*), a devastating, creepy deconstruction of the small town family and the director's own personal favorite.[19] This deconstruction was continued in Orson Welles' *The Stranger* (1946), in which even the small-town college professor's wife (Loretta Young) did not know her husband (Welles) was a Nazi war criminal. The trend was prefigured, in terms of implied incest, in *Kings Row* (1942, Sam Wood). The theme was carried forward by Hitchcock in *Psycho* (1960), where the viewer suspects that Mrs. Bates had something to do with the creation of Norman Bates, though Norman's madness remains "inscrutable, capricious, apparently unpresentable."[20] In Hitchcock's *Strangers on a Train* (1951) we actually meet the family of the psychotic Bruno Anthony, though the connections between the family relationship and his homicidal psychosis are not readily apparent.

### *FRANCES* (GRAHAM CLIFFORD)

In the 1982 film *Frances,* the first of several powerfully critical counterportraits of alleged family values, American audiences were introduced to a terrifying narrative showing the lengths to which one family member could go to literally demolish the personality of another—all with the enthusiastic support of the legal and medical establishments. The film recounts the story of actress Frances Farmer, an early member of the Group Theater and a fresh Hollywood talent. (Howard Hawks called her "the finest actress I ever worked with.")[21] By the early 1940s the public image of the real Frances Farmer was of a hotheaded, beautiful young film actress, a political radical who drank too much, had several run-ins with police, the most publicized landing her in jail. Few knew that her mother secretly arranged—in complicity with hostile police and a legal system eager to silence her—to have her committed to several mental institutions. There, given various barbaric forms of insulin shock and electroshock "therapy," she still persisted in her noncompliant behavior, trying to run away from the "snake pit" mental prisons. Her struggle reached a climax at the Western Washington State Hospital at Steilacoom, where, after six years of electroshock, massive drug experiments, and repeated rapes, she probably fell victim to the then fashionable experimental transorbital lobotomy treatments of Dr. Walter Freeman, who was known as "the father of American lobotomy."[22] Freeman performed over four thousand such operations of the over one hundred thousand that took place in North America between 1944 and 1960.[23]

In this barbaric and bizarre period of post–World War II psychiatry and neurosurgery, Freeman's treatments involved assembly-line lobotomy procedures on "difficult" patients suffering from "apprehension, anxiety, depression, compulsions, obsessions, as well as drug addicts, sexual deviants, and of course schizophrenics. He was convinced the frontal lobes of the brain were somehow responsible for aggression or, ultimately, a patient's refusal to cooperate in what he termed an "acceptable way."[24] The brains of his "patients" were entered under the eyelid—supposedly less risky than earlier prefrontal lobotomies, which left victims in near-vegetative states. (However, no detailed records of the man's "successes" exist.)[25] Freeman's version of the transorbital lobotomy, or leukotomy, involved the insertion of a

> thin calibrated instrument, resembling an ice pick, between the patient's eye and eyelid, and driving it through the orbital plate and into the brain to a final depth of about one and one-half inches, where it was moved only slightly to sever the nerves connecting the cortex with the thalamus. The whole operation could be performed in less than a few minutes, with not a good deal more fuss than the administration of a penicillin shot.[26]

Patients experienced a permanent disabling—literally a disconnection—of some mental functioning, making them much more compliant. Freeman was extremely enthusiastic about his technique, claiming it would surgically control schizophrenia, habitual forms of criminality, homosexuality, and virtually all so-called neurological illnesses. A real showman with a dramatic flair, Freeman once lobotomized thirty-five women in a single day; another time, he lobotomized thirteen women in a few hours.[27]

Fascinated by the case of Frances Farmer, probably the most famous person in confinement at a mental hospital in the United States, Freeman examined her several times, finding her "defiant and uncooperative"—and thus a good candidate for his procedure. Here is how Freeman explained his rationale at the time:

> The patients for whom this operation brings the best results are tortured with self-concern, who [*sic*] suffer from terribly painful disabling self-consciousness, whether it expresses itself in pains in the body organs or terrible distress from feelings of persecution. . . . In ordinary language, the technique severs the nerves that deliver emotional power to ideas. Along with a cure comes some loss in the patient's imaginative power. But that's what we want to do. They are sick in their imaginations.[28]

Frances Farmer, once a young, rebellious, imaginative, and visionary actress, as well as a political radical, was never to be the same after this treatment, which was probably performed (there were no witnesses present) in 1949.

Already as a teenager, Farmer was an outspoken, often rebellious young woman, winning an essay contest with a composition entitled "God Dies." At twenty-one she won a contest sponsored by a local Communist newspaper, the prize being a trip to the Soviet Union. Her mother, quoted on the front page of the *Seattle Post-Intelligencer* for March 29, 1935, said, "If I must sacrifice my daughter to Communism I hope other mothers save their daughters before they are turned into radicals in our schools. . . . Something should be done immediately to clean the schools of radical teachers before they sway other girls and boys away from American ideals."[29] By the time Farmer's mother and the male medical, political, and cultural power structures of the day were through with her fourteen years later, Frances would entertain few thoughts of any sort, though she vainly tried to resume an acting career.

The 1982 film of her life was based on several sources, mainly relying on William Arnold's biography *Shadowland* (though he was not credited)[30] and Farmer's ghostwritten autobiography, *Will There Ever Be a Morning?*[31] From the evidence available over half a century later, compared with most women of her day Farmer was a brash, outspoken, wild, and vibrant stage presence, as well as a striking film actress. (Her one really fine film role was as the female lead in Hawks's 1936 *Come and Get It.*) She had the misfortune to run up against virtually every secret network and power structure of her day: local schools; the university; state power elites (apparently including a secret Washington state vigilante network with members high in the judiciary); Hollywood film executives and gossip columnists; possibly the FBI (whose massive surveillance of other Hollywood leftists is well documented); the sexism of male New York dramatists in the Group Theater, and—probably worst of all—her obsessively controlling mother. As Michel Foucault has argued, "the entire existence of madness, in the world now being prepared for it, was enveloped in what we may call, in anticipation, a 'parental complex.' The prestige of patriarchy is revived around madness. . . . [Psychiatrists] isolated the social structure of the bourgeois family, reconstituted it symbolically in the mental asylum, and set it adrift in history."[32] Farmer experienced the imposition of her mother's conception of just such a bourgeois "family."

The 1982 film version of Farmer's life (1914–70) features a screenplay by Nicholas Kazan and others. Jessica Lange was nominated for an Academy Award for her performance as Frances, which (aside from some dramatic additions) follows the overall outlines of Farmer's life. The film is an understandably grim, unrelenting portrait of a world that is not a paranoid delusion but a multileveled repressive reality closing in on a woman who persisted in nonconformist behavior. Yet the reality of Farmer's experiences at the Western Washington State Hospital were probably far worse than the horrific film images. Trustee prisoners were used as staffers and prostituted female inmates. Soldiers from a nearby base were recruited by these trustees to use the helpless women for their sexual needs—at bargain prices. Acting as pimps and assistants, the trustees held down the terrified, struggling female inmates to permit institutionalized, for-pay rapes. Farmer, still a physically attractive woman, was repeatedly gang-raped. While the film briefly portrays this aspect of her experience, it was apparently more extensive and extreme.

According to Arnold, the character called Harry York (played by Lange's real-life friend and sometime companion Sam Shepard) has no real counterpart in Farmer's actual life.[33] While she was involved with several men over the years—she was married three times—the continuity and supportive depth of her relationship with the fictitious Harry York character were never matched by anyone in her daily life. Farmer's actual father, a weak, financially unsuccessful individual, lived apart from the family for twenty-five years and had little or no effect on her mother's influence.

Dalton Trumbo—screenwriter, blacklist victim, and defiant and unrepentant Hollywood "Red"—knew Farmer during her Hollywood years. When William Arnold interviewed him, Trumbo said, "You have to realize that they were out to get Frances and she knew it. Who? The cops. Why? The political thing. The migrant worker thing. [Farmer supported efforts to aid striking agricultural workers, among many other causes.] You name it. They wanted to bust that kid wide open and they finally had the opportunity."[34]

Clearly Farmer was a deviant and a rebel in a corporate society concerned to keep women compliant and quiet. She was hounded into "psychic oblivion," according to Harry M. Cheney, "because she didn't care whether the ink on the balance sheets was black or red. She played by her own rules, never realizing until it was too late that everyone else was playing an entirely different game. Criminally betrayed by her mother, her lover, her society, Frances Farmer ended up on an operating table with an ice pick in her frontal lobe simply because she was different."[35]

In an illusory dreamworld of family values extolled by Reagan supporters, *Frances* reflected only a small part of the media's widespread and expanding critique of the traditional family. The family was becoming a battleground, yet one that—despite the happy images of much of television and mainstream Hollywood—had long been recognized as a site of horrors. This was significantly so in the explicit "horror film" genre, as Robin Wood's famous essay illustrated, where the family itself became the site of the unspeakable, the ghastly, and the evil in the films of the preceding decade.[36]

## *BLUE VELVET* (DAVID LYNCH)

A cult film that came to have a mass following,[37] *Blue Velvet* (1986) depicts a world of explosive brutality, seething corruption, and murder lurking beneath a deceptively innocent and benign image of everyday life. If "family" in film embodies a range of traditional values and functions[38]—including love of father, father as ruler, love of country, mother love, mother duty, the good mother, the good or dutiful wife—these are both represented and exploded in Lynch's film. In retrospect, it is arguably the most significant, most influential, most crucially important American film of the 1980s.[39]

*Blue Velvet* presented a take on family and small-town life (with obvious implications for all of society), portraying it as sick and noxious. The film is the definitive representation of traumatized innocence and—particularly in Dennis Hopper's over-the-top portrayal of Frank Booth—the most agonized representation of the product of a dysfunctional family. What kind of grotesque family could produce, in Frank Booth, one of the sickest, most violent characters in the history of film?

The celebrated opening shots in Lynch's film portray a street with picket fences in a stylized and idealized small town, complete with a fire truck moving in dreamlike slow motion, hyperreal birds, kids playing and crossing a street under the watchful eye of a crossing guard, and well-tended gardens. However, as the camera closes in on the world beneath the lawn, the viewer is assaulted by images of a seething world of ravenous, crawling, slithering insects. The middle-aged man busy watering his lawn falls down, an apparent heart attack or stroke victim, his dog barking frantically as the hose writhes about him like some poisonous green snake.

Jeffrey Beaumont (Kyle MacLaclan), dressed in artist's black and sporting one gold earring, has been called home from college after his father's illness to help in the family hardware store. He finds a recently severed human ear covered with ants. It was, Lynch suggested, "like finding a ticket to another world—you know, it would change your life."[40] So begins a classic American film story structure—the investigative narrative—here used to write a clandestine history of America during the Reagan era.[41]

Jeffrey takes the ear to the local police station, where a detective by the name of Williams brings it to the coroner, who says it will reveal a great deal once it is analyzed. (He thinks it was cut off with scissors.) After this exchange—which seems right out of a 1950s "B" movie[42]—the scene abruptly cuts to a close-up of scissors snipping a yellow police ribbon encircling the field where the ear was found. Later Jeffrey goes directly to the detective's home for more information. There he meets Sandy (Laura Dern), the detective's daughter, a blond high school senior, who tells Jeffrey that a woman singer is involved. The two hatch a plan to get into the apartment of the woman (Dorothy Valens, played by Isabella Rossellini) in order to hunt for clues. Dressing up as an insect exterminator, Jeffrey gains admittance and simulates spraying Dorothy's kitchen. He finds keys hanging beneath the counter, which he pockets. While he is there, a man in a yellow jacket enters and talks to Dorothy. This "Yellow Man," who is also a police detective, serves as a link between the legal order and the dark side of this small-town society.

The plan is to search the apartment for clues when Dorothy is out. Jeffrey and Sandy follow her to work, where she performs as the "Blue Lady" and sings "Blue Velvet," "Blue Star," and other torch songs at an anachronistic and very strange roadhouse called The Slow Club. Then Jeffrey and Sandy return to her apartment. Their agreed-upon signal fails, Dorothy arrives, and Jeffrey is trapped, hiding in her louvered front closet. After hearing a noise and grabbing a large kitchen knife, Dorothy opens the closet and orders Jeffrey out, demanding to know what he wants, to which he replies that he just wanted to "see" her. In an interview, Lynch once said, "I always wanted to sneak into a girl's room and watch her into the night and that, maybe at one point or another, I would see something that would be the key to a murder mystery.")[43] Abruptly ordering Jeffrey to undress, Dorothy pulls down his shorts and fondles his genitals, apparently performing oral sex on him (and probably triggering major castration anxiety among male viewers). Then she abruptly screams, "Don't look at me!" as Frank Booth arrives at the door.

Hustled—naked—back into the closet, Jeffrey watches one of the most bizarre scenes in film history. Seeming like an hour but lasting only a few minutes, Frank, screaming such choice expletives as "f——k" and "f——king," demands, "where's my bourbon." As Dorothy hands him the glass she dims the lamps and lights a candle. Booth, expressing nervous relief, says, "Now it's dark," suggesting that things have reached a new stage, though not, as one might expect, a more relaxed one. Ordering Dorothy to face him, seated on a chair, her legs spread, with the blue velvet robe open, Frank takes out a clear plastic gas mask and turns on a gas canister he wears on his belt, inhaling nitrous oxide (laughing gas). He strikes her, but, apparently impotent, then frantically humps on her as if he were having an orgasm. Then it is over. As Frank leaves, he says cryptically to Dorothy, "You're still alive; do it for Van Gogh," a reference to the severed ear, which belonged to Dorothy's husband—though why this was done is never made clear—who is, with her young son, Frank's captive. Dorothy, in bondage as Booth's sex slave, must be on the edge of suicide or expecting to be murdered by the volatile and psychotic Frank.[44] After he leaves, Jeffrey emerges to try to comfort Dorothy, who waves him off. He leaves, though he will return several times before the film's bloody conclusion.

A story capturing the mystery and repressed madness that lies beneath what is called "the normal," *Blue Velvet* evokes "a secret history, both personal and social, literal and psychological,"[45] a representation of small-town America as a seething underworld of permanently twisted personalities, perversity, corruption, and denial. The film shows "an extremity of imagined human behavior, a submersion in infernal appetites."[46]

In the character of Frank Booth, one sees how far film images of evil have come, beginning with such Hitchcockian Hollywood monsters as Uncle Charlie (Joseph Cotten) in *Shadow of a Doubt* (1943), Bruno Anthony (Robert Walker) in *Strangers on a Train* (1951), and Norman Bates (Anthony Perkins) in *Psycho* (1960).[47] They are all the products of families that are clearly dysfunctional. However, Lynch's character is in a class by himself, representing a "shrieking, algolanic compound of frottage, rape, sadism, torture, fetishistic obsession, helpless incestuous anxiety, delusion, and infantile rage . . . a sexual dynamic several steps beyond the diagnostic potentialities of DSM-III or other conventional psychoanalytic measurements, and therefore, perhaps, beyond our experience."[48]

Yet if Frank Booth is nearly beyond imagining, the power of Lynch's film makes him real because knowledgeable viewers know everything he does has already been done somewhere to somebody.

The personal power relations described in *Blue Velvet* are brutally offensive in their portrayal of the treatment of women (and some men). Jeffrey gains an awareness of their horror when he is abducted by Booth and his associates and taken to a surreal place called Ben's, where Ben (Dean Stockwell), a preening, garishly made up bisexual, upstages even Hopper. Driven to an industrial area, Jeffrey is kissed and smeared with lipstick by the psychotic Booth, then beaten to a pulp and left bleeding and unconscious—mirroring the fate of millions of battered women over the decades. This scene can be viewed as a kind of parable about men's growing awareness of the violence experienced by women.[49]

The ostensible but ambiguous femme fatale Dorothy Valens is much more than a victim. She is so degraded that she appears to enjoy the sexual violence inflicted on her by both Booth and (at her urging) by Jeffrey, who is himself horrified by the depths of perversity that well up in him. Late in the film, in a scene many reviewers found offensive but which quite effectively represents all the horrible acts done to her, she emerges from the bushes at Sandy's house completely naked, bruised, hysterical, and incoherent—the quintessential victimized and battered woman.

The film climaxes with a gory slew of deaths at Dorothy's apartment complex. Jeffrey arrives to discover the corrupt "Yellow Man" police detective dead; next to him is the lifeless body of Don Valens, Dorothy's earless husband, his brains splattered on a table. Frank arrives, his handgun equipped with a silencer to kill Jeffrey (who again hides in the louvered closet, armed with the detective's gun). When Frank pulls open the closet door, Jeffrey blasts him right between the eyes, blowing off the back of his head. Detective Williams arrives too late to do much but comment "it's all over." His possible implication in police corruption involving the Yellow Man and complex drug dealing and payoffs is never explained, leaving a gnawing doubt about the whole police apparatus.

The concluding scenes of the film are a bizarre reaffirmation of traditional family values—or maybe just a weird Lynchian take on them. Jeffrey is shown relaxing in the yard at Sandy's place. His father—apparently miraculously recovered—is busy talking to Detective Williams. Inside the house, Jeffrey's and Sandy's mothers—looking virtually identical—sit facing each other on the living room couch. Jeffrey and Sandy examine a mechanical robin holding a bug in its beak, while Sandy exclaims that the real robins have returned (for her an image of reaffirmed goodness). In a weird Lynchian touch, the beetle trapped in the beak of the obviously mechanical robin seems literally to be alive. The film concludes as it began, with the added image of Dorothy, playing with her son, superimposed.

In his next major film, *Wild at Heart* (1990), Lynch carried the deconstruction effort further, while still not providing any way out for his characters. Lynch once remarked that "there are lots of strange things in the woods," later claiming that "Kafka gives me a good mood." Continuing to plumb new depths of evil and mystery in his terminally weird worldview, Lynch concluded that "this is the way America is to me. There's a very innocent, naïve quality . . . and there's a horror and a sickness as well."[50]

All this should be viewed in terms of Lynch's larger total deconstruction or illumination of the "secret history" of American life implied not only in *Blue Velvet* but also the *Twin Peaks* television series and the films *Twin Peaks* and *Twin Peaks: Fire Walk with Me* (1992) spanning more than a decade.[51] Lynch was apparently very interested in Reagan, his family, and his administration.[52] His films found a counterpart in a president who was in many ways an artificial construction, who simply chose to deny unpleasant realities. A political figure (justifiably) charged with never publicly uttering a word that was not prescripted by others, he completed this bizarre scenario by literally effervescing mentally—he was diagnosed with Alzheimer's five years after leaving office—moving from dissociation from reality to a permanent mental "vacation."

### *THE STEPFATHER* (JOSEPH RUBEN)

This counterportrait of American family values during the Reagan era presents a strong, valorized image of a new family—that of the single mother and her daughter—mirroring the positive experience of millions of single-mother households. The "family" in the Reagan era became one of those "commodities, fetishized [*sic*], sentimentalized, and gutted of substance in political discourse, sold on television and in film as something viewers must desire, that they might . . . own if they purchased its images."[53] No character embodies the situation better than Jerry Blake in *The Stepfather* (1987), a dark horror-comedy deconstructing the alleged utopia of family and small-town life.[54]

Described by one critic as a "commercial psychological thriller modeled after Hitchcock's *Psycho,* Ruben's film offers a progressive take on the subject matter used in many of the horror films of the 1980s, again addressing the darker side of small-town America and voicing criticism of the supposed benefits of the male-dominated family. Basing his screenplay on a news item about a New Jersey man who murdered his family, then changed his name, and remarried, Donald E. Westlake (working with Carol Lefcourt and Brian Garfield) fashioned a darkly comedic scenario based on the premise of witnessing events from the perspective of the killer's new family.[55]

The film opens with a peaceful, tree-lined street in a Seattle suburb. Then there is a characteristic "evil house" forward tracking shot of what outwardly seems a fine older home. Inside the house, in the upstairs bathroom, a man (Terry O'Quinn) methodically rinses off blood, showers, shaves his beard, and dresses in preparation for his new life. Heading downstairs, he spots a child's toy and carefully puts it away. (The character is obsessive about "order," repeatedly mumbling "We've got to have a little order around here" when things are not quite the *Happy Days* sitcom he envisions the world to be.) The bloody body of a woman is glimpsed in the living room, and a child's corpse is visible in the foreground. As he exits the house, he begins to whistle "Camptown Races" as he picks up the morning paper and walks off on a beautiful autumn day.

A year later, the man, renamed Jerry Blake, is married to Susan (Shelley Hack), a widow with a teenage daughter, Stephanie (Jill Schoelen). To Susan Jerry represents a "new beginning," but to Stephanie there is something "too weird" about him: "He wants us to be like the families on TV . . . Grin and laugh and be having fewer cavities all the time." In fact, Jerry quotes old TV sitcoms like *Mr. Ed* and *Father Knows Best.* He reflects all the outward trappings of an ideal family man and a nice guy, but there is an underside to him that emerges, for example, when Stephanie has trouble at school, where Jerry makes her feel "like he wanted to erase me off the face of the earth." Everyone interprets Stephanie's suspicion as the result of unresolved grief over her father's death and rivalry with Jerry for her mother's attention. Only the audience can see the real danger the young woman discerns.

For Jerry Blake all the images of the Reagan-era happy nuclear family are like a religion. Only Stephanie—along with the audience—sees it as a "fantasy thing." Up to this point there is nothing that does not square with a Norman Rockwell vision of the patriarchal American family, which is precisely the writer's and director's point: a serial killer can live completely within such outward expectations of normality, just like the families he sees on TV. In fact, Jerry's "fantasy thing" is exactly the medicine publicly extolled in the late 1980s version of the American Dream by such conservative "family" experts as Dr. James Dobson, the Christian Right, President Ronald and Mrs. Reagan, and many others as an answer to the litany of social problems allegedly associated with the evils of single motherhood.

Even when Jerry's views outwardly appear somewhat crazy, they are easily subsumed within a family values ideology. Perhaps the most genuinely chilling moment in the film occurs during a barbecue Jerry hosts for a few "friends." Someone points to a follow-up story concerning the murder of the family a year earlier. To the question, "How could a man kill his whole family?" Jerry replies, "Maybe they disappointed him." Nobody questions his diagnosis.

Later, at the same barbecue, Jerry goes into the basement, where he engages in one of the psychotic dialogues only the audience has seen, apparently reliving some past childhood disciplinary abuse and, like Norman Bates conversing with "Mother" in *Psycho,* verbally enacting the part of the abusive parent.

When Stephanie spots him while getting some ice cream from the freezer, he abruptly switches off. From Stephanie's expression it is immediately obvious to Jerry that she now definitely "knows," that all her fears were correct, and that Jerry truly is an evil interloper in her mother's house. He realizes he has to cover his tracks and prepare to move on.

Stephanie wants to expose him, but only her psychologist, Dr. Bondurant (Charles Lanyer), seems ready to listen. Using an assumed identity, he arranges a meeting with Jerry to view a house. The psychologist tries to pump Jerry for information about his past. Jerry erupts in a psychotic rage, beats him to death, drags the body to his car, runs it off the road and down a hill. All signs of the murder go up in flames as Jerry walks away again whistling "Camptown Races."

Despite saving Stephanie from expulsion from school, things begin to come apart for Jerry. He accuses Stephanie's date of trying to "rape" her, but Susan intervenes and for the very first time openly criticizes him in front of Stephanie, creating some kind of psychotic reaction in Jerry. He cannot accept that he has failed; it is they who disappointed him, and appropriate measures must be taken.

Jerry slowly begins to fashion a new identity in another town in the Seattle region. He leaves his old job (but does not tell Susan), finds another selling "family" insurance (of course), and rents a condo next to another single mother he immediately seeks to befriend.

Susan, unaware of the abrupt change in Jerry's personality, tries to go on as usual, baking a cake and preparing meals like a good TV mom. When she tries to call Jerry at the American Eagle real estate office, she is told that he no longer works for them. When Jerry comes home, she tells him of her call, but he denies there is any problem, suggesting she asked for the "wrong name." She looks puzzled. He grabs the phone, saying there is no problem. Then he stops, confused, and says, "Wait a minute, who am I here?"

They all now know and, according to his twisted logic, must be eliminated. He abruptly smashes Susan's face with the phone and dumps her, unconscious, down the basement stairs. Then, carefully choosing a chef's knife, he goes after Stephanie, who is just emerging from her bath. An amusing—though deathly—chase ensues through doors, broken mirrors, closets, and the attic, with visual references to *Psycho* and *The Birds,* with Stephanie at one point grasping a piece of a large mirror and plunging it into the arm of the enraged and frenzied stepfather.

A subplot involves the brother—Jim Ogilvie—of Jerry's murdered former wife, who throughout the film is shown vigorously investigating and tracking down her murderer. Just as he arrives at Susan and Jerry's, gun in hand, Jerry plunges the knife he is wielding into Jim's gut and up into his heart, killing him before he can get off a shot. Then he goes after Stephanie, who effectively evades him.

Susan, now conscious but badly beaten, drags herself up to the main floor, where she finds Jim's gun. Seeing Jerry on the stairs, Susan shoots him, after which her the gun jams. Jerry struggles for the knife, but Stephanie manages to grab it and stab him. He rolls down the stairs, apparently dead (until the inferior sequel *Stepfather II*). The final scene shows a reunited mother and daughter, with Stephanie, in black leather, looking taller and stronger. She brandishes an electric saber saw as she cuts down the tall, phallic birdhouse Jerry had built for a bird "family." The two are shown entering their home arm in arm.

What is unusual about *The Stepfather,* Patricia Ehrens writes, is its "foregrounding patriarchal power but positing the maternal order in opposition to the destructive elements of patriarchy."[56] In a genre notorious for exploiting images of helpless women confronting monstrous males seeking to injure or destroy them, here one finds a strong and revitalized mother-daughter head of household as a satisfying alternative to the male-dominated family.

Writing on American "horror" films, Robin Wood notes that the older film construct of a "monster"—as simply the projection of repressed fears on some grotesque figure—was replaced in this era by "the family," in the broadest sense, as the embodiment of horror, expressing repressed elements of American life, in particular childhood and female sexuality. Images of the "terrible house," of women as objects of the evil male protagonist's hatred, of sexuality's release as a monstrous perversion, of ambivalence toward the family, and of "the double" all figure in horror and related films and are clearly evident in *The Stepfather.*[57]

Unlike the manner in which viewers are channeled into seeing nearly everything from the male perspective in *Fatal Attraction* (which appeared the same year), what is remarkable about *The Stepfather* is that here "the film's structuring devices do not lock us into Jerry's subjective point of view."[58] It is possible—indeed, it is the film's intention—to critique Jerry's behavior through Stephanie's more skeptical emotional distance from him.

The debt to Hitchcock is overwhelming. *Shadow of a Doubt* is an obvious reference point, with its critical take on small-town life and a beloved family member who turns out to be profoundly evil and deranged. *The Birds* is present in numerous avian associations (Jerry works for American Eagle Realty; a stuffed bird appears behind him at dinner; he is shown making a birdhouse). *Psycho* is even more directly referenced in Jerry's conversations with an imaginary parent; in the use of disguises; and in the private space in a cellar. There is even a nude shower sequence with an overhead shot.

Yet *The Stepfather* is unique in its reworking of all the major Hitchcockian elements and themes, presenting, as Ehrens convincingly points out, "a new premise about American life" that combines bewilderment, fear, and hostility of American males resulting from the loss of a sense of place with—thanks to the transformation of women's roles over a thirty-year period—"an affirmation of female bonding which has emerged as a viable alternative for many women."[59]

Echoing *Shadow of a Doubt, The Stepfather* quite remarkably pursues the parallel development of Stephanie's character, here as Jerry's rival for the affections of the mother. Stephanie wants her mother all to herself, and the film is so structured as to present this as a viable and positive alternative to the sick and illusory images of the happy family Jerry harbors. Jerry's efforts to create the traditional bond with the mother, usually viewed as normal, are here presented as motivated by sadistic and psychotic drives. While there are some parallels between Stephanie and Teresa Wright forty-four years earlier, Stephanie never wants a connection with Jerry the way Teresa wanted to bond with her serial murderer uncle (Joseph Cotten) in *Shadow of a Doubt.* In fact, the directly opposing efforts of Stephanie and Jerry for "control" of the affections of Susan make *The Stepfather* a remarkable and important departure from the standard Hollywood product of this era and a revolutionary alternative to the Reagan-era family values ideology.

When Stephanie, dressed in black leather to connote a new female power, saws down Jerry's "family" birdhouse, Ehrens argues, the film "has destroyed the American home with its male head of household, leaving it impotent on the ground. Likewise, [it] has reconstituted the family couple as two women, seemingly sufficient unto themselves (certainly safer). In one image [the film] has represented men's worst fears and perhaps many women's fondest hopes."[60] In marked contrast to Jerry's desire to dominate, the mother-daughter relationship depicted shows great mutual respect. Thus *Shadow of a Doubt* and *Psycho* are profoundly reshaped, reversing the original dynamics and outcomes. While it is not unheard of in horror films for a virginal heroine to save herself, the final outcome of *The Stepfather* breaks the conventional pattern of a heterosexual couple surviving the horror. In fact, no male authority figures at all survive. *The Stepfather* remains one of the most remarkable critiques of patriarchal family ideology to appear in the Reagan era.

### *FATAL ATTRACTION* (ADRIAN LYNE)

Variously interpreted as a neo-noir film, a parable for the age of AIDS, an allegory about international terrorism, a grotesque and perverted patriarchal portrait of vengeful feminism, a diabolically clever reassertion of male power, a new take on old slasher movies—but most certainly a quintessential expression of Reagan era family ideology—*Fatal Attraction* (1987) has been the object of an extensive body of literature.[61] The film's main strength is that it has something for everyone. It provides a remarkable example of the multivocality of a film text and illustrates how the viewer can actively construct his or her own meaning.

There is little doubt that in *Fatal Attraction* director Adrian Lyne wished to present an image of a woman that would typify a man's worst nightmare. Though commonly described as one of the femmes fatales of neo-film noir, the character is much more problematic, less a fatal woman than a fatality in the continuing war between the sexes.

The ground was covered often enough in earlier films such as *Pitfall* (1948, Andre de Toth), which has been described as "the key film noir detailing the fall of the errant husband from the grace of bourgeois respectability."[62] In this film Lizabeth Scott plays the "bad" but sexy woman, while Jane Wyatt plays Dick Powell's boring but "good" wife. While Scott did not die, she did go to jail. Wyatt suffered on as the dutiful wife despite her realization that the relationship would never be the same (unlike the wife four decades later).

*Fatal Attraction* comes closer, in the final version, to Clint Eastwood's *Play Misty for Me* (1971). In fact, the central plot might literally have been lifted from this film about a woman who just won't take no for an answer. Evelyn (Jessica Walter) goes after a man (Eastwood) who, like Michael Douglas, just wanted a little fun, priding himself on his attraction for women. The ex-fan of the late-night radio disc jockey played by Eastwood, Evelyn called regularly to request Erroll Garner's "Misty." (Anyone, like the present writer, who has worked as a night d.j.—wondering who is out there listening—will relate to Eastwood's character, who fantasizes that perhaps a real dream woman is out there; in this instance it appeared she was, though the dream became a nightmare.) When he finally meets Evelyn, she is eager to sleep with him, so they spend the night together. But then she literally won't go away. Evelyn is at first overly needy, then desperate, and eventually homicidally psychotic, stopping at nothing, including murder, to get her man. Eastwood, though not married, does wish to reestablish a former relationship with a woman (Donna Mills). *Play Misty for Me* does not present enough information on Evelyn to understand why her personality is as it is, unlike *Fatal Attraction,* where there is more to work with.

*Fatal Attraction* is essentially the story of a family besieged. Dan Gallagher (Michael Douglas) is a Manhattan lawyer, (supposedly) happily married for nine years to Beth (Anne Archer, in a career-making role), a stay-at-home wife with beauty, talent, and boundless enthusiasm for her husband's career, their home, and their six-year-old daughter, Ellen.

One weekend, while Beth is visiting her parents, Dan becomes involved sexually with Alex Forrest (Glenn Close), an editor in a publishing house his firm represents. For Dan it's a one-night stand, but Alex wants a lot more. Showing signs of emotional instability (she slashes her wrists to keep him at her place after their second night together), Alex stalks Dan and then his family. Events escalate, culminating in a horrific bloodletting in the second-floor bathroom of the Gallagher's home, where Dan unsuccessfully attempts to drown the knife-wielding ex-lover (now pregnant with his child) in the bathtub. Beth shoots Alex dead, effectively cleaning up Dan's mess and preserving the family. The final scene shows Dan, happily waving to the police and ambulance removing Alex's corpse (and the now-dead fetus he fathered), as if bidding goodbye to dinner guests. The only remaining question would seem to be whether Dan or Beth would ever want to take a bath again in their tub.

*Fatal Attraction,* like many thrillers, is heavily indebted to the "master of suspense." Described by one critic as starting like *Vertigo* and ending like *Psycho,*[63] the film actually starts more like *Psycho.* It opens with an establishing shot of the Manhattan skyline at dark and then closes in on a cozy family-at-home scene showing the Gallaghers relaxing in their underwear. *Psycho* began with a shot of the Phoenix skyline, closing in on Janet Leigh and boyfriend John Gavin in their hotel room, finishing up after some lunchtime lovemaking. *Fatal Attraction* also adds bits from *Frenzy* on its way back to *Psycho.* (The barefoot Alex seems to have carried an exact copy of Mother's [Anthony Perkins'] chef's knife all the way from her Manhattan loft to the upstairs bathroom of the Gallagher's country home.)

A representation of the family as a "haven in a heartless world," *Fatal Attraction* repeatedly contrasts cozy images of the Gallaghers in warm, homey splendor with Alex Forrest's lonely white loft apartment, located in the heart of a hellish-looking meat-packing neighborhood complete with flaming burn barrels. The intended associations—the relations between the sexes as a meat market, a kind of interpersonal hell—seem obvious enough.

Dan, a lawyer on the way up, is about to become a partner in the firm headed by Arthur (Fred Gwynn). At the start of the film, Dan, Beth, and Ellen live in a comfortably elegant Manhattan apartment with their yellow Lab, Quincy, though Beth is aching to live in the country. One evening Dan and Beth join his work buddy, a chubby guy named Jimmy (Stuart Pankin), and his wife (played by sometime rock vocalist Ellen Foley) at a book-signing party, where Jimmy ogles a woman in black (Close), who returns a withering stare of loathing. Dan later runs into her at the bar, where they exchange knowing grins and introduce themselves. When Beth waves to Dan that it is time to leave, Alex, like an older woman sending away a child, remarks, "You better run along," but her looks betray her interest in him.

The affair starts a few days later. With Beth away, Dan attends a Saturday conference to iron out legal matters concerning a manuscript. Alex, now dressed in creamy white, revealing a vivacious, humorous side, flirts with Dan. In one of the film's few clever or light moments, she indicates to him he has some cream filling left over from a donut on his nose. After the meeting, they run into each other in a rainstorm and decide to have a drink, which leads to an early dinner and a scene crucial for reading their characters: Dan tells a story, the point of which is he doesn't do "family" law and therefore can't represent his mother in her divorce. Alex offers that being a lawyer must be like being a doctor. "You have to be discreet. Are you?" Dan answers affirmatively, and Alex says she is as well. Alex: "Where's your wife?" Dan: "In the country." Alex: "And you're here, being a naughty boy." Dan: "We haven't done anything illegal." Alex: "Not yet." Dan: "It will definitely be up to you." Alex: "I haven't made up my mind yet." The scene clearly indicates that both are intensely aware of the sexual possibilities.

Alex, a thirty-six-year-old professional single woman, has obviously been this way before; so, apparently, has Dan, though perhaps not as often as Alex. They shortly end up at Alex's loft apartment, ripping off clothes and having rough sex on the kitchen sink and then coupling in her bed. After going out for some salsa dancing, it's back to oral sex in her freight elevator and more coupling in bed.

Dan's predawn departure the next morning brings an immediate call from Alex to his home. She wants him to come back. Dan finally agrees to meet her in a park on a bright fall afternoon. He feigns a heart attack and Alex is apparently terrified, saying her father died in front of her when she was in grade school. Dan apologizes, calling her "honey," whereupon Alex pretends she was joking and says her father is "alive and well, and living in Phoenix." (Later it is revealed that he did die.)

In another key moment at Alex's apartment late that afternoon, while eating a spaghetti dinner and listening to Puccini's *Madame Butterfly,* Dan opens up, talking about himself and his past—to Alex's obvious pleasure. She asks about his family. Dan talks positively about his wife and child, when Alex suddenly asks him the crucial question: "What are you doing here?" Dan can only say, "You sure know how to ask 'em."

Events degenerate into a series of gothic images involving Alex: wrist-slashing; pouring acid on Dan's car; murdering Ellen's pet rabbit; kidnapping Ellen for an afternoon but returning her unharmed (Beth has a car accident while frantically searching for Ellen). Alex is finally driven over the top by Dan's near-strangulation of her in a kitchen scene the obverse of their first frantic sexual coupling, followed by the final bathroom bloodbath.

In a film that can be read many ways and upon which one can project almost any meaning one wishes, Dan Gallagher might stand for an average upper-middle-class Reagan era American male, with all the accompanying anxieties about professional competence, sexual performance, aging, and self-worth. Moreover, like many men who treasure the security of family and marriage, Dan fantasizes about something wilder, more profoundly passionate.[64] Though his wife seems exceptionally sexy and more attractive than Alex, they are—as with most married couples in movie history—never shown making love; something always seems to get in the way.

If *Fatal Attraction* presents what has been seen as a dystopian female revenge fantasy, it is all viewed from the perspective of the male character. In this sense, the film makes a significant contribution to sexual paranoia, viewing everything from Dan's viewpoint. In this respect, the film might more accurately be titled "One Man's Avoidance," for Dan is an other-directed people pleaser who apparently does not want anyone to dislike him, elevating dysfunctionality and denial to a high art. A master of mixed messages, he can't say "no" to Alex even when he wants her to go away. He's a lawyer who doesn't know anything about "family" law. A supposedly loving husband and father, Dan lies repeatedly to his wife, her parents, and his boss. He misrepresents himself to the local police, manipulates his secretary into covering for him, and illegally enters Alex's apartment, roughs her up and nearly strangles her. Not a very positive portrait of the average American professional man.

Everybody has a history, but Alex's past is cloudy. The death of her father, provided as a bit of motivation, doesn't say enough. With her biological clock ticking, Alex obviously wants a marriage and child in the worst way. A veteran of the predatory date/sex wars of the big city (we learn she had a "bad miscarriage" and thought she couldn't get pregnant, but the circumstances surrounding how and by whom she got pregnant are not explained), she's clearly facing a lonely future if she doesn't grab Dan. Even with her power shoulders and Cosmo-girl lace undies, she really just wants to settle down with a nice guy. She sees in Dan a guy who can open up, loves opera as she does, likes kids, and has a thing for dogs. Significantly for its era, given that about fifty percent of marriages end in divorce—Alex might legitimately ask, "How married is this guy?" Emotionally clearly a candidate for one of the hundreds of "Women Who Love Too Much" groups—founded after Robin Norwood's pop psychology book of that era[65]—or more systematic "codependency" treatment and maybe some psychomeds, Alex does not belong in the femme fatales hall of shame. However "bad news" a woman Alex is, does it really require a fatal bullet? Audiences, identifying with the film's utopian image of the dream family besieged, seemed to think so.[66]

Beth, played to perfection by Anne Archer, is the heroine (and victim) of the whole sordid tale. In one critic's brilliantly bizarre analysis of the film, Alex represents one of the legions of third world revolutionary "terrorist" movements confronting the U.S. in the 1980s, with Dan representing the inept American ruling class of the Reagan era, building on the imperialistic relations of the past and blaming the victims for fighting back. In the face of the leadership's incompetence, Beth, like "gender gap" women voters, wants to do whatever she can to hold the family together.[67]

If *Fatal Attraction* is about facing (or not facing) responsibility, Beth is both victim as well as heroine. Playing the trophy wife correctly all the way, she looks great, entertains her husband's friends (who become her friends), prepares delightful nouvelle cuisine meals, is a great mother to Ellen, hunts for a house in the country and then paints it, and still finds the time to offer brandy and back rubs to her busy lawyer hubby. Then he tells her he has been having "an affair" with Alex and that she's pregnant. First Beth is stunned, then she shrieks—expressing her fury by flailing at him with her arms and fists—"What's the matter with you!" While Dan's actions are quite explicable in terms of male fantasies and might seem necessary for the narrative, they make absolutely no sense to Beth, who has done all that society says should be done, fulfilling every role the "feminine mystique" said she should. (She doesn't have a job, but she did in the earlier James Dearden story and short film "Diversion" on which his screenplay is based.)[68] Since nothing is known about Beth's prior life, the audience can project whatever it wants onto her character.

By the end of the film, Alex has been construed as an evil feminist temptress, spouting the rhetoric of equality and fair treatment. In reality, her character is a reflection of all the anxiety independent women inspired in much of contemporary culture of the time. A feminist villain assaulting a utopian family, she is a perfect reflection of Reagan era illusory family ideology.[69]

The films discussed in this chapter all reflect dimensions of paranoia at its most critical and visionary, presenting alternative, often profoundly subversive, perspectives on "family values" in American society. Their deconstruction of what was virtually "official" Reagan era family ideology suggests that reality was often more surreal than one's conception of it. Given the representation of the dark side—the hidden and denied part of American life in *Blue Velvet* and succeeding films and television series created by David Lynch, the public might be unwilling to explore this dimension. Yet numerous and richly diverse alternatives to the official nuclear-family ideology of the period were obviously possible, as is evident in these and other filmic examples from the era, which provided striking portraits of the Jungian "shadow" of "family values," an underside of the "shining city on the hill" extolled by Reagan's speechwriters.

CHAPTER SEVEN

# "She Was Bad News"

## Male Paranoia and Femmes Fatales

Given the virtually total male control of the Hollywood film industry during much of the twentieth century, it is commonly observed that images of women in movies reflect a "male gaze," revealing the hopes and anxieties of American men of this period. Such has been the standard interpretation of images of women in films of the 1940s, particularly the fatal women of film noir.[1] Alternative readings of such images, however, reveal interesting subtexts that help to explain the enduring fascination of classic-period femmes fatales as well as several contemporary models.[2]

The tendency to characterize film noir as a masculine form is challenged in recognizing the extent to which these films afford women roles that are "active, adventurous and driven by sexual desire."[3] These "black widows" and "spider women" of film noir are quintessentially "deadly but sexy, exciting, and strong."[4] Among the most striking but problematic femmes fatales of the classic period is Jane Greer's intriguing, enigmatic portrayal of Kathie Moffett in *Out of the Past* (1947, Jacques Tourneur). Tuesday Weld as Sue Anne Stepanick in *Pretty Poison* (1968, Noel Black) is one of the most gleefully evil surprises any male has ever encountered. Among neo-noir femmes fatales, Kathleen Turner's performance as Mattie Walker in *Body Heat* (1981, Lawrence Kasdan) expresses a deviously manipulative quality many men fear, typified in her comment to her victim, small-town Florida lawyer Ned Racine (William Hurt), "You're not too smart, are you—I *like* that in a man." Theresa Russell's *Black Widow* (1987, Bob Rafelson) remains a haunting presence, as does Virginia Madsen's lusty traducer/husband killer in *The Hot Spot* (1990, Dennis Hopper). This chapter will also consider Linda Fiorentino's most notable versions of the quintessential "bad news" woman, Bridget Gregory/Wendy Kroy in *The Last Seduction* (1994, John Dahl), and Sharon Stone in *Basic Instinct* (1992, Paul Verhoeven). The chapter concludes with a discussion of Mädchen Amick's tantalizing fusion of erotic beauty and deception as Lena in Nicholas Kazan's *Dream Lover* (1994), which sums up male hysteria during the era, suggesting—from a male perspective—that what one assumes is paranoia could actually be a justified heightened awareness.

The femme fatale reflects the problematic nature of classic Hollywood film products as a domain of what Laura Mulvey has termed the "male gaze." Psychoanalytic feminist film theorists see movies as part of an "apparatus" that evokes and attempts to resolve Freudian postulations of male traumas around the mother as a sexual object.[5] In classic Hollywood productions, for the male spectator the "woman stands as a signifier for the male . . . as a bearer of meaning, not maker of meaning."[6] Stated more broadly, the image of women presented in such movies—especially the representation of the femme fatale—functions as a sign for something in the male unconscious rather than having anything to do with actual historical female subjects. Such representations of women, the products of a cinematic "gaze," rely on the mechanisms Freud originally delineated as voyeurism and fetishism. Such images function as devices that permit the male spectator to avoid the particular threat to power and privilege women present.

In the classic Hollywood era of the quintessential femmes fatales, one can note three main ways in which the "woman" is portrayed.[7] First there is the idealized, asexual mother figure who nurtures the male hero. This can range from the bountiful and immense figure of strength of Ma Joad (Jane Darwell) in *The Grapes of Wrath* (1940, John Ford) to the bizarrely wacky female character portrayed by Janet Leigh in *The Manchurian Candidate* (1962, John Frankenheimer) who, minutes after meeting the emotionally ravaged Major Marco (Frank Sinatra), inexplicably says she is breaking her engagement to another man in favor of Marco.[8]

A second model is that of woman as fetishized object, who is given attributes that lessen her threat to male power, such as physical weakness. Dana Wynter as Becky in the original *Invasion of the Body Snatchers* (1956, Don Siegel), is a good example. Though softly beautiful and nurturing (until she is "invaded"), she is also physically weak and extremely emotional. Becky and all the other women in the film are quick to respond to the orders of men, whether human or alien.

Extreme, almost grotesque caricatures are evident in such 1950s sexpots as Jayne Mansfield, Jane Russell, and the more complex images of Marilyn Monroe.[9] Paradoxically, males might have felt anxiety when confronted with the extreme aspects of such fetishized objectification, fearing to be seen as men who "couldn't handle" such women. Both Monroe and Mansfield, of course, saw their onscreen personas as something of a put-on. Monroe, an object of male desire in real life, found the screen Marilyn a fun place to visit but a horrifying place to live.[10] Judging from all the available evidence, Mansfield exulted in her brief years of stardom. In a 1997 televised interview, Russell spoke of most of her films as what "the guys" wanted to see.

In a third category, the female body is set up in films as a mere object of sexual desire, without intrinsic meaning. The woman becomes not a person but a plot device that stimulates action on the part of the central male character. Kim Novak's double character in Hitchcock's *Vertigo* (1958) seems especially representative of such a functional category.[11]

Many of the original arguments made by feminist critics have been modified in recent years, with more attention being paid to the position of female spectators and a greater recognition that "gendered address" is far more complicated than originally thought. For example, it is now agreed that multiple identifications probably take place for both male and female spectators.[12]

Although movies remained the domain of voyeuristic male pleasure for much of the twentieth century, the female voice or "womanly subtext" in a film continues to exist as a secondary, embedded dimension. To illuminate it requires an appropriate interpretive practice of reading "through" the dominant, intended, male-defined discourse to locate a subtextual alternative female discourse. This "reading against the grain" of the film text[13] is especially useful in explaining the motivation of such characters as Kathie Moffett, the femme fatale in Tourneur's noir classic *Out of the Past,* or deconstructing the images of the binary women in the neo-noir misogynist blockbuster *Fatal Attraction.*

## Femmes Fatales

Femmes fatales are usually powerful, attractive women. Their power is based on sex, which they use to manipulate men in order to get what they want. Men who fall for them usually come to grief, often ending up dead or in jail. Occasionally the men don't even seem to mind being manipulated—until it is too late. If they don't die, they spend the rest of their lives trying to figure out how they could have been so stupid and hoping "to be lucky enough to forget"[14] the woman that played them for a chump. The problematic nature of the femme fatale often results from the contradictory manner in which she is perceived by the (male) hero and the audience rather than her actual person.[15] This description holds for many of the most notorious examples of such women—from Barbara Stanwyck's icy portrayal of Phyllis Dietrickson in *Double Indemnity* (1944, Billy Wilder) through Glenn Close's borderline psychotic Alex Forrest in *Fatal Attraction.*[16]

Most of the later, neo-noir characterizations of fatal women are so evil they are often caricatures of any recognizable women. Sharon Stone as Catherine

Tramell in *Basic Instinct* (1992) and Linda Fiorentino as Bridget Gregory and Wendy Kroy in *The Last Seduction* (1994) are quintessentially fetishistic and misogynist portrayals reflecting male sexual fantasies and the worst aspects of male paranoia; from the perspective of the males they manipulate, they are truly "bad news."

Femmes fatales usually reject the roles the dominant society prescribes for women. In the end, their rejection of social norms is supposed to lead to their demise or harsh punishment. Given the Production Code of the 1940s, these women had to die. But as powerful, independent women men lust after, they remain intriguing after more than half a century.

From another perspective, classic femmes fatales can be seen as expressions of the same kinds of sexual and other personal freedoms enjoyed by men in their eras. They can also be viewed as the products of unspoken or suppressed horrors: incest; rape; spousal or child abuse; or intense, long-term psychological cruelty. They feel "confined by the roles traditionally open to them . . . the restrictions that men place on them."[17] From *their* perspective the world is dangerous, corrupt, irrational, and ruled by men. Where once they might have been victimized, now they have "wised up." Because they have the one thing men want, it is a source of potential power for them. Their film images present a stark contrast to the bland, cloying, conventional women who people these same films.

## *OUT OF THE PAST* (JACQUES TOURNEUR)

With a title that could stand as a metaphor for the whole noir cycle, Jacques Tourneur's *Out of the Past* (1947) has a screenplay by Geoffrey Homes (the pseudonym of Daniel Mainwaring) based on his novel *Build My Gallows High.* Other (uncredited) writers also worked on the story.[18] The character of Kathie Moffett is one of the most beautiful but lethal femme fatales in the history of film noir."[19]

The film features Robert Mitchum as Jeff Markham, a New York City private eye hired to find and bring back a mobster's runaway woman. Having shot her manipulative, cruel boyfriend Whit Sterling (played with smiling venomousness by Kirk Douglas), she has fled to Mexico with his money. Prior to this, he had hired Markham and his associate, Fisher (Steve Brodie), to find her. When he locates her in Acapulco, Markham immediately falls in love with her and double-crosses Sterling, never informing his employer he has found his fatal woman.

The film, initially set in Bridgeport, California, on the eastern slope of the Sierras, opens with a man in black, driving a black convertible, riding into town and wondering if the Jeff Bailey on a service station sign could be Jeff Markham, now in hiding, whom he has been sent to find. The man is Joe Stephanos, the chief enforcer for Sterling. He finds Bailey, who indeed turns out to be the missing Markham, now living under an assumed name. Stephanos gently reminds him Sterling wants to see him because Markham owes the man: Realizing he can't escape his past, Markham, who has a new woman friend, Ann (Virginia Huston), accepts his fate. He changes from his outdoor clothes and his assumed identity back into his detective's fedora and trench coat, and the tragic persona of a world-weary private eye. On a nighttime drive to Tahoe, he tells Ann the whole story, which makes up the first half of the film. His sleepy narration has the quality of a dream from which he can't escape and almost doesn't want to. As he relates the tale, the story unfolds on the screen.

Kathie Moffett, played by the then twenty-three-year-old Jane Greer, radiates an arresting, voluptuous child-woman kind of sexuality that makes her irresistible to men. Kathie can obviously mobilize her sexual allure to control men for whatever purposes she has in mind. Motivationally she remains problematic. Why, other than money, does she do what she does? One might surmise that the young Kathie is a woman who has found a life that frees her from a routine existence and working for a living, permitting her to maintain the lifestyle she has come to enjoy.

Sterling, in Kirk Douglas's characterization, can be cruel. He smiles a lot, but the lingering threat of violence and a kind of involuntary servitude to him is always present. (He tells Jeff, "I may fire somebody, but nobody quits me.") He gets whatever he wants and will use violence if necessary. His obsessively loyal enforcer, Joe Stephanos, is always at his side, ready to execute whatever actions the boss requires. (Some critics have even seen a homoerotic attachment between the two.)

Similarly, Kathie is always calculating how to maintain her lifestyle by using her sexual power—or more extreme means, if necessary. Whatever control she has over Sterling, from the moment Jeff Markham sees her walking in out of the sunshine in Acapulco he decides he must "have" her. For him, nothing else matters. His lust—or their temporary mutual passion[20]—conquers all his misgivings.

The sexual attraction between the two simmers like a powerful undercurrent. Unlike the explicit images of later films, such as *Body Heat,* because of Production Code restrictions, one never sees the two of them do anything but kiss—certainly never with their clothes off. But the erotic tension and sexual longing is always present. One gets the impression that when they were completely alone their love-making was frequent, hot, intense, addictive, dirty—the kind of all-enveloping sex that would make a man not really mind dying because he knew it could never get any better. In one scene the couple return to her place to escape from a tropical thunderstorm. There is a forward tracking shot looking out into the downpour that, with subtle indirectness, conveys more erotic power and sex—while showing nothing—than most of the elaborately composed, steamy, sweaty sex scenes in *Body Heat* three decades later.[21]

Months later—after she has abandoned him and he has grown almost to hate her—he still remembers how much he had wanted her. Near the very end of the film, when he returns to the mansion at Tahoe to find Sterling's lifeless body on the floor, she appears behind him and denies his charge of betrayal with the following key insight: "I never told you I was anything but what I am. You just wanted to *imagine* I was. That's why I left you. . . . " He reluctantly agrees to go back to Mexico with her. While Kathie is packing for their supposed getaway, Jeff calls the police, an act that proves suicidal. He dies from bullets fired by Kathie when she realizes he set up the police blockade, while she dies in the hail of automatic weapon and rifle fire at the police roadblock, with both their bodies tumbling out of the wrecked car.

Clearly Kathie, the perfect femme fatale, is "articulated with all the fetishism and misogyny characteristic of the genre,"[22] yet, as another critic has noted, the "incoherence of the motivations ascribed to the woman is a direct product of the contradictory ways in which she is perceived by the hero, rather than in terms of what she actually 'is,' in herself."[23] As James Maxfield perceptively notes, "Kathie shares the dream of most normal women (and men): she wants to be loved for what she truly is."[24] It has also been argued that "the contending 'images' of Kathie . . . derive from oppositional tendencies within male desire, with which she is framed."[25] Kathie's character can be seen in terms of an unresolvable triple conflict: her desire for personal autonomy in a cultural context that will not permit it; her and Jeff's initial mutual passion for one another, which is also unacceptable to society; and, finally, Jeff's projection of all his hopes and fantasies onto her.

Is Kathie a "battered" woman? Late in the film, when Sterling says to Kathie, "I took you back when you came whimpering and crawling, but I should have kicked your teeth in," it is as vivid and direct a threat of violence as any ever made. Here one glimpses the possibilities confronting Kathie. Seeing Kathie as the woman smashed in the face and disfigured by Marty Augustine in Altman's *The Long Goodbye* twenty-six years later makes her shooting of Sterling more understandable. In the words of one critic, he is "a man too rich, too young, too ruthless,"[26] whose capacity for violence emerges late in the film.

Kathie's "multiplying excesses" as the film unfolds make her ultimate death "narratively as well as ideologically necessary."[27] Unlike Mattie Walker in *Body*

*Heat,* the Production Code and existing political ideology dictated that Kathie could not be allowed to "get away with murder," no matter how evil the men were whom she has killed—at least up to Jeff.

But where and how did it all start? Is she a softer, sexier version of Ann Savage in *Detour* (1945, Edgar G. Ulmer), or a meaner, tougher, truly evil version of Julia Roberts in *Pretty Woman* forty-five years in the future?

In the notoriously confusing San Francisco section late in the film, the rapacious Sterling is revealed as guilty of major tax fraud and willing to kill to avoid prosecution. He is considering framing Jeff Markham for two killings. Sterling's chief thug, Stephanos, is sent—probably by Kathie acting on her own in yet another bizarre twist of her character—to kill Jeff. He is hiding from the police in the Sierras; they are after him on the framed-up murder charges. The execution plans fail when Jeff's young deaf-mute employee spies and deftly snags Stefanos with a fishing rod, slinging him to his death in full view of the surprised, amazed Markham. It is important for understanding Kathie's subsequent motivation that she thinks it was Jeff Markham who killed Stephanos.

Like many noir films, *Out of the Past* presents both a critique and a representation of the crisis on the social and political order of post-World War II America.[28] The world the film portrays is "one in which the social order and its laws are unable to protect the ordinary citizen from predatory economic forces."[29] This is a defining subtext of many noir features. After Kathie flees—and goes back to Sterling—Jeff assumes his new identity as Jeff Bailey. But Markham has no weapons to fight the manipulative Sterling. He can't go to the police because Sterling has been able to use the force of the law against him in framing him for murder. Markham thus becomes a hunted man. Caught up in his passionate obsession for Kathie, there is for Jeff no way out. His call to the police is suicidal; a self-imposed death sentence.

Kathie ultimately embodies a kind of paranoia about men based upon her knowledge of the way things are in her world. If "at the heart of paranoia lies anxiety over a loss of autonomy"[30] it is just such—in this case justified—paranoia that sends Kathie on her fatal journey that ends in her (and Jeff's) death at the police roadblock.

## ***LOLITA*** **(STANLEY KUBRICK)**

In the 1990s the term "lethal Lolita" entered the news in connection with the case of Amy Fisher, the Long Island, N.Y., teen who shot the wife of mechanic Joey Buttafuoco, with whom she was apparently sexually involved and who, according to some reports, led her into prostitution. The Lolita reference comes from Stanley Kubrick's *Lolita* (1962), based on the novel by Vladimir

Nabokov, in which the main character is consumed with lust for a teenage girl. With Kubrick's admission to the pantheon of eminent directors, the film—which caused a scandal among critics when it was first released—looks better and better. A number of other directors (Eric Rohmer, Woody Allen) have also dealt with the theme of an older man (like Allen himself) obsessed with an underage girl, and the public and critics have become quite used to the topic.

Kubrick's film, a darkly comedic study in what once might have been termed "degeneracy" and a kind of pedophilia, features James Mason as Humbert and Sue Lyon as the twelve-year-old Lolita with whom he is obsessed. Shelley Winters plays her mother and Humbert's landlady. Peter Sellers at his manic best is Quilty, a drama coach and secret rival for Lolita's affections. The film begins with the novel's violent end—Humbert shoots Quilty—and then utilizes the flashback technique to tell the tale of Humbert's foolish but dire obsession. Although Humbert, a professor, speaks with apparent intelligence, throughout he behaves like a child. Lolita appears to know exactly what he's up to. When her mother dies in an accident, Humbert whisks her away. Though he tries to make everything appear moral and "normal," both his behavior and the situation are not, nor are most of the wacky people he meets, who also pass judgment on him. Lolita eventually escapes Humbert and settles into marriage with a very ordinary guy. In the end, Humbert is the victim of his own obsession. Today he would be described as a child abuser and Lolita a "victim" of a quasi-incestuous relationship. She would most likely appear on TV talk shows and write a book about her victimization—which might be made into a movie.

### *PRETTY POISON* (NOEL BLACK)

In the 1950s William March wrote a dark novel called *The Bad Seed,* which was subsequently turned into a Broadway play and film, whose premise was that evil tendencies are inherited. In the film a little girl named Rhoda Penmark (Patty McCormack) uses her powers to murder (through plausible "accidents") people she doesn't like. If one imagines that diabolical character now grown up and transformed into a nubile high school majorette, one has Sue Ann Stepanick (Tuesday Weld) in perhaps her definitive movie role. Together with Anthony Perkins (by this time forever identified as Norman Bates), Weld is one of the two main characters, but she is clearly the embodiment of the title, *Pretty Poison.* Like Rhoda in *The Bad Seed,* Sue Ann learned how to manipulate people through an apparently sweet but truly diabolical cuteness and charm. The film—with a screenplay by Lorenzo Semple, Jr. that provides a perverse twist on conspiracy themes worthy of Cornell Woolrich or Richard Condon—remains one of the dark, sardonic gems among American films released in the late 1960s.

The story involves a young man named Dennis Pitt (Perkins), who has been institutionalized for several years for setting fire to his aunt's house, resulting in her death. Released on probation, he finds work in a small Massachusetts mill town. Dennis makes up stories, takes secret photographs, and spins all sorts of lies about being a secret agent involved in a variety of national security missions. (It's not clear whether he seriously believes all this.) He is strongly attracted to the sexy Sue Ann, who he sees marching at her high school. Her sexiness is not only physical (she is a platinum blond with gorgeous legs) but the result of a sparkle in her eyes and a nervous edginess in her speech and vocal inflections. She is smarter than she appears, but this is not immediately apparent to viewers, who are meant to see her as a sex object.

Both Dennis and Sue Ann make up stories, but he knows he is lying and usually gets caught. Though Sue Ann gives every impression of believing him, she has a secret agenda to use Dennis for her own ends. Because Sue Ann craves excitement and seems sexually turned on by it, Dennis feeds her craving by spinning more elaborate fictional conspiracies, telling her he is a CIA agent assigned to investigate the company he works for, which he claims is polluting the river—perhaps at the urging of some evil foreign power. Dennis's strategy is rewarded and eventually they do make love. Sue Ann's suspicious and very strict (single) mother (Beverly Garland) sees through Dennis' stories and forbids Sue Ann to see him. Disobeying her mother, she enlists Dennis in a plan of her own involving running away to the Gulf of Mexico—perhaps to get married—if they can overcome one obstacle—her mother.

Meanwhile Dennis, in a plot he may only half believe himself, enlists Sue Ann in "ecotage" against the mill. After sabotaging a tower supporting the mill's outlet into the river, Dennis is confronted by the kindly night watchman, whom Sue Ann gleefully clubs over the head with heavy metal pliers, knocking him unconscious. Unseen by Dennis, she pointedly takes the man's gun and puts it in her bag. She slides the dazed man into the river, making sure his head is underwater. Everything seems to change from this point on as Sue Ann gleefully bounces up and down on his unconscious body until he drowns.

The ensuing investigation of the death and sabotage points to Dennis, who flees into the woods near town. Sue Ann invites Dennis over to her house on the pretext that her mother is away, but she appears unexpectedly and confronts them. Handing the gun she took from the night watchman to Dennis, Sue Anne urges him to shoot her mother. When he is unable to do it, Sue Ann takes the gun and coolly shoots her mother several times. Sexually turned on, she wants to make love to Dennis—who is sickened and nauseated by the brutal murder—with her mother's bleeding body lying only a few feet away.

Sue Ann now orders him to put her mother's body in the back of her little sports car and dump it in a lake. Unable to carry out her orders, he drives back and phones the police, asking them to come and get him.

During his interrogation Dennis tries to explain what really happened, but Sue Ann had already called, explaining how Dennis had brutally murdered her beloved mother. In her own interrogation she tearfully portrays Dennis as a monster. Given his history and the damning testimony of his probation officer (John Randolph), Dennis is committed to an institution. The final scene shows Sue Ann taking up with another man recently arrived in town.

The small Massachusetts town, on one level, is meant to represent an America that is sick and self-destructive, mirroring domestic developments in the late 1960s. Significantly, the apparent paranoia of the fantasy-prone Dennis—who conjures up secret plots about foreign enemies yet still seems to know what he is doing—is supplanted by a much more devious and profound amorality, a hidden agenda of diabolical perversity set in motion by the young femme fatale.

Representing a microcosm of the American economy and society of the late 1960s, the mill in the film pollutes a treasured New England river,[31] yet it is "foreigners" who are blamed. Sue Ann and her outwardly benign little town can be seen as an analogue of the sick and violent nation that witnessed, in the years leading up to this film, the assassinations of JFK, Malcolm X, Martin Luther King Jr., and Robert F. Kennedy, and was responsible for the deaths of millions in Vietnam, yet still cleverly denies the systemic violence endemic in the nation's history.[32]

### *BASIC INSTINCT* (PAUL VERHOEVEN)

In Paul Verhoeven's 1992 erotic thriller, Sharon Stone's career-making portrayal of femme fatale Catherine Tramell represents "female monstrosity,"[33] the character being a projection of the worst male fears, in this case the fervid nightmares of screenwriter Joe Esterhazy. The film pits troubled, substance-abusing, too-quick-to-shoot San Francisco police detective Nick "Shooter" Curran (Michael Douglas) against Tramell, a bisexual, mystery-writing heiress with a manipulative bent and a purely instrumental view of sex with men, who may be a sociopath and serial killer. From her very first interrogation—the overrated scene in which she crosses her legs, providing a glimpse of pubic hair—Tramell mocks, manipulates, and taunts the authorities, including Curran and his associate, played by George Dzundza. The investigation is prompted by the ice-pick murder of nightclub owner Johnny Boz, a man with whom Tramell openly admits she regularly had "very pleasurable" sex. In addition to falling prey to Tramell's wiles, Curran also has brutal sex with sometime girlfriend and police shrink Beth Garner (Jeanne Tripplehorn), who is supposedly his therapist but seems untroubled by ethical niceties.

*Basic Instinct* is the preeminent study of male paranoia in media culture of recent decades. At one level it represents a kind of game involving red herrings and false—consciously implanted—leads in which viewers are left with two distinct explanations and perpetrators for each of the plot's murders. Roger Ebert, for example, commented at the time of the film's release, "Each and every shred of evidence throughout the entire movie supports two different conclusions. . . . The plot has been constructed so that every relevant clue can be read two ways. That means the solution, when it finally is revealed, is not necessarily true. . . . I left the movie feeling depressed and manipulated."[34] However, Verhoeven's comments in an interview included in the "Director's Cut Edition" of the video make it clear that Catherine Tramell was guilty of *all* the murders in the film.

*Basic Instinct* is a prime example of the "erotic thriller," whose main female character is usually psychotic and evil, a "direct heir of the mysterious and destructive femme fatale of the noir films, who becomes . . . the most potent focus of the spectator's fascination/repulsion."[35] If *Fatal Attraction* represented a dystopian horror show about the threat to the utopian male-dominated family posed by a single female, *Basic Instinct* speaks to the worst male fears of single women. It does so, first, by expressing male anxieties concerning their own sexual performance. Second, it posits the threat of abandonment by removing the "need" for the male in lesbian sex; finally, there is the sheer danger of casual, "free" sex with someone who just might be mentally deranged.

The opening scene of the film depicts a blond woman—her hair obscures her face but she looks very much like Catherine Tramell—astride a man whose hands are bound, engaged in sexual intercourse. Suddenly the woman grabs an ice pick and stabs the man about the face and head. One blow seems to pierce his nose, while others repeatedly puncture the arteries in his neck, which emit copious quantities of blood. (It is as horrific a scene as any this viewer has seen in a mainstream feature, excepting war movies.) It immediately establishes the unidentified woman as some kind of psychokiller.

*Basic Instinct,* though not a film noir, does project the male fear of female transgression against patriarchal power. Catherine Tramell is terrifying because she does not need men—she has a live-in lesbian lover whom she encourages to watch her encounters with men. The latter are merely objects, as all people seem to be for her. Catherine is in a struggle with Detective Curran, the primary male protagonist, who is also seemingly into brutal sex on a regular basis. But sex, as portrayed here, seems quite *un*erotic, a kind of aggressive contact sport that is unconvincingly staged and simulated in the manner of "soft porn."

In *Basic Instinct* Catherine's case is either the product of the screenwriter's misogynist imagination or, as one critic has suggested, "boredom and perversity caused by having too much money."[36] Tramell, the focus of the spectator's rapt attention and repulsion, becomes the fetishistic object of Nick Curran during the course of his investigation. As Laura Mulvey suggests, "The fetish acknowledges itself like a red flag, symptomatically signaling a site of psychic pain."[37] Movie culture is the one place where such disturbances and struggles can be represented and staged. As Mulvey puts it, it functions as "a massive screen on which collective fantasy, anxiety, fear, and their effects can be projected." Moreover, as she suggests, "it speaks to the blind spots of a culture and finds forms that make manifest socially traumatic material, through distortion, defense, and disguise."[38]

Historically, in so-called women's films of the 1940s and '50s, it was a *male* sexually oriented predation (though never explicitly shown), which is here reversed in Joe Esterhazy's screenplay. Catherine goes far beyond the noir femme fatale, a primary cause of male alienation in the original cycle—the result, Anne Kaplan has said, of "the excesses of female sexuality (natural consequences of female independence)" and, in the film noir, punished "in order to re-place it within the patriarchal order."[39] But in *Basic Instinct,* after Catherine has literally gotten away with murder several times over, the "punishment" presented is the quite bizarre suggestion by Nick Curran, made near the conclusion, that they "fuck like minks, raise rugrats, and live happily ever after." If, as Verhoeven has stated, everything in the film—in *his* view—was meant to point to Catherine's guilt, it is no wonder the film fades out at the very end and then returns to focus on an ice pick under the bed. Catherine Tramell's pen name "Woolf" represents a profound threat to patriarchal power and ideology. Such women—like the creatures in the natural world—must be tamed as fetished objects of the "male gaze" or literally caged. Clearly, Catherine's character would never permit that to happen. For Nick Curran—like his brutally murdered partner—it is only a matter of time.

### *THE LAST SEDUCTION* (JOHN DAHL)

In John Dahl's 1994 film Linda Fiorentino plays Bridget Gregory, one of the most memorable femme fatales in the annals of "bad news" women. Bridget, a cynical, selfish, ruthless phone sales lead generator with a caustic wit and a pitiless killer instinct for male anxieties and weaknesses, is married to a sleazy, drug-dealing New York City doctor named Clay Gregory (Bill Pullman). At her instigation he arranges a large sale of pharmaceutical cocaine, the proceeds of which Bridget immediately steals. She flees to a small town in upstate New York, assuming the alias Wendy Kroy (New York spelled backward). She is pursued by a black detective (Bill Nunn) hired by her husband, who is in debt to a ruthless loan shark.

Mike Swale (Peter Berg), an insurance claims adjuster, has just returned to town after a brief, humiliating "marriage" to a person named Trish, who turned out to be a female impersonator. Eager to reassert his manliness, he comes on to Bridget in a local bar and buys her a drink. She tries to brush him off, but his claim to be well endowed is proven true and they shortly end up in bed. The next day she walks out without so much as a good-bye, but not before calling her attorney (J. T. Walsh, in a cameo role) to begin divorce proceedings and to get advice on her claim to the stolen drug proceeds. She lands a job as director of the phone sales division of a large insurance company nearby—the same company where Mike is employed. She informs her boss that she is fleeing her abusive husband and must maintain her alias. Impressed by her résumé and eager to be politically correct, her boss agrees.

A new life begins. Uninvolved but expert sex with Mike brings him under her total control. She plans to use him to get rid of her husband. After a series of darkly humorous encounters with her husband's agents, a complex plan to manipulate Mike emerges.

When Bill Nunn, the black private detective, arrives in town, people at work—who act as if they had never laid eyes on an African-American—tell her in horrified tones that "a black man" was asking for her. One night Nunn surprises her in her car and demands the stolen drug-deal money. She first says it's in a bank but then admits she has it. As they drive off, she taunts him about the size of his penis and agrees to surrender and give up the money only if he will expose himself. As she has found his (common male) weakness—anxiety over size—he agrees, unzipping his pants. Knowing her side is equipped with an airbag, she veers off the road and smashes into a power pole, catapulting Nunn through the windshield, whereupon he dies instantly. Lying in a hospital bed, dressed all in white, Wendy explains to an investigating police officer that the black man used foul language and exposed himself. The officer understands completely. "Like in the movies," he agrees.

After evading several investigators hired by her husband, she sends Mike a letter written by her but allegedly from Trish, who says she is coming to town to work at the same firm in order to be near him. Fearful of being humiliated and exposed to ridicule, Berg agrees to a bizarre scheme to murder her husband back in New York City. Berg will enter what he thinks is a ruthless slumlord's apartment, handcuff him, and then stab him to death. Bridget tells him they will get a lot of money from his widow and live happily ever after. In a grimly humorous confrontation, Mike is unable to kill Bridget's husband, who shows him a photo proving that Wendy is actually his wife, Bridget. Outraged at her deception and his manipulation, he gives Bridget the prearranged signal to enter the apartment. She finds the handcuffed Clay and sprays something into his throat, immediately killing him. Then she taunts Mike to "rape" her, which he does out of anger. She reaches for the phone, and dials 911 in order to capture his verbal obscenities on tape. The police arrive and arrest the naïve Mike Swale for "rape" and also for the murder of Clay Gregory, to which Bridget testifies.

Incredulous at his victimization, Mike, now in jail, is next shown with his public defender, who tells him everything points to his guilt because there is no evidence—she has carefully destroyed the phony label affixed to her husband's mailbox—to support his tale that it all was set up by Bridget. She gets away with the money and Mike is sentenced to jail—perhaps to his death by execution. Like Matty Walker in *Body Heat,* Bridget Gregory brings off the ultimate femme fatale caper, leaving the victimized and bewildered male to take the rap.

*The Last Seduction* remains a darkly humorous satirical exercise in black humor in which the femme fatale character demonstrates with consummate cynicism how to manipulate both the public's sympathy for battered and abused women and the immediate police response to charges of rape. Most men, their consciousness raised, want to do the "right" thing, to be politically correct on issues of abuse, harassment, rape, and violence. Bridget knows how to make them *want* to please. She also has a keen eye for male anxieties and feelings of sexual inadequacy, controlling men by leading them around by their libidos. *Why* she behaves this way we are not told—and for good reason. Bridget Gregory—while a playful, sardonic version of the femme fatale—embodies some of the worst fears of men. She, like most men, wants to make a life—but solely on *her* own terms, representing a total reversal of traditional roles.

### *DREAM LOVER* (NICHOLAS KAZAN)

Among contemporary victims of fatal women, James Spader's Ray Reardon in *Dream Lover* presents a kind of role-reversal of Ingrid Bergman's part in *Gaslight* fifty years earlier. Reardon, a successful architect, finds a woman he thinks is perfect. Lena (Mädchen Amick) is everything he has ever wanted. Recently divorced, on the rebound, and looking for the right woman, Ray is fascinated by the slim, darkly beautiful young woman after their initial meeting, but she leaves without giving him her phone number, so he stakes out her classy loft apartment. When they finally connect again, she seems cool and distant, claiming that she likes him "too much"—just the kind of thing a lonely single man might like to hear. They begin an intense sexual relationship that is graphically captured by the camera.

Soon they are married, though none of her family and very few of her (apparent) friends are present. A year later they have a child. Lena seems a devoted lover, wife, and mother, though her sexual desire seems to have diminished after the birth of the child. Ray's career is so successful and busy that he doesn't have much time to think about it. When Lena fails to remember the death of her college president—an incident related to Ray by someone who graduated from the same school the same year—he gradually becomes suspicious.

From this point on Lena begins to act more mysterious. One night at a restaurant a woman asks her if she isn't Sissy from some town in Texas. Lena claims the woman is mistaken, but Ray isn't so sure. Claiming to be on a trip to Hawaii, Ray stops in Texas, where he finds a very tall, well-muscled, long-haired, gas station attendant who looks like a Hells Angel. He says Lena is his former girlfriend, who "did things" to him he "still can't name." He provides directions to her parents' house. They appear to know Ray immediately and are very effusive. Ray brings the parents back home and they all surprise Lena and the baby. She apologizes, saying she felt inadequate and unequal to Ray and wanted to hide her poor background and admitting she lied about her abusive childhood.

After another child is born, friends make comments about how the baby doesn't look at all like Ray, engendering more suspicion. Ray is increasingly puzzled and irritated when credit card statements list numerous charges to a hotel. Confronting Lena, she admits to having an affair, though with whom is never made clear. Enraged at her apparent betrayal, Ray strikes her. Leaving and then returning later, Ray finds a man in their apartment who says he is Lena's psychiatrist. A police officer arrests Ray as an abusive spouse.

It turns out that Lena has filed charges of domestic abuse and has been photographed with numerous "bruises"—all apparently self-inflicted or even created with the artful application of makeup. Amazed and outraged at the false charges, Reardon hires a lawyer. At the hearing he explodes in anger again, confirming the elaborate network of charges Lena has set forth. Restrained by attendants, he is declared insane and faces a life of confinement. Lena remains in control of the children and the finances. It turns out that she stalked him for a long period, determining his preferences and refashioning herself to match his fantasy of an ideal woman.

The screenplay (also by Kazan) masterfully utilizes recent developments in law enforcement meant to protect women against abusive spouses and shows how those same practices can be used to spin a web of false charges. Unfortunately, the film's subtle insights into the potential legal overkill of present-day politically correct practices are diminished by the film's ending, with the plot verging on the absurd. Luring Lena to an isolated part of the sanitarium grounds while on a visit, Reardon slowly strangles her to death while explaining that as a certified lunatic he will be found "not guilty by reason of insanity." In a twisted ending, Ray's full recovery leads to his discharge. He is also awarded custody of his children.

*Dream Lover* demonstrates much more than the devious power of a fatal woman. It shows graphically how in a few short decades the concepts of "sexual harassment," or spousal "abuse" became all pervasive, affecting the workplace, the family, and the larger society.[40]

For example, in one area where important counterresearch has appeared, modern sexual-harassment law increasingly places the liability burden on employers rather than harassers. This creates somewhat perverse economic incentives to restrict speech and behavior more than the law actually dictates in order to avoid expensive lawsuits and judgments. As Jeffrey Rosen has pointed out, "Prudent companies have little choice but to restrict a great deal of sexual expression that no jury would ultimately condemn. The law has transformed inquisitions into the emotional lives of employees into an ordinary matter of corporate self-interest."[41]

Now—screenplays such as *Dream Lover, The Last Seduction,* or *Disclosure* (1994, Barry Levison), suggest—there is a situation of overkill. It now appears that feminism has been remarkably successful in creating a climate of suspicion and near hysteria in which men's words and gestures are automatically suspect and women's charges are given utter credibility, suggesting a complete reversal of hard-won standards of due process and freedom of speech. A few years ago philosopher John Fekete presented a number of cases (largely drawn from Canadian universities) that demonstrated the level of hysteria that could be generated against men accused of "sexual harassment," and the ways academic careers could be derailed or even destroyed on thin or nonexistent evidence simply because the accusation had been raised.[42] *Dream Lover* suggests a similar dynamic is possible surrounding charges of "abuse." Clearly charges of "molestation" and "child abuse" have been wildly exaggerated in a number of celebrated cases.

The "hostile environment" doctrine based upon the subjective experience of "unwanted" or "offensive" conduct—including speech—as perceived by the accuser and tested by the "reasonable woman" standard transfers the burden of proof from the accuser to the accused, in violation of long-standing American concepts and practices of due process. It also has profound and deleterious repercussions on the conduct of daily life in businesses and other large organizations in terms of the potential intimate personal relations of men and women, as well as same-sex relationships.

Whether such "harassment" actually occurs, Daphne Patai has argued, increasingly comes down to the *perception of the accusers.* A "man as the enemy" view has come to the fore in feminism, not just among lesbians but among many other women who are presented as feeling their heterosexuality itself is somehow politically incorrect. Patai's study points to disturbing legal trends and internal administrative practices in American organizations that are negative outcomes of the alleged gains of what she has called the "sexual harassment industry." It is especially disturbing if even the small minority described in Patai's study see the First Amendment as an oppressive device for perpetuating male privilege. This is not to deny the very real dimensions of interpersonal violence in society (which still was weighted toward males approximately 85 to 15 percent, according to statistics available in 2000). There remains, however, a potential for malicious and false accusations in the vast new web of corporate practices and governmental legislation.

The "women as victims" approach ultimately infantilizes not merely all women who have persistently sought greater social autonomy but all responsible adults by undermining long-standing principles of due process and freedom of speech. The headlong lunge of the legal system to protect women from male violence similarly provides opportunities for false and malicious accusations. It is such emergent trends that are reflected in *Disclosure, Dream Lover,* and *The Last Seduction.*

# Women and Sexual Paranoia

While men may experience anxieties about women, women might have many more reasons to be suspicious of men. Since World War II the film industry has catered to their fears, creating a subgenre originally intended for the large market of women who attended movies on a regular basis during wartime. In this cycle of films, gothic melodramas merged with the stylistic elements of film noir to produce what one critic has described as "uniquely feminine cine-dramas of suspicion and distrust."[1] A standard theme of these 1940s films was "you can't trust your husband," which would be echoed by women over the next six decades. The emergence of theoretical feminism into popular culture by the late 1960s and early '70s made increasing numbers of women wary of all men—and marriage in general.

In microcosm, Hitchcock's *Rebecca* (1940) might be taken as a starting point, continuing with *Suspicion* (1941), and ending with his *Notorious* (1946). *Shadow of a Doubt* (1943) contributed a "you can't trust your uncle" variation. The following is a rough composite plot for such women's pictures of distrust and paranoia:

> After a whirlwind courtship, a [usually] rich, naïve, and sheltered young woman marries a somewhat mysterious but charming man. At first he seems the ideal spouse, loving, sensitive, and protective. Yet his civilized facade masks a brooding rage. After the "honeymoon" (which may last from a month to a few years), his behavior shifts. Clue upon clue begin to appear, leading the woman to suspect that her husband plans to murder her or drive her insane. . . . Her home has become not a secure haven, but a prison. . . . Will he murder her? Or is she only imagining this horror?[2]

Such representations of paranoia grow out of the audience's knowledge that the female character's fears are real, engendering a bond of vicarious terror. George Cukor's faux-Victorian, woman-in-distress thriller *Gaslight* (1944) is a prototypical example of such a film.[3] Here the young wife, played with almost saintly innocence by Ingrid Bergman, is manipulated and terrorized by her older husband, played by the always elegant and cosmopolitan Charles

Boyer, whose intention is to drive her insane, have her institutionalized, and gain access to her fortune.[4] *Gaslight* remains a remarkable study of how a man can manipulate, dominate, and abuse his wife through purely psychological means, anticipating by several decades the theoretical insights of feminist critiques of conventional male dominance in the family. Such productions continue to the present day in theaters and on cable TV programs and whole cable channels devoted to women's issues.

The first cycle, from *Rebecca* through *Sudden Fear* (1952, David Miller) includes and intersects with the classic film noir cycle. Virtually all of these women's films were conceived, produced, written, and directed by men. But some of the strongest women actors of the 1940s and '50s were involved in them, investing tremendous energy in often mundane plots: Joan Crawford (*Mildred Pierce* [1945, Michael Curtiz] and *Sudden Fear*), Barbara Stanwyck (*Sorry, Wrong Number* [1948, Anatole Litvak]), Katherine Hepburn (*Undercurrent* [1946, Vincente Minnelli]), and Barbara Bel Geddes (*Caught* [1949, Max Ophuls]).

### *THE HOUSE BY THE RIVER* (FRITZ LANG)

Fritz Lang's unjustly neglected Victorian gothic melodrama intersects with the woman-in-distress films. With a screenplay by Mel Dinelli, striking photographic images created by Edward Cronjager, and deft touches by the director, *The House by the River* (1950) examines the ambiguous nature of guilt, evolving into a full-blown case study of psychopathic evil.

The film is set on a tidal river somewhere in the United States during the late 1890s or early 1900s. Louis Hayward plays Stephen Byrne, a novelist of limited success who apparently lives on money inherited through the good graces of his accountant brother, John (Lee Bowman), who gave up his share of their inheritance so Stephen would be free to write. Stephen is married to Marjorie (Jane Wyatt).

While containing gothic elements, *The House by the River* also expresses the somewhat perverse view that great writing grows out of the writer's experience. Early in the film an older neighbor, Mrs. Ambrose, suggests to Byrne that he "spice up" his writing to make it more salable. In the next scene the attractive blond maid Emily (Dorothy Patrick) asks him if it would be all right if she took a bath in the upstairs bathroom since Mrs. Byrne is away and the plumber has not yet arrived to fix the downstairs bath. Stephen obsessively watches her walk all the way into the house, apparently oblivious to Mrs. Ambrose, who is standing there talking to him. Then, while writing, he watches as the light in the upstairs bathroom is turned off. He enters the house and gulps down a large glass of brandy, followed by another. Emily emerges from her bath, wipes the steam from the mirror, dabs her neck and chest with Mrs. Byrne's perfume, slips on a robe over her nude body, and descends barefoot down the stairs. Lurking within the dark shadows beside the stairs, Stephen watches as Emily's knees and thighs peek through the open front of the robe. Having observed her body earlier as she walked into the house, and having two large drinks, he is free of inhibition, quite aroused, and consumed with lust for the sexy young woman. He moves to the bottom of the stairs and grabs her as she comes down, kissing her full on the mouth. She pulls back, screaming. Through the window, the nosy Mrs. Ambrose looks toward the noise. Stephen covers Emily's mouth with his hand and then grabs her throat and strangles her.

When his brother suddenly appears, Stephen convinces John that it was all an accident and that the police would never believe him. They agree to dispose of the body by dumping it in the river. Stephen finds a huge canvas sack in the basement and they put the body into it and drag it out toward the boat. Just then the neighbor appears and talks to Stephen, with the sack lying behind the wall between the houses and John crouching in darkness. When she leaves, they row out into the river, drop anchor, and dump the sack containing Emily's corpse. However, as a result of the tide, a day or so later the sack is seen floating by, serving as a grim reminder of the crime, which profoundly depresses John but seems to have energized Stephen. When his wife returns, he says Emily must have gone off with a boyfriend and falsely accuses her of having stolen his wife's jewelry.

But the sack and its cargo float by again, a visual representation of the murder. Stephen goes out in the boat, seeking the sack, which he finds stuck on a log. He tries to snag it with the boat hook, unleashing a long lock of blond hair that floats in the water. This section as well as all the other scenes on the river are photographed to convey a dark, ominous, mysterious atmosphere; there are startling—even hallucinatory—moments where the white bellies of jumping fish glow in the dark, and where vegetation in the water resembles human hair. Finding the sack, Stephen tows it out farther and dumps it again.

When John's housekeeper mentions that the sack she lent to Stephen has John's name stenciled on it, he realizes he is conclusively implicated as an accessory to murder. When a detective (Will Wright) reports that Emily's body has been found in the sack with John's name on it, Stephen claims it had been stolen from the house. A coroner's inquest is held. The prosecutor (Howland Chamberlain) tries to implicate John. Stephen repeats his made-up tales of Emily's thefts and loose living. The neighbor, Mrs. Ambrose, vouches for the character of both men. Although the court rules that Emily's death was due to murder by "person or persons unknown," John remains under community suspicion. Both Byrne men are hounded by detectives. Stephen, excited by the attention, even conducts a book signing, his sales stimulated by all the newspaper reports.

Stephen grows more distant from Marjorie and verbally abusive, refusing to let her read his latest novel-in-progress, *The River*, which is all-consuming. Marjorie, hurt and rejected, seeks out John, who grows more depressed as his clients begin to leave. Marjorie asks Stephen to watch out for his brother, suggesting that he might be suicidal. One night Stephen follows John to an isolated wharf area by the river, where John assures him he is not contemplating suicide. When John accuses Stephen of being mentally ill, Stephen retaliates by accusing him of having an affair with Marjorie. John swings at him, knocking him down, and then turns to go away. Stephen grabs a piece of heavy chain, smashing it into the back of John's head, knocking him unconscious. He then dumps him into the river.

Returning home, Stephen finds Marjorie reading his manuscript, which has been retitled *Death on the River*. She is horrified, finding revelations beyond her worst suspicions and clearly implying that Stephen murdered Emily. In matter-of-fact tones he outlines his attraction to Emily and the events leading up to the crime. Then, with a distracted look in his eyes, he begins to strangle Marjorie. A noise is heard as the camera follows a track of muddy footprints and John appears in the doorway. Stephen recoils at what he thinks is an apparition and runs, next imagining the ghost of Emily coming through another door. He runs in the opposite direction, becomes entangled in blowing curtains, and falls to his death down the stairwell.

For Marjorie, the truth was even worse than her vague suspicions. It appears that her husband was a psychopath who could kill and hide his crime by making up all sorts of tales about his victim to explain the latter's disappearance. He was even capable of murdering his own brother and wife! Lang's interrogation of the notion of guilt in this unjustly neglected, almost lost film suggests how minor events can lead to more serious acts.

Lang's exploration of guilt, coupled with the theme of erotic obsession and its consequences, is central to many noir classics. The gullibility of the legal system is another common theme. The film also comments on bourgeois respectability and our reliance on outward appearance (recall Mrs. Ambrose's testimony on behalf of the brothers). The deceit and evil to which people are prone is deftly handled in the courtroom inquest. As with other Lang features, the usual suspects again reveal their propensity to do some kind of wrong if given the chance. Although the audience is in the know all along, poor Marjorie is unaware, until the last five minutes, that her husband is "very, very ill," a psychopathic killer who will do anything to advance his literary career. While among the least known films belonging to Lang's American period, *The House by the River* remains an intriguing compendium of the master's themes.[5]

### *ROSEMARY'S BABY* (ROMAN POLANSKI)

*Rosemary's Baby* initiates a stream of horror/paranoia films suggesting the power of evil in modern society, with the home and family as sites of unspeakable horrors.[6] In this popular feature film, based on the even more popular Ira Levin novel of 1965 that sold over 5 million copies,[7] Mia Farrow and John Cassavetes play Rosemary and Guy Woodhouse, a childless couple in their thirties who want to start a family. They move into an old New York City apartment building. (Called the Bramford in the film, it was actually the Dakota, in front of which John Lennon was assassinated in 1981.)

The film opens with a slow camera sweep across Manhattan, finally gliding over the roof of the landmark Dakota. The huge structure is filled with a cast of eccentric older characters, sometimes cast against type, who eventually are revealed to be linked in an evil enterprise. Looking at their large, dark apartment, the Woodhouses are guided by a caretaker played by Elisha Cooke Jr. (veteran character actor of film noir), who explains that the previous occupant had recently died after a long illness. They are shown her possessions and desk, and there is a close-up of a letter with the phrase, "I can no longer associate myself with . . ." written in large letters. After they move in, Rosemary meets Terry, a young woman staying with an old couple, the Castevets, who live right next door to Guy and Rosemary. Terry shows Rosemary a small metal globe on a chain she wears about her neck. The ball is filled with an herb—tannis root—given to her by the couple.

Later, at a dinner in their apartment with Hutch, an old friend of Rosemary's, the couple are informed that the building was the site of Victorian-era witchcraft, led by a man named Adrian Marcato. Before and after this and other revelations, strange noises echo in the halls, and Beethoven's haunting "Für Elise" is repeatedly heard from somewhere in the building.

After a night in which they hear strange chanting coming though the wall, the couple discover that Terry has fallen from an upper floor to her death on the sidewalk outside the building. Her body is shown lying in a pool of blood. Shot from ominous low angle, the old neighbor couple, Minnie and Roman Castevet (played by Ruth Gordon and Sidney Blackmer), come along on the sidewalk and see the crowd, including the police as well as Rosemary and Guy, that has formed around Terry's now-covered body. Rosemary introduces herself to the old couple, who do not seem very disturbed over the death of the young woman they had taken into their home. But later that day Minnie comes by to invite them to dinner in order to help them all forget the unfortunate death.

The Castevets turn out to be beyond eccentric. Minnie is alternately acerbic and outspoken, then preoccupied and withdrawn. Roman, who says he is seventy-nine and has been everywhere in the world, represents himself as a critic of organized religion. Although Rosemary says she was raised a Catholic, he irascibly criticizes the church, saying, "You know, the Pope will never visit a city where the newspapers are on strike." While Roman at first appears to be merely an eccentric old-time rationalist or atheist, there is a more ominous quality about him. (He reminds me of my virulently anti-Catholic late great-aunt who, over fifty years ago, told us horrendous tales about nuns who allegedly gave birth and then killed their infants and buried the bodies in the walls of convents.)[8] It is Ruth Gordon's Oscar-winning performance as Minnie Castevet that is most impressive. Appearing initially as an insinuating, yet well-meaning, busybody, she becomes genuinely terrifying as her neighborly inquisitiveness is revealed to be integral to a most evil design.

As the plot unfolds, Guy's acting career is not going well, but after he visits the Castevets alone—supposedly to hear more of Roman's stories—it seems to go much better. Guy receives a phone message about landing a part in a play when a competitor is mysteriously struck blind. During a romantic dinner with Rosemary to celebrate his new part, she and Guy discuss having a baby. As if on cue, Minnie arrives at the door with two cups of what purports to be chocolate mousse. Rosemary samples some of the dessert (it has, she remarks, "a chalky undertaste") and is shortly overcome by drowsiness.

In a scene that may be a hallucination or an actual memory flashback, Rosemary dreams of being in a large, empty room that might be in the Bramford, surrounded by a number of naked, distorted figures, who are photographed with a wide-angle lens. She is on a bed and told that her legs have to be tied down. Guy is seen making love to her, but his appearance now changes into a bestial, dark, hairy, and scaly creature thrusting into her.

Rosemary wakes up and finds scratches on her body, for which Guy apologizes, claiming they came from his fingernails during their lovemaking. Shortly after, Rosemary discovers she is pregnant. Minnie Castevet gives her the same locket Terry wore, containing the odiferous tannis root.

Rosemary begins to suspect that her husband and the whole cast of characters in the building are somehow linked. Cued by Hutch's stories about the Bramford and her own strange intimations, she begins a parallel investigation of the building and its inhabitants. After visiting the old couples' apartment and meeting Roman, Hutch is suddenly stricken with a mysterious fatal illness. He leaves Rosemary a book entitled *All of Them Witches,* with instructions on how to decipher the name "Adrian Marcato" and the book title. Old photos in the book confirm Hutch's story that Adrian Marcato heads a satanic cult. She discovers that Roman Castevet is the son of the late 1800s cult leader.

Rosemary's paranoia now has a foundation. Building on the fear and anxiety of a first-time mother, the film becomes terrifying—one of the most riveting representations of female paranoia in film history—as the web of her husband and his satanic controllers closes around Rosemary. Viewers see everything through her eyes, yet also watch as she grows pale and sickly, suffering from blotches under her eyes, weight loss, and increasing psychological torment as she begins to sense she has some kind of unholy thing growing in her womb.

The escalating paranoia has a logic based on the manner in which everyone Rosemary turns to eventually turns against her—ostensibly caring neighbors, her obstetrician (genial Ralph Bellamy cast against type as the satanists' Dr. Sapirstein), and another physician, Dr. Hill (Charles Grodin), to whose office Rosemary flees for help. Momentarily, as Grodin seems to accept her story, the audience feels she has finally found someone who will help her. Pretending to agree with her tale of satanic conspiracy, Grodin hides his diagnosis of "prepartum hysteria;" from another room, he summons Dr. Sapirstein and Guy, who quickly arrive to take the terrified woman back into their control.

After a painful labor and the birth of (what Guy says is) a healthy male child, Rosemary is kept in bed, heavily sedated, and separated from the baby. Although informed by Dr. Sapirstein that the baby died following "complications," Rosemary *knows* that she hears it, healthy and alive, crying next door. She hysterically accuses everyone about her of stealing her baby. That same night, she breaks through the back of a mysterious closet that had been blocked by a chest of drawers before they moved in. She discovers secret rooms attached to the Castevets' apartment, where Guy and a large gathering of familiar neighbors—all of them obviously satanists—are hovering around a black-draped cradle. Rosemary looks closer at the baby and recoils, screaming, "What have you done to its eyes?" As she writhes in horror, close-up shots on either side of her face show what appear to be nonhuman, catlike eyes. Roman Castevet explains the horrific truth, "He has his *father's* eyes. Satan is his father, not Guy." Guy pleads, "They said you wouldn't be hurt." Rosemary, aghast and furious at his betrayal, spits in his face. In a somewhat bizarre turnabout—an ambiguous recognition of motherly duty—Rosemary is shown seeming to want to care for her hybrid offspring, brushing aside an older satanist woman who is too rapidly rocking the black-draped cradle. The film concludes with the patriarchal Roman ordering the woman away, pleased that Rosemary has assumed her appropriate role of caring for the devil's offspring.

*Rosemary's Baby* was Roman Polanski's first American film and his second horror film, preceded by the riveting female paranoia study *Repulsion* (1965), a British production. *Rosemary's Baby* remains the quintessential study of inexorably developing female paranoia, inspiring sympathy and genuine anger at Rosemary's victimization. The paranoia in *Rosemary's Baby* arises out of the fact that the film outwardly appears to be set in the everyday world but is actually, as Kim Newman noted, a "vast nightmare parallel [world] where intellects vast, cool and unsympathetic" are out to get the central character.[9] A protofeminist revisioning of the 1940s gothic woman-in-distress theme, the film anticipates the genuine horror that many women would eventually feel about "the family," as feminist investigations peeled back layers of repressed denial about spousal abuse. Central to her betrayal is Rosemary's husband, the man she believes loves her and whose life she supposedly shares. Guy uses Rosemary to advance his career, trading her body to the devil for a part in a play. The family, a cultural utopia of warmth, closeness, and caring, becomes in *Rosemary's Baby* a dystopia of terror. From this point in movie history, expectant motherhood was added to the repertory of film horror themes.[10]

### *KLUTE* (ALAN J. PAKULA)

This 1971 film built upon and recast noir suspense thriller traditions in an effort to explore the contemporary situation of women.[11] Director Pakula borrowed from the noir cycle many of its terrifying clichés, effectively working them into his "paranoia trilogy," the other films being *The Parallax View* (1974) and *All the President's Men* (1976). As Pakula said of the film shortly after its release,

> At the outset *Klute* has all the characteristics of a forties thriller. For me, starting to direct quite late, the attraction was in using a genre for my own ends; it wasn't pastiche which interested me but, on the contrary, making a contemporary exploration through the slant of a classic form. What's also marvelous about the suspense film is it allows for a stylization or theatricalization, which is not possible in more simple films. . . .[12]

Central to *Klute* is the story of Bree Daniels (Jane Fonda), an independent call girl with dreams of becoming either an actress or an artist/designer. While the film includes elements from film noir, Bree is not a femme fatale. By the standards of the time, she is a strong, assertive character in search of her identity.

The film begins with a dinner in a middle-class suburban home, the residence of Tom Gruneman, who is missing and suspected of being a psychopathic killer who targets New York City prostitutes. His wife is present, as is Peter Cable (Charles Cioffi), head of Gruneman's firm, and John Klute (Donald

Sutherland), a detective and friend of the family who volunteers to search for Gruneman with Cable's enthusiastic support.

The appeal of the film lies less in the obvious efforts by the male screenwriters and the director to express a feminist sensibility with regard to Bree Daniels, poised—as one critic described her, "at a possible turning point in her existence"[13]—than in its implicit critique of the ruling male power structure represented by Cable. A corporate psychokiller, Cable stalks Bree Daniels throughout the film. Played with an edgy psychotic intensity, Cable represents the dark, evil half of the male power structure. The film was released at the peak of opposition to the Vietnam War, with a significant reservoir of popular paranoia among those on the Left concerning faceless "higher circles." Cable fits neatly into such a category, though I have encountered few confirming interpretations.[14] He possesses a kind of Jack the Ripper morality (anticipating serial killer novels and films of the 1990s), projecting onto this woman all his sick fantasies and blaming her for the ills of a world which, in actuality, he and people like him have created. Shown in his office high in a Manhattan tower, Cable represents the kind of masculine power that can operate outside the law and get away with it, while, at the same time, judging a woman like Bree Daniels, who indulges in all kinds of paid "permissiveness" with men not unlike himself.

Cable represents only half of the patriarchal power structure. Bree Daniels is similarly kept under surveillance by detective John Klute, who represents the "good" men of society who want wives and children. He can also be seen as representing the relative innocence of the country versus the evil projected upon the city.

The film is misnamed because it concerns Bree Daniels, her life, and her efforts to become the person she wants to be. (Fonda was perfect in the lead, given her political activism and her transformation from sex kitten to outspoken political actor.)[15] The classic investigative narrative of film noir here merges with the struggle of a woman to exist freely and to control her own life. As the audience sees her, this struggle occurs largely through her relations with her clients, for it is with them, as she tells her therapist, that she finds a kind of freedom and feels in control. Prostitution becomes for her an almost compulsive route to personal identity, thanks to her skill at role-playing, as well as a source of income. (Contrast Julia Roberts's romanticized version of a "call girl" in *Pretty Woman* [1990, Garry Marshall]).

Bree's struggle is between herself, Cable, and Klute, though Cable's aim is to dominate, terrorize, and ultimately kill her.[16] The narrative presents a harrowing journey through the various circles of a prostitute's hell as Bree, with Klute's aid, searches for a missing call girl friend who was one of Cable's victims. Their search involves three distinct levels of the profession: a high-class madame, a sleazy cat house, and a burned-out streetwalker. Bree even considers rejoining the girls managed by her former pimp, Frank Ligourin (Roy Scheider) but is dissuaded by Klute.

At the film's climax, Cable dies while being pursued by Klute, crashing through the plate glass of a high office window. Bree Daniels survives a terror-filled stalking scene in a garment factory and decides to go off with Klute. (They became romantically involved while he was keeping her under surveillance). At the conclusion, she's ambivalent, her future open. She's now under Klute's protection, ready to try to go off and live with him. Near the end there is a glimpse of what she might become: a woman shown sitting at Klute's feet, her small-town cop, holding a cat. Fonda obviously wanted to understand the character and literally seemed to become her. But any optimism in the film seems at best of a tentative, hurting kind. (At the time of its release, Robin Wood saw the ending as not in keeping with the conventions of film noir, given its optimism, a view that is debatable.) One is left with a feeling of openness and possibility based on the simple fact that the woman remains alive after the horrifics of the preceding two hours, and that Cable, the psychokiller, is supposedly dead—though in films a mere two decades later the psychokiller would be reincarnated as Hannibal Lecter.

## Hannibal Lecter and the Age of Sex Crimes

While critics could not have realized it at the time (and nobody seems to have noted it since), *Klute*'s images of a serial killer anticipated the popular cultural explosion of women-killing psychos during the last two decades of the century, the emergence of what one critic has called an "age of sex crime."[17] Hannibal Lecter became a virtual culture hero and attained mythic status in the 1990s. While one could go back to Hitchcock's killers—Norman Bates in *Psycho,* Uncle Charlie in *Shadow of a Doubt*—or even further back in time to Jack the Ripper, there were enough psychokillers in fiction, film, and television in the last twenty years to constitute a major cultural trend marking the ascendancy of the serial killer to heroic status.

In the United States, nicknamed killers—the Boston Strangler, the Son of Sam, the Hillside Strangler, the Green River Killer—slaughtered "socially powerless and scapegoated victims [using] a signature style of murder or mutilation."[18] Because of intense media involvement, they were elevated almost to the status of sports heroes. Something very significant was revealed by the public's cultural infatuation with such madmen. The killers were virtually all male and their victims were usually women, though sometimes young men.

Sexual politics was obviously intertwined in such killings and in the public's fascination with them. It is difficult not to accept Jane Caputi's compelling argument that the murders are

> rooted in a system of male supremacy in the same way that lynching is based in white supremacy. Moreover, whether the victims are female or male, when murder itself becomes a sexual act, this is the paradigmatic expression of a belief system that has divided humanity into two erotically charged and unequal gender classes . . . constructing sex itself as a form of masculine domination and defeat of the feminine.[19]

## *THE SILENCE OF THE LAMBS* (JONATHAN DEMME)

Hannibal Lecter, a fictional psychotic killer, became a culture hero after the release of *The Silence of the Lambs* (1991), which was based on Thomas Harris' 1988 best-seller. In a rare event, the film was named Best Picture, Demme Best Director, Anthony Hopkins Best Actor, and Jodie Foster Best Actress. Some critics—the film generated scores of significant commentaries[20]—attributed the appeal of the novel and the film to an inherent cultural "feminism" responding to the allegedly strong female characters. Yet any reasoned assessment must also consider the larger cultural context.

The first appearance of Hannibal Lecter occurs in Harris' novel *Red Dragon*,[21] which was subsequently filmed as *Manhunter* (1986, Michael Mann). In that film Lecter plays only a subsidiary role, though similarly functioning as a source of information on other serial killers. In *The Silence of the Lambs* he is locked up for life in a hospital for the criminally insane. Lecter is like some devouring extraterrestrial creature with not the slightest concern about his cannibalism. His intellect is immense, as is his inexplicable appetite for the internal organs of his victims. ("I ate his liver with fava beans and a nice chianti.") Where or how his taste for Bach and human flesh developed is never explained. Coleridge once described Iago's evil as one of "motiveless malignity" so deep and foul it needed no other cause. Hannibal Lecter is the purest example.[22]

The role of FBI trainee Clarice Starling (Jodie Foster), while clearly drawn in the novel, is supplemented by touches modeled on a real FBI agent with whom Foster spent time in preparing for her role.[23] Everything else is arguably the product of the male power structure—from her memories of her father, through her FBI superior Jack Crawford (Scott Glenn), and especially the psychotic killer Hannibal Lecter (Anthony Hopkins). Starling must petition him for aid in finding Jame Gumb, another serial killer who kidnaps, tortures, and kills young women, flaying them in order to make a "girl suit" for himself. Starling is sent to Lecter in the vague hope he will find her appealing, having resisted all earlier efforts. Curiously, Lecter is drawn to Starling's simple integrity. Over the course of four separate interviews, Lecter assumes the role of teacher, psychotherapist, and even father figure and psychic lover.[24]

Ever since Jack the Ripper, serial killers have been romanticized in popular culture. Lecter becomes a culture hero, "genius, artist, core soul of mankind, preternatural demon, outlaw hero, an undefeatable and eternal entity."[25] While he has murdered both sexes, only those of men are described in the novel and film, perhaps making him more palatable to women readers and viewers, who are positioned, incredibly, to identify with a "good" serial killer (Lecter) rather than a "bad" serial killer (Buffalo Bill/Jame Gumb).

But where are the purported feminist values in this immortalization of such a brutal, sadistic killer? Starling, the main female character, must somehow gain self-awareness through a grotesque process of bonding with Lecter. Lecter eventually brings his supposed genius to bear in analyzing the evidence on Gumb and enabling Starling and her handlers to solve the case. Even though Starling is the supposed heroine, she must consent to an idiosyncratic form of psychotherapy from the demented "doctor" (he is a psychiatrist). Their meetings thus become a kind of psychic rape, with Clarice selling "her core constitutive memory" (Caputi's phrase) to this repellant, venomous, supposedly superhuman killer with whom the audience is asked to identify.

Lecter (in the novel) agrees to provide assistance only if Clarice reveals to him her "worst memory of childhood." By sharing this experience with Lecter, Clarice supposedly comes to understand how her whole adult life was shaped by her horrifying childhood experience of witnessing the death of lambs and horses. She seeks to "silence the lambs" she hears screaming in her memory, now symbolized by women threatened by sex offenders. Her psychic rape by Lecter is thus supposed to be a revelatory experience, though several critics have noted that the slaughter of innocent lambs might well stand for the experience of childhood rape or incest, even though she denies this.

At the conclusion of the novel and the film, it is not Clarice who has been liberated from her fear but Lecter, who calls her from a Caribbean island where he is in hiding, assuring her that he does not intend to harm her. The film's final scene shows Lecter, seeing his old nemesis deplaning, put on his Panama hat and disappear into a crowd in search of his "dinner."

Thomas Harris published his first Lecter novel in 1988. Eleven years later, in 1999, a sequel, *Hannibal*, appeared. The film rights were quickly sold, and in the spring of 2000 Julianne Moore was cast as the new Clarice Starling after Jodie Foster refused to repeat her role. Like Jack the Ripper, Dr. Lecter now seems a pop-culture immortal, perhaps riding on a wave of human self-loathing that seems increasingly evident at the dawn of the twenty-first century.[26]

# Bad Cops and Noir Politics

Innocent suspects brutally beaten; fabricated evidence used to justify sweeping antigang programs; cops dealing dope, covering up for each other, and delivering perjured testimony; an elite anticrime unit running amok as police higher-ups avert their eyes; "kill" parties, where officers get together to celebrate police killings. This is recent history in Los Angeles,[1] not something out of another neo-noir film set there. The unblinking savagery with which such actions were carried out was mirrored in scenes from the film *L.A. Confidential* (1997, Curtis Hanson), whose events occurred in 1953, as well as *Devil in a Blue Dress* (1995, Carl Franklin), which is set in 1948—both of which demonstrated some of the historical roots of the 1965 Watts and South Central riots following the Rodney King beating verdicts in 1992.

Bad cops and police corruption are not new. But real evil emanating from sources of authority—especially official law enforcement—is profoundly terrifying, calling into question the very foundations of the social order. Although some corruption and abuse of power is inevitable where public employees are involved, many police officers lay their lives on the line for a lot less than your average plumber or electrician.[2]

Such contradictions have long been recognized in the movies. In *Rogue Cop* (1954, Roy Rowland) senior detective Chris Kelvaney (Robert Taylor) lives the good life, thanks to extra income from payoffs through his undercover connections to crime kingpin Beaumonte (George Raft). However, unlike such contemporary films as *L.A. Confidential*, the "5,000 brothers" of the San Francisco police force are seen as honorable and dedicated.

In *City That Never Sleeps* (1953, John H. Auer), Johnny Kelly (Gig Young), a Chicago cop in blue is about to hand in his resignation and work for a crooked big-time lawyer named Penrod Biddell (Edward Arnold), who promises him the kind of money that will "give your life dignity." Viewers see Johnny's shame—consistent with early 1950s cultural values—in the fact that his wife earns a lot more than he does. In the end, Kelly stays on the job, apparently only to honor the memory of his father, a veteran cop.

Police compensation has increased significantly since these and other "bad cop" movies appeared in the 1950s, but the level of corruption in big-city police departments—if one is to believe news reports—is greater than ever. Reports of false arrests, coerced confessions, false testimony, and the overuse of lethal firepower to carry out virtual extrajudicial executions in New York, Pittsburgh, Chicago, Philadelphia, and especially Los Angeles suggest that the fictional, often paranoiac representations of the past were prescient, darkly visionary commentaries on present-day realities.

## Media Images and Urban Corruption

The film version of *L.A. Confidential* (1997, Curtis Hanson), based on James Ellroy's 1990 novel, largely confines itself to late 1953 and early 1954 (in contrast to the original novel's 1950–58 time span), marking the beginning of the TV era. In 1950 and 1951 Senator Estes Kefauver had demonstrated how to rivet the attention of nearly half of the population with television sets through televised hearings of his U.S. Senate Special Committee to Investigate Crime in Interstate Commerce, known as the "Kefauver Committee." The Kefauver hearings presented to the largest television audience yet achieved "a sordid intermingling of crime and politics, of dishonor in public life."[3]

Simply by watching their TV sets Americans in the early 1950s experienced the revelatory power of the medium to confirm and legitimate what many already knew—despite J. Edgar Hoover's opinion to the contrary[4]—namely, that organized crime existed and that police and politicians were linked to it. However, where the influence of the mob on politics ended and the authority of government began was difficult to determine. The years that followed the Kefauver hearings were filled with documentary-style, semifictional film exposés of crime. For two decades (1930–50) the Production Code—created at least partially in reaction to perceived glorification of gangsters in films of the 1930s—discouraged both explicit linkages to politics and "crime pays" messages.[5]

One outcome of the Kefauver hearings in the movie culture of the 1950s was the "confidential" series of films purporting to tell the inside story of supposedly corrupt cities, including *Kansas City Confidential* (1952, Phil Karlson), *Chicago Deadline* (1949, Lewis Allen), *Chicago Confidential* (1957, Sidney Salkow), *The Phenix City Story* (1955, Phil Karlson), *New York Confidential* (1955, Russell Rouse)—all serving as early models for *L.A. Confidential.* After the initial explosion of such "confidential" film exposés, it would be nearly two decades before the clear implication of organized crime as a representation of the whole political-economic system became a central theme in such popular films as Francis Ford Coppola's *Godfather I* (1972) and *II* (1974), *Serpico* (1973,

Sidney Lumet), and *Chinatown* (1974, Roman Polanski). The latter were anticipated by Abraham Polonsky's remarkable 1948 film *Force of Evil* (discussed in chapter 3), and the images of political collusion with organized crime evident in *The Racket* (1951, John Cromwell), which attempted to cash in on the organized-crime craze following the Kefauver hearings. One should also mention Welles' *Touch of Evil* (1958), often considered the terminus of classic period film noir.[6]

## *THE BIG HEAT* (FRITZ LANG)

Explicit and corrosive images linking politics to crime are evident in *The Big Heat*,[7] Fritz Lang's searing 1953 film, with a screenplay by Sydney Boehm based on William P. McGivern's popular 1952 novel, which fuses distinctive Langian motifs of mirrors and burning flesh—and the human propensity for evil—to create a crucial film link between 1940s noir and 1950s crime exposés. In Lang's film Glenn Ford portrays Detective Sergeant Dave Bannion, who is asked to investigate the suicide of a man named Tom Duncan, a supposedly honest cop who worked in the police records department. In the opening moments of the film, viewers see Duncan shoot himself. His gun falls on a thick envelope addressed to "The District Attorney." Before the police arrive, his widow Bertha (Jeannette Nolan) opens the envelope and apparently hides the letter in a safe deposit box. Bannion suspects that Duncan was on the payroll of the rich and respected but corrupt civic leader Mike Lagana (Alexander Scourby), especially after the dead cop's mistress, Lucy Chapman (Dorothy Green), is found dead shortly after being interviewed by Bannion. Her claim that Duncan was happy and in good health contradicts Mrs. Duncan's account, who claims that her husband's suicide was the result of failing health.

Ignoring both higher-up police orders and anonymous phone threats to get off the case, Bannion continues his investigation, going after Lagana and his thugs, only to have his wife (Jocelyn Brando) killed as a result of a car-bomb explosion obviously intended for him. Driven by rage and grief, he descends into near paranoia as he pursues the criminals responsible for his wife's death. The film's compelling images and situations underscore the logic of his conclusion that everybody is on the take and the whole system is corrupt.

The film is remarkable for its time—especially given the apparent strictures of the Production Code—in explicitly portraying the linked corruption of the police and the political system; local political figures, including the commissioner of police, are shown playing cards with Lagana's thugs, among them the sneering and sadistic Vince Stone (played with malevolence and psychopathic relish by Lee Marvin). Lagana's paid police higher-ups—including Bannion's commanding officer—also seek to steer him away from his investigation. Bannion's moral outrage and—as the widespread corruption becomes evident—justified paranoia leads him into several reckless confrontations. After one of these outbursts, he is suspended from the force, but, like the driven, true crime fighter, he still dogs Lagana and his gang.

To smash this setup—which might well have reminded Fritz Lang of the Nazi Germany he fled—Bannion has to find allies in strange and unlikely places, among people who have little to lose. The most fascinating of these is Debbie Marsh (Gloria Grahame), the gorgeous yet morally clueless girlfriend of Lagana's chief enforcer, Vince Stone. Debbie is frequently shown admiring herself in mirrors—trademarks of many of Fritz Lang's films.

Debbie is attracted to the stoic, overcontrolled Bannion. She returns to Bannion's hotel room with him, partly out of sheer curiosity but really to get to know him romantically. Debbie's physical beauty—and the setting, with her reclining on Bannion's bed—makes one sense the possibilities, but she is surprised and disappointed that Bannion fails to make the pass she seems to expect and want. (The novel intimates a much stronger attraction to Debbie on Bannion's part.)

Debbie is seen in Bannion's company—Vince Stone gets a full report from one of his underlings. Thinking she has given away inside information or "played footsie" with Bannion, when she returns to their apartment, Vince abruptly throws boiling coffee in her face, permanently scarring her. This remained one of the most savagely brutal treatments of a woman in the grim annals of film noir—at least until Robert Altman's film version of *The Long Goodbye* (1973) where mobster Marty Augustine smashes his girlfriend's face with a soda bottle, cutting her badly.

Debbie flees back to Bannion's bleak hotel, where he gets her another room and, over several days, nurses her. Half of her face is scarred—a literal representation of her conflicted character, torn between the vicious Vince of her past and her newly discovered sense of right, embodied in Bannion. To aid Bannion's crusade, Debbie confronts Bertha Duncan at her home, both wearing their hard-won mink coats, symbols of a woman's status in the 1950s. Using a gun Bannion had given her for protection, Debbie shoots Bertha, killing her. Because of this act, according to the rules of the culture and the strictures of the Production Code, Debbie's death now becomes almost inevitable.

Returning to the criminals' luxury apartment headquarters, Debbie prepares a boiling pot of coffee. When Vince comes in, she throws it in his face. The agonized Stone shoots Debbie twice, just prior to Bannion's arrival. In an exchange of gunshots Bannion gets the drop on Vince and has the chance to blow him away, but he cuffs and arrests him instead. As Debbie dies in

Bannion's arms, he finally recognizes that when he stepped outside the law he became just like the criminals he was fighting.

At the end of the film Bannion is welcomed back to the police force, temporarily cleansed by the "big heat" who have apparently come in from the outside, suggesting the possibility of political or legal remedies for the police-crime connection represented in the film. The knowing audience, however, is still left with the suspicion that nothing has permanently changed.

### *SERPICO* (SIDNEY LUMET)

Based on the Peter Maas book cowritten with Frank Serpico—the undercover New York City cop who in the late 1960s blew the whistle on systemic corruption in the police force—*Serpico* (1973) is a study in growing menace and rational paranoia that still manages to grip the viewer three decades after its release. Lumet subsequently made several grim, noir-influenced crime films,[8] each characterized by their gritty realism and critique of the corruption attendant to big-city police and politics: *Dog Day Afternoon* (1975), *Prince of the City* (1981), *The Verdict* (1982), *Q & A* (1990), and *Night Falls on Manhattan* (1997).

*Serpico,* based on a screenplay by Waldo Salt and Norman Wexler, is a study in naïve idealism, disillusionment, disaffection, and growing isolation, conveying an all-encompassing menace and mounting paranoia as idealistic cop Frank Serpico (Al Pacino) finds virtually everyone around him on the take.

The film opens on a rainy night in New York City as an ambulance transports the critically wounded Serpico, who has been shot in the face. Serpico's Christlike positioning on the emergency room bed suggests he is dying—a crucified victim. Two brief flashbacks follow—first a clean-shaven, short-haired Serpico in his police academy rookie class and then at his graduation, where he hears inspiring words about serving the public, which he obviously took to heart.

A series of events follow that demonstrate to him and the viewer how "the system" operates and how rookie cops are supposed to act—and revealing Serpico's distinctive approach. On his first assignment with a veteran partner, he gets a "free" lunch at a deli in return for their not ticketing vehicles double-parked in front. On another night two officers get a "rape in progress" call, which they pass on but Serpico takes, rescuing a young black woman from a gang rape. After an exhausting foot pursuit, Serpico captures one young black man, whom he convinces to give up the other "perps." After arresting and cuffing them single-handedly, Serpico is told "thanks" by the detective in charge. Indignantly protesting that it is *his* "collar," he learns "normal" practice is not to allow a rookie officer to get arrest credit since it will make the veteran detectives "look bad."

Serpico next decides to take a fingerprint course—supposedly to improve his chances of getting a detective's gold shield. He winds up at the Bureau of Criminal Investigations for three boring years, during which he takes courses at New York University in various liberal arts areas and pursues his interest in opera and ballet. After a failed relationship with a willowy blond dancer, he meets a neighbor who is a nurse and also likes opera. They move in together.

Soon Serpico becomes an undercover cop. Early in his new post at the Ninety-ninth precinct Serpico is handed an envelope containing three hundred dollars in cash—apparently part of the usual payoff to all the undercover cops. Uncertain how to respond, he contacts his Princeton-educated friend Bob Blair (Tony Roberts), who works in a special investigations unit attached to the mayor's office. Blair arranges a lunchtime meeting with the deputy commissioner, Kellogg (John McQuade). Over a fancy lunch, Kellogg, nibbling on his huge lobster, reminisces knowingly that "things like this were common practice in the old days." He suggests Serpico can either risk being brought up on charges or ignore the whole thing. Frank decides to drop the matter.

Later, after being transferred to a Manhattan division, he is greeted by an old classmate and undercover cop named Keough (Jack Kehoe), who offers him two hundred dollars as his share of a shakedown of a gambler. Serpico refuses the money. Keough is amazed at Serpico's refusal, voicing the message Serpico is supposed to get: "Who can trust a cop that doesn't take money?" Here he seems to mirror—in reverse—the skeptical opposing judgment of the veteran safecracker "Doc" (Sam Jaffe) in *The Asphalt Jungle* (1950, John Huston), who claims, "You can never trust a cop; just when you think he's paid off, he turns legit."

Serpico is now partnered by a man who is the bagman, collecting payoffs for the whole division. He goes to his superior and supposed friend, the sanctimonious Captain McClain (Biff McGuire), who assures him that the matter is being investigated. Unwilling to wait any longer, Serpico and his friend Blair go to the mayor's office (John V. Lindsay was the mayor of New York City at the time), who at first agrees to investigate the matter and then reverses himself, unwilling to alienate the police force because of expected summer riots.

Unable to find a partner who will work with him because of his reputation for being both clean and a rat (informer), he is transferred to still another division, reporting to commanding officer Inspector Lombardo (Ed Grover), who is as decent a cop as Serpico has met in his whole career. They eventually go to the chief of police (played by white-haired M. Emmet Walsh) with more tales of corruption, but he merely suggests that an "internal" investigation might be best.

Eventually Serpico and Blair tell their story to the *New York Times*, which publishes a major exposé. Shortly thereafter a major investigation is undertaken by the district attorney. Now the word is out on Serpico. Transferred to a narcotics division in South Brooklyn, he is threatened by another cop wielding a knife as soon as he enters the station house. In one of the most memorable action moments of the film, Serpico throws the man to the floor, disarms him, and is surrounded by other hostile officers, whom he warns away with his gun. The confrontation clearly indicates that he can trust nobody and must now rely only on himself.

On a drug stakeout (featuring F. Murray Abraham in a bit part as one of the other officers), three men try to bust a drug dealer, with Serpico entering first. When Serpico's calls for help from his fellow officers go unanswered, the dealer shoots Serpico in the face. Finally the other cops enter the apartment—too late for Serpico. Was it their cowardice, or a setup, or a little of both? One can't quite tell, though it's obvious from the film's opening that something like this was bound to happen.

The film now returns to the opening scenes. Serpico is not dead, but he is critically wounded. His parents visit him in the hospital. The doctor tells him he will be permanently disabled. Captain Green, one of his few allies, holds a gold (detective's) shield out to him. Serpico responds, "What's this for? Being stupid enough to get shot in the face?"

Mayor Lindsay subsequently established the Knapp Commission. Serpico was questioned at length, and a major investigation took place. In a postscript, viewers are informed that Serpico resigned from the force in 1972 and left for Switzerland, though he returned to New York to serve as a technical advisor on the film. Today he's an artist living in upstate New York.

What is especially striking about the Serpico case is not that corruption was exposed but that it existed within the New York City police department systemwide, through several generations of police officers involved in rake-offs and extortion from gambling, loan-sharking, prostitution, narcotics—even murder. The clear implication, crime novelist Larry Beinhart suggested, is that

> *thousands* of people knew about it and *participated* in it without exposure. . . . [A]lthough New York City embarked on an extensive and possibly successful reform, the vast majority of those officers who had been "on the pad" virtually all their police lives retired in their own time as if nothing had happened, to enjoy both the fruits of their corruption and their pensions.[9]

Crime—for them—obviously paid enormous dividends.

## *DEVIL IN A BLUE DRESS* (CARL FRANKLIN)

In many ways the body of novels and films created by African-American writers and directors in the 1990s—particularly Bill Duke's striking *Deep Cover*

(1992), Carl Franklin's *One False Move* (1992) and *Devil in a Blue Dress* (1995), and Charles Burnett's *The Glass Shield* (1995)—are important contributions to noir discourse and, perhaps more significantly, powerful political statements about what Charles Mills has called "The Racial Contract" in his similarly titled book.[10] African-American directors have utilized film noir conventions—especially its black subspecies, ranging from the novels of Chester Himes in the 1940s though Walter Mosley's Easy Rollins series set in Los Angeles—making them effective ways for "portraying the consequences of a supremacist system of knowing and acting in which many whites hardly realize they participate."[11] Each of these films illustrates the "epistemology" of noir films and literature as discourse.[12]

*Devil in a Blue Dress,* based on Walter Mosley's 1991 novel, opens with Ezekiel "Easy" Rawlins (Denzel Washington) in voice-over relating that "it was summer 1948 and I needed a job." Easy Rawlins is not, as director Carl Franklin stated in an interview, one of those noir protagonists comfortably adapted to operating in a "world of cynicism." To Franklin, most noir protagonists give the impression that "anyone who doesn't understand that cynicism is a sucker. Our protagonist is the sucker . . . the guy who's learning about this cynical world and somehow leads a double life. So in a way we've almost taken the noir genre and turned it inside out."[13]

In the novel and the film, Easy Rawlins is an upwardly mobile black man. As Joppy, his supposed friend and the bartender-owner of his favorite hangout says, "Easy is always trying to better himself." One day Joppy introduces Easy to a noirish character named Dewitt Albright (Tom Sizemore). Offering his card to Easy, Albright says he does "favors" for people. Albright suggests that Easy call him if he wants a gig. The work—which Rawlins desperately needs—involves finding a woman named Daphne Monet (Jennifer Beals). Easy Rawlins blunders into his investigator's role, making a lot of mistakes before he "solves" the case. Along the way he—and the film—uncovers the racist post–World War II social atmosphere of southern California and consequently redirects our attention to the historical roots of much more recent racial conflicts in Los Angeles.[14]

What is remarkable about *Devil in a Blue Dress* is its effective mobilization and use of the repressive politics of race and its representation of the terrors of racism for an ordinary black man caught between two cultures. Easy Rawlins has that kind of dual consciousness W. E. B. DuBois described a century ago, giving him powers that no white man could have. African-Americans experience an inevitable alienation, being simultaneously in and outside mainstream American culture. While such alienation could cripple, it could also liberate the brightest (the "Talented Tenth") intellectuals, who could act on their perceptions of the obvious contradictions between the evident high ideals of, say, the Declaration of Independence and the equally obvious racism and discrimination apparently in society.[15] As applied to Easy Rawlins, he is hired because he is black, intelligent, and can move in circles a white man cannot—and he really needs the hundred dollars proffered by Albright.[16]

Rawlins is hired by Albright—though precisely on behalf of whom is not made clear—to find the mysterious Daphne, who is described as having predilections for soul food, black music, and "dark meat" (black men). Rawlins straddles both communities, especially after it becomes evident that Monet, who is engaged to wealthy white mayoral candidate Todd Carter (Terry Kinney), is a product of an interracial union—she is a partially black though light-skinned and quite beautiful woman who can easily pass as white.

The most striking narrative moments in the film occur when Rawlins experiences real or possible racially motivated violence, though there are several black-on-black violent encounters as well. The precarious position of a black man in a white environment is conveyed in several situations. Early in the film Easy gets a phone call telling him to meet the sleazy Albright at a nearby beach. Arriving before Albright, Rawlins is approached by a young white woman who engages him in conversation. Her white male companions attempt to gang up on Rawlins, who is saved by the arrival of Albright. A racist authoritarian, he obviously revels in threats of violence and is seemingly turned on by the terror he causes to the other racist whites, whom he scares away, forcing one of them to abase himself before the black Rawlins. Later Albright assaults Rawlins himself, holding a large knife to his eye while threatening to have one of his hirelings shoot him—all intended to get Rawlins to reveal information Albright thinks is being withheld.

At one point, Rawlins is taken in for questioning by two white detectives following the death of Coretta James (Lisa Nicole Carson), a fact unknown to him until the detectives break the news. Her murder apparently occurred shortly after Easy left her place, following a night of liquor-induced intense sex on her couch while her drunken boyfriend lay passed out in the next room. The portrayal of the white cops' violent and racist treatment of Rawlins reflects a knowing "subjugated" knowledge of racist double standards and hidden racial violence typical of large urban police forces throughout much of the past century. In a moment echoing the then recent O. J. Simpson trial, the police threaten to plant evidence on Rawlins that would ensure his conviction for the several murders they are investigating. After a violent interrogation and numerous threats—they give him twenty-four hours to come up with information—he is released. As he walks away from the police station, a police car drives by, one cop leaning out and making lewd gestures and racist taunts. Several other cop cars in the background suggest the possibility of racist police violence confronting any black man who finds himself on their "wrong" side.

On his way home, Rawlins is stopped by yet another sleazy white man, whose sedan blocks his path. Seated next to a young boy is mayoral candidate Matthew Terrell (Maury Chaykin), who seeks information about his opponent, Todd Carter. Presenting himself as a friend of "the colored people," he laments Rawlins' recent bad treatment by the police. Later it is revealed that Terrell is a pedophile.

Arriving back at his house, Rawlins is amazed to get a call from the elusive Daphne Monet asking him to meet her that night at the Ambassador Hotel. Rawlins discovers that this "devil in a blue dress" is quite beautiful. After some sexual banter, Monet says she wants to be taken to see a certain Richard McGhee, who lives way out in an all-white area. When they arrive at the house, McGhee is found dead—the smell suggests his body has lain there for awhile. Daphne abruptly flees in a car, leaving Easy Rawlins with the corpse. Easy calls in his friend Mouse (Don Cheadle), a near-psychotic killer from Houston's underworld. Mouse's arrival at a crucial moment saves Rawlins from having his throat slit by Monet's black half-brother. From this point on the film largely becomes an action shootout. Monet is kidnapped by Albright and associates and then found by Rawlins and Mouse. The abductors are all killed, Monet is freed, and Albright dies in a final grisly but banal death scene.

Informed of Daphne's mixed racial background, Todd Carter rejects Monet, breaking their engagement, but his rich family provides her with a large cash settlement, part of which she shares with Mouse, who gives half to Rawlins then departs. Provided with snapshots of his opponent's pederasty—purchased for a huge sum by Daphne—Todd Carter resumes his political career. It turns out that Monet is actually a girl named Hanks from Lake Charles, Louisiana, "just trying to move up in the world." The film ends with Easy Rawlins back in his segregated neighborhood. He remains an ironic figure—certainly no burned-out private eye suffering existential dread. Rather, he is an ordinary guy in what was a much simpler time in American life for both whites and blacks. The film effectively communicates that—along with the stark scenes vividly representing interlinked, deep-seated racism and constant threats of violence aimed at those not respecting the color line in the Los Angeles of 1948. None of these insights, of course, would ever have appeared in films belonging to the original film noir cycle.

## *L.A. CONFIDENTIAL* (CURTIS HANSON)

*L.A. Confidential,* released in 1997, is set in 1953 (the same year Fritz Lang's *The Big Heat* was released). It presents a portrait of an intertwined criminal, legal, and police apparatus that is in some ways even more corrupt than organized crime. The complex plot—perhaps stretching credulity—only becomes clearer by the end of the film, and may even require two or three viewings to fully appreciate its intricacies. Like *Chinatown* a quarter century earlier, it comments on the political system and law enforcement in terms of the whole society. It depends on racism—both historical representations and contemporary incidents—for its cohesiveness. It is rooted in the rich associations of Los Angeles with earlier decades of crime fiction and films central to noir discourse.

### *Los Angeles in Noir Film and Fiction*

Instead of a largely fictional community that, as in *The Big Heat,* is rescued by the outside intervention of larger political forces, Los Angeles represents something entirely different. As a setting for films and novels, Los Angeles has great symbolic resonance. If L.A. embodies the future of America, its representations in novel and film may be taken as an implied though indirect social critique of the whole of American culture.[17] In the history of crime films, Los Angeles locations have been central to the film noir and neo-noir canon.[18] A place of virtually endless (if smoggy) sunshine, it is also the site of a great American "countermyth."[19] If it is a place where "dreams come true," it is also the place where dreams fail[20]—flattened against the Pacific shore, the dead end of the continent. Earlier Nathaniel West, in his novel *The Day of the Locust* (1939), saw L.A. as a place where people come to die. The dance marathon in Horace McCoy's novel *They Shoot Horses, Don't They?* (1935) is set in a rundown depression-era ballroom overlooking the Pacific. Both novels were later made into memorable movies by John Schlesinger (1975) and Sidney Pollack (1969), respectively.

Consistent with the strands of noir discourse on Los Angeles, *L.A. Confidential* revisits the scene of what Paul Arthur has described as "earlier crimes"[21] to paint a portrait of evil. The film is especially insightful on the growing role of television in the early 1950s and the symbiotic—sometimes corrupting—interaction of print and TV media, law enforcement, and political image-making. The film is also filled with narrative strands that, like *True Confessions* (1981, Ulu Grosbard), *Chinatown* (1974, Roman Polanski), and its sequel *The Two Jakes* (1990, Jack Nicolson), seem to reference an America burdened by illusions about its flawed origins and its fundamental corruption.

In the dark, often paranoid epistemology of noir, nothing is to be trusted and everything is suspect. For many, that is a defining attribute of noir discourse. *L.A. Confidential* only intersects in certain places with some canonical films in the noir cycle; perhaps in this sense it is a "post" noir and certainly a "retro" noir. But in other respects *L.A. Confidential* represents a unique hybrid of past and present. Its director wanted "to keep the period stuff in the background. . . . [W]e avoided set up [*sic*] that would draw attention to the window dressing of the period, whether it be the cars or the clothes or the set dressings. . . . Character and emotion [are brought] to the forefront, and ideally let the audience, on a scene by scene basis, forget that it's a period movie."[22] For anyone with even the remotest familiarity with the culture and social history of Los Angeles in the 1950s, that view is difficult to accept.

*Bad White Men and Racist Violence*

The characters in James Ellroy's novel often seem inspired by cases in Krafft-Ebing's *Psychopathia Sexualis* (1886). Many of the worst of these—and some of the more disgusting behavior of the central protagonists—do not appear in the film. *L.A. Confidential* is distinctive—though not unique—among contemporary films for its often grim representation of reciprocal levels of violence at both personal and institutional levels.[23] We are familiar with some of the more recent examples of L.A. police violence, and there is a body of literature describing earlier episodes.[24]

The main protagonists of the film version of *L.A. Confidential*—to some degree the "bad white men" in novelist Ellroy's oft-cited definition of noir as "bad white men doing bad things in the name of authority"[25]—all depend on the application of violent, often lethal, force to validate their status. Each character represents an alternate path of career development strewn with obstacles. Each makes unique adaptations demonstrating a tenacity and determination despite a complex maze of corruption reaching to the highest levels. The public is cynically portrayed as gullible to the point of incredulity. Perhaps the failure of the highly hyped film to generate the immense box-office receipts that were anticipated is a reflection of the public's rejection of that view. Here the problem is more complex, involving almost a denial—through misdirection—of the full dimensions of the violent racism upon which the story depends. As the great sociologist Max Weber once remarked, ultimately the "decisive means for politics is violence."[26] And violence certainly can be a *very* decisive means—crucially linking the framing and killing of several black people in the film. In the larger noir tradition violence is but one of the decisive tools, along with "fraud, deceit, treachery, betrayal, and general, endemic unscrupulousness."[27] While such means were never alien to Dashiell Hammett's detectives, they are now the tools of the trade of modern police detectives, who have become the "public" agents supplanting the private eye.

Bud White (Russell Crowe) witnessed his father's fatal beating of his mother with a tire iron while still a boy. For three days he remained next to his mother's body until a truant officer found him. One might expect that he would be haunted—even psychologically crippled—by such horrors, but instead he is driven by a profound, violent hatred of wife-beaters and anyone who abuses women. In his daily work he relies on physical violence, beating recalcitrant "perps" and enacting a kind of vigilante justice, serving for a time as the chief extralegal muscle for Captain Dudley Smith.

Dudley Smith (James Cromwell) is the outwardly wise and fatherly but inwardly cold, manipulative, and, as it turns out, boundlessly corrupt mastermind of covert illegal rackets being run from within the police department. As James Ellroy described him in the novel,

> When Dudley Smith brought you along you belonged to him—and he was so much smarter than everyone else that you were never sure what he wanted from you or how he was using you—shit got lost in all his fancy language. . . . Dudley could bend you, shape you, twist you, turn you, point you—and never make you feel like some dumb lump of clay. But he always let you know one thing: he knew you better than you knew yourself.[28]

Edmund Exley (Guy Pearce) is the son of a celebrated murdered cop hero. In the novel his father is a major character running for the Senate. The senior Exley's best lines and mentoring function in the novel are given to Smith's character in the film. In the novel Exley senior has a hidden past involving child victimization and murder; at the novel's end he winds up an apparent suicide, along with a character named Dieterling, a thinly disguised version of Walt Disney, who owns a theme park. In the screenplay he is replaced by a plot involving the Zachary Scott–like promoter named Pierce Patchett (David Strathairn), who runs an elegant call-girl operation. Exley wants to get to the top whatever it takes—even if it means ratting on his police brothers by testifying against them in court. Like the character of Serpico, Exley—obsessed with what he repeatedly describes as "absolute justice"—pointedly refuses payoffs and kickbacks, but unlike Serpico he eventually proves himself to others on the force by inflicting that regenerative violence so endemic to American culture. In a carefully choreographed scene midway in the film, Exley blows away several black men in a shotgun-style execution. What begins as an act of self-defense escalates into a mass murder. The scene is capped off with Exley pursuing an unarmed man down a long hall and then, as the fleeing man tries to escape into an elevator, sticking his shotgun into the crack in the elevator door and atomizing the trapped suspect, literally blowing his head off in the novel. In the film Exley emerges with half his face covered with the executed man's blood and gore. This multiple execution is hugely acclaimed by most of the detectives on the force and is sensationalized in the news media. Exley is reborn, regenerated through violence, earning the nickname "Shotgun Ed."

Jack Vincennes (Kevin Spacey) can't even remember how or why he became a cop, but he is a "celebrity crime fighter," a kind of Jack Webb with a soft heart. His ambiguous sympathy for a bisexual male actor he introduces to deep-in-the-closet D.A. Ellis Lowe (Ron Rifkin) seems a precondition of his elimination well before the film's end, suggesting that he is made to pay for this "weakness." A technical adviser to a TV show called "Badge of Honor" (similar to Jack Webb's long-running TV series *Dragnet*), Vincennes' job is to advise on how the cops should "look"—their public image being most important—and not necessarily how they should behave. In this function Vincennes operates in a symbiotic relationship with sleazy though often amusing Sid Hudgens (Danny DeVito), editor of a tabloid rag called *Hush Hush* (modeled on the old *Confidential* magazine) that lives off scandal yet ironically helps the careers of the aspiring stars whose drug busts they publicize. (Robert Mitchum is among the more celebrated actors busted for pot—he is pointedly mentioned in the film—and his career arguably benefited, as did those of other stars of the 1940s.) Hudgens first feeds Vincennes info on illegal activities by Hollywood's minor celebrities, and then Vincennes arranges to bust them, with Hudgens present at the busts to photograph the events, in return for which he passes money to Vincennes.

None of these men are failed, compromised, noir protagonists at existential dead ends. Except for Hudgens's intro, there are no voice-overs of dead men—as in *Double Indemnity* ("I couldn't hear my footsteps"), *Out of the Past* (where we hear the dead PI, played by Mitchum, sleepily describing how madly in love he was with the woman who killed him), or *Sunset Boulevard* ("It was all very queer" says the voice of the dead Joe Gilles). Nor are these characters neurotic vets or burned-out ex-cops working as seedy PIs—shabby lower-middle-class men with worn out heels working in nondescript-looking offices with a frosted glass partition and a bottle in the bottom drawer of the desks. On the contrary, these characters are strong, young, highly motivated, and driven public employees. Almost one-dimensional, they are sometimes puzzled, genuinely curious, and always seeking excitement.

It is ironic that the emergence of film noir was immediately preceded by the publication of one of the classic studies of the race problem in America, Gunnar Myrdal's *An American Dilemma*,[29] which was also the release date of Billy

Wilder's *Double Indemnity*, one of the canonical examples of film noir.[30] Race was long considered one of the most socially destabilizing factors in American society, as blacks migrated from the South to cities like New York, Detroit, Los Angeles, or Chicago. Although there was a marked absence of African-Americans in classic film noir,[31] they are certainly present in *L.A. Confidential.* In a way they are central to it, though they play subsidiary roles as low-life *victims* of the white protagonists.

*The Nite Owl Murders*

The central plot device of *L.A. Confidential*—the ramifying mysteries connected with the execution-style murder of six white men at a place called the Nite Owl Café—relies on racism and supposed willingness of the 1950s public—as well as present-day audiences—to believe that three young black men could slaughter six white men in cold blood. Without this willingness to accept what turns out to be an elaborate frame-up, the film would not be as involving as it is. *L.A. Confidential* absolutely depends on the dominance of "bad white men" in noir ideology—at least until very recent years.

The film is built on, yet paradoxically underplays, what has been called an "epistemology of ignorance" and "telling white people things they do not know and do not want to know."[32] The crucial racial aspect of the narrative, the so-called Nite Owl murders, begins after a scene-setting opening on Christmas Eve 1953. Bud White—after subduing a wife-beater in a scene designed to establish his proclivity for extreme physical violence—is in a liquor store, where he meets beautiful Lynn Bracken (Kim Basinger), a high priced call girl. The extorted liquor is for the LAPD Christmas party. Its (illegal) imbibing is followed by a vicious racist beating of some Hispanic detainees by the drunken cops.

After the introduction of the major characters, the crucial event occurs. It appears that a multiple, execution-style murder has taken place at an all-night greasy spoon in downtown L.A. called the Nite Owl Café. Edmund Exley is the first detective to arrive at the scene. In the film's best cinematic moment, detail is used to create a specific place, mood, and setting. Exley enters the restaurant, which looks just like a 1950s functional all-night eatery. The camera lingers over the half-eaten burger platters, the order pad, the body of a dead man—the cook—behind the counter, with a blood-spattered chest (presumably a shotgun-blast victim), a .38 near his hand. He still leans against the gas grill on which there are greasy, blackened burgers sizzling, as well as a pan with a gas flame still lit under it. The cash register is open and appears to have been cleaned out. It looks like it might have been an armed robbery that got out of hand or turned violent when the cook pulled his gun. A feeling of dread hangs in the air as Exley follows a bloody trail into the men's room, where he discovers dead bodies piled up like so many slabs of beef. Abruptly Captain Dudley Smith arrives to inform Exley—who protests that he was there first and the case is "his"—not only that Exley cannot "have" the case but that he "doesn't want it." Despite his disappointment, Exley pointedly removes his glasses in order to be photographed by the gathering media. Is Smith's action a reflection of the departmental pecking order or something more insidious? Why doesn't he wish Exley to be in charge?

While it does not become evident until the final half hour of the film, the avuncular Captain Dudley Smith is at the center of the complex plot, which involves killing off Smith's early associates in his former career of crime, blaming young African-American men for the killings, and then arranging for those same men to escape in order to facilitate their almost certain murder.

*Social History versus Cliché: Noir, Kafka, or Action Entertainment?*

James Ellroy, author of the brooding novel *L.A. Confidential,* has suggested that "most of noir is a cliché. I differed from other noir writers by giving you noir as social history . . . about bad white men doing bad things in the name of authority."[33] If earlier expatriate Europeans—particularly Germans—shot L.A. "through a lens of Weimar and made it look like a city invented by Kafka,"[34] there are still extensions of Kafka—and some Cornell Woolrich twists—in this end-of-millennium film version of the Los Angeles of 1953. The plot, though not literally a flashback, almost accomplishes the same thing in the final thirty minutes as White and Exley go back well over a decade to scrutinize old daily duty logs, revealing more than incidental contacts between Dudley Smith and his now dead former associates, Leland "Buzz" Meeks and Dick Stensland.

Dudley Smith's depravity throughout the film represents a kind of methodical, almost banal evil that comes about as a result of a series of initial compromises that continue to evolve into an ever-widening conspiratorial web. To maintain it, Smith becomes surgically clinical about the killings. This dimension of his character is evident in the late-night scene in his kitchen. Jack Vincennes has come for advice on his "unofficial" investigation. After being asked by Vincennes about his connection to the recent events as well as those that occurred over a decade earlier, Smith abruptly turns and shoots Vincennes through the heart. Bending down—almost like an emergency-room physician—to clinically examine Jack's eyes, he asks, "Do you have a valediction, lad?" He is genuinely puzzled when Vincennes gasps, "Rollo Tomasi" and then dies.

*"Epic Pop History": The Novel and Film as Flashback*

In some ways *L.A. Confidential* is itself a gigantic flashback on an era. According to Ellroy, "The 1950s to me is darkness, hidden history, perversion behind closed doors waiting to creep out." Reputedly described by the *Times of London* as "the aspiring Balzac of America's slimy underbelly," he is a kind of "secretary of society"—specifically the L.A. of the 1940s and '50s. Ellroy thought of *L.A. Confidential* as the centerpiece of his L.A. quartet, the other three novels being *The Black Dahlia, The Big Nowhere,* and *White Jazz.* He described it all as

> an epic pop history of my smog-bound fatherland between the years 1947 and 1959. . . . My essential design was to cram real-life events and established historical characters into a series of complexly structured story-lines, add fictional protagonists and antagonists, and rebuild and rewrite my hometown . . . to my own specifications.[35]

It suggests that the past was just as corrupt as the present. Even though the novel recounts events from a fictional point of view, the story of the LAPD's blood-stained past suggests that corruption could be traced back to the 1930s, when some of the largest police scandals occurred.[36] In one case, dating back over sixty years, the brother of then mayor Frank Shaw was selling LAPD jobs and answers to promotion exams right out of City Hall while vice-squad members roamed the city as collectors for organized vice operations and their political patrons. The narrative of the film itself thus presents nothing new; the screenplay for *Chinatown* had transposed events to 1938. Ellroy created his own panorama of novelistic impressions and the screenwriters simply drew from it to make the film.

The examples of police corruption in *L.A. Confidential* reflect a period when, as one law enforcement specialist described it, "corruptibility and violence were rewarded skills of police recruits, veteran cops were often 'promoted' from the beat to the mob, and the LAPD was shifting from a frontier mentality to one modeled on the military."[37] Numerous scenes seem to celebrate the rich diversity of such police corruptions.

The film's ostensible message or lesson seems to be that "corruption is not extraordinary in its evil, but rather comes about as a series of initial compromises that evolve into greater compromise," that power ultimately corrupts and yet "there are some things a police officer cannot do and live with himself."[38]

These lessons are not forgotten in the stunning climax of the film at the Victory Motel, a bloodbath in which Bud White is critically wounded. Here Exley seemingly rejects Smith's ironic offer of shared heroism and, as the sirens signal arriving police reinforcements, he abruptly and fatally shoots Captain

Smith in the back. While explosively brutal, it is the one extrajudicial execution in the film the audience can cheer.

The events that follow the "execution" of Smith constitute an ironic double coda to the stunning climatic shootout and final elimination of the central villain. Recognizing that the department will need more than one manufactured hero to cover the unbelievable slaughter and extensive conspiracy and corruption, Exley, having blown away the primary evildoer, *retrospectively* accepts Smith's offer—to protect his own future—by participating in the collective deception of the public, resurrecting the now-dead leader of the conspiracy as a "hero," along with himself and the wounded White—an apt example of the most cynical propagation of "necessary illusions."[39] In the film's ironic denouement, Exley seems destined for another promotion in what appears to be the same racist, corrupt system. Ultimately it is a cynical, bleak, and empty resolution. Here, consistent with the noir tradition or vision, one sees the isolation and ultimate insecurity of the (white) male protagonist.

*The Crisis and Recovery of White Racist Masculinity*

In different ways a "crisis and recovery of masculinity"[40] is presented in the three competing images of Bud White, Ed Exley, and Jack Vincennes. The film essentially distributes audience sympathy among them in ways that subvert traditional entertainment models of a "perfect" masculine hero yet still ensure the preservation of white male privilege within society, of which the film's LAPD is representative. While Vincennes dies horrifically at the hands of Captain Dudley Smith, the name "Rollo Tomasi" he whispers to Smith before dying—which only Exley and Vincennes knew about—provides Exley with a crucial clue in his and White's quest to unravel the Nite Owl killings. Bud White, while a physical wreck after suffering multiple gunshot wounds, survives and has his "virgin whore" Lynn Bracken to look after him. Exley, with still another phony hero medal, is on the way up in what now appears as a totally corrupt system.

All these events place *L.A. Confidential* within the tradition of noir discourse. Yet elements of contemporary cynicism and postmodern irony—rather than noir's historical and darker existential vision—also permeate *L.A. Confidential.* Even given its ambiguous qualities, the film is only partially "denatured" noir—half empty of radical content, its crucial insights almost but not quite thrown away. It reminds one of the weary mood of *Farewell My Lovely* (1975, Dick Richards). It's not the failure of Michael Winner's curious remake of *The Big Sleep* (1978), nor is it as glib as Kenneth Branagh's elegantly constructed *Dead Again* (1991), nor such an empty, turgid exercise as the confused *Mulholland Falls* (1996, Lee Tamahori), which one critic has deprecatingly described as "ambiance shorn of its 1940s radical affinities."[41]

Eric Lott sees a moral and racial charge in classic film noir—a racialization of the inner life of the white protagonists, which he characterizes as "a sort of white-face dream of social anxieties with explicitly racial sources, condensed on film into the criminal undertakings of abjected whites."[42] *L.A. Confidential* paradoxically reinforces racism by reinstilling belief in the criminal undertakings of abjected *blacks*. This is accomplished early on by having the three black men rape a Hispanic woman, which makes it much easier for the audience to believe they might also be guilty of the Nite Owl killings.[43] It also makes their unnecessary killing—an extrajudicial execution, the result of poor planning and almost nonexistent backup—seem more acceptable.

Ultimately, one of the most important contributions of the film is in effectively representing images of cynically manufactured illusions and manipulated consent in the homeland of the dream factories. Its "print the legend" finale has even been described—in an allusion to the classic 1962 western *The Man Who Shot Liberty Valance*—as "John Fordian."[44] More significantly, it tackled the larger issues of hidden racist history, of the culturally denied and repressed. Hispanic and African-American racial stereotyping is seemingly criticized in ways that appear ambiguous and conflicted.

If one focuses too closely on the film's final double coda, it might *seem* to be only a noir-influenced "entertainment"—somewhere between period soap opera and retro-action flick—with which those who are historically informed might identify but, sadly, the mass audience might easily forget. The *real* climax of the film—savvy viewers must ultimately recognize—is Exley's summoning the resolve to murder Smith at the Victory Motel, killing those evils not only in Smith but in himself and, hopefully, society at large. Viewed in this light, *L.A. Confidential* gains greater depth and potentially shattering impact.

## *DEEP COVER* (BILL DUKE)

Manthia Diawara, Dan Flory, and others have noted how contemporary African-American directors have utilized and redeployed the powerful images of earlier film noir features, recognizing that in classic gangster flicks and the earliest film noir lawbreakers are not simply one-dimensional "bad guys," and that audience identification with them is inevitable. Based on an early recognition of the effects of gangster films on the audience, which led to the creation of the Hays Office and the Production Code,[45] the newer tendency evident among black filmmakers is to fuse the distinctive African-American cultural view that breaking the law "is to fight one's captivity, and to claim the right to invent oneself," thereby creating new "symbolic possibilities."[46] By presenting such powerful images of criminals, these filmmakers—Bill Duke, Carl Franklin, Charles Burnett, Spike Lee, Mario Van Peebles, John Singleton, Allen and Albert Hughes, among others—appropriated the centuries-old image of the outlaw. While equating street gangleaders of the black drug subculture with Robin Hood and other varieties of primitive bandits and rebels might seem to stretch analogies, oppositional subcultural images—from blues and jazz early in the century, through "Zoot" in the 1940s,[47] to the emergence of hip-hop and "gangsta" rap in the 1980s and '90s—remain significant and powerful icons in American popular culture.

The appropriation of noir stylistic conventions by African-American filmmakers and writers is a logical use of available cultural resources as weapons to express what Manthia Diawara has described as "black rage" against white colonization of black communities. Diawara defined this black rage as "a set of violent and uncontrollable relations in black communities induced by a sense of frustration, confinement and white racism,"[48] taking the form of eroticized violence on the part of some characters against others they want to control.

Making a far darker statement than *L.A. Confidential* and presenting a more conclusive indictment of a legal system that tolerates and encourages the very criminality it purports to combat, *Deep Cover* (1992), by African-American director Bill Duke, is based on a screenplay cowritten by two white screenwriters: Michael Tolkin, who wrote the screenplay for *The Player* (1992, Robert Altman) and wrote and directed *The Rapture* (1991); and Henry Bean, who wrote the 1990 neo-noir "bad cop" film *Internal Affairs,* directed by Mike Figgis. By appropriating traditional film noir elements of characterization, visuals, and narrative style, *Deep Cover* contemporizes earlier noir political themes to fashion a noir politics of black rage. As a film, it expresses that rage by critiquing American society and social structure in ways that make it among the grittiest and darkest examples of neo-noir of the 1990s.

According to a Drug Enforcement Administration (DEA) lecture on undercover drug surveillance:

> Deep Cover is an undercover assignment in which the operative completely abandons the protection of his official identity and adopts a new one as a criminal, isolating himself in the dominion and complete control of his target. This type of assignment is rare in law enforcement and even rarer in overseas operations, where exposure will almost always be fatal.[49]

Narratively *Deep Cover* explores the very thin line separating those enforcing the law and those who deviate from it in the so-called drug war. Profound moral issues are raised. The film is unique in that here there is real moral anguish. When the central protagonist is faced with killing, it is not some video game shootout but a wrenching, agonizing experience. Death involves real pain and agony for anyone who comes into contact with it, not simply its victims.

In *Deep Cover* Laurence Fishburne assumes a distinctly film noir double identity as Cincinnati cop Russell Stevens, recruited to assume the deep undercover narcotics agent identity of "John Q. Hull,"[50] who operates in Los Angeles in the center of the cocaine trade. Stevens is recruited during a racist interview conducted by a nerdy white federal DEA operative named Jerry Carver (Charles Martin Smith, best known for his role as a quintessential nerd in *American Graffiti* [1973, George Lucas] and bearing a marked resemblance to 1950s *Mad* magazine character Alfred E. Neuman). Carver selects his candidates from a pool of African-American police officers by means of the following riddle: "Tell me, do you know the difference between a black man and a nigger?" Nobody among the interviewees seems to have the answer he wants. (One interviewee is even moved to violence, grabbing Carver by the throat.) Officer Stevens supplies the answer Carver apparently seeks: "The *nigger* is the one who would even *answer* that question."

Carver tells Stevens he is an ideal candidate for deep undercover work because his psychological profile—his anger, repressed violence, resentment and hostility toward authority, and rigid code of values—is virtually indistinguishable from that of a criminal. John Q. Hull gradually moves up the drug hierarchy in order to discover the top suppliers in control of L.A. operations.

Using a classic film noir voice-over, Stevens/Hull relates his undercover history, his struggle to make sense retrospectively of a series of moral compromises in what he sees as his deeply mistaken decision to work for the DEA, which is part of the white power structure that separates him from the best elements of the black community and compromises his long-held conviction that he must live his life and act in ways that initially led to his becoming a cop. As he tells Carver, "I wanted to be of some use. I wanted to make a difference." He clearly wants to transform the worst aspects of the victimized and colonized African-American community. In this sense, the film represents a radical, essentially black nationalist perspective.

Statements about "family"—or its absence—in African-American culture are also central to the film's ideology. In what might well be described as a "Frank Capra in Hell" flashback, viewers hear Stevens' resonant voice-over stating, "My father was a junkie." As a boy of ten he accompanied his cocaine-addicted father on an abortive effort to rob a liquor store. As they pull up outside the store, his father snorts some coke, warning him, "Don't ever do this shit!" He asks young Russell what he wants for Christmas. When the boy says he doesn't know, his father reminds him—in what turn out to be his last words—"Always know what you want. Else, how you gonna *get* what you want, if you don't *know* what you want?" We see him entering the store with a handgun, a shot is heard, and he emerges—gleefully brandishing a fistful of cash—only to be gunned down from behind by a shotgun blast from the wounded white store clerk. The horrified boy watches as his father falls backward and dies in the snow. The boy is left alone, with a wad of blood-soaked, stolen money. In a voice-over the character played by Fishburne says, "My father. When I saw him like that, I only had one thought—it wasn't gonna happen to me!" As a reminder, he always carries some of the blood-soaked money with him for the next twenty years.

Like Bud White in *L.A. Confidential,* who as a young boy witnessed his mother's beating death at the hands of his father, young Stevens never forgot his father's horrifying end, personally vowing to change the situation that led to it, to seek the transformation of an endemically racist American society. That the character adopts such a posture seems the whole point of the film.

Having assumed his new identity, Stevens is sent to L.A. to begin to work his way into the drug hierarchy. First he is to establish contact with cocaine supplier Felix Barbossa (played menacingly by Gregory Sierra). As Carver explains the strategy to Stevens/Hull, once they get Barbossa they can also nail his importer, Gallegos, and the latter's even more influential uncle Guzman, who travels on a diplomatic passport issued by an unnamed Latin American country.

Stevens/Hull first teams up as an assistant to a white Jewish lawyer, David Jason (played by Jeff Goldblum with a reptilian edginess), who apparently specializes in drug cases and does a very significant amount of dealing as well. He handles Hull's first drug bust in court and gets him off. Jason has a beautiful blond wife and a young child in grade school. His duality and marginality are everywhere apparent—he's a white Jewish lawyer working drug cases and simultaneously dealing drugs from Barbossa to street-level dealers, in a sense representing the boundary between whiteness and blackness, Jewish ethnicity and black racialism.[51] In addition to his attractive wife, Jason has more than one beautiful black mistress, as well as a mistress/business associate named Betty McCutcheon (Victoria Dillard), who owns a very expensive African crafts shop that serves as a front for laundering his drug money.

Two subplots in the film are also important in terms of its larger meaning. When Hull first checks into his Hollywood apartment as John Hull, he meets a drugged-out neighbor, Belinda Chacon, with a young son—obviously meant to represent the young Stevens—whom he tries to befriend. Hull rejects Belinda's sexual advances and an offer to "sell" her boy to him for two thousand dollars and walks away in silence. The other subplot involves a black nationalist and born-again Christian narcotics cop named Taft (Clarence Williams III, who, early in his career, was the only African-American on the old "Mod Squad" TV series and was perhaps the first black undercover cop in media culture of recent memory). Hauling Hull in for questioning—he does not know his real identity—Taft says that through Christ he will be forgiven and gives him a miniature New Testament. Hull, still playing his part, laughs and throws it across the room. In a transforming symbolic act, Taft is killed by Hull's associate Jason, provoking and signaling Hull's reemergence from rogue status to that of genuine upholder of the law.

An important line is crossed only thirty minutes into the film at a billiards parlor when Hull and Jason stand by helplessly as Barbossa beats to death one of his couriers, who has been using the drugs for himself and also giving information to the police, ultimately leading to Hull's arrest. Taking a pool cue, Barbossa pounds Eddie to a bloody pulp right before their eyes. Wiping the blood off the now dead Eddie—whose battered body lies before them on the pool table—Barbossa suggests they "try it sometime," adding that "it's very liberating" to kill a man. From being present at a murder, Hull goes on to commit murder, gunning down a street dealer who killed a woman who was one of his and Jason's dealers.

Events soon put Hull in danger from all sides. A complicated police bust and double-cross leads Jason, Betty McCutcheon, and Hull (contrary to Carver's orders) to seize Barbossa as a hostage, leading to a harrowing high-speed nighttime car chase through L.A. streets, ending with Jason forcing Barbossa to jump from the speeding car right into the path of a pursuing police cruiser, instantly killing him.

After disobeying a direct order from his handler, Hull is abruptly told by Carver to shut down the whole operation. Incredulous and outraged at what he sees as a government sellout ("I sold drugs, I watched people die—people like me; I didn't do anything. I killed people . . ."), he refuses to stop his activities and quit, vowing to himself to continue his drug war as a rogue agent and, together with Goldblum, expanding his drug-dealing empire.

Yet Carver seems to agree with Hull, cynically admitting, "It's *all* shit. . . . Come along with me to Washington. We'll have a budget. We'll have some clout. That's all there is. The spoils of war." Hull is disgusted. In a voice-over—summing up his feelings of utter self-loathing at his corruption and manipulation by the government—Hull says, "This whole time I ain't nothing but a cop pretending to be a drug dealer, when I was a drug dealer pretending to be a cop . . . The whole game was a joke . . . I was a fool. I'd been turned out like a two dollar 'ho'. Used, abused, no towel, no kiss." Fleeing Carver, he drives down an alley and snorts from a bag of coke, marking the first time he has used the stuff.

Gallegos, the next higher-up in the drug mafia, arrives in L.A. to take over Barbossa's territory, ordering Hull and Jason to pay $1.8 million for having killed Barbossa, his supplier to dealers. They meet Gallegos at a theater. Hill shoots and kills Gallegos, seizes his drug profits, and orders his henchmen to arrange a meeting with Hector Guzman, who controls the cocaine coming into L.A. A night meeting at the docks is arranged. After sampling a designer drug Jason is seeking capital to produce and agreeing to invest, Guzman and his armed guards are about to leave when the manic born-again Taft, who had arrived earlier, leaps out and tries to stop them. Jason abruptly shoots Taft, who is critically wounded. Hull is horrified—clearly reliving his father's bloody death. Hull, shaken by this needless slaughter, reemerges as a true cop with his values restored. In a shootout with Hull, Jason falls to the ground—apparently fatally hit. By the end of the film Hull emerges with a seared conscience, millions in drug money, and nominal custody of the young boy whose drugged-out mother, Belinda, is found dead of an overdose. In a final cemetery scene, he places the old bloody bills his father stole over twenty years ago on Belinda's headstone. As the film's closing credits roll, Stevens strides out of the cemetery, uncertain of his future at the hands of both the international drug mafia—from whom he stole millions—and the secret agencies of the U.S. government he double-crossed.

By the film's conclusion, corruption has been traced to the highest levels of the U.S. government. At a Congressional hearing Hull turns against his corrupt DEA handlers, carrying off a supreme act of whistle-blowing by presenting a video of U.S.-backed Latin American ally Hector Guzman in the midst of a drug deal, multiple copies of which have already been sent to TV and print media. At least here one senses the possibility of some kind of *political* action as a response.

*Deep Cover,* a grim and convincing neo-noir film by an African-American director, reflects not simply the phony and futile "drug war" but corrupt bureaucracies that ultimately prove ineffective and are easily manipulated for immediate political ends. Major drug suppliers are dealt with according to political priorities, with drug trafficking by "friends" of the U.S. government merely winked at. This is obviously not a new insight. Several studies have shown that there is much more to the general theme informing the film than the imagination of screenwriters Tolkin and Bean.[52]

If one accepts Charles Mills' general argument in *The Racial Contract* that white supremacy is the system of domination that has made the world what it is today, some filmic representations of the victims of that system must inevitably become part of one's consciousness—especially given Mills' belief in the genuine inability of whites to recognize their privilege. *Deep Cover* effectively assists in such recognition, going far beyond distinguishing between white and black worlds, and white power and privilege—evident in such neo-noir or retro-noirs as *Devil in a Blue Dress* and *L.A. Confidential*—instead presenting a dark, bleak, and cynical view of a virtually faithless world in which African-American protagonists—in order to generate the new symbolic possibilities central to a renewed radical politics—are forced to choose "between being criminals or fools, between transgressing white power or dumbly serving it."[53]

The survival of Fishburne's character in *Deep Cover* to a large degree represents an individualistic adaptation to an utterly corrupt situation—although he has the luxury of the skimmed drug profits. Other African-Americans might similarly be moved to try to get their part of the pie before rejecting the whole corrupt system, though virtually none would succeed on such a scale—most likely ending up dead, like the central figure of the Hughes brothers' grim 1993 portrait of Los Angeles gang warfare in *Menace II Society.*

All of the films discussed in this chapter embody and reflect the darkest noir political themes and provide only a limited hope that any larger political transformations of the society that produced such criminals are even possible. Beginning with *Chinatown* (1974), a more disengaged and offhanded postmodern variety of cynicism is evident in *L.A. Confidential,* which argues that the source of evil and racist oppression may be traced back to those in authority, whose sworn duty it is to uphold law and order for everyone in society. *Deep Cover,* through the moral anguish of the manipulated African-American protagonist, argues that since the whole political-legal system is corrupt—its policies making sense only in terms of narrow bureaucratic imperatives—the only solution is to start all over again by choosing another good young man to carry on the struggle.

# From Assassination to the Surveillance Society

## "Mazes That Extend Toward Infinity": Assassinations, Conspiracies, and the Quest for Coherence

The assassination of President John F. Kennedy remains the most significant moment in American history of the latter half of the twentieth century—"seven seconds that broke the back of the American Century"[1]—after which historical possibilities and events were profoundly altered. Its media and popular cultural representations over the decades contributed to what has become a kind of epistemological break, making both the general populace and a significant subgroup of intellectuals question their ability to *know* the truth rather than merely to believe or sense it.[2] The more one studied it, the less one seemed to know. It was truly "dangerous knowledge."[3]

The JFK assassination and the controversial, often fantastic, frequently tendentious inquiries surrounding it are cultural phenomena so vast that extensive discussion of all the relevant issues is quite beyond the scope of this book, but the topic and the event may serve as a convenient starting point for much of the theorizing on conspiracy during the past four decades. On the twentieth anniversary of the event, novelist Don DeLillo—whose novel *Libra* is one of the finest fictional interpretations of the JFK assassination—wrote an article for *Rolling Stone* magazine in which he suggested that the assassination resulted in a new way of perceiving—or failing to perceive—reality: "What has become unraveled since that afternoon in Dallas is not the plot, of course, not the dense mass of characters and events, but the sense of a coherent reality most of us shared. We seem from that moment to have entered a world of randomness and ambiguity."[4]

Whatever particular version of an assassination conspiracy one cares to explore, one aspect is clear: the whole truth will never be known—perhaps never can be known—because of a generalized obsession with "secrecy."[5] This involves conscious efforts by officials in diverse governmental agencies to limit disclosure, withhold information, reclassify documents, deny allegations, and misdirect investigations—all practices which have bred a well-justified paranoia growing out of the widespread recognition that all the components of the most fantastic conspiracy theories regarding the assassination have already been admitted by U.S. government agencies or are self-evident as a result of four decades of research.[6] At a broader, cultural level, the inability to discern the truth about the events surrounding JFK's death may reflect the postmodern condition itself.[7]

A number of perceptive, devastating critical commentaries on the assassination and the 1964 *Warren Report* (Report of the President's Commission on the Assassination of President Kennedy) were published within months of the events and that document's appearance. Several influential early studies were written by Philadelphia attorney Vincent J. Salandria. They were followed by Edward Jay Epstein's book-length investigation,[8] which transformed the way the *Warren Report* was subsequently viewed by the intellectual community. Through his interviews with several commission members and many staff, Epstein revealed the conscious effort on the part of the Commission to create and establish a kind of widely believed *political* truth concerning the events surrounding the assassination of the president. Epstein concluded that in presenting its version of the event, the Warren Commission was attempting to protect the national interest.

This, of course, was the *intention* of many officials in the U.S. government, who—apparently fearful of international repercussions growing out of the linkage of the assassination to Cuba or the Soviet Union—urged the creation of what became the Warren Commission within days of the assassination. FBI Director J. Edgar Hoover told White House aide Walter Jenkins, "The thing I am most concerned about . . . is having something issued so we can convince the public that Oswald is the real assassin."[9] Assistant Attorney General Nicholas Katzenbach wrote Bill Moyers, then an aide to President Lyndon B. Johnson:

> 1. The public must be satisfied that Oswald was the assassin; that he did not have confederates who are still at large; and that the evidence was such that he would have been convicted at trial.
>
> 2. Speculation about Oswald's motivation ought to be cut off, and we should have some basis for rebutting thought that this was a Communist conspiracy or . . . a right wing conspiracy to blame it on the Communists.[10]

The commission's task—unspoken in its official charge—was clear: reassure the public.

Among the many early works critical of the striking omissions, excisions of testimony, and carefully worded, elaborately constructed "truths" of the *Warren Report* was Mark Lane's diligent, meticulously researched critique entitled *Rush to Judgment,*[11] which was published the same year (1966) as the documentary film version directed by Emile d'Antonio. Josiah Thompson, a professor of philosophy, also became interested in researching the assassination. His book formed part of a second wave of in-depth analysis—it was published in 1967, four years after the assassination—making use of the forty-six books published in the four preceding years, as well as the meticulous analysis of a legion of critics of the *Warren Report* and its twenty-six volumes of supporting information.[12] Thompson's investigations led him away from academia to become a private investigator, operating out of an office in San Francisco.

Epstein's, Lane's, and Thompson's studies reflected the growing disbelief in the carefully patched together "political truth" concerning a lone assassin and a single, fatal bullet that was presented in the *Warren Report.*[13]

In later decades it became commonplace to see through the carefully-constructed compromises of the Warren commissioners and their staff. That their effort failed so profoundly is evident in the overwhelming public disbelief in the commission's central findings. Nearly forty years later—and, significantly, because of the cumulative effect of the kinds of questions raised, though certainly not initiated, in Oliver Stone's *JFK*—profound skepticism and disbelief concerning those findings are still experienced by an overwhelming majority of the U.S. population. Such popularly held views also reveal more than simple disbelief, reflecting a profound sense of powerlessness in the face of events people are unable to control, based upon decades of secrets and lies that inevitably generate public paranoia.

A Gallup poll held in December 1993—marking the thirtieth anniversary of the event—asked, "Do you think that one man was responsible for the assassination of President Kennedy or do you believe that others were involved in a conspiracy?" Only 15 percent of those polled believed that only one man was responsible. Fully 75 percent of respondents said others were involved in a conspiracy. The remaining 10 percent expressed no opinion.[14] Such opinion figures were actually exceeded a decade earlier (1983)—eight years *before* Oliver Stone's movie on the JFK assassination—when 80 percent of those surveyed in a national poll carried out by ABC News and *The Washington Post* said they thought the assassination, though involving Lee Harvey Oswald, was part of a larger conspiracy.[15]

Other than the leading news organizations and TV news anchors, who seemingly continued to assert their monopoly on defining history,[16] few ordinary Americans have *ever* accepted the central contentions of a lone gunman and a single fatal bullet. Thus, in direct opposition to the likes of Lyndon

Johnson, Nicholas Katzenbach, and J. Edgar Hoover—each of whom urged the establishment of the Warren Commission to forestall rampant rumors of conspiracies (and to prevent international conflict with the Soviet Union)—for more than three decades the overwhelming political consensus on the events (held by at least three-quarters of the U.S. public) has been that some sort of conspiracy *did* exist—though the majority of the public also believe accused assassin Lee Harvey Oswald was in some way associated with it.

Oswald, the alleged assassin, remains one of the most mysterious and enigmatic characters in recent history.[17] Was he merely a grotesque mediocrity, a crazy, psychotic "lone nut," or was he part of a complex web of forces, each possessing the *motive* to kill the president, all with vast resources that would provide the *means* and the *opportunity?* The latter possibility does not mean Oswald was the killer or even the only shooter; indeed, there is no direct evidence that on November 22, 1963, he even fired the weapon that killed the president. Even among those who believe the evidence points to Russian or Cuban Communist involvement in the assassination, compelling questions concerning Oswald's involvement continue to be raised.[18] As one critic has suggested, Oswald's "guilt" often seems to be viewed as a product of the whole society—as *collectively* shared.[19]

## *JFK* (OLIVER STONE)

Given the elusiveness of any definitive conclusion, the profound ambiguities and intriguing mysteries surrounding the assassination, it is no wonder that it has figured in so many movies over the decades (see Art Simon's study *Dangerous Knowledge*). It should come as no surprise that the major recent effort to represent aspects of the assassination on film—Oliver Stone's 1991 film—created such a firestorm of criticism after its release. It remains the preeminent embodiment of the political film and, in a more limited sense, is also the finest "conspiracy thriller" of recent decades.

After an opening capsule history of the struggle for the soul of America in the early days of the cold war and JFK's place in that struggle, there is a brief, fleeting image of an unidentified woman—hysterical, bleeding, her clothes torn—who has been thrown from a vehicle on a lonely Texas country road, and is now in a hospital, surrounded by unidentified men, who hear her warn, "These guys are serious . . . they're going to kill the President!" While viewers only see the woman again in a brief, almost subliminal, flashback, her image haunts the film. Perhaps she symbolizes the nation's psychic wound, one of the first victims sacrificed for trying to speak the truth.

*Recollections of an Era*

It is difficult for those who did not live through it to recall the symbolism of the thousand days of JFK's presidency, during which a significant minority of the nation was profoundly moved by his call to a generation to commit itself to public service, to something beyond self-interest. In a PBS documentary shown in 1988—marking the twenty-fifth anniversary of the assassination—the great violinist Isaac Stern recollected what was lost with the death of John F. Kennedy:

> With him went *a time*—a time of *possibilities.* . . . It's so easy—after the fact—to cast aspersions and doubts. With him, you could always *believe*—in the ninth inning home run; in winning the fifth set at Wimbledon; running a three-and-a-half-minute mile; . . . in having all the children in America reading and writing, painting and dancing, speaking many languages, knowing everything one could know about the world. . . . To be a part of *one* world that had a positive look for the next three, four, five decades. [He was a man with] *a positive attitude*—with *hope,* with *clarity;* with *intelligence;* with *compassion;* and an immensely broad understanding of history—and an understanding of people. . . .[20]

According to one critic, Stone's film can "show us what no one saw, can give us not only what did happen but what *could have happened.*" Viewers are "positioned by the film to participate in a speculation about history, which is an even more powerful fantasy of history, beyond the fantasy of knowing what happened to the possibility of knowing what might have been."[21] The film and controversies in its wake galvanized public opinion to act on those beliefs and feelings, resulting in the *JFK Assassination Records Act,*[22] the creation of the Assassination Records Review Board,[23] and the declassification of millions of pages of documents. Thousands of pages of commentary have been written on the film itself.[24]

Stone's *JFK* is perhaps the most *influential* political film in U.S. history, in the sense that the assassination of Kennedy affected other historical outcomes—such as the expansion of the Vietnam War and the shattering of national political consensus in its wake. The film has also catalyzed and focused the activism of a new generation of assassination researchers, which in turn has led to the declassification of a huge amount of previously classified material. Whether those documents will ultimately change historical views on the events or their consequences remains for future historians to determine, but one can think of no work that better embodies the following characterization of how movies influence society and history: "Films take the raw material of social history and of social discourses and process them into products which are themselves historical events and social forces."[25]

Brilliantly realized—with multiple, quick cuts; rakish angles; an often indistinguishable fusion of documentary and pseudo-documentary or newsreel film; restaged historical events; and occasionally deafening sound bursts—the film is a technical masterpiece of postmodern cinema. Although often overpowering in its force, the film can sometimes be maddening in what its narrative implies or leaves unsaid. It has been much maligned because of its often bizarre visions of complex conspiracies within the government. One should bear in mind, however, that it is an *artistic* rendering that is highly selective and does not purport to be an actual documentary.

Like the best film noir mysteries, Stone uses the classic investigative narrative device, asking the viewer to identify with an individual's quest into one of modern history's more enduring enigmas: Who *really* killed John F. Kennedy? The central character can easily be seen as the audience, representing the inquisitive citizen who seeks the truth. The problem many observers have with the film is that the central character—New Orleans District Attorney Jim Garrison (Kevin Costner)—was discredited at the time of his 1969 investigation, despite the fact that he brought the only indictments, resulting in the sole trial of an individual for the actual killing of President Kennedy. That the accused, Clay Shaw, was easily acquitted does not lessen the significance of Garrison's original efforts.[26] The film creates a fictional Garrison not unlike the naïve James Stewart in Frank Capra's *Mr. Smith Goes to Washington* (1939). While criticism outweighed praise for this narrative decision, Stone's Garrison does provide someone with whom viewers can identify, following him from his early puzzlement over inconsistencies in the *Warren Report* to his quest for the possible killers, with instructive onscreen visits to the assassination site in Dallas and to the meeting with Mr. X (Donald Sutherland), based on onetime covert operative and now retired U.S. Army Col. Fletcher Prouty.

*JFK* is probably the most maligned film ever produced for a mass audience. It started receiving negative reviews months before it was released. The fact that so many in the political and media establishment were made uncomfortable—even outraged—by it suggests that Stone's film struck a raw nerve in these media guardians of the body politic,[27] intruding into the self-appointed, self-defined interests of establishment media figures, who had built their careers based on having "been there" in Dallas, maintaining a kind of monopoly over the interpretation of the assassination. They simply did not want somebody else usurping their initial definition and subsequent proprietary sense of guardianship of politically correct "history."

The author recalls an episode of "This Week—with David Brinkley" around the time of the film's release featuring a panel of program regulars, including conservative George Will (who subsequently published some of the most scathing critiques of the film), centrists Cokie Roberts and Sam Donaldson, and retired *New York Times* columnist Tom Wicker (a political liberal and an acquaintance of JFK). All of them condemned what they termed historical distortions in the film, though Roberts failed to indicate that she was the daughter of a Warren Commission member, the late Louisiana Democratic congressman Hale Boggs.

*JFK* is not pure history but rather an artistic statement about the events that serves historical functions, artfully constructing—almost subliminally deconstructing—usual understandings, representing alternative possible scenarios and raising far-reaching questions about the "official truths." As a result, most critics misinterpreted and misunderstood what the film could definitively say as a historical document.[28] It is, after all, a *movie,* but one about history that itself has made history. Despite what many critics have described as its distortions, it is a movie based upon meticulous research, weaving known facts into possible or hypothetical scenarios. The film's suggestion—in Mr. X's conversation with the overly credulous Garrison at the Washington Monument—that the assassination came from *within* some agency of the U.S. government seemed particularly infuriating to mainstream journalists.

However, anyone who has studied the hidden and officially denied history of the twentieth century knows that successive U.S. administrations *have* systematically lied about a wide range of covert, secret policies and programs, which has generated an extensive body of literature on this topic.[29] One could suggest any number of operations carried out by the CIA, the FBI, or military intelligence units on domestic operations—including activities of the mafia and other international crime organizations—which *could* have been connected to the events in Dallas in November 1963. Even the family of slain South Vietnamese dictator Ngo Dinh Diem—who was killed in a coup sanctioned by JFK in early November 1963—has been named in more than one scenario as being linked to—even ordering—the Kennedy assassination three weeks later. Lyndon Johnson once told Richard Helms of the CIA that he thought there was a connection between JFK's death and the Diem assassination three weeks earlier.[30] Any single group or combination of groups—including such oft-cited "suspects" as pro- or anti-Castro Cubans, rogue CIA agents, disgruntled former contract agents, possible "Manchurian Candidate"—style programmed assassins, or Texas oil men and their associates—suggested in the film *Executive Action* (1973, David Miller) could have been connected to the assassination of John F. Kennedy. The screenplay of *JFK* itself suggests a central enigma about the event when it has David Ferrie (Joe Pesci) claim that "not even the *shooters* know"—or would need to know. Given such a range of possibilities, Stone ought to be forgiven for whatever artistic excesses still remain in his striking film.

One heavily criticized dimension of Stone's *JFK* is the linking of the homosexual underworld of New Orleans to the assassination through Clay Shaw, David Ferrie, and a fictionalized composite of gays represented by Willie O' Keefe (Kevin Bacon). The following comment is typical: "*JFK* is its own evidence for homosexual panic. . . . Gayness itself is *JFK*'s evidence of conspiracy."[31] Though no critics seemed to want to deal with possible revelatory aspects of this theme—accusing Stone of contributing to the worst public fears and stereotypes concerning homosexuals—there is one aspect of this politically incorrect theme that might bear closer scrutiny. While the images may appear offensive to many, the gay underworld in the film can be said to function metaphorically, representing a secret world analogous to the clandestine world of intelligence and covert action politics out of which the JFK assassination probably developed.

If, as the character Davie Ferrie suggests, "We're through the looking glass here . . . a mystery wrapped in a riddle inside an enigma," where are we after *JFK*? Stone's film asks us to confront the dark realities of our own national past. In doing so, *JFK* has performed a valuable service, constituting a socially significant, symbolic political act and keeping alive for yet another generation the quest for answers to the enduring mystery surrounding the death of a president—the truth about, and the ultimate meaning of, those seven seconds in Dallas.[32]

### *The Public View*

Supposedly manipulated and controlled by mass media and, according to numerous conspiracy thinkers and elite theorists, consistently lied to for over fifty years by various administrations, it is remarkable that the American public for so many years has been able to summon the independence of mind to maintain such a critical and oppositional stance on the question of the Kennedy assassination. According to political scientist Sheldon Appleton, this widespread belief in a conspiracy reflects "a political world view which sees the government as failing to provide its citizens with help they feel they need to cope with the problems of modern life."[33] Indeed, numerous surveys in recent decades reveal a marked—and deepening—cynicism about public participation in government and a feeling by many that the latter is more responsive to the needs of the upper classes than working- and middle-class citizens.

Given such a perceived lack of responsiveness on the part of government, it follows from the opinion data that most people think government simply

> cannot be trusted to tell the truth about major political events like the Kennedy (and Martin Luther King Jr.) assassinations. The same small group of powerful people who seem to control that government may well have decided to take action to cut down those who, like Kennedy, seem in retrospect to have been willing to act in the interests of the average American.[34]

Given the fact that for over thirty years three-quarters to four-fifths of the U.S. population have viewed *both* the JFK and Martin Luther King Jr. assassinations as the products of conspiracies, the high level of cynicism and powerlessness connoted by such belief suggests that an absolute majority of the population no longer believes it lives in a democratic system. Aside from the JFK assassination, some of the other sources contributing to modern conspiracy thinking and theorizing lie in events that conventional history and political science have never adequately investigated or resolved. Within a five-year period in the 1960s one president (JFK), a probable future president (RFK), and the two most important black leaders since World War II (Malcolm X and Martin Luther King Jr.) were victims of assassinations.[35] One reason such conspiracy theories are so compelling is the fact that they *seem* to clarify very complex, ambiguous historical and social situations, forces, and events.

The more one studies such events, the less plausible one finds the standard stories and official explanations. In this sense, the more one knows, the less one seems to know, for the knowledge one amasses becomes "dangerous knowledge"—both to the existing order and one's own sense of what one can know.

## Conspiracy Thinking and the Political Unconscious

Fredric Jameson has postulated the existence of a "political unconscious" evident in a diverse variety of social texts. If every film and television text representing conspiracy is, at its most fundamental level, representative of the Jungian "visionary," part of a political unconscious, such texts are also manifestations of underlying *collective* perceptions of the nature of contemporary citizenship.[36] Not only do the majority of citizens no longer vote, but the National Election Studies and other opinion data strongly suggest that most have lost a real sense of personal agency or efficacy and find themselves unable to conceive of social alternatives.

A process of circular causation has been at work for nearly forty years, which becomes evident as one traces the relations and political psychology of a number of social groups and the textual manifestations of their unconscious political thinking in the large number of texts devoted to conspiracy in popular media culture. Such trends have become part of everyday discourse in American society.[37] Television documentaries treat the phenomenon.[38] Many books on the subject provide overviews which sympathetically and intelligently review the various theories, seeking to determine factual elements and underreported aspects of virtually any plot or conspiracy.[39] Throughout the 1990s—and into the new century—there were proliferating conspiracy sites on the Web. One could ask any Internet search engine to look for "Conspiracies" or "Assassinations" and spend days tracing out the connections; some of these even provided "do-it-yourself" conspiracy construction options, offering to list any plausible plot one could suggest that was not already included. Academic conferences as well as a research center[40] also mushroomed.

Conspiracy discourses also appeared in popular novels (and movies based on them), such as John Grisham's *The Firm* and *The Pelican Brief.* They also surfaced in film biographies such as *Hoffa* (1992, Danny DeVito); *Ruby* (1992, John Mackenzie); and *Nixon* (1995, Oliver Stone), as well as Clint Eastwood's *Absolute Power* (1997) and *Conspiracy Theory* (1997, Richard Donner). The latter almost playfully skirted the very real issues posed by the CIA MKULTRA program, which was designed to produce a programmed assassin through drugs and conditioning, issues explored in depth in two book-length studies.[41]

### *THE X-FILES*

Coextensive with such developments was the growth to cult status of the Fox network's *The X-Files,* as well as clones such as NBC's *Dark Skies.* The central premise of the latter was the attempt by extraterrestrials to implant alien larvae in humans, as well as a secret military agency called MAJESTIC.[42]

*The X-Files,* which began in 1993, was the most distinctive of such television series, generating numerous books, scholarly articles, and websites. At one level, the program was essentially a pastiche or parody of virtually every alleged and fantasized notion of government, corporate, criminal, and/or extraterrestrial conspiracy that has arisen during the past fifty years. The series is unique for its carefully controlled, intelligently written characterization and engagingly unconventional central protagonists, FBI agents Fox Mulder (David Duchovny, whose departure at the end of the 2000/2001 season made these qualities appear less apparent) and Dana Scully (Gillian Anderson).[43] Their characters violate and reverse cultural stereotypes of male rationality and female emotionality. Beyond that, over the years both seem to have developed complex personal varieties of spiritual insight or even mysticism, Scully from her Catholic upbringing combined with her training as a doctor and an extensive scientific education that knows its philosophical limits. The latter are evident in one episode, which aired during the third season, entitled "Revelations," in which a small boy who has blood welling out of his hands and side prompts Scully to go to confession for the first time in years, telling the priest she is most afraid that "God really may be speaking. And no one's listening." Mulder, known as "Spooky" in the Bureau, has a degree in psychology from Oxford University and a mystical obsession with the unknown, as revealed in the "X," or unsolved, FBI case files.

Neither Mulder nor Scully fit cultural stereotypes of the authoritarian-submissive FBI agents of the Hoover era. Orders from their superiors are routinely evaded or ignored. Over the years, Scully witnesses Mulder's often bizarre hypotheses and provides backup—if her cellphone is on and functioning. (The series relies so heavily on this form of communication that it would have been impossible to develop the complex and intimate relationship existing between them prior to its invention.) A complex sexual-spiritual chemistry exists between the two. It is as if they were members of some religious order or cult, or comrades in a radical political sect. Transcending any common notions of sexual attraction or love, it is quite unlike anything in the history of popular entertainment.

*The X-Files* combines a distinctively postmodern amalgam of elements of the occult, horror films, and political conspiracy thrillers. Story "arcs" involve alien abductions and UFOs, possible alien colonization of Earth, cold war conspiracies, and government cover-ups of virtually everything connected with such plot elements. All these elements, combined with a dark visual look and elaborate production values, helped to make it a popular culture cult item.

### *Visual Images of Government and Political Conspiracy*

*The X-Files* features images of government activity unlike anything in the history of television. These images enhance the undercurrent of paranoia sustaining the series through a dark, neo-noir "look": wet, slick streets; night-for-night photography; and the use of artificial light such as dimly lit interiors; flashlights; and characters dressed in dark colors. These are all standard elements of color film noir and horror films of the past thirty-five years. There is an obvious visual and thematic debt to Alan Pakula'a *All the President's Men* (1976)—characters bear names like "Deep Throat"—as well as to other conspiracy films from the 1970s. A playfully respectful use of such elements makes their use much more of an homage than simply a borrowing. (Charles Cioffi—the psychokiller executive Peter Cable in *Klute* (1971, Alan J. Pakula) and Ray Tower in *Missing* (1982, Costa Gavras)—was cast in the pilot episode as a high FBI official who recruits Dana Scully to monitor Fox Mulder.) Frequent settings in garages and basements—central images of the Watergate era and its films—draws one (at least in the explicitly political episodes) back into the paranoia and suspicion of power of that era.

*Conspiracy and the Cigarette-Smoking Man*

Fifty years of domestic political conspiracy theories and speculations converged during the fourth season of *The X-Files* in an episode entitled "Musings of a Cigarette-Smoking Man." The Cigarette-Smoking Man (CSM) plays a crucial role in the mythology of the series, appearing whenever the story arc concerns matters of national security. He is the embodiment of all the men-in-black of the past half century. William B. Davis, who plays the CSM, has argued in interviews that he is the real "hero" of the whole series, a claim the series leads would find hard to admit. Although the CSM has few lines, metaphorically he represents all the secret U.S. operatives of the cold war and after.

First broadcast November 17, 1996, just prior to the thirty-third anniversary of the JFK assassination, this historical overview begins in 1996 (the then present) but flashes back to October 30, 1962, just after the Cuban Missile Crisis. In this episode Scully and Mulder do not appear on camera until the final ten minutes. (According to the character biographies established for the show, Scully was not yet born and Mulder was just a baby.) Their voices are heard at the outset, prior to the first flashback, as they are spied on by the CSM by means of surveillance microphones. The program is in four parts.

Part 1, which bears the title "Things Really Did Go Well in Dealy Plaza," opens with a close-up, floor-level image of a rat scurrying across the floor of what appears to be an abandoned warehouse. From the same menacing low angle appear first the feet and then the familiar face of actor William B. Davis, known as the CSM, who is eavesdropping electronically on a conversation across an alley in the office of the "Lone Gunmen" (the trio of computer geeks/nerds and assassination buffs who regularly though unofficially aid Mulder and Scully). In the office/workshop of the Lone Gunmen, Scully and Mulder are listening as Frohike (Tom Braidwood)—the oldest of the three, who lusts after Scully—relates through historical flashbacks the secret past of the CSM.

We are at the Center for Special Warfare, Fort Bragg, North Carolina, where the young CSM is an Army captain. It is October 30, 1962, just after the Cuban Missile Crisis. The plot fills in his background: his mother died of lung cancer and his father was a convicted Communist spy, supposedly electrocuted in a Louisiana prison. In hazy scenes meant to convey the historical past, members of a secret right-wing group within the military and government are interviewing the young CSM, reviewing his extended résumé/rap sheet of covert action, including his connections to the assassinations of Patrice Lumumba in the Congo and Rafael Trujillo in the Dominican Republic (now documented as having significant CIA involvement).[44] After flatly and convincingly denying his participation in any such activities (as he was trained to do), he is given the first of his history-making assignments: the assassination of a forty-six-year-old man, a World War II PT boat commander (obviously JFK, though the name is never spoken). Next, Mulder's father is shown in conversation with the CSM in their barracks, remarking that his young son, Fox, has just uttered his first word: "JFK." (Later in the episode the CSM ponders a snapshot of Mulder's mother holding her—and possibly his—young son.)

Realistically and believably filmed in Dallas at the Texas School Book Depository building and Dealy Plaza, the rest of this episode effectively plays off of Oliver Stone's recreation of the assassination scene in his 1991 film *JFK*, but with new and added twists: the young CSM (operating under the name Mr. Hunt, an obviously allusion to E. Howard Hunt of CIA and Watergate burglary notoriety who, some suggest, had connections to the events in Dallas) is the handler of the frontman/patsy—clearly meant to be accused assassin Lee Harvey Oswald, since his rooming house is identified on screen as Oswald's Rooming House and he is addressed as "Lee." However, it is Hunt who is portrayed as the actual assassin and "second gun."

Shown entering Dealy Plaza from the drainage outlet emptying into the Trinity River, the CSM fires from a street-level gutter opening, delivering the explosive frontal head shot that killed the president. The series here develops one of the engaging subplots of the JFK assassination, namely the search for locations where alternative assassins might have been located.[45] In addition to the incorporation of this minor subplot, the episode features an actor portraying Lee Harvey Oswald shown fleeing the Book Depository and heading to his rooming house, where he retrieves his handgun, affirming loudly and vehemently to himself, "I won't be a patsy!" After shooting a police officer who stops him, he is arrested at the Texas Theatre, where Mr. Hunt said he would be going to see a movie (and where they were supposed to meet).

Part 2 is entitled "Just Down the Road Aways from Graceland." It is early 1968. Martin Luther King Jr.'s voice is simulated by an actor in the background. The CSM has obviously gained tremendously in stature and influence, making disparaging comments to an actor portraying J. Edgar Hoover and ridiculing the FBI surveillance of the civil rights leader and the FBI-crafted letter urging King to take his own life. At a meeting with Hoover he and several others agree that the situation requires King's "elimination." The CSM says he will do it himself but will need "a cracker patsy" (meaning alleged assassin James Earl Ray)."

Adding to the verisimilitude, this section, like the one in Dallas, appears to have been filmed in Memphis, first at the church at which King delivered his last speech and then at the rooming house where James Earl Ray resided and in front of which he supposedly ditched the assassination weapon. The Ray character is shown presenting the CSM with the rifle he ordered Ray to purchase, being given money, and then being ordered out of the room to "take in a movie," leaving the CSM free to do the shooting alone and unobserved. The CSM thus fits all the particulars of the alleged mastermind of the King assassination who—James Earl Ray claimed until his death in 1998—was a man he knew only as "Raul" or "Raoul." (Later in the episode viewers discover that Raul Bloodworth is the mystery-writing pen name of the CSM). Taking a position in the bushes behind the rooming house—a position favored by some alternative scenarios of the King assassination which suggest someone other than James Earl Ray did the shooting—the CSM delivers the fatal shot to King. After King's death he is shown watching Robert F. Kennedy's speech following King's death.[46] In the speech RFK quotes from Aeschylus: "In our sleep pain which cannot forget falls drop by drop upon the heart until, in our own despair, against our will, comes wisdom through the awful grace of God." The CSM picks up the quote exactly, silently mouthing the words, as if they also expressed his own understanding of his life.

Through all this, the CSM has his own dream. Like many of the figures of the 1960s and '70s (such as ex-CIA agent and later White House "plumber" E. Howard Hunt) who wrote spy novels and political thrillers, he wants to be a published author, but he gets nothing but rejections—many scathing in their disparagement of his writing abilities.

Part 3, entitled "The Most Wonderful Time of the Year," is set in Washington, D.C., just before Christmas 1991. The CSM discusses with his secret group of operatives the events he has supposedly covertly stagemanaged: assassinations; the Anita Hill case; rigged elections; manipulation of the Academy Awards and the Olympic hockey match (by secretly drugging the Russian goalie); fixing it so the Buffalo Bills will never win the Super Bowl; and moving the Rodney King beating trial to Simi Valley. Then a newsflash reveals that Gorbachev has resigned, ending the Cold War. For all his powers to manipulate events, the CSM remains a desolate and isolated man with no family, who cannot get his novels published.

In Part 4, entitled "The X-Files," the CSM is with Deep Throat (Jerry Hardin), who appeared in earlier episodes of the series. An alien spacecraft has crashed and an alien being has survived. The CSM and Deep Throat argue over who will execute the alien. They flip a coin. Deep Throat enters the sealed chamber where the alien is on life support and shoots it several times with his handgun.

The CSM now has a new purpose: he has a vast range of conspiracies and plots to conceal. Mulder and Scully enter the story. The CSM is glimpsed in the background as Charles Cioffi interviews Scully in order to recruit her to develop written "reports" on Mulder and his exploration of the X-Files. Scully and Mulder unknowingly become part of the CSM's plans.

Finally we are in the present. A magazine has accepted one of the CSM's stories. As Raul Bloodworth he has become a published author. Jubilant, he types his letter of resignation. Upon rushing out to buy a copy of the publication, he discovers it is a sleazy "girlie" magazine. To make matters worse, the editors have changed the ending of his story. Embittered, his dreams of literary fame dashed, he sits on a park bench musing how life is "like a box of chocolates. A cheap, perfunctory gift that nobody asks for. When it is gone all you've got is an empty box filled with brown paper wrappers." A filthy and aged street person of indefinable gender appears, picks a candy box out of the garbage, sits next to him, and eats the remaining candies. The CSM lights up another cigarette, back in character. The final moments return to the beginning of the episode.

This episode sums up the political conspiratorial "arc" of the series as well as the hidden history of the United States in the cold war era. The CSM, arguably—and certainly metaphorically—represents the secret operatives of the U.S. national security state who were asked to carry out (and willingly performed) tasks. In the words of the once secret Doolittle Committee report[47] to the Hoover Commission in 1954:

> It is now clear we are facing an implacable enemy whose avowed objective is world domination by whatever means and at whatever cost. There are no rules in such a game. Hitherto acceptable norms of human conduct do not apply. If the United States is to survive, long-standing American concepts of "fair play" must be reconsidered. We must develop effective espionage and counterespionage services and must learn to subvert, sabotage and destroy our enemies by more clever, more sophisticated, and more effective methods than those used against us. It may become necessary that the American people be made acquainted with, understand and support this fundamentally repugnant philosophy.[48]

From this passage it is evident that at the same time the U.S. Senate was censuring Senator Joseph McCarthy for his overzealous pursuit of alleged communists, a more influential, though secret, power center within the national executive was advocating and essentially condoning *whatever means were deemed necessary* in the long-term struggle with the national enemy, however the latter was defined. There were no ground rules. Anything—any technique, any weapon—was acceptable.[49]

Although *The X-Files,* like much of the conspiracy mania of the late 1990s and early twenty-first century, was fashionable, the series presented a serious, though sometimes playful, examination of the unexplained or repressed aspects of U.S. politics and culture during the past half century, beginning with the National Security Act of 1947 and the Roswell incident of the same year.[50] Its importance lies in its visionary and revelatory insights into collectively felt public fears of a hidden history, of darker secrets. The series thus tapped deeper elements of popular psychology, complementing and reflecting both widespread anxieties and hopes for something beyond our materialistic consumer society. The hope for life and life forms beyond what is immediately apparent is echoed in the following comment by Mulder in one *X-Files* episode: "Perhaps the belief in otherworldly mysteries gives me some hope."[51]

## New Technologies and New Forms of Paranoia in a New Century

Another emerging impulse that stimulated paranoid visions lay in a new politics of illusion. Here paranoia was engendered by a media-fashioned "reality." The recognition that all we know and see is a product—a media construction—or even mere simulations of reality created by computer programs explains the appeal of such millennium-end films as *Wag the Dog* (1997, Barry Levinson), *The Game* (1997, David Fincher), *The Truman Show* (1998, Peter Weir), *Dark City* (1998, Alex Proyas), *The Matrix* (1999, Wachowski Brothers), *The Thirteenth Floor* (1999, Josef Rusnak), *Pleasantville* (1998, Gary Ross), *Enemy of the State* (1998, Tony Scott), or *Ed Tv* (1999, Ron Howard). This variety of political paranoia arguably has less to do with traditional bases of political anxiety than with public fears that movie images and techniques, carried over into politics and news, would now mean that seeing is no longer believing. "Reality" may simply be a construct.[52]

*Wag the Dog,* Barry Levinson's timely 1997 essay on the politics of simulation and media image manipulation quickly entered everyday political discourse. It features Robert De Niro as Conrad Brean, a kind of political fixer/media mastermind who, the plot suggests, can command a small army of "men in black" to kill anyone who reveals the truth about his constructed "pageants." Dustin Hoffman plays Stanley Motss, a fictional Hollywood producer, modeled on such men as Ray Stark and Robert Evans, hired to make the president—a thinly disguised version of Bill Clinton—survive allegations of sexual abuse of a teenage girl visiting the White House. Brean and Motss do so by attempting to stage a "war" with Albania. When that fails, they try to concoct a phony war hero—obviously modeled upon airman Scott O'Grady, who became a public hero after his rescue from Bosnia in 1995. Based very loosely on Larry Beinhart's satirical novel *American Hero* (1994)—which suggested that the 1991 Persian Gulf War was largely a staged media event—*Wag the Dog* cynically illustrates how political illusion makers could hoodwink a public only dimly aware of distant events and totally dependent on television news reports for knowledge of events. During the last years of the Clinton administration, members of Congress routinely mentioned the film in speeches, wondering if military actions by the Clinton White House were simply intended to divert public opinion from the president's sexual peccadilloes and subsequent impeachment woes. Based on several well-researched reports, the purported retaliatory U.S. bombing of a chemical and pharmaceuticals plant in Sudan in 1998 had no justification other than symbolic diversion. During the NATO bombing of Yugoslavia in the spring of 1999, *Wag the Dog* was routinely played on Belgrade television; earlier it was shown on Iraqi television during U.S. bombing raids. Everybody was in on the joke—though for the ordinary citizens of Serbia and Iraq who experienced the "collateral damage" it was rarely funny.

Films produced at the end of the millennium presented audiences with heightened forms of "cinematic unreality" qualitatively and significantly different from traditional pictures crafted by cinematic illusion makers.[53] The simulation by computers of events, situations, or environments was so unnerving that it helped stimulate a more generalized paranoia and a pervasive cynicism.

If earlier visionary paranoia raised questions of "who" could be trusted, viewers now had to consider whether their most basic senses could be trusted. Historically, this was not a radically new phenomenon. The emergence of propaganda techniques on a grand scale began in the United States with the creation in 1917 by President Woodrow Wilson of the Committee on Public Information (CPI)[54] under the leadership of journalist George Creel. Blending advertising techniques and a sophisticated understanding of psychology, its efforts probably represent the first instance of a modern government's dissemination of propaganda on a large scale. It emerged in an ostensibly "democratic" state. Invoking the supposed dangers posed by German propaganda, the committee implemented "voluntary" guidelines for the news media and contributed to the atmosphere that led to the creation of the Espionage Act of 1917 and the Sedition Act of 1918. Very much like modern reporters who participate in Pentagon-managed press pools, journalists of the time had to comply with official guidelines to stay connected to the information loop.

### ***THE TRUMAN SHOW*** **(PETER WEIR)**

Peter Weir's 1998 film, with a screenplay by Andrew Niccol, delivers a pointed, often satirical commentary on the ersatz reality the mass public has, through its viewing choices spanning half a century of commercial television, symbiotically created—aided, of course, by those who measure audience size and preferences and then program television content to maximize the number of viewers. The film's antecedents are many, including legendary sci-fi writer Richard Matheson's *I Am Legend* (1954), in which only one man remains on earth not affected by the bacterium causing vampirism. The novel was adapted for Boris Sagal's film *The Omega Man* (1971), with Charleton Heston as the last non-vampire man. It was also obviously a source of the quintessential modern horror film *Night of the Living Dead* (1968, George Romero), in which flesh-eating zombies besiege a rural farmhouse. Matheson's novel expressed the ultimate paranoia of a single individual facing a world of vampires. His *Twilight Zone* teleplay "A World of Difference" featured Howard Duff as a businessman who comes to perceive that his office is really a movie set and that he is only an actor. Even his home and wife are contrivances. The point, seemingly, is that life is an imposed illusion, that people are deluded into thinking they are more than actors on a stage.

Other precursors include Paul Bartel's 1966 short film *Secret Cinema,* in which a young woman begins to suspect her associates are making a film of her life to be shown at a theater on weekends. Even her shrink is in on it, serving as the producer of the secret movie.[55] This plot seems directly inspired by Freud's interpretive 1931 essay on female paranoia, where he describes the supposed delusions of a female paranoiac who believed her lover was secretly photographing their sexual liaisons.[56] One critic has noted the resemblance of the film to Robert Heinlein's story "They" (1941), a paranoid fantasy in which a patient in an asylum believes—correctly, according to the story—that virtually everything that happens in the world is staged for his benefit. According to the same critic, the second half of the film seems to echo Frederik Pohl's satirical story "The Tunnel Under the World" (1954), in which the central character finds the town he has been living in is really a site for testing ads.[57] Bill Moyers' 1989 PBS series *The Public Mind* provided a detailed account of an actual American city in which a sample of television viewers participated in a study in which the content of everything they watched on television was linked to their grocery purchases. The literary and social-psychological antecedents of Truman's fears seem endless.

*The Truman Show* is thus only the latest in a long line of representations of paranoia, media criticism, and media satire. Here an individual discovers that for the past thirty years he has been living a totally confected, false "reality." The film presents a solipsistic view in which the viewer is asked to identify with the one "true" person in a constructed world where everyone else is in on the deception. In this case the paranoia is really heightened awareness. *The Truman Show* could be seen as a kind of perverse inversion of *Citizen Kane*, as Truman attempts to discover the true nature of the world around him, just as viewers and the investigator in Welles' film engage in deconstructing the public man Kane.

With so many sources and antecedents,[58] one could legitimately ask whether *The Truman Show* was really much of a revelation or whether it simply tried to play off the market created by social awareness of the self-absorption of an upper-middle-class culture in which a significant and growing minority seemed to care mostly about themselves in their frenzied fever of overconsumption and overcommitment. Even if the film significantly represents baby boomer solipsism, its attempted revelatory qualities place it within a distinguished line of literary and filmic explorations of truth and reality.

Truman Burbank (Jim Carrey), prompted by a stage light that falls out from the "sky," slowly realizes that he and everyone and everything in his world are constructions and—in a classic paranoid delusion that in this case proves true (as viewers and eventually Truman himself come to see)—that everything in it is directed at him alone. The first aspect of his realization forms part of a long tradition going back to Plato's classic allegory of the cave in his *Republic*. Reflecting a fundamental philosophical view concerning the nature of reality and the limits of the human mind, the cave allegory anticipated the world of mass-media image construction and—more recent still—the world of computer-generated images.

Focusing on a particular individual who unknowingly plays a role in a television program supposedly watched by millions, the film is a fiction in which only the central character remains unaware. A bizarre parable straining credulity, it still speaks to a society (the United States at the end of the millennium) addicted to mass-mediated "information," both cynically critiquing that society yet also attempting to entertain its mass audience. Like serious (clinical) paranoia, the truer it is, the less humorous and the more terrifying it seems. The film's theme is nothing less than an exploration of "reality"—of who creates and controls it.

Ed Harris portrays Christof, the master creator/manipulator/producer-director. While echoing the self-promoting performance artist Christo, the name's religious associations and the absolute power of the character seem obvious: he symbolizes the godlike figures of our society. Aside from objections arising out of well-conceived Judeo-Christian moral strictures against representing the unrepresentable,[59] there is a more general metaphorical utility of such an image: Christof represents the "high priests" of media, entertainment, government, and politics—like Stanley Motss (Dustin Hoffman) and Conrad Brean (Robert De Niro) in *Wag the Dog,* or even the less omnipotent NSA official portrayed by Jon Voight in *Enemy of the State*—who, like Plato's guardians and their auxiliaries, create images (television programs, in the particular case of *The Truman Show)* for a mass audience. The programs created must have enough appeal to keep the audience glued to their screens so they see the nearly one-third of on-air time devoted to commercial messages.

One could thus view the entire film as a metaphor for the various ways capitalist media culture seeks to mold and exploit each personality in its symbiotic war of greed to hold and control its audience[60] with programs that, ironically, also present what the majority of viewers secretly want to see. In *The Truman Show,* however, the "commercials" are built right into the story through numerous artfully conceived and positioned product placements. (In Ron Howard's less successful populist inversion of some of the themes in *Ed Tv* (1999), the commercial messages run continuously in a banner along the bottom of the screen.)

Sometimes what is thought to be paranoia is really heightened awareness. *The Truman Show* uses classic themes usually associated with paranoia in almost pleasurable ways to which anybody can effectively relate. The paranoiac, as a meticulous metaphysician, finds everything a clue, empirical data potentially confirming the plot in which he or she is enmeshed, confirming intimations that outside forces—indeed, the social-political order itself—are malevolently concentrating their efforts against the victim.[61]

In *The Truman Show* a certain pleasure can be derived from the way in which Truman's community, with apparently benign ingenuousness, sees to all his needs: arranging traffic to conform to his whims; composing newspaper headlines that respond to his perceived bewilderment; discouraging his travel; diligently accommodating his desires for friendship, love, and (off-camera) sex. His "wife" (Laura Linney) is—for perhaps the first time in a major Hollywood production—essentially an actor-prostitute who can step out of her character long enough to ask the producer for more money.

At other times the film is quite terrifying, a real postmodern horror tale resembling *Invasion of the Body Snatchers*—particularly in the nighttime scenes in which long lines of his "neighbors" search for Truman, arms locked together, marching through the dark and calling out his name—echoing real fascist brownshirts or filmic alien invaders. Here the initially clever paranoia of the film becomes palpable and truly visionary in its expression of the "psychic dread" one individual begins to experience as he questions the order and reality of his world.[62]

Proceeding into ever deeper circles of a kind of media hell, *The Truman Show* and Truman's hometown, Seahaven, begins to resemble "The Village" in the classic TV series *The Prisoner.* Patrick McGoohan played "Number 6," a former British intelligence agent held captive in an idyllic seaside resort. The series was viewed by many as a parable about the real political status of a freedom-seeking individual who, seeking to opt out of worldly and absurd conflicts, found he could never truly be free—nor ever know why.

*The Prisoner,* justifiably regarded as among the most engaging and mystifying dramatic series ever broadcast on network television, is not even surpassed by *The X-Files* in terms of its impenetrable enigmas. By contrast, Truman Burbank, while also a prisoner, is an insurance salesman, rather than a secret agent, possessing no important or classified information. He is a valuable commodity with which viewers are expected to identify. Are they thus being asked to laugh at themselves? *The Truman Show,* like *Wag the Dog,* reflects a kind of sneering, condescending elitism that is duplicitous in suggesting that the public as portrayed is both gullible and—as an audience to which such films are directed—very intelligent for watching and somehow being in on the joke. One critic has pointed to the curious double standard that has become an industry staple: "[T]o suggest simultaneously that the audience inside the movie is a pack of blithering idiots and that the audience outside—the one watching *The Truman Show*—is a cultivated community of media-savvy individuals that knows what's real and what's bogus."[63]

After smashing his sailboat into a concrete wall painted to look like the sky, Truman can—once he finds it—choose to leave his constructed phony world through the door in the wall. The more nightmarish reality, however, is that for the rest of us there is no way out since we depend for our information about the known world on centralized mass media. One critic has suggested that *The Truman Show* "expresses a powerful nostalgia for an age in which the all-powerful auteur actually created things, in real time and real space, film sets as big as the world they portrayed: a rather more romantic image than that of the film maker as bureaucrat, overseeing hordes of workstation-bound programmers."[64]

A still more terrifying choice for Truman and viewers both within the television world portrayed in the film and in movie theaters would have been for him to remain in his artificial world. At least he would have been "one of us." The legitimate premise of the film might even have had greater impact: the shock and internal crisis experienced by a person seeing for the first time the world as it is—and seeing through it. Uncovering a fake world comprised of fake people and scripted events is not delusional paranoia but the beginning of knowledge. The filmic devices of contrived and illusional paranoia thus become truly visionary, illuminating the human condition through a dystopian vista not, as Max Weber nightmarishly projected, of a world of total bureaucratization, "a polar night of icy darkness and hardness,"[65] but of an endless series of contrived *spectacles*—whether of Orwellian one-way imposed images devastatingly descried by Guy Debord in the 1960s[66] or the burgeoning pseudoparticipatory interactivity of expanding TV cable and satellite companies, the Internet, Web TV, and the ever-faster personal computer. We have more channels, but has there actually been an increase in genuine choices? Given the increasing rapidity of media corporate mergers, maybe it *is* a conspiracy in which we are all increasingly in the position of Truman Burbank.

## The Total-Surveillance Society and the End of Citizenship

### *ENEMY OF THE STATE* (TONY SCOTT)

This 1998 film presents a view of contemporary citizenship where society is fully capable of complete remote electronic surveillance and manipulation of any database, where nothing is left of genuinely private life. Will Smith plays Robert Clayton Dean, a rising Washington, D.C., labor attorney who inadvertently finds himself in the middle of a frantic search for a digital-tape record of an assassination passed to him without his knowledge. Dean's wife, Carla (Regina King), who is also a lawyer, is much more concerned with civil liberties and is troubled by a new piece of legislation coming up for a vote in Congress that would give the National Security Agency (NSA) the license to undertake surveillance of virtually anyone, using whatever advanced electronic circuitry and equipment it wishes.

The film suggests that an unscrupulous NSA official named Thomas Reynolds (Jon Voight) would—and could—have a U.S. congressman (Jason Robards) killed by his agents for opposing the legislation backed by NSA. Symptomatic of the ubiquity of information collection in this surveillance society, a digital camera set up to study duck migration captures the assassination. The naturalist who finds the event on his digital tape is observed by a NSA informant and eliminated by men-in-black—having just enough time to make a copy of the disk and drop it in former classmate Dean's bag in a chic lingerie store, where he was shopping for a Christmas gift for his wife. Through detailed analysis of images on the store's ubiquitous surveillance camera, NSA knows Dean has the tape, although he doesn't suspect anything until much later. He suddenly becomes the object of an intense search without understanding why. His whole life begins to crumble under Voight's surveillance: his credit cards are canceled; his wife gets anonymous reports he's having an affair;

and he loses his job. The alleged affair is with beautiful Rachel Banks (Lisa Bonet), a former girlfriend who arranges electronic surveillance of clients for Dean, carried out by someone named Brill (Gene Hackman), a brilliant, crusty, reclusive "screw you" kind of ex-NSA electronic-surveillance specialist. Brill (intentionally) looks just like the Harry Caul character he played in Francis Ford Coppola's 1974 film *The Conversation.* (He even has a studio in an old warehouse that appears to be an updated version of his old lab.) Here he has conquered all the moral anguish and ambivalences that so paralyzed him in the earlier film; he's like Harry Caul on speed. Operating in a kind of paranoid warp speed, he knows precisely what "they" can do to a person and what to do to combat them. Using twenty-five years of underground electronics lore and handyman skills, he directs Dean's astute electronic guerrilla counterattack.

*Enemy of the State* is high-tech Orwell for the twenty-first century. It feeds off the paranoia and fear the total surveillance society now makes possible. Moving at a frenetically kinetic pace, it makes use of multiple jump cuts, time-lapse surveillance camera and satellite photos, and dizzying camera angles and perspectives to heighten the edginess to the point where one can barely follow the film's complex narrative, which has Dean victimized by remote electronic manipulations of relevant databases, much like Sandra Bullock's character experienced in *The Net* (1995, Irwin Winkler) and Michael Douglas's character in *The Game* (1997, David Fincher), though in the latter case the central character fails to inspire much viewer identification, whereas one cares about Dean and his family.

The film demonstrates how *anyone* can fall victim to a nightmarish application of available technology and information networks. The ability to track anyone, whether by a "big brother" government or the security operatives in the private sector, currently exists. Electronic eavesdropping is everywhere, we are all under constant satellite surveillance, and our computers can easily be hacked into. In 1999 it was revealed that special access codes for use by the NSA have secretly been built into all versions of the Windows operating system.[67] While the government and the private sector possess the technology and the techniques, it is those—in government and outside—who would use such means for their own particular ends that the film sees as the primary problem. But the threat is even greater. Reynolds, the rogue NSA administrator, is ruthless, yet he is acting in his own interest to get the communications bill passed to advance his career. The ruthless violence of the NSA agents is not as absurd as some critics have suggested. The agents are simply doing their jobs, just following orders, using whatever level of force is required to get the "bad guys." The victims of Waco and Ruby Ridge know that only too well.

According to news reports on CNN, CBS's "60 Minutes," the American Civil Liberties Union website, and scores of other monitoring websites, Project

ECHELON—a massive electronic intercept system sponsored by the U.S. National Security Agency (NSA) and counterpart agencies in the United Kingdom, Australia, Canada, and New Zealand—scans *all* Internet traffic, faxes, cell-phone conversations, international long distance calls—virtually *all electronic communication in the world.* According to John Pike of the Federation of American Scientists (*www.fas.org*), they are looking for "thugs and drugs." However, most of what they are scanning are the private communications of ordinary individuals.

Using a filtering system that flags messages containing certain key words, ECHELON can process one million message inputs processed every thirty minutes. According to reports commissioned by the Scientific and Technological Options Assessment program—a research arm of the European Parliament—the system filters *everything,* selecting ten inputs out of a million for closer analysis.[68]

Because ECHELON is a highly classified operation, with no oversight by courts or legislative bodies, nobody knows precisely what is done with the information and how it is used. According to reports collected by the ACLU in the United States, ECHELON has been engaged in significant instances of invasion of privacy, including secret surveillance of such organizations as Amnesty International. It has also been engaged in industrial espionage, passing information to U.S. companies about their competitors, such as Airbus Industries. The most sensational of the revelations concerning ECHELON dealt with the late Princess Diana. According to *The Washington Post,* the NSA admitted it possessed files on the princess, including intercepted phone conversations. Although the Princess was not a "direct" target, the retention of files and the surveillance itself reflects the intrusive, completely surreptitious manner in which the ECHELON system operates.[69]

Information about ECHELON's activities is only one privacy concern, though it is a vivid indication that the paranoia represented in *Enemy of the State* is a rational reflection of real trends. The advertising for *Enemy of the State* contained the slogan "It's not paranoia if they are really after you." Revelations about ECHELON prove that "they" are after *everyone.* What is dismissed by some as paranoia, then, is often an intimation of a real threat, a justifiable, rational reflection of heightened awareness concerning our precarious state.

# Afterword

## New Political Possibilities in Film Culture

In the last four decades Americans have come to believe their government is not to be trusted. Back in 1958, most U.S. citizens felt their government was basically honest. When asked in national polls, "Do you think that quite a few of the people running the government are crooked, not very many, or do you think that hardly any of them are crooked?," only 24 percent responded "quite a few." The proportion of the public showing such distrust increased in the 1960s and '70s, leveling off in the 1980s but then reaching an all-time high in 1994, when an absolute majority (51 percent) of participants in a national survey responded "quite a few."[1]

An even more striking trend in U.S. public cynicism and distrust was evident in responses to the question, "Would you say that the government is pretty much run by a few big interests looking out for themselves, or that it is run for the benefit of all the people?" In 1964 only 29 percent saw the government as "run by a few big interests." The figure rose sharply in succeeding years until 1980, then leveled off, but by 1994 it had risen to an all-time high of 76 percent.[2] People also increasingly felt the government simply did not care about people like them. What do such responses suggest about public attitudes? How are such responses reflected in the audience or market for media images and narratives—in movies and television?

According to political scientist Ronald Inglehart, such opinion figures reflect the transformation of American society. The United States—along with most of the industrial democracies of the North Atlantic, Japan, New Zealand, and Australia—has entered a period of "postmaterialist values." No longer exclusively focused on economic well-being, citizens now apply new, increasingly critical, standards to their evaluation of the government and its officials. This has led to a decline in the basis of authority throughout the industrial, liberal democracies surveyed.[3] It seems particularly evident in the political culture of the United States.

Among an increasingly active minority, this decline reflects abhorrence of both past and more recent state policies, as well as a diminished sense of control before the ever-increasing power of globalizing corporations and the governments whose authority they diminish.

Into this postmaterialist atmosphere, the products of American media industries—the films discussed in the preceding chapters—have been projected. Conspiracy images and discourses in these films and television programs also play a role in shaping such public attitudes, though the process of influence and reflection is so circular that it is often difficult accurately to trace these paths of influence. At another level, such media texts might also reflect a collective—almost unconscious—search for *meaning* in a fragmented, postmodern mass culture. Against this postmaterialist, postmodern political-cultural background, what was once simply taken for granted—the sanctity and integrity of the individual personality—also seems increasingly in doubt. The very model of "personhood" and individuality has come into question—clearly anticipated by the existential anxiety evidenced by the central protagonists of the film noir cycle, as well as its extensions in more recent "neo" and "retro" varieties of noir films. The traditional, classically liberal view of the individual as a "rational, motivated agent with a protected interior core of beliefs, desires and memories"[4] now seems a relic of another age.

## Paranoia and the Postmodern Situation

If the postmodern period is marked by paranoia, at least in part this reflects a public crisis in epistemology regarding truth claims, the status of knowledge, and the determination of truth. It is now a commonplace that the contemporary postindustrial, post–cold war, post-Marxist, *postmodern* society has produced a continuing crisis over what is "real" and how "reality" is determined and authorized. The traditional division between historical (elite) memory and unhistorical—even ahistorical—(popular) memory has been increasingly displaced by the normalization of mass-mediated communication, simulation, and an avalanche of "information"—all of which is evident in the public's inability to discern—or perhaps even to care about—what is real and what is not. Part of this is a product of conscious corporate mystification and misdirection, playing into what Noam Chomsky and others correctly see as a tendency in current political culture to pay attention to everything but that which is fundamentally important—the transformation of an imperfect representative democracy into a system of corporate rule—though there are genuinely new dimensions to the process.

Moreover, in the "globalizing" world capitalist economy everyone watches American movies and television programs and eats American fast food. Such encroaching standardization of human experience paradoxically also diminishes emotional returns, with people wanting more and better *feelings* as a result of their consumption. According to one sociologist, "The homogeneity of rationalized settings seems to diminish our lives and leaves us craving some form of enchantment." Such efficient—perhaps overefficient—food-delivery systems as McDonalds, Wendy's, and Burger King have no room for anything smacking of uniqueness, novelty, or creativity. "Anything that is magical, mysterious, fantastic, dreamy . . . is apt to be inefficient." All such "cathedrals of consumption" will inevitably fail to satisfy.[5]

In their study of postmodern cinema, Carl Boggs and Thomas Pollard argue that media culture and mass consumption in general may be used by people to "re-enchant" their lives in a wider effort to make existence more satisfying and livable in this ruthlessly capitalist culture and society. They suggest, that "modes of hyper-consumption, available to broadening sectors of the population, function to soften the harsh and alienating features of advanced capitalist production and work, 're-enchanting' an economic system that people otherwise experience as oppressive."[6] Yet such efforts provide only an illusory, inauthentic satisfaction.

Some may find or seek re-enchantment in such mass sports spectacles as the World Series, the Super Bowl, or the NBA Finals, which provide serial goals and temporary, seasonal quests for meaning and significance. Still others may engage in an almost limitless consumption of commodities in an environmentally destructive postindustrial system of "consumer populism" that encourages shopping virtually as an end in itself, one in which consumers become only slightly more animated versions of the zombies lumbering though the shopping center in George Romero's *Dawn of the Dead* (1978). All participate in a system of production based on planned obsolescence, which encourages throwing away items whose repair often costs more than the initial purchase, or the disposal of anything functional but now "boring," no longer exciting or the very latest model.

For still others, enchantment may arise from gossip about the lives of stars and celebrities. By extension, for a significant and vocal minority a perverse form of enchantment might be found in a belief in conspiracy discourses. Perhaps for them a form of enchantment results from *not* feeling they can ever definitively, *officially* know what they overwhelmingly suspect they already do know, thereby deriving a form of satisfaction from knowing the denied, unadmitted, "inside" story, the underside of history.[7]

## COMPUTERS, THE INTERNET, AND VISIONS OF CONSPIRACY

The explosion of computer technology and the exponential growth of the Internet over the past decade are major contributing factors to the appeal of conspiracy theories and a broadening cultural paranoia. The increasing availability of cheaper, more sophisticated, yet easier to use computer technology has led to an increase in skeptical, suspicious—even truly delusional—screeds (often with supporting videos) now available on the Internet.[8] Such technological developments did not necessarily lead to an increase in conspiracy theories themselves, but they did enable those in circulation to reach a wider audience. No longer did one have to wait for mainstream periodicals to legitimize a story.[9] Ironically, such developments permitted important nonmainstream discourses to evade traditional media gatekeepers, permitting suppressed stories to reach a wider public.

On television, the quest for shrinking yet increasingly diverse audiences narrowed the gap between tabloid publications and network newsmagazines in recent years. For example, in 1992 the Gennifer Flowers story—involving her alleged long-term affair with then governor Bill Clinton of Arkansas, who was the Democratic candidate for president—moved rapidly from the supermarket tabloid *The Star* to the major networks as they tried to compete with the rapidly emerging cable tabloid-style news outlets.[10] (This story was followed by the Clinton-Lewinsky "zippergate" scandal, which occupied much of 1998 and 1999.) Another example concerned the charge by Pierre Salinger (JFK's former press secretary) that he had the inside story on the July 16, 1996 explosion and crash of TWA flight 800. At a press conference Salinger claimed he had "information" that *proved* the plane was shot down by an errant U.S. sea-based missile. The story, which was picked up by all the media within hours, apparently started on the Internet when Richard Russell, a retired United Airlines pilot and former crash investigator, sent e-mail messages to fewer than a dozen friends August 22, 1996, suggesting the possibility of a government coverup in the crash (or shooting down) of TWA flight 800. These messages, repeatedly recopied and resent on the Internet, acquired so much legitimacy that the story was described by FBI and U.S. Navy officials as an "outrageous allegation" in their daily briefings on the TWA 800 crash investigation. Such cases suggest that *circulation*—even in the form of denying a story as inaccurate—has become a functional form of legitimation.[11]

## The "Society of the Spectacle" and the Obliteration of History

Globalized television and the Internet have created new spheres of public involvement—"virtual" communities[12]—organized around various forms of simulation. Given the increased opportunities for manipulation of mass opinion through propaganda, such forces reflect the art of directed simulation and the propagation of illusion. This is essentially the same critique—made decades earlier by Guy Debord and the Situationists—of the "society of the *spectacle*." Here is how Debord enunciated his first thesis:

> The whole life of those societies in which modern conditions of production prevail presents itself as an immense accumulation of *spectacles*. All that once was directly lived has become mere *representation*. . . . Understood on its own terms, the spectacle proclaims the predominance of appearances and asserts that all human life, which is to say all social life, is mere *appearance*.[13]

This theory anticipates Jean Baudrillard's later views on emergent mass media as generating a world of simulation essentially immune to rational critique.[14] Baudrillard has argued that the media present and represent a superfluity of alleged information, thereby excluding the possibility of a meaningful response by recipients. Increasingly, the simulated reality created and presented has no referent, ground, or source but simply *is*. The public response seems to be passivity, a strategy involving silence and passive consumption. Such public disengagement—while simultaneously participating vicariously through watching the TV spectacle—makes obsolete traditional bases of politics based on class conflict or contending interests. Television news is a perfect example of such a new world of more information and less meaning. If, as Baudrillard suggests, television is simply a succession of surface images, of signifiers for the viewer to experience, then the latter will be unable to recall the previous day's news because there is nothing to recall but images.

What is today presented as "news" is largely a collection of images, a constructed, synthesized *hyper*reality. As most viewers experience it in the United States, the news involves a characteristic, postmodern *denial*—an easy and casual obliteration of history through constant reediting and sampling—in which history (the past) is reduced to a resource bank of images for easy reuse, collapsing everything into the present.[15] In this postmodern culture, Fredric Jameson has suggested, everyone confronts

> the disappearance of a sense of history, the way in which our entire contemporary social system has little by little begun to lose its capacity to retain its

own past, has begun to live in a perpetual present and in a perpetual change that obliterates traditions of the kind which all earlier social formations have had in one way or another to preserve.[16]

Contemporary news media facilitate a kind of brainwashing in which their very function appears to be "to relegate such recent historical experiences as rapidly as possible into the past. The informational function of the media would thus be to help us *forget,* to serve as the very agents and mechanisms for our historical amnesia."[17] In many of the films I have discussed one can still seek out a historical context by using such media texts to diagnose past conflicts represented in them, and by seeking to "read" emotions of past eras inscribed in the film images. In the media culture of our postmodern society, "history" is the past, representing all that is useless or irrelevant, material for mere nostalgic or generational quizzes ("What year was *this* song popular?") to briefly hold the attention of TV viewers of a predetermined demographic audience while four thirty-second commercials run. In such a context, "You're history!" has become the definitive put-down epithet.

## Implanted Memories and the Demise of Citizenship?

Citizenship in such a history-less "society of the *spectacle*" increasingly becomes a form of participation in a kind of "virtual" American or world community in which social relations are mediated by images, representative characters and, significantly, mass-mediated "rememberings" of "the real,"[18]—virtually "implanted" through so-called news and "info-tainment," not capturing preexisting reality so much as generating and expressing, through the construction of a world (as it appears in the media) considered real or historically "true" at any given moment, yet subject to easy and increasingly casual revisioning in news and advertising keyed to viewer demographics.

While such insights are widely held and even central to recent cultural studies, it is important to look more closely at the *political* implications of two interrelated problems they bring into focus: (1) the increasingly rapid and diverse creation of what passes for "information" and the validation of that information into "knowledge"; and (2) what this implies for the "virtual" democracy or the "representation of" democracy that now exists in the United States.

In the last two decades of the twentieth century political scientists devoted more attention to the implications of such developments—especially in light of the increased awareness and explicit consciousness of domestic manipulation of the public that began in the last years of the Ronald Reagan era.[19] Not enough attention was directed at the arrival of new forms of what can only be described as *cultural amnesia*—far outpacing George Orwell's vision of a constantly rewritten history. The emergent electronic communities of the postmodern present are populated by citizens operating with what are, in effect, "implanted" memories. Of course, science-fiction films such as *Blade Runner* (1982, Ridley Scott) and *Total Recall* (1990, Paul Verhoeven) anticipated this trend, presciently representing or predicting the emergent developments. This implantation process could also be represented less subtlely and more physically, as in Alex Proyas's film *Dark City* (1998), where actual injections into the brains of humans are shown, though this film image might be seen as a metaphorical trope for the old "hypodermic" model of opinion formation through repetition that originated in post–World War II propaganda studies, suggesting a simplistic model of injection of ideas into the public mind.[20]

In her study of the Marilyn Monroe phenomenon in American popular culture, the late Paige Baty has suggested that "Most Americans have what might be called 'memories' of mass-mediated lives they have never 'lived.'"[21] While the similarity of such an image to the implanted memories of *Blade Runner* and *Dark City* might be the closest analogue, such television sitcoms of the 1950s as *Leave It to Beaver, Ozzie and Harriet,* and *Father Knows Best* all attained cult status as reruns in the 1980s and 1990s, creating and maintaining a timeless 1950s of "happy days," with no issues not solvable within the confines of each episode. In reality, as more serious historical treatments suggest, the 1950s was a time of FBI surveillance, political suspicion, and fear of nuclear war. As recreated nearly a half century later in the film *Pleasantville* (1998, Gary Ross), the 1950s era in the United States is represented as a bleak society devoid of color and characterized by emptiness and repressed feelings. Eventually all the social transformations and political movements of the late 1950s and '60s emerge in the film in an explosion of colors accompanied by a stirring soundtrack of classic pop music and jazz that makes one treasure having lived through it.

The political implications of all this would have made such historical practitioners of propaganda as Adolf Hitler and Joseph Goebbels gasp with envy. If George Orwell saw any of this coming, it was not in such a user-friendly, "virtually" consensual form. Perhaps Jean-Jacques Rousseau's insight (which I paraphrase) that people then and now often "run headlong to their chains" is more apposite to such an emergent "virtual" society.[22]

## History as Plot and Conspiracy

The foregoing merely provides a contextual background to the meaning and appeal of conspiracy theories and generalized paranoia as significant "modes of remembering" and understanding. Such developments have been accompanied by extreme transformations, volatility, and puzzling contradictions in public opinion concerning matters of trust and efficacy—at least as evidenced in the half century since such opinions have been systematically solicited in national election studies. Whereas nearly 75 percent of a national Gallup survey conducted just prior to the assassination of John F. Kennedy trusted the government to do the right thing most or all of the time, thirty years later the number hovered in the low-to-mid-20 percent range.[23] Although there has been a similar trajectory of citizens' sense of governmental efficacy, the primary issue still remains trust in government.[24] As corporate power becomes indistinguishable from what was once thought to be a "democratic" state, there are many real and justifiable reasons for such distrust.

This cartographic—plot-based or "emplotted"—mode of remembering is increasingly circulated and authorized by the mass-mediated info-economy. Essentially this involves the legitimating appearance on one of scores of TV talk shows or thousands of local radio talk shows, integration into an episode of *The X-Files,* or the "reenactment" of an event on *Unsolved Mysteries.*

In the contemporary, postmodern, mass-mediated political culture of totally constructed appearances, paranoia becomes generalized throughout the culture. In such a context, conspiracy and its corresponding plot structure might seem to provide a kind of coherence. But what is proffered is only the *promise* of "meaning, historical coherence, of genealogy, of location."[25] It simply cannot provide what is most sought after: a foundational model of "truth," fixed or consistent in conventional "scientific" terms, through intersubjectively verifiable methods and evidence. While that may be so, a surface appearance of scientific trappings and illusions, plagiarized from traditional "high" science, still legitimates much that is published, including the most tendentious Internet "documents." Such discourse creates, in Foucault's terms, the "*effects* of truth."[26]

## Visionary Paranoia and New Symbolic Possibilities

In the twenty-first century there is increasing evidence of a new kind of historical "literacy" in which history is not viewed as an outcome of struggles over or consistent with divergent strategies for enacting historical grand narratives of human emancipation, whether through visions of capitalist possessive individualism or the new social relations arising out of construction of (anachronistic) visions of genuinely socialist or other kinds of utopian society. Rather, history is reduced to a series of *plots* in a context where less and less seems to make sense in terms of earlier modes of understanding. This emplotted history becomes a means of charting and navigating reality, simultaneously turning what is "historical" into new forms of the simulated—conspiracies and corresponding plot structures, in effect, enacting coherence in postmodern realms of appearance and representation. For many such "plotting" of the historical becomes a preferred means of charting and navigating an increasingly complex reality, as well as turning—in a downward spiral from any previous semblance of "reality"—what was once historical into what is now simulated and constructed.[27]

On the one hand, sustained by the tension between public fears and personal desires, filmic visions of palpable menace and a vaguely paranoiac yet often prescient sense of conspiracy may provide a kind of psychological comfort or closure for those for whom just believing they *know* what happened is empowering—even if they can't affect the outcomes of past struggles or apparent plots. More significantly—and quite paradoxically—through their *visionary* function as prescient premonitions or promptings of a political collective unconscious reflective of the "return" of *hidden* history in films and media culture generally, of the now well documented repression of historical movements once struggling for human emancipation, these films can also stimulate and perhaps even empower the political imaginations of those who view them. They may do so by calling attention to all the unknown, hidden, repressed, and denied dimensions of human history—of the repressed struggles in the United States to realize, through now largely defunct, barely remembered political movements, the much-maligned narratives of human liberation so foreign or demeaned in contemporary political culture. The history of these attempts continues to resurface, returning to haunt the present in the over sixty years of film and television examples explored throughout this study. It is through such socially symbolic artistic acts embodied by films—which truly make artifacts of moments, turning the repressed desire for social and political alternatives into filmic memories of what has been repressed or abandoned—that one glimpses a potential for reinvesting social life with deeper meaning by not simply expressing nostalgia and regret at what has been lost but by giving audiences the cultural materials necessary to generate new symbolic possibilities and alternative future visions.

# Notes

## INTRODUCTION

1. Indeed, as Timothy Melley argues (pp. 7–16) in *Empire of Conspiracy: The Culture of Paranoia in Post-War America* (Ithaca: Cornell University Press, 2000), the American public experiences a veritable "agency panic" as all traditional notions of individual control diminish.
2. C. B. Macpherson, *The Political Theory of Possessive Individualism: Hobbes to Locke* (New York: Oxford University Press, 1962). For a persuasive argument on the relevance of Macpherson's ideas to the emerging twenty-first century, see Peter Lindsay, *Creative Individualism: The Democratic Vision of C. B. Macpherson* (Albany: State University of New York Press, 1996).
3. Louis Hartz, *The Liberal Tradition in America* (New York: Harcourt, Brace, 1955).
4. Melley, *Empire of Conspiracy,* p. vii.
5. Fredric Jameson, *The Political Unconscious: Narrative as a Socially Symbolic Act* (Ithaca: Cornell University Press, 1981), pp. 19–20.
6. Jameson, *Political Unconscious,* p. 19.
7. Marshall Berman, *All That's Solid Melts into Air: The Experience of Modernity* (New York: Penguin, 1988).
8. Sara Evans, *Personal Politics: The Roots of Women's Liberation in the Civil Rights Movement and the New Left* (New York: Vintage, 1980).
9. On the surveillance of the feminist movement, see Ruth Rosen, "When Women Spied on Women," *The Nation,* September 4–11, 2000, pp. 18–25.
10. King's surveillance is described in excruciating detail by David J. Garrow in *The FBI and Martin Luther King, Jr.* (New York: Penquin, 1989) and in the more provocative thesis of attorney William F. Pepper in *Orders to Kill* (New York: Warner, 1998), which views the state surveillance of the Nobel prize–winning civil rights leader culminating in state-sponsored or -approved orders to kill him.
11. See Angus Mackenzie's *Secrets: The CIA's War at Home* (Berkeley: University of California Press, 1997), for a meticulous account of how government agencies—particularly the CIA—infiltrated student movements and the alternative press, intimidated mainstream journalists and civil liberties organizations, and suppressed and manipulated those who sought information.
12. Ross Gelbspan, *Break-Ins, Death Threats, and the FBI: The Covert War Against the Central America Movement* (Boston: South End Press, 1991).
13. On "subjugated knowledge," see Michel Foucault, *Power/Knowledge: Selected Interviews and Other Writings, 1972–1977* (New York: Pantheon, 1980), pp. 80–85.

14. This took the form of a paper presented by the author at the annual meeting of the American Political Science Association, Washington, D.C., September 1997, entitled "Conspiracy and the Quest for Coherence in Popular Culture."
15. See, for example, Melley, *Empire of Conspiracy.* Earlier studies include: George Johnson, *Architects of Fear: Conspiracy Theories in American Politics* (Los Angeles: Tarcher, 1983); Richard Hofstadter, *The Paranoid Style in American Politics and Other Essays* (New York: Knopf, 1965); Richard O. Curry, ed. *Conspiracy: The Fear of Subversion in American History* (New York: Holt, Rinehart and Winston, 1972).
16. This is effectively argued by Robert Justin Goldstein (in a chapter bearing the same title) in his massive study *Political Repression in Modern America: 1870 to the Present* (Boston: Schenckman, 1981; rpt. Champaign: University of Illinois Press, 2001), pp. 285–396.
17. See the critique of the legislation, Public Law, pp. 104–32, signed by former President Bill Clinton on April 24, 1996, posted by the Center for National Security Studies at <http://www.cdt.org/policy/terrorism/cnss_habeas.htm>.
18. These include: Michael Rogin's "Political Repression in the United States," in his *Ronald Reagan: The Movie and Other Episodes in Political Demonology (*Berkeley: University of California Press, 1987), pp. 44–80, which influenced my original conceptualization of the present study; Goldstein's *Political Repression in Modern America;* Frank J. Donner, *The Age of Surveillance: The Aims and Methods of America's Political Intelligence System* (New York: Knopf, 1980), and his *Protectors of Privilege: Red Squads and Police Repression in Urban America* (Berkeley: University of California Press, 1992); David Caute, *The Great Fear: The Anti-Communist Purge under Truman and Eisenhower* (New York: Simon & Schuster, 1978); Richard Fried, *Nightmare in Red: The McCarthy Era in Perspective* (New York: Oxford University Press, 1990); Ellen Schrecker, *Many Are the Crimes: McCarthyism in America* (Boston: Little, Brown, 1998); and, on a more popular level, Jonathan Vankin and Jonathan Whalen, *The 60 Greatest Conspiracies of All Time* (Secaucus, N.J.: Citadel, 1996) and Michael Parenti, *Dirty Truths* (San Francisco: City Lights, 1997). For a theoretical treatment of these issues—which, ironically, Alan Wolfe now reject but which I have found very suggestive—see his book *The Seamy Side of Democracy: Repression in America,* 2nd ed. (New York: Longman, 1978).
19. Charles W. Mills, *The Racial Contract* (Ithaca: Cornell University Press, 1997), p. 18.
20. William Gibson, *Neuromancer* (New York: Ace Books/Berkeley, 1986), p. 51.

### 1. "OUR GREATEST EXPORT IS PARANOIA"

1. The quote that serves as the chapter title occurs in Bill Pullman's voice-over.
2. Teresa Brennan, "The Age of Paranoia," *Paragraph* 14, no. 1 (March 1991): 20–45. Bran Nichol, "Reading Paranoia: Paranoia, Epistemophilia and the Postmodern Crisis of Interpretation," *Literature and Psychology* (Spring–Summer 1999): 44.
3. For a discussion of the dimensions and implications of the surveillance society, see Mark Boal, "Spycam City—The Surveillance Society: Part One" *The Village Voice,* September 30–October 6, 1998; and "Spycam Chic—The Surveillance Society: Part Two" *The Village Voice,* December 2–8, 1998.
4. See Patrick O'Donnell, "Engendering Paranoia in Contemporary Narrative," in *Na-*

*tional Identities and Post-Americanist Narratives*, ed. Donald E. Pease (Durham: Duke University Press, 1994), pp. 181–204.

5. The notion of "structures of feeling" comes from Raymond Williams, *Marxism and Literature* (New York: Oxford University Press, 1977), pp. 128–35.
6. O'Donnell, "Engendering Paranoia," p. 184.
7. On the alleged Libyan "hit" squads in the United States, perusal of *Time* and *Newsweek* from late 1981 through early 1982 reveals several accounts. For a discussion of the limited realities and widespread delusions surrounding the charge, see chapter 9 in Bob Woodward's *Veil: The Secret Wars of the CIA, 1981–1987* (New York: Pocket, 1988).
8. See Murray Edelman's discussion of the construction of foreign enemies in *Constructing the Political Spectacle* (Chicago: University of Chicago Press, 1988).
9. For a meticulous and devastating critique of the emergence of the "heterophobia" phase of the movement against sexual harassment of women, see Daphne Patai's *Heterophobia: Sexual Harassment and the Future of Feminism* (Lanham, Md.: Rowman & Littlefield, 1998). Two 1994 neo–films noirs, *The Last Seduction* (John Dahl) and *Dream Lover* (Nicholas Kazan), make use of overeager, politically correct males who are easily manipulated by unscrupulous femmes fatales claiming spouse abuse and sexual harassment.
10. Jeffrey Rosen, review of *Heterophobia*, by Daphne Patai, *The New Republic*, June 29, 1998, pp. 25–32.
11. Patai's study reviews a large number of such cases. John Fekete's *Moral Panic: Biopolitics Rising* (Toronto: Robert Davies, 1995) presents case studies of numerous males, largely in Canadian academic settings, who were victims of false charges of harassment.
12. Anita M. Waters, "Conspiracy Theories as Ethnosociologies: Explanation and Intention in African-American Political Culture," *Journal of Black Studies* 29, no. 1 (September 1997): 112.
13. Waters, "Conpiracy Theories," p. 113.
14. Richard Hofstadter, "The Paranoid Style in American Politics," in his book *The Paranoid Style in American Politics and Other Essays* (New York: Knopf, 1965).
15. Michael Kelly, "The Road to Paranoia," *The New Yorker*, June 19, 1995, pp. 60–75.
16. The best sociological study is by John Mirowsky and Catherine E. Ross, "Paranoia and the Structure of Powerlessness," *American Sociological Review* 48 (April 1983): 228–39.
17. Surveys by Princeton Survey Research Associates for Pew Research Center for the People and the Press presented in "Deconstructing Distrust: How Americans View Government, available online at <*http://www.people-press.org/trustque.htm*>.
18. Data for years 1952–1998 reflecting responses to national surveys on the topic "Public Officials Don't Care What People Think" is available online at <*http://www.umich.edu/~nesguide/toptable/tab5b_3.htm*>. Graph available online at <*http://www.umich.edu/~nesguide/graphs/g5b_3_1.htm*> (accessed March 20, 2001).
19. Sheldon Appleton, "The Mystery of the Kennedy Assassination: What the American Public Believes," *The Public Perspective* 9, no. 6 (October–November 1998): 12–17. One of the most insightful explorations of conspiracy theories in the JFK assassination is Christopher Sharrett's "Conspiracy Theory and Political Murder in America: Oliver

Stone's *JFK* and the Facts of the Matter," in *The New American Cinema,* ed. Jon Lewis (Durham: Duke University Press, 1998), pp. 217–47.

20. The most recent edition is *Diagnostic and Statistical Manual of Mental Disorders: DSM IV* (Washington, D.C.: American Psychiatric Association, 1994). A description of paranoia and related disorders can be found on pp. 637–38. The National Institutes of Health's National Institute of Mental Health has an online booklet entitled *Useful Information on Paranoia* (rev. 1989) available at <*http://www.mentalhealth.com/book/p45-paran.htm*>.
21. A vivid evocation of this delusion can be found in Philip K. Dick's novel *A Scanner Darkly* (New York: DAW, 1977), which opens with a man trying to shake bugs from his hair, then showering for eight hours, still thinking he has bugs crawling all over him. A month later he thinks he has bugs in his lungs.
22. These examples are taken from the National Institutes of Health's National Institute of Mental Health, *Useful Information on Paranoia,* rev. 1989.
23. Mirowsky and Ross, "Paranoia and the Structure of Powerlessness," p. 237.
24. These National Election Studies data tables and graphs are available online at <*http://www.umich.edu/%7enes/nesguide/top tables*>. Given the suggestion of Mirowsky and Ross that the development by paranoid thinking is a stepwise, ladderlike process, public opinion surveys suggest the movement of a large proportion of the U.S. electorate toward such an outlook in the 1970s, '80s, and early '90s.
25. See the survey of public-opinion polling data on the JFK killing by Appleton, "The Mystery of the Kennedy Assassination," and Sharrett, "Conspiracy Theory and Political Murder in America." A wide range of criticism and discussion of Stone's film includes the special issue ("Through the Looking Glass: A Critical Overview of Oliver Stone's *JFK*") of the political film journal *CINÉASTE* 19, no. 1 (1992). The director, together with Zachary Sklar, collected a large and balanced selection of reviews, including the screenplay, as *JFK: The Book of the Film (*New York: Applause, 1992). An overview of the controversy may be found in Robert Brent Toplin's "JFK: Fact, Fiction, and Supposition," in his *History by Hollywood: The Use and Abuse of the American Past (*Chicago: University of Illinois Press, 1996), pp. 46–79. See also Robert Brent Toplin, ed., *Oliver Stone's USA: Film, History, and Controversy* (Lawrence: University Press of Kansas, 2000), for extensive commentary on the film and Stone's own detailed responses. Marita Sturken's "Re-enactment, Fantasy, and the Paranoia of History: Oliver Stone's Docudramas," *History and Theory* 36, no. 4 (December 1997): 64–79, is, with Sharrett's essay, most reflective of my own orientation. Art Simon's *Dangerous Knowledge: The JFK Assassination in Art and Film* (Philadelphia: Temple University Press, 1993) is the most extensive discussion of the majority of the films referencing the event.
26. Mirowsky and Ross, "Paranoia and the Structure of Powerlessness," p. 229.
27. *The Standard Edition of the Complete Psychological Works of Sigmund Freud,* trans. and ed. James Strachey (London, 1953–73), 12: 79.
28. Eric L. Santner, *My Own Private Germany: Daniel Paul Schreber's Secret History of Modernity* (Princeton: Princeton University Press, 1997).
29. Elias Canetti, *Crowds and Power* trans. Carol Stewart (New York: Seabury, 1978); Gilles Deleuze and Felix Guattari, *Anti-Oedipus: Capitalism and Schizophenia,* trans. Robert Hurley, Mark Seem, and Helen Lane (Minneapolis: University of Minnesota

Press, 1983); William Niederland, *The Schreber Case: Psychoanalytic Profile of a Paranoid Personality* (Hillsdale, N.J.: Analytic Press, 1984); and Morton Schatzman, *Soul Murder: Persecution in the Family* (New York: Random House, 1973).

30. Santner, *My Own Private Germany,* p. ix.
31. Ibid., p. xiii.
32. Ibid., p. xiv.
33. See Carl Freedman, "Towards a Theory of Paranoia: The Science Fiction of Philip K. Dick, *Science Fiction Studies* 11 (1984): 16.
34. Ibid., p. 16.
35. For a wide range of material on the transformation of Dick's story into the film, see Judith B. Kerman, ed., *Retrofitting "Blade Runner": Issues in Ridley Scott's "Blade Runner" and Philip K. Dick's "Do Androids Dream of Electric Sheep?"* (Bowling Green, Ohio: Popular Press, 1991).
36. Philip K. Dick, *Clans of the Alphane Moon (*New York: Carroll & Graf, 1988).
37. Quoted by Lawrence Sutin in *Divine Invasions: A Life of Philip K. Dick* (New York: Harmony, 1989), p. 302.
38. On infantilization, see Lauren Berlant, "The Theory of Infantile Citizenship," *Public Culture* 5 (1993): 395–410; idem, *The Queen of America Goes to Washington City: Essays on Sex and Citizenship* (Durham: Duke University Press, 1997). Marita Sturken's insights on this topic may be found in *Tangled Memories: The Vietnam War, The Aids Epidemic, and the Politics of Remembering* (Berkeley: California University Press, 1997) and the previously cited essay "Oliver Stone's Docudramas."
39. See Berlant, "The Theory of Infantile Citizenship."
40. The first "men-in-black" reference I can recall appeared in the now obscure 1984 film *Flashpoint (*which I discuss in chapter 2). Ignored by most surveys of JFK assassination films, such as Art Simon's otherwise comprehensive *Dangerous Knowledge,* the film is worth viewing.
41. After several rereadings of the book and in light of contextual historical knowledge, it is difficult not to accept the argument of the film that U.S. officials were complicit in the literal "execution" of a U.S. citizen who knew "too much."
42. See the excellent discussion of *Missing* in John J. Michalczyk's *Costa Gavras: The Political Action Film* (New York: Associated University Presses, 1984), pp. 217–35. See also Stephen Prince's *Visions of Empire: Political Imagery in Contemporary American Film* (New York: Praeger, 1992), pp. 86–94.
43. Sturken, "Oliver Stone's Docudramas," p. 77.
44. Ibid.
45. Ibid.
46. On public knowledge of and views about lying by the government, see Sissela Bok, *Lying: Moral Choice in Public and Private Life* (New York: Vintage, 1989).
47. Joshua Meyrowitz, *No Sense of Place: The Impact of Electronic Media on Social Behavior* (New York: Oxford University Press, 1986).
48. Ibid., p. 89.
49. Gerry Mander, *Four Arguments for the Elimination of Television* (New York: Morrow, Quill, 1979), pp. 97–99.
50. Stanton Peele, The *Diseasing of America: Addiction Treatment Out of Control* (Boston: Houghton, Mifflin, 1989), pp. 236–37.

51. See Douglas Kellner, *The Persian Gulf TV War* (Boulder, Colo.: Westview Press, 1992) and John R. MacArthur, *Second Front: Censorship and Propaganda in the Gulf War* (New York: Hill & Wang, 1992).
52. Hedrick Smith, "The Image Game: Scripting the Video Presidency," *The Power Game: How Washington Works* (New York: Bantam, 1989), pp. 388–440.
53. The statement in the 1973 documentary film *I. F. Stone's Weekly,* produced and directed by Jerry Bruck Jr. See also Andrew Patner, *I. F. Stone: A Portrait—Conversations with a Non-Conformist* (New York: Anchor, 1990).
54. Sturken, "Oliver Stone's Docudramas," p. 74.
55. Fredric Jameson, "Reification and Utopia in Mass Culture," *Social Text* 1 (Winter 1979): 130–48.
56. Donner's perceptive and comprehensive overview of tendencies that, while already in existence, took on added impetus under the aegis of of the twenty-four-year-old Hoover in 1919, appears in *The Age of Surveillance.* He continues the story, focusing on local repression, in *Protectors of Privilege: Red Squads and Police Repression in Urban America (*Berkeley: University of California Press, 1992). A brief exposition of Donner's theories is provided by Chip Berlet, "Government Intelligence Abuse: The Theories of Frank Donner," which may still be available online at <http://www.publiceye.org/pra/liberty/donner.htm>.
57. Contemporaneous reflections on the growth and development of filmic paranoia in the years between classic film noir and the conspiracy films of the 1970s and later may be found in Paul Jensen, "The Return of Dr. Caligari: Paranoia in Hollywood, *Film Comment* 7, no. 4 (Winter 1971–72): 36–45; George Wead, "Toward a Definition of Filmnoia," *Velvet Light Trap* 13 (1974): 2–6.
58. On the science-fiction film and complementary literature, see J. P. Telotte, *Replications: A Robotic History of the Science Fiction Film* (Urbana: University of Illinois Press, 1995). Also see Scott Bukatman, *Terminal Identity: The Virtual Subject in Post-Modern Science Fiction* (Durham: Duke University Press, 1993). Intersecting with these themes is Jodi Dean, *Aliens in America: Conspiracy Cultures from Outerspace to Cyberspace* (Ithaca: Cornell University Press, 1998).
59. Insightful commentary on these political films as conspiracy texts may be found in Steven Prince, *Visions of Empire: Political Imagery in Contemporary American Film* (New York: Praeger, 1992).
60. In addition to Donner's *Age of Surveillance,* see the immensely detailed and comprehensive study by Robert Justin Goldstein, *Political Repression in Modern America* (Boston: Schenkman, 1978; rpt. Champaign: University of Illinois Press, 2001). A briefer critical study of the same trends, often relying on Goldstein's account, is Michael Rogin's "Political Repression in the United States," in his *Ronald Reagan: The Movie* (Berkeley: University of California Press, 1988), pp. 45–80.
61. See Donner, *The Age of Surveillance,* pp. 33–51.
62. See the detailed account of the secret surveillance and harassment of the IWW and other groups in Joan M. Jensen, *The Price of Vigilance (*Chicago: Rand, McNally, 1968). Also see Jensen's survey of the long history of U.S. Army surveillance in *Army Surveillance in America, 1775–1980 (*New Haven: Yale University Press, 1991).
63. Donner, "Military Surveillance of Civilian Politics—Countersubversion in Uniform," *Age of Surveillance,* pp. 287–320, provides an excellent overview of domestic

use of military intelligence from 1917 through the revelations of Christopher Pyle in 1970. Jensen, *Army Surveillance in America, 1775–1980,* pp. 231–67, discusses some of the same trends.

64. Christopher Pyle's first article, "CONUS Intelligence: The Army Watches Civilian Politics (pp. 4–16) appeared in January 1970. His doctoral dissertation on the same topic, "Military Surveillance of Civilian Politics, 1967–1970," Columbia University, Ph.D., 1974, was published in a Garland Press edition in 1976.
65. Donner, *The Age of Surveillance,* p. 320. In a private letter to this author, Christopher Pyle suggested that even if the vast archive had been preserved, most of it was so vague and out of date to have no current or future utility to anyone. New reports of uses of military-intelligence surveillance against anti–World Trade Organization demonstrators in Washington, D.C., appeared in the spring of 2000.
66. Roy M. Talbert Jr., *Negative Intelligence: The Army and the American Left, 1917–1941* (Jackson: University of Mississippi Press, 1991).
67. See Frank Morales, "Report on Federal Anti-Activist Intelligence Network," *Covert Action Quarterly* 69 (Spring–Summer 2000).
68. One good collection is Griffin Fariello, *Red Scare: Memories of the American Inquisition—An Oral History* (New York: Avon, 1995). Also see Ellen Schrecker, *Many Are the Crimes: McCarthyism in America* (Boston: Little, Brown, 1998).
69. William Arnold, *Shadowland* (New York: McGraw Hill, 1978), pp. 172–75. Much of Arnold's book was used—apparently against his wishes—as a source for the 1982 film *Frances* (Graeme Clifford), which underplays the political dimensions of actions against Farmer.
70. Griffin Fariello, *Red Scare: Memories of the American Inquisition* (New York: Avon, 1995); Joel Kovel, *Red Hunting in the Promised Land: Anticommunism and the Making of America* (New York: Basic Books, 1994); David Caute, *The Great Fear: The Anti-Communist Purge Under Truman and Eisenhower* (New York: Simon & Schuster, 1978); David Caute, *Joseph Losey: A Revenge on Life* (New York: Oxford University Press, 1993).
71. Angus Mackenzie, *Secrets: The CIA's War at Home* (Berkeley: University of California Press, 1997).
72. Jon Weiner, *Come Together: John Lennon in His Time* (New York: Random House, 1984), especially pp. 220ff.
73. Ross Gelbspan, *Break-ins, Death Threats and the FBI: The Covert War Against the Central America Movement* (Boston: South End Press, 1991).
74. On the extent and dimensions of U.S. involvement in the El Salvador civil war, see the excellent brief account by William Blum, *Killing Hope: U.S. Military and CIA Interventions Since World War II* (Monroe, Me.: Common Courage Press, 1995), pp. 352–69.
75. On the dimensions of secret U.S. involvement in Guatemala, see Blum, *Killing Hope,* pp. 72–82, and Michael McClintock, *The American Connection: State Terror and Popular Resistance in Guatemala* (London: Zed Books, 1985).
76. For a study of the militia of Montana, see Kelly, "The Road to Paranoia."
77. See Robert S. Hamm, *Apocalypse in Oklahoma* (Boston: Northeastern University Press, 1997), for a perceptive analysis of the Waco events that provides a comprehensive critique of FBI actions.

## 2. FILM POLITICS

1. Robin Wood, *Hollywood from Vietnam to Reagan* (New York: Columbia University Press, 1986), p. 78.
2. Wood, "The American Nightmare," *Hollywood*, pp. 78, 4.
3. Quoted by Stuart Samuels in "The Age of Conspiracy and Conformity: Invasion of the Body Snatchers (1956)," in *American History/American Films: Interpreting the Hollywood Image*, ed. John E. O'Connor and Martin A. Jackson (New York: Unger, 1979), pp. 204–5.
4. Brecht's period in Hollywood is profiled in Anthony Heilbut's *Exiled in Paradise: German Refugee Intellectuals in America from the 1930s to the Present* (Boston: Beacon, 1984), pp. viii, 174–94.
5. Quoted by Heilbut, *Exiled in Paradise*, p. 183.
6. Fredric Jameson, *The Political Unconscious: Narrative as a Socially Symbolic Act* (Ithaca: Cornell University Press, 1981), p. 20. The most useful exposition of his concept for understanding paranoia and conspiracy discourses is his discussion in *The Geopolitical Aesthetic: Cinema and Space in the World System* (Bloomington: Indiana University Press, 1992), especially the part entitled "Totality as Conspiracy," pp. 9–84. The preface by Colin MacCabe clarifies some of Jameson's difficult, sometimes opaque, and often impenetrable prose.
7. See Sheldon Appleton, "The Mystery of the Kennedy Assassination: What the American Public Believes," *The Public Perspective*, October–November 1998, pp. 12–17.
8. Samuels, "The Age of Conspiracy and Conformity, pp. 204–5.
9. On the complex question of the "auteur" in contemporary Hollywood, see Timothy Corrigan, "Auteurs and the New Hollywood," in *The New American Cinema*, ed. Jon Lewis (Durham: Duke University Press, 1998), pp. 38–63.
10. The acceptance/negotiation/opposition formulation comes from Stuart Hall's essay "Encoding/Decoding," in *Culture, Media, Language*, ed. Stuart Hall et al. (London: Hutchinson, 1980), pp. 128–38.
11. There are many analyses of these films, though the most insightful is still the one by Samuels on the 1956 version essay (see n. 3). J. Hoberman's review articles in *The Village Voice* (February 18, 1994) and *Sight and Sound* (May 1994) analyze the 1994 version but also compare all three. Danny Peary, *Cult Movies* (New York: Delta Books, pp. 154–58, 1981), emphasizes the nonconformity and anti-anticommunism (fear of McCarthyism) reading. Peter Biskind, "The Mind Managers: *Invasion of the Body Snatchers* and the Paranoid Style," in his *Seeing Is Believing* (New York: Pantheon, 1983), pp. 137–44, also sees the wider implications.
12. Samuel Stauffer, *Communism, Conformity, and Civil Liberties* (Garden City, N.Y.: Doubleday, 1955), pp. 43, 177–78.
13. See these figures in David Caute, *The Great Fear: The Anti-Communist Impulse Under Truman and Eisenhower* (New York: Simon and Schuster, 1978), p. 215.
14. C. Wright Mills, *White Collar* (New York: Oxford University Press, 1951; rpt. 1956).
15. The term is used by Alan Gowans, *Learning to See* (Bowling Green, Ohio: Popular Press, 1983).
16. Herbert Marcuse, *Eros and Civilization: A Philosophical Inquiry into Freud* (New York: Vintage, 1962), p. xvii.

17. This distinction is made by Christian Bay, *The Structure of Freedom* (New York: Atheneum, 1965), p. 6.
18. Clayton R. Koppes and Gregory D. Black, *Hollywood Goes to War: How Politics, Profits, and Propaganda Shaped World War II Movies* (New York: The Free Press, 1987), p. vii.
19. Robert Sklar, private communication. Sklar's *Movie-Made America: A Cultural History of American Movies,* rev. ed. (New York: Vintage, 1994), is the standard social history of the American movies.
20. Stephen Prince, *Visions of Empire* (New York: Praeger, 1992), explores at length both the failure to confront the Vietnam War in film in its earlier phase and the ideological tendencies in some of the major postwar films set in Vietnam.
21. This film is one of very few assassination films not discussed in Art Simon's *Dangerous Knowledge: The JFK Assassination in Art and Film* (Philadelphia: Temple University Press, 1993).
22. See Greil Marcus, *Mystery Train,* rev. ed. (New York: Dutton, 1982). In their 1988 concert film *Rattle & Hum,* the rock group U-2 asserted their "reclamation"of the song from Manson prior to their performance of it.
23. See Simon Frith, "Brit Beat: On and On and On," *The Village Voice,* July 14, 1987, p. 77.
24. Hinckley is discussed by Gary Wills in *Reagan's America* (New York: Penguin, 1988), pp. 247–51.
25. Dave Grossman, *On Killing: The Psychological Cost of Learning to Kill in War Society* (Boston: Little, Brown; Back Bay Books, 1996).
26. An early but still useful discussion of this process is Dick Hebdige's *Subculture: The Basis of Style* (London: Methuen, 1979).
27. The most persuasive arguments along these lines occur in Steven Marcus' discussion of the fiction of Dashiell Hammett. See his introduction to Hammett's, *The Continental Op* (New York: Vintage, 1972).
28. Stuart Hall, "Notes on Deconstructing 'the Popular,'" in *People's History and Socialist Theory,* ed. Samuel Raphael (Boston: Routledge & Kegan Paul, 1981), p. 228.
29. Douglas Kellner, *Media Culture* (New York: Routledge, 1996).
30. Hall, "Notes on Deconstructing 'The Popular,'" p. 235.
31. On the trajectory of public opinion concerning the Vietnam War, see William L. Lunch and Peter W. Sperlich, "American Public Opinion and the War in Vietnam," *Western Political Quarterly* 33, no. 1 (March 1979): 21–44. The literature on images of Vietnam as depicted in film is too voluminous to list here, though this study does mention specific sources in relation to particular films.
32. On the way popular-music references relate to the shifts in public opinion, see Ray Pratt, "There Must Be Some Way Outa Here": The Vietnam War in American Popular Music," in *The Vietnam War: Its History, Literature and Music,* ed. Kenton Clymer (El Paso, Tex.: Texas Western Press/University of Texas Press, 1998), pp. 168–89.
33. Michael Ryan and Douglas Kellner, *Camera Politics* (Bloomington: University of Indiana Press, 1988).
34. Siegfried Kracauer, *From Caligari to Hitler: A Psychological History of German Film* (Princeton: Princeton University Press, 1947), p. 218.
35. Douglas Kellner, "Hollywood Film and Society," *The Oxford Guide to Film Studies,* ed. John Hill and Pamela Church Gibson (London: Oxford University Press, 1998), p. 355.

36. Ibid.
37. Alan Gowans, *Learning to See: Perspectives on Modern Popular/Commercial Arts* (Bowling Green, Ohio: Popular Press, 1981).
38. Walter Lippmann, "The World Outside and the Pictures in Our Heads," *Public Opinion* (rpt. New York: Free Press, 1965), pp. 3–22. This classic study remains in print in multiple editions. For a discussion of the context and background leading up to its publication, see Ronald Steel, *Walter Lippmann and the American Century* (New York: Vintage, 1980), pp. 171–85.
39. Jameson, *The Political Unconscious,* p. 20. See also Jameson, *The Geopolitical Aesthetic.*
40. Fredric Jameson, "Reification and Utopia in Mass Culture," in *Signatures of the Visible* (London: Routledge, 1990), p. 25.
41. Jameson, *The Political Unconscious,* p. 20.
42. Jung describes the "visionary" work of art in "Psychology and Literature" (originally published in 1933), in *Modern Man in Search of a Soul* (New York: Harcourt, Brace/Harvest Books, 1960), pp. 152–72. For a more extensive exposition of Jung's relevance to film analysis, see Susan Mackey-Kallis, *Oliver Stone's America: Dreaming the Dream Outward* (Boulder, Colo.: Westview Press, 1996); see also the website of the *HI-Q FILM REVIEW,* devoted to film analysis from a Jungian perspective, at *<http://www.cgjung.com/films>.*
43. Jung, "Psychology and Literature," pp. 159, 162, 165. Emphasis added.
44. Michael Parenti, *Dirty Truths* (San Francisco: City Lights, 1997).
45. Carl Oglesby, "Paranoia as a Way of Knowing," in his *The JFK Assassination: The Facts and the Theories* (New York: Signet, 1992), pp. 27–30.
46. Carl Oglesby, "Seeing the Invisible State," *The JFK Assassination,* pp. 25–51.
47. Foucault defines the term as "historical contents buried and disguised" but known to "those disqualified from the hierarchy of knowledges and sciences." See his essay "Two Lectures," in *Power/Knowledge: Selected Interviews and Other Writings, 1972–1977* (New York: Pantheon, 1980), pp. 81–82. This body of literature—which constitutes the historical-political background of the film texts considered in the present study book—includes: Frank J. Donner, *The Age of Surveillance: The Aims and Methods of America's Political Intelligence System* (New York: Knopf, 1980), and *Protectors of Privilege: Red Squads and Police Repression in Urban America* (Berkeley: University of California Press, 1992); Michael Rogin, "Political Repression in the United States," in his *Ronald Reagan: The Movie and Other Episodes in Political Demonology* (Berkeley: University of California Press, 1987), pp. 44–80; and Robert Justin Goldstein, *Political Repression in Modern America: 1870 to the Present* (Boston: Schenckman, 1981; rpt. Champaign: University of Illinois Press, 2001); William Preston Jr., *Aliens and Dissenters: Federal Suppression of Radicals, 1903–1933,* 2nd ed. (Chicago: University of Illinois Press, 1994), especially pp. 277–96, which updates the work through the cold war period.

### 3. THE DARK VISION OF FILM NOIR

1. On the discursive nature of "noir," see James Naremore, "American Film Noir: The History of an Idea," in his *More Than Night: Film Noir in Its Contexts* (Berkeley: University of California Press, 1998), pp. 9–39. Dan Flory's article "Black on White:

Film Noir and the Epistemology of Race in Recent African American Cinema," *Journal of Social Philosophy* 31, no. 1 (Spring 2000): 82–116, provides an incisive overview of the discursive status of noir and its distinctive epistemology, as well as extensive and perceptive analysis of African-American uses of the style. Mike Davis' discussion of L.A.-based noir in *City of Quartz* (New York: Vintage, 1990), remains one of the most engaging studies on the topic. Jonathan Munby's *Public Enemies, Public Heroes: Screening the Gangster from "Little Caesar" to "Touch of Evil"* (Chicago: University of Chicago Press, 1999) touches on all the noir films and criticism, providing novel insights and unique connections.

2. The term "film noir" was apparently first used by Nino Frank in *Écran Française* 61, 28, August 1946, in a discussion of the U.S.-made films noted. Interestingly, three of the five films were directed by European expatriate directors. The first published U.S. reference to "black cinema" occurred over two decades later in a book by Charles Higham and Joel Greenberg, *Hollywood in the Forties* (New York: A. S. Barnes, 1968).
3. On the effects of McCarthyism, see Ellen Schrecker, *Many Are the Crimes: McCarthyism in America* (Boston: Little, Brown, 1999) especially the extensive notes and bibliography.
4. One of the best efforts is Brian Neve's "Film Noir and Society," in his *Film and Politics in America: A Social Tradition* (New York: Routledge, 1992), pp. 144–70. Also see Munby's *Public Enemies, Public Heroes.*
5. Douglas Kellner, "Hollywood Film and Society," *Oxford Guide to Film Studies* (New York: Oxford University Press, 1998), p. 355.
6. Richard Maltby, "The Politics of the Maladjusted Text," in *The Book of Film Noir,* ed. Ian Cameron (New York: Continuum, 1993), p. 39.
7. See Todd Erickson, "Kill Me Again: Movement Becomes Genre," in *The Film Noir Reader,* ed. Alain Silver and James Ursini (New York: Limelight Editions, 1993), p. 307.
8. Maltby, "The Politics of the Malajusted Text," p. 41.
9. Douglas Kellner, *Media Culture* (New York: Routledge, 1995).
10. Geoffrey O'Brien's "The Return of Film Noir," *New York Review of Books* 38, no. 14, August 15, 1991, is for me among the more engaging brief efforts to determine the reasons for the resurgence of interest in these films, although the author finds little or no political significance in them. In Alain Silver and Elizabeth Ward's *Film Noir: An Encyclopedic Reference to the American Style,* 3rd ed. (Woodstock, N.Y.: Overlook Press, 1993)—the key reference for film lovers—nearly fifty books and major journal articles are listed for the period 1979–91 (various appendixes list perhaps fifty more since Silver and Ward's latest revision). Ian Cameron, ed., *The Book of Film Noir* (New York: Continuum, 1993) is comprehensive in scope and an important guide to classic and current neo-noir films. Naremore's *More Than Night* incorporates previous insights and has becomes—as much as any single work can—the standard text on the style.
11. A succinct discussion of the tiresome question of whether film noir is a distinct genre may be found Elizabeth Cowie's "Film Noir and Women," *Shades of Noir,* ed. Joan Copjec (New York: Verson, 1993), pp. 121–32.
12. O'Brien, "The Return of Film Noir," p. 45.
13. While the "canon" of noir includes as many as five hundred films from the classic

period, there have been hundreds of remakes and homages from the 1960s through the '90s. *Chinatown, Farewell My Lovely, Body Heat, Blood Simple, The Hot Spot, Blue Velvet, The Grifters,* and many others might be included in the numerous subcategories of "neo-noir" films. On the latter, see Silver and Ward's *Film Noir* and the articles on "neo-noir" in Silver and Ursini's collection *The Film Noir Reader.*

14. For an informative technical discussion of these lighting techniques and effects and the equipment utilized in achieving them, see Paul Kerr, "Out of What Past? Notes on the B Film Noir," *Screen Education 13* (Autumn–Winter 1979): 32–33. Also relevant is Janey Place and Lowell S. Peterson, "Some Visual Motifs of Film Noir," *Film Comment* 10, no. 1 (January–February 1974): 30–35. Both essays are reprinted in *The Film Noir Reader,* pp. 107–28 and 65–76, resp.
15. Silver and Ward, "Introduction" *Film Noir,* p. 5.
16. Laura Mulvey, *Citizen Kane* (London: BFI Film Classics, 1992), p. 17. On narrative patterns, see J. P. Telotte, *Voices in the Dark: Narrative Patterns in Film Noir* (Chicago: University of Illinois Press, 1989).
17. See Robert G. Porfirio, "No Way Out: Existential Motifs in the Film Noir," *Sight and Sound* 45, no. 4 (Autumn 1976): 212–17; reprinted in *The Film Noir Reader,* pp. 77–94.
18. On the flashback and the psychological meanings associated with it, see Foster Hirsch, *Film Noir: The Dark Side of the Screen* (New York: A. S. Barnes, 1981; rpt. New York: Da Capo Press, 1983), pp. 72–78. See also Frank Krutnik, "Film Noir and the Popularization of Psychoanalysis," *In a Lonely Street: Film Noir, Genre, and Masculinity* (New York: Routledge, 1991), pp. 45–55.
19. E. Ann Kaplan, ed., *Women in Film Noir,* 2nd ed. (London: British Film Institute, 1999) is the standard study. See also James Maxfield, *The Fatal Woman: Sources of Male Anxiety in American Film Noir, 1941–1991* (London: Associated University Presses, 1996). An engaging online source is John Blaiser's *No Place for a Woman* available at <*http://www.lib.berkeley.edu/MRC/NOIR*>.
20. Here is how Chandler described his character while commenting on the detective novel in his classic essay "The Simple Art of Murder": "Down these mean streets a man must go who is not himself mean, who is neither tarnished nor afraid . . . a complete man, and a common man, an unusual man . . . a man of honor—by instinct, by inevitability, without thought of it . . . the best man in his world and a good enough man for any world." *Atlantic Monthly* (December 1944): 59. Racism and xenophobia in Chandler's—and other writers'—characters in the late 1940s and '50s are noted by Mike Davis in his review of Los Angeles–based noir in *City of Quartz,* p. 91, n. 42.
21. As reported in Ellroy interview in *Salon,* December 1996, at <*http://www.salon1999.com/dec16/interview2961209.htm*> (emphasis added).
22. The best studies of the Production Code are Leonard Leff and Jerrold Simmons' *The Dame in the Kimono: Hollywood, Censorship, and the Production Code from the 1920s to the 1960s* (New York: Anchor, 1991), and Jonathan Munby's *Public Enemies, Public Heroes.* An earlier treatment of the issues involved is Murray Schumach's *The Face on the Cutting Room Floor* (New York: Morrow, 1964).
23. Steven Marcus, "Dashiell Hammett," in *The Poetics of Murder: Detective Fiction and Literary Theory,* ed. Glen W. Most and William W. Stowe (New York: Harcourt Brace Jovanovich, 1983), pp. 201–2.
24. Flory, "Black on White," pp. 85–89.

25. Marcus, "Dashiell Hammett," pp. 201–2.
26. Ibid., p. 202.
27. Flory, "Black on White," p. 87 Charles Mills, *The Racial Contract* (Ithaca: Cornell University Press, 1997).
28. Flory "Black on White," p. 87.
29. See Jonathan Munby's perceptive essay, "The 'Un-American' Film Art: Robert Siodmak, Fritz Lang, and the Political Significance of Film Noir's German Connection," in his *Public Enemies, Public Heroes,* pp. 186–220.
30. Flory, "Black on White," p. 88.
31. Numerous biographies and video documentaries exist of of Hammett and of his relationship with Hellman. See, for example, Diane Johnson, *Dashiell Hammett: A Life* (New York: Random House, 1983). Also worth reading are Dennis Dooley, *Dashiell Hammett* (New York: Frederick Ungar, 1984); and William F. Nolan, *Hammett: A Life at the Edge* (New York: Condon & Weed, 1983). Joan Mellen persuasively argues the case for Hammett's virtual authorship of much of Hellman's work; see *Hammett and Hellman: The Legendary Passion of Lillian Hellman and Dashiell Hammett* (New York: HarperCollins, 1996).
32. Tom Hiney, *Raymond Chandler: A Biography* (New York: Atlantic Monthly Press, 1997), p. 94.
33. See the biography by Francis M. Nevins Jr., *Cornell Woolrich: "First You Dream, Then You Die"* (New York: Mysterious Press, 1988). See also Mark T. Bassett, ed., *Blues of a Lifetime: The Autobiography of Cornell Woolrich* (Bowling Green, Ohio: Popular Press, 1991). Foster Hirsch, in *Film Noir,* provides a a good discussion of his importance to the body of films noirs. Lastly, see David Reid and Jayne L. Walker, "Strange Pursuit: Cornell Woolrich and the Abandoned City of the Forties," in *Shades of Noir,* ed. Joan Copjec (London: Verso, 1993).
34. Nevins Jr., *Cornell Woolrich,* p. 110.
35. Ellery Queen, introduction to Cornell Woolrich, *The Ten Faces of Cornell Woolrich: An Inner Sanctum Collection of Novelettes and Short Stories* (New York: Simon & Schuster, 1965), p. 12.
36. See the brief but engaging discussion of Woolrich's influence on film noir in Eddie Muller's *Dark City: The Lost World of Film Noir (*New York: St. Martin's, Griffin, 1998), pp. 118–23.
37. The term occurs in Jim Cook and Alan Lovell's *Coming to Terms with Hollywood* (London: British Film Institute, 1981), p. 2. The relation of such a sensibility to American society of the cold war era and the factors producing film noir is perceptively discussed in Brian Neve's *Film and Politics in America: A Social Tradition* (London: Routledge, 1992).
38. On Chandler's alcoholic amnesia, see Hiney, *Raymond Chandler,* pp. 61–63.
39. See Hirsh, "The Literary Background," *Film Noir,* pp. 23–51. Also see William Marling, *The American Roman Noir: Hammett, Cain, and Chandler* (Athens: University of Georgia Press, 1995).
40. George Steiner, "Franz Kafka," in *Atlantic Brief Lives: A Biographical Companion to the Arts,* ed. Louis Kronenberger (Boston: Little, Brown/Atlantic Monthly Press, 1971), p. 425.
41. The section heading is taken from Anthony Heilbut's *Exiled in Paradise: German Refugee Artists and Intellectuals in America from the 1930s to the Present* (Boston:

Beacon, 1984), p. 230. This work is remarkable for its comprehensive view of the 1930s and 1940s and the crucial role the German expatriates played in shaping "American" popular culture, particularly through the infusion of their perspectives into Hollywood films of the era.

42. The connections between German expressionist films and film noir have long been noted. For a brief overview, see John D. Barlow, "The Heritage of German Film Expressionism," *German Expressionist Film* (Boston: Twayne, 1982), pp. 169–206.
43. Quoted by Heilbut, *Exiled in Paradise,* p. viii.
44. See Thom Andersen, "Red Hollywood," in Suzanne Ferguson and Barbara Groseclose, eds. *Literature and the Visual Arts in Contemporary Society* (Columbus: Ohio State University Press, 1985), pp. 141–96; Larry Ceplair and Steven Englund, *The Inquisition in Hollywood: Politics in the Film Community,* 1930–1960 (Garden City, N.Y.: Anchor Press/Doubleday, 1980); and Naremore, *More Than Night,* pp. 96–135.
45. On Lang's films, see Tom Gunning, *Films of Fritz Lang: Allegories of Vision and Modernity* (London: British Film Institute, 2000), and Lotte Eisner, *Fritz Lang* (New York: Da Capo Press, 1986).
46. Andrew Sarris, *The American Cinema: Directors and Directions, 1929–1968* (New York: E. P. Dutton, 1968), pp. 63, 65. See also Jonathan Munby's essay "The 'Un-American' Film Art."
47. Peter Bogdanovich, *Fritz Lang in America* (New York: Praeger Film Library, Frederick A. Praeger, 1967), p. 14.
48. O'Brien, "The Return of Film Noir," p. 48.
49. The importance of Preminger and *The Moon Is Blue* is discussed in detail in Leff and Simmons, *The Dame in the Kimono,* pp. 189–203.
50. Lang, quoted in Bogdanovich, *Fritz Lang in America,* p. 84.
51. One of the earliest discussions of filmic manifestations of these developments is Marjorie Rosen's *Popcorn Venus: Women, Movies, and the American Dream* (New York: Coward, McCann & Geoghegan, 1973), pp. 189–206.
52. David Caute's biography *Joseph Losey: A Revenge on Life* (New York: Oxford University Press, 1994) reveals the incredible extent and number of surveillance files on a single individual. Multiplied by the tens of thousands who came under direct FBI or military-intelligence surveillance—as described in Frank J. Donner's *The Age of Surveillance* (New York: Knopf, 1980)—the names in files may have implicated as many as twenty million Americans. The quantity of alleged information must have occupied vast amounts of space in the era before computers and electronic-information storage. Given the expansion of computer technology in recent years, Donner suggests, there is no telling where the information might be stored.
53. The effects of the German influx are perceptively chronicled in Heilbut's *Exiled in Paradise.*
54. Philip Kemp, "From The Nightmare Factory: HUAC and the Politics of Noir," *Sight and Sound* 55 (Autumn 1986): 266–70.
55. On the contexts and meanings of *Red River,* see Robert Sklar's essay "Empire to the West: *Red River* (1948)" in *American History/American Film: Interpreting the Hollywood Image,* ed. John E. O'Connor and Martin A. Jackson (New York: Frederick Ungar, 1979), pp. 167–82.
56. The film is remarkable for its expression of idealism and humanistic commitment

on the part of the older Communists active in this period. Although they were probably selected with such a retrospective objective in view, they are nonetheless vividly portrayed, conveying great emotion and personal distress as they recall international and domestic crises.

57. This is somewhat ironic given Wood's direction of *For Whom the Bell Tolls* (1943), which retrospectively supported the Republican side in the Spanish Civil War, which was supported by all shades of the Left in the United States. See the description of Wood in Otto Friedrich's *City of Nets: A Portrait of Hollywood in the 1940s* (New York: Harper Perennial Books, 1986), pp. 166–69. See chapter 7 for a detailed discussion of the MPA and its operations and relations with HUAC.
58. On Disney's ties to HUAC, Hoover, and the FBI, see Marc Eliot's *Walt Disney: Hollywood's Dark Prince* (New York: Birch Lane, 1993).
59. See Friedrich, *City of Nets,* pp. 166–69.
60. These Developments are detailed in Ceplair and England's *The Inquisition in Hollywood,* pp. 209–25.
61. See James Naremore, "The Trial: The FBI vs. Orson Welles," *Film Comment* 27 (January–February 1991): 22–27.
62. This episode is described in Barbara Leaming's *Orson Welles* (New York: Viking, 1985), pp. 290–94.
63. This episode is related in David Thomson's *Rosebud: The Story of Orson Welles* (New York: Vintage, 1997), p. 257.
64. Ceplair and England, *The Inquisition in Hollywood,* consider this issue at length, reviewing all the earlier literature. For a comprehensive discussion of the formation, politics, and orientation of the Screen Writers Guild and its most influential members in the 1930s and '40s, see Nancy Lynn Schwartz, *The Hollywood Writers' Wars* (New York: McGraw-Hill, 1983).
65. The definition occurs in Jim Cook and Alan Lovell's *Coming to Terms with Hollywood* (London: British Film Institute, 1981), p. 5.
66. Paul Schrader, "Notes on Film Noir" (1972), reprinted in *Film Noir Reader,* pp. 53–64.
67. On Polonsky's critique of capitalism, see Christin Noll Brinckman, "The Politics of *Force of Evil:* An Analysis of Abraham Polonsky's Pre-Blacklist Film," *Prospects* 5, no. 6 (1981): 357–86.
68. A good discussion of the orientation of the Browderites at the end of World War II can be found in Thom Andersen's "Red Hollywood," p. 187. For an even more detailed history, see Maurice Isserman, *Which Side Were You On? The American Communist Party During the Second World War* (Middletown, Conn.: Wesleyan University Press, 1982).
69. See Harvey Klehr and John Earl Haynes' *The American Communist Movement* (New York: Twayne, 1992); idem, *The Secret World of American Communism* (New Haven: Yale University Press, 1995).
70. For the background behind the firing, see Allen Yarnell's *Democrats and Progressives: The 1948 Election as a Test of Postwar Liberalism* (Berkeley: University of California Press, 1974), pp. 10–13.
71. For specific data, see Norman D. Markowitz, *The Rise and Fall of the People's Century: Henry A. Wallace and American Liberalism, 1941–1948* (New York: The Free Press, 1973), pp. 81–123.

72. Edward L. and Frederick H. Schapsmeir's *Prophet in Politics: Henry A. Wallace and the War Years, 1940–1965* (Ames: The Iowa State University Press, 1965), p. 189.
73. A brief balanced account of the 1948 campaign can be found in Joseph C. Goulden's study *The Best Years, 1945–1950* (New York: Atheneum, 1976), pp. 342–425. A comprehensive and sympathetic treatment of the Henry Wallace campaign is presented in Curtis MacDougall's *Gideon's Army*, 3 vols. (New York: Marzani & Munsell, 1965). Also see Karl Schmidt, *Henry A. Wallace: Quixotic Crusader* (Syracuse: Syracuse University Press, 1960). The 27 percent high point of Wallace support comes from Joseph Goulden's interview with pollster Louis H. Bean, who related that Harold Stassen had done a poll showing Wallace at 27 percent, but that Wallace himself was aware he had slipped significantly from there to 10 percent. See Goulden, *The Best Years*, p. 351.
74. On the origins of McCarthy's anticommunism, see Thomas C. Reeves, *The Life and Times of Joe McCarthy* (New York: Stein and Day, 1982), pp. 187–233.
75. On Clark Clifford's role in the Democratic Party campaign against Wallace, see Richard J. Walton, *Henry Wallace, Harry Truman and the Cold War* (New York: Viking, 1976), pp. 228–344. Walton quotes much of Clifford's 1947 memo, which contributed to the domestic Red Scare of the late 1940s. Also see Richard M. Freeland, *The Truman Doctrine and the Origins of McCarthyism* (New York: Alfred A. Knopf, 1972), pp. 191–92, 293–306. Ironically, Clifford was represented as one of the heroes of the 1974 documentary film *Hearts and Minds* (Peter G. Davis), describing his own "revolutionary" transformation of views on Vietnam policy during internal administration reviews in the 1967–69 period. This reassessment would halt the planned two hundered thousand troops to be sent to Vietnam and lead to LBJ's decision not to run in 1968.
76. Clifford memorandum, quoted by Markowitz, *The Rise and Fall of the People's Century*, p. 257.
77. These events described in detail in E. and F. Schapsmeir's *Prophet in Politics*, pp. 180–209.
78. See Goldstein, *Political Repression in Modern America*, pp. 285–396.
79. Interview (late 1970), quoted in Andersen, "Red Hollywood," p. 187.
80. The best general discussion of these developments can be found in George Lipsitz's *A Rainbow at Midnight: Labor and Culture in the 1940s* (Chicago: University of Illinois Press, 1994). Also see Goulden, *The Best Years*, pp. 108–31. Specific data on strikes may be found in David Reid and Jayne L. Walker's "Strange Pursuit: Cornell Woolrich and the Abandoned City of the Forties," in *Shades of Noir*, p. 61.
81. For a year-by-year listing, see Silver and Ward, *Film Noir*, pp. 333–36.
82. Jon Tuska, *Dark Cinema* (Westport, Conn.: Greenwood, 1988), p. xvi.
83. See Andersen, "Red Hollywood," pp. 141–96.
84. The entire process is described in Christine Noll Brinckmann's article "The Politics of *Force of Evil:* An Analysis of Abraham Polansky's Preblacklist Film," *Prospects* 6 (1981): 357–86.
85. The term occurs in Carl Macek and Alain Silver's entry on *Force of Evil;* see Silver and Ward, eds., *Film Noir*, pp. 105–6.
86. Brinckmann, "The Politics of *Force of Evil*," p. 381.
87. Polonsky in a letter to Brinckmann, p. 380.

88. Polonsky, in a letter to Christine Brinckmann, p. 380.
89. See Robert Sklar, *City Boys: Cagney, Bogart, Garfield* (Princeton: Princeton University Press, 1992) for a comparative study of the careers of Bogart and Garfield. The comparison with Bogart appears in the profile of director John Berry in *Tender Comrades: A Back Story of the Hollywood Blacklist,* ed. Patricia McGilligan and Paul Buhle (New York: St. Martin's, 1997), p. 74.
90. Polonsky, "Introduction" to *The Films of John Garfield,* by Howard Gelman (Secaucus, N.J.: Citadel, 1975), p. 8.
91. Cited in Eric Sherman and Martin Rubin, eds., *The Director's Event: Interviews with Five American Filmmakers* (New York: Atheneum, 1970), p. 20.
92. The urban settings are rhapsodically described by Martin Scorsese in the PBS *American Cinema* series episode on "Film Noir," which was first broadcast in 1996.
93. Joseph Starobin, "Preface," *American Communism in Crisis, 1943–1957* (Cambridge, Mass.: Harvard University Press, 1972), p. ix. Starobin also served as foreign editor of *The Daily Worker,* the national Communist Party newspaper.
94. Among the best of these are: William Pecter, "Abraham Polonsky and *Force of Evil,*" *Film Quarterly* 15, no. 3 (spring 1962): 47–54; interview in *Film Culture,* 50–51 (Fall–Winter 1970): 43–44; David Talbot and Barbara Zheutlin, *Creative Differences: Profiles of Hollywood Dissidents* (Boston: South End Press, 1978), pp. 55–99; Brinckmann, "The Politics of *Force of Evil*"; and see Polonksy's interview with J. D. Pasternak and F. W. Howton in *The Image Maker,* ed. Ron Henderson (Richmond, Va.: John Knox Press, 1971), pp. 21–25.
95. The consequences of this repressive activity are succinctly analyzed in Goldstein, *Political Repression in Modern America,* pp. 285–396.
96. Andrew Sarris, *The American Cinema: Directors and Directions, 1929–1968* (New York: Dutton, 1968), p. 220.
97. See *Tender Comrades,* pp. 55–89, for a discussion of Garfield's significance and subsequent virtual obliteration in media memory. Robert Sklar's *City Boys* provides the most comprehensive discussion of Garfield's film career. Howard Gelman's book *The Films of John Garfield* presents stills, plot summaries, and brief quotations from reviews of every film, as well as many plays, in which he appeared.
98. See Tom Flinn and John Davis, "The Breaking Point," *The Velvet Light Trap* 14 (Winter 1975): 17–20, for an analysis of this minor masterpiece.
99. A transcript of Garfield's testimony is available in an appendix to Gelman, *The Films of John Garfield,* pp. 216–22.
100. See the interview with Dassin in *Tender Comrades,* pp. 199–224. In the furor over the bestowning of a special Lifetime Achievement Academy Award to Elia Kazan in 1999 (who named names of former Hollywood comrades), Dassin's name was advanced by some, such as film critic Stuart Klawans, as having produced an equivalent body of outstanding films equally deserving of a special award, especially given his work outside the United States after being forced into exile by the blacklist. See Klawans, "Films—Oscar Who?" *The Nation,* March 15, 1999, available at <*http://www.thenation.com/issue/990315/0315klawans.shtm*>.
101. For a good study of the total body Mann's work, see Janine Basinger, *Anthony Mann* (Boston: Twayne, 1979).
102. See Basinger, *Anthony Mann,* under of each of Mann's noir features.

103. See Caute's *Joseph Losey,* pp. 70–181, for the magnitude and complexity of FBI surveillance of Hollywood leftists from the late 1930s through the HUAC-McCarthy era.
104. On the paradoxical quality of noir versus the vast majority of films of the classic (1941–59) period, see Richard Maltby, "The Politics of the Maladjusted Text," in *The Book of Film Noir,* pp. 39–48.
105. See Joseph Goulden's *The Best Years.*
106. See Leonard Quart and Albert Auster, *American Film and Society Since 1945* (New York: Praeger, 1984), pp. 28–29.
107. Ibid.
108. For an analysis of the development and promotion of this film, see Martin A. Jackson's essay "The Uncertain Peace: *The Best Years of Our Lives* (1946)," in *American History/American Film,* pp. 147–66.
109. Cited by Jackson, "The Uncertain Peace," p. 154.
110. Robert Warshow, "The Anatony of Falsehood," *The Immediate Experience* (Garden City, N.Y.: Doubleday, 1962), p. 155.
111. Ibid, p. 159.
112. Dana Polan, *Power and Paranoia* (New York: Columbia University Press, 1986), p. 223.
113. See also Raymond Carney, "American Dreaming: *It's a Wonderful Life,*" *American Vision: The Films of Frank Capra* (London: Cambridge University Press, 1986), pp. 377–438; Robert B. Ray, *A Certain Tendency of the Hollywood Cinema, 1930–1980* (Princeton: Princeton University Press, 1985), p. 200.
114. Ray, *A Certain Tendency,* p. 203.
115. Ibid., p. 213.
116. Ibid., p. 215.
117. The affirmational discourse in these 1940s films is discussed by Polan, *Power and Paranoia,* pp. 9–11; for suppressed countertrends in *It's a Wonderful Life,* see pp. 222–23.
118. For an overview of women's experiences in World War II and immediately thereafter—especially regarding the enforced demobilization of "Rosie the Riveter" from the workforce—see Andrea S. Walsh, *Women's Film and Female Experience, 1940–1950* (New York: Praeger, 1984), pp. 49–88. The public-opinion data provided by Walsh demonstrates the almost unanimous desire of female workers to remain in their wartime jobs following their forced demobilization. See also Marjorie Rosen's "The Rise and Fall of Rosie the Riveter" in *Popcorn Venus,* pp. 201–20, which provides a good overview of the period and its filmic representations of women.
119. Dmytryk, a Communist since 1944, was one of the "unfriendly" Hollywood Ten witnesses who appeared before HUAC in 1947, was charged with contempt, jailed, and blacklisted. Unlike the others, he agreed under pressure to "name names" in return for a chance to direct again. *The Caine Mutiny* (1954) and *Mirage* (1965) represent his best post-blacklist work. His case is discussed at length in Victor Navasky's *Naming Names* (New York: Viking, 1980).
120. See George Lipsitz's analysis of the film in "The Working Class and Hollywood," in his book *A Rainbow at Midnight,* pp. 289–91.
121. This is related in the American Movie Classics Channel program "Blacklist: Hollywood on Trial," which was originally broadcast in 1996.
122. On the effects of censorship and precensorship in the era of the Production Code

see Munby, *Public Heroes, Public Enemies; Robert* Sklar, *Movie-Made America: A Cultural History of American Movies,* rev. ed. (New York: Vintage, 1994), pp. 294–96; James Monaco, *How to Read a Film* (New York: Oxford University Press, 1981), pp. 230–33; and Murray Schumach's *The Face on the Cutting Room Floor,* which examines the blacklist and includes in an appendix the 1956 version of the Production Code as well as an official explanation of the rationale behind it. Censorship of political content is provided by the case of Polonsky's *Force of Evil,* which is discussed in Sklar, *City Boys,* pp. 206–10.

123. See Polan, *Power and Paranoia,* p. 222.
124. Barbara Deming, *Running Away from Myself: A Dream Portrait of America Drawn from Films of the Forties* (New York: Grossman, 1969), p. 201.
125. See Sylvia Harvey's "Women's Place: The Absent Family of Film Noir," in *Women in Film Noir,* pp. 22–34. Harvey presents an illuminating series of linkages between the apparently retrogressive images of women in the films and wider, often denied, systemic conflicts and crises that reflect back on the ways women were portrayed.
126. For an analysis of the structure of the film industry and the system of production that created the features retroactively termed "film noir," see Paul Kerr, "Out of What Past? Notes on the B Film Noir," in *The Film Noir Reader,* pp. 107–28.
127. These figures are based on lists published in Cobbett Steinberg's *Reel Facts* (New York: Vingage, 1982). The nine films include: *The House on 92nd Street* (1945), *Mildred Pierce* (1945), *Gilda* (1946), *Notorious* (1946), *Spellbound* (1945), *Nora Prentiss* (1947), *Possessed* (1947), *Key Largo* (1948), and *Detective Story* (1951). See also Jack Nachbar, "Film Noir," in *Handbook of American Film Genres,* ed. Wes D. Gehring (New York: Greenwood, 1988), p. 70 and n. 11, p. 79.
128. See Place and Peterson, "Some Visual Motifs of Film Noir."
129. See Nachbar, "Film Noir," p. 70.
130. See the detailed figures provided by Paul Kerr, "Out of What Past?" p. 119.
131. See Sklar, "The Disappearing Audience and the Television Crisis," *Movie-Made America,* pp. 269–85.
132. David M. Oshinsky, *A Conspiracy So Immense: The World of Joe McCarthy* (New York, The Free Press, 1983), covers the Wisconsin senator's rise and fall. The section on the censure vote (pp. 472–94) is especially informative in assessing the varieties of Senate opinion at the time.
133. See Naremore, *More Than Night,* pp. 1–39, and Flory, "White on Black," pp. 84–85, 89.

## 4. THE CULTURE OF RESISTANCE IN THE FILMS OF THE 1960S

1. On surveillance and covert operations against domestic movements and individuals in the period 1960–75, see Robert Justin Goldstein, *Political Repression in Modern America: 1870 to the Present* (Boston: Schenkman, 1981; rpt. Champaign: University of Illinois Press, 2001); Frank Donner, *The Age of Surveillance: The Aims and Methods of America's Political Intelligence System* (New York: Knopf, 1980), especially chapters 5 ("The Bureau in Action," pp. 125–176) and 6 ("Aggressive Intelligence," pp. 177–240). Both of these works are essential reading for an understanding of the hidden history of the 1960s through Watergate.
2. On the concept of "adversary" or "resistance," culture, see Charles Maland," *Dr.*

*Strangelove* (1964): Nightmare Comedy and the Ideology of Liberal Consensus," in *Hollywood as Historian: American Film in a Cultural Context,* ed. Peter C. Rollins (Lexington: University Press of Kentucky, 1983), pp. 190–210.

3. The concept of "fusion paranoia" seems to have originated in Michael Kelly's essay "The Road to Paranoia," *The New Yorker,* June 19, 1995, pp. 60–75, which reported on the militia of Montana.
4. See Lawrence Suid, "The Pentagon and Hollywood: *Dr. Strangelove* (1964)," in *American History/American Film: Interpreting the Hollywood Image,* ed. John E. O'Connor and Martin A. Jackson (New York: Frederick Ungar, 1980), pp. 219–35.
5. William Adams, "War Stories: Movies, Memory, and the Vietnam War," *Comparative Social Research* 11 (1989): 167.
6. Richard Slotkin, *Regeneration Through Violence: The Mythology of the American Frontier, 1600–1860* (Middletown, Conn.: Wesleyan University Press, 1973). Also see his *Gunfighter Nation: The Myth of the Frontier in Twentieth-Century America* (New York: HarperCollins, 1993).
7. A succinct treatment of Vietnam War–era films is presented in Steven Prince's chapter "Hearts and Minds," in his *Visions of Empire* (New York: Praeger, 1992), pp. 115–53. Also see Michael Anderegg, ed., *Inventing Vietnam: The War in Film and Television* (New Brunswick, N.J.: Rutgers University Press, 1990); Linda Dittmar and Gene Michaud, eds., *From Hanoi to Hollywood: The Vietnam War in American Film* (Philadelphia: Temple University Press, 1991); and Robin Wood's comments on *Taxi Driver* and *The Deer Hunter* in *Hollywood from Vietnam to Reagan* (New York: Columbia University Press, 1986), pp. 50–55 and 270–98, resp.
8. On the power and utility of the "indignation" concept, see Peter Lupsha, "Explanation of Political Violence: Some Psychological Theories Versus Indignation, " *Politics and Society* 2, no. 1 (Fall 1971): 89–104.
9. See Morris Dickstein's *Gates of Eden: American Culture in the Sixties* (New York: Penguin, 1977).
10. Quoted from an Associated Press news release, December 14, 1999.
11. *The Political Companion to American Film,* edited by Gary Crowdus (Chicago: Lakeview Press, 1994), contains a good overview of the cycle of assassination thrillers to which I am indebted. See especially Andrew Horton, "Political Assassination Thrillers," pp. 310–18.
12. Art Simon's, *Dangerous Knowledge* (Philadelphia: Temple University Press, 1993) remains the most comprehensive treatment of film images of the JFK assassination.
13. These elements are taken from the "political assassination thrillers" entry in Crowdus, *The Political Companion to American Film,* pp. 310–18.
14. See Susan L. Carruthers, "'The Manchurian Candidate' (1962) and the Cold War Brainwashing Scare," *Historical Journal of Film, Radio and Television* 18, no. 1 (March 1998): 75–95, for an analysis of the film and topic of brainwashing. Also see Charles S. Young, "Missing in Action: POW films, Brainwashing and the Korean War, 1954–1968," in the same issue, pp. 49–75.
15. John Frankenheimer interview in Gerald Pratley's *Frankenheimer: The Films of John Frankenheimer* (Bethlehem, Pa.: Lehigh University Press, 1998), p. 40.
16. Quoted in *Halliwell's Film Guide, 8th ed.,* ed. John Walker (New York: HarperCollins, 1991), p. 705.

17. John Marks, *The Search for the Manchurian Candidate: The CIA and Mind Control—The Secret History of the Behavioral Sciences* (New York: Norton, 1991); Gordon Thomas, *Journey Into Madness: The True Story of Secret CIA Mind Control and Medical Abuse* (New York: Bantam, 1990).
18. See William Turner and Jonn Christian, "*The Manchurian Candidate*," *The Assassination of Robert F. Kennedy: The Conspiracy and Cover-up* (New York: Thunder's Mouth Press, 1993), pp. 192–229.
19. Fletcher Knebel and Charles W. Bailey, *Seven Days in May* (New York: Harper & Row, 1962).
20. Kirk Douglas, *The Ragman's Son* (New York: Pocket, 1989), pp. 320–25.
21. See Gordon Sander, *Serling: The Rise and Twilight of Television's Last Angry Man* (New York: Penguin/Plume, 1994), pp. 188–89.
22. See Peter Wyden, *Bay of Pigs* (New York: Simon & Schuster, 1979), for a comprehensive historical treatment. Also informative on the Bay of Pigs invasion and the conspiracies spawned in its aftermath is Warren Hinkle and William Turner's *Deadly Secrets: The CIA-Mafia War Against Castro and the Assassination of JFK* (New York: Thunder's Mouth Press, 1993).
23. Arthur M. Schlesinger Jr., *The Imperial Presidency* (Boston: Houghton, Mifflin, 1973), p. 198. On JFK and Seven *Days in May,* see Charles Higham and Joel Greenburg's book *The Celluloid Muse: Hollywood Directors Speak* (Chicago: Henry Regnery, 1971), p. 92; and Anthony Summers, *Not in Your Lifetime: The Definitive Book on the JFK Assassination* (New York: Marlowe, 1998), pp. 170, 473, 467.
24. See Heather A. Purcell and James K. Galbraith, "Did the U.S. Military Plan a Nuclear First Strike for 1963?," *The American Prospect,* no. 19 (Fall 1994), which is available online at <*http://www.prospect.org/archives/19/19galb.html*>.
25. Quoted in McGeorge Bundy, *Danger and Survival: Choices About the Bomb in the First Fifty Years* (New York: Random House, 1988), p. 354.
26. Summers, *Not in Your Lifetime,* pp. 48–49, 170, 467.
27. The film ranked fourteenth in film revenues for 1964, just below *A Hard Day's Night.* See Maland, "*Dr. Strangelove,*" pp. 190–210 for a survey of critical responses.
28. This not to deny the importance of several politically relevant books published in this period: Rachel Carson's *Silent Spring,* which helped jump-start the environmental movement; Michael Harrington's *Other America,* the first recognition of poverty in the 1960s; Betty Friedan's *Feminine Mystique,* which stimulated the growth of feminism; and Ralph Nader's *Unsafe at Any Speed,* which marked the start of the consumer-safety movement.
29. See Maland's illuminating discussion in "*Dr. Strangelove,*" pp. 190–98.
30. Joshua Meyrowitz, "The Exposure of Backstage Group Behavior," *No Sense of Place: The Impact of Electronic Media on Social Behavior* (New York: Oxford, 1985), pp. 135–43.
31. Quoted in Joseph Glemis, *The Film Director as Superstar* (New York: Doubleday, 1970), p. 309.
32. Ibid.
33. Dickstein, *Gates of Eden,* p. 97.
34. Hannah Arendt, *Eichmann in Jerusalem: A Report on the Banality of Evil* (New York: Viking, 1963).

35. See Maland, "*Dr. Strangelove*," p. 198ff. Also see similar remarks by Suid, "The Pentagon and Hollywood," pp. 219–35.
36. For a thoughtful examination of the way westerns were used to critique American society, see John Lenihan, *Showdown: Confronting Modern America in the Western Film* (Chicago: University of Illinois Press, 1985). Also see Richard Slotkin's wide-ranging discussion of such films in *Gunfighter Nation.*
37. On these films, see the discussion in Lenihan, *Showdown.*
38. See Douglas recollections of the film in his autobiography *The Ragman's Son,* pp. 306–14.
39. According to Douglas, the man, Bill Raisch, was a former Ziegfeld Follies dancer who lost an arm. He had a regular job as Burt Lancaster's stand-in. He was, Douglas emphasizes, a very easygoing person, unlike the character he played. See Douglas' discussion in *The Ragman's Son,* pp. 308–14.
40. James Bishop Jr., *Epitaph for a Desert Anarchist: The Life and Legacy of Edward Abbey* (New York: Simon & Schuster, Touchstone Books, 1995), p. 109.
41. Ibid., p. 11.
42. *The Los Angeles Times,* 1989.
43. Quoted in Bishop, *Epitaph for a Desert Anarchist,* p. 110.
44. This statistic is found in Henry Blinder's "*Seconds,*" in *Cult Movies 3,* ed. Danny Peary (New York: Simon & Schuster, Fireside Books, 1988), pp. 212–17.
45. The best example is the 1988 "Badgeman" blow-up and colorization of a section of the Mary Moorman photograph of the Kennedy assassination, which is examined at length in an episode that forms part of the series *The Men Who Killed Kennedy,* an original BBC production, reedited and shown with new narration by Bill Kurtis on the A&E network in 1991–92 and repeated several times on the History Channel in the summer of 2000.
46. I am indebted to Danny Peary's entry (pp. 61–62) on *Blow-Up* in his *Guide for the Film Fanatic* (New York: Simon & Schuster, 1986) for some suggestive insights mentioned here.
47. Marshall Berman, *All That's Solid Melts into Air: The Experience of Modernity* (rpt. New York: Penguin, 1988), p. 59.
48. The remark occurs in a Learning Channel "Great Books" documentary on *Catch-22* and the film based on it that was aired originally in 1996.
49. On Stone's *Born on the Fourth of July,* see Susan Mackey-Kallis's *Oliver Stone's America: Dreaming the Dream Outward* (Boulder, Colo.: Westview Press, 1996) and Robert Brent Toplin, ed., *Oliver Stone's USA* (Lawrence: University Press of Kansas, 2000).
50. Penn was interviewed on the American Movie Classics series *The Moviemakers,* which aired December 1999, from which these comments are taken.

## 5. "YOU MAY THINK YOU KNOW WHAT'S GOING ON HERE"

1. Thomas Powers, *The Man Who Kept the Secrets: Richard Helms and the CIA* (New York: Knopf, 1979; rpt. New York: Pocket, 1981).
2. Kathryn S. Olmsted, *Challenging the Secret Government: The Post-Watergate Investigations of the CIA and FBI* (Chapel Hill: University of North Carolina Press, 1996).

3. Daniel Schorr, "My 17 Months on the CIA Watch: A Backstage Journal" *Rolling Stone,* April 8, 1976, pp. 32–38, 80–98; idem, *Clearing the Air* (Boston: Houghton Mifflin, 1977).
4. Quoted in Morton H. Halperin et al., *The Lawless State: The Crimes of the U.S. Intelligence Agencies,* Center for National Security Studies (New York: Penguin, 1976), p. 235.
5. See the chapter "The Seventies: Under Control?" in Zinn's *A People's History of the United States* (New York: Harper & Row, Harper Perennial, 1980), pp. 529–69.
6. Pauline Kael, "*The Godfather:* Alchemy," *The New Yorker,* March 18, 1972; rpt. in *For Keeps: Thirty Years at the Movies* (New York: Penguin, Plume, 1996), p. 438.
7. Douglas Kellner, "Hollywood Film and Society," *The Oxford Guide to Film Studies,* ed. John Hill and Pamela C. Gibson (New York: Oxford University Press, 1998), p. 360.
8. Roman Polanski, *Roman* (New York: Morrow, 1984), p. 348. On the making of the film, see Peter Biskind, "The Low Road to *Chinatown,*" *Premiere,* June 1994, pp. 68ff. See, in general, Biskind's *Easy Riders, Raging Bulls* (New York: Simon & Schuster, 1999).
9. Polanski, *Roman,* p. 346.
10. See Fredric Jameson's essay "Postmodernism and Consumer Society," in *The Anti-Aesthetic: Essays on Postmodern Culture* ed. Hal Foster (Port Townsend, Wash.: Bay Press, 1983), pp. 111–26.
11. James Naremore, *More Than Night: Film Noir in Its Contexts* (Berkeley: University of California Press, 1998), pp. 207, 206.
12. Stephen Marcus' comments on Hammett's demystification of the false stories presented to investigators like the Continental Op. and Sam Spade should be reemphasized in this context. See Steven Marcus, "*Dashiell Hammett,*" in *The Poetics of Murder: Detective Fiction and Literary Theory,* ed. Glenn W. Most and William W. Stowe (New York: Harcourt Brace Jovanovich, 1983), pp. 196–209.
13. On these developments, see Doug Henwood, "The Americanization of Global Finance," *NACLA Report on the Americas* 33, no. 1 (July–August 1999): 13–20; idem, *Wall Street: How It Works and For Whom* (New York: Verso, 1998). See also John R. MacArthur Jr., *The Selling of "Free Trade": NAFTA, Washington, and the Subversion of American Democracy* (New York: Hill & Wang, 2000).
14. Marc Reisner, *Cadillac Desert: The American West and Its Disappearing Water* (New York: Penguin, 1987), pp. 15, 54–107.
15. Marshall Berman, *All That's Solid Melts into Air* (New York: Penguin, 1988).
16. See John Cawelti's influential and widely cited essay "Chinatown and Generic Transformation in Recent American Films," in *Film Theory and Criticism,* 2nd ed., Gerald Mast and Marshall Cohen (New York: Oxford, 1979), pp. 559–99.
17. See Kael's original insightful take on *The Long Goodbye* in "Movieland, The Bums' Paradise," *The New Yorker,* October 22, 1973; rpt. in *For Keeps,* pp. 514–20.
18. This image is borrowed from Kael's *New Yorker* review.
19. Robert P. Kolker, *A Cinema of Loneliness* (New York: Oxford University Press, 1988), p. 66.
20. This theory is suggested by Kolker (p. 68).
21. For example, see Michael Ryan and Douglas Kellner, *Camera Politica: The Politics and Ideology of Contemporary Hollywood Film* (Bloomington: Indiana University Press, 1988), pp. 85–87, 95–101.

22. Anthony Lewis, "Farce of Tragedy," *New York Times,* February 2, 1976, p. 23. Pike is quoted by Oriana Fallaci, "Otis Pike and the CIA," *The New Republic,* April 3, 1976, p. 9. See Kathryn S. Olmsted's *Challenging the Secret Government: The Post-Watergate Investigation of the CIA and FBI* (Chapel Hill: University of North Carolina Press, 1996), especially chapters 6 and 7, for a comprehensive overview of the Pike committee investigations and public and congressional opinion on the Pike and Church (Senate) committees and their revelations.
23. In his book *Orders to Kill* on the Martin Luther King assassination (New York: Carroll & Graf, 1996; rpt. New York: Warner, 1998), attorney William Pepper suggested that domestic military intelligence operations resulted in some seven million files on Americans containing over twenty million names.
24. Timothy Corrigan, "Auteurs and the New Hollywood," in *The New American Cinema,* ed. Jon Lewis (Durham, N.C.: Duke University Press, 1998), pp. 38–63. The Coppola quote is cited by Lewis, p. 55.
25. For a thoughtful review of the film within its political and social context, see Stephen Farber's "A Nightmare World With No Secrets," *New York Times,* May 12, 1974.
26. These aspects are especially well noted in Danny Peary's entries on *The Parallax View* in his *Guide for the Film Fanatic* (p. 321) and *Cult Movies 2* (New York: Delta, 1983), pp. 115–18.
27. Quoted by Peary, *Cult Movies 2,* p. 118.
28. Thomas T. Noguchi, M.D., "Medical Examiner's Case No. 68–5731, Robert F. Kennedy," *Coroner* (New York: Simon & Schuster, 1983), pp. 86–108. According to Noguchi, "Scientific evidence of soot and divergent angles, and a host of witnesses who did not actually see Sirhan fire the fatal shot, all seemed to indicate there may have been a second gunman. Moreover, even the most sophisticated forensic techniques were unable to prove that the fatal bullet was fired from Sirhan's gun" (p. 107).
29. See Douglas Valentine, *The Phoenix Program* (New York: William Morrow, 1990). See also Alexander Cockburn and Jeffrey St. Clair, *Whiteout: The CIA, Drugs, and the Press* (New York: Verso, 1998).
30. These films are discussed in Stephen Prince's *Visions of Empire: Political Imagery in Contemporary American Film* (New York: Praeger, 1992).
31. "Mr. Pakula Goes to Washington—Alan J. Pakula on *All the President's Men,*" *Film Comment* (Sept.–Oct. 1976): 16. Also see Richard T. Jameson, "The Pakula Paradox," in the same issue, pp. 8–12.
32. See Peary's discussion of *The Parallax View* in *Cult Movies 2,* pp. 115–118.
33. See Schorr's account of the events in his memoir *Clearing the Air.*
34. Carl Bernstein, "The CIA and the Media," *Rolling Stone,* October 20, 1977, pp. 55–67. Kathryn Olmsted, in *Challenging the Secret Government,* covers the extensive literature on CIA media connections and *New York Times* articles that attempted to refute the charges, written by John Crewdson and Joseph Treaster, *New York Times,* December 25–28, 1977. Another important study of domestic CIA efforts to suppress or influence the content of books is Angus Mackenzie's *Secrets: The CIA's War at Home* (Berkeley: University of California Press, 1997).
35. "Mr. Pakula Goes to Washington," p. 16.
36. Ibid., p. 13.
37. Jim Hougan, *Secret Agenda* (New York: Random House, 1984), p. 373; Len Colodny

and Robert Gettlin, *Silent Coup: The Removal of a President* (New York: St. Martin's, 1992), p. 464. See also the postscript, "Protecting the Myth—*The Washington Post* and the Second Watergate Cover-Up," pp. 451–75.

38. Roger Morris, foreword to *Silent Coup,* p. xxiv.
39. Two good studies of the Silkwood affair cover similar ground. Howard Kohn, who covered the case for *Rolling Stone,* has written a detailed journalistic narrative, *Who Killed Karen Silkwood?* (New York: Summit, 1981), which sadly contains no notes or index. A new edition is available of Richard L. Rasheke's *The Killing of Karen Silkwood,* 2nd ed. (Ithaca: Cornell University Press, 2000). Also see Peter Carlson, "Silkwood's Real-Life Characters Find Much to Praise—and a Few Inaccuracies—in the Hit Film," *People Weekly,* February 20, 1984, pp. 74–75.
40. A good discussion of the dangers posed by the incident at Three Mile Island is Ernest Sternglass' *Secret Fallout: Low Level Radiation from Hiroshima to Three Mile Island* (New York: McGraw-Hill, 1981), pp. 197–239. Other relevant works include: Philip L. Catelon and Robert C. Williams, *Crisis Contained: The Department of Energy at Three Mile Island* (Carbondale: Southern Illinois University Press, 1982); Robert F. Willson Jr., "On the Air/ON the Line: Parallel Structure and Contemporary History in 'The China Syndrome,'" *Journal of Popular Film and History* (September 1979): 49–53.
41. See John Hellman, "The Hero Seeks a Way Out," *American Myth and the Legacy of Vietnam* (New York: Columbia University Press, 1986), pp. 139–69, for an analysis of these three works.
42. On the transformation of the novel into the film, see Stephen Zito, "*Dog Soldiers:* Novel into Film," *American Film* 2, no. 10 (1977): 8–15.
43. Gary Arnold, "'Rain': A Knockout Adventure Destined to Become a Classic," *The Washington Post,* August 9, 1978, p. B1.
44. See Hellman's discussion of the "returned hero" genre in "Epic Return," in his *American Myth,* pp. 171–204.
45. This image is suggested by Hellman's analysis in *American Myth,* p. 148.
46. For extended discussions of *Dog Soldiers,* see Robert Solotaroff, *Robert Stone* (New York: Twayne, 1994), pp. 52–81, and Hellman, "The Hero Seeks a Way Out," pp. 139–69.
47. Gary Arnold, "Menacing 'Cutter's Way,'" *The Washington Post,* November 19, 1981, p. C15.
48. See Peary's effusive entries in his *Cult Movies 2,* pp. 50–52; also see his *Guide for the Film Fanatic* (New York: Simon & Schuster, Fireside, 1986), p. 109.
49. (New York: Harcourt Brace Jovanovich, 1979); rpt. (New York: Avon, 1982).
50. The title of my dissertation was *Organizational Participation and Political Orientations: A Comparative Study of Participation in Community Organizations in Lower-Class Urban Settlements in Santiago, Chile, and Lima, Peru,*" University of Oregon, 1968. Two articles that grew out of my research were: "Parties, Neighborhood Associations, and the Politicization of the Urban Poor in Latin America" *American Journal of Political Science* 15, no. 3 (August 1971): 495–524; "Community Political Organizations and Lower-Class Politization in Two Latin American Cities, *Journal of Developing Areas* 5, no. 4 (July 1971): 523–42.
51. This conceit was suggested by Edward Said's discussion of Joseph Conrad in his *Culture and Imperialism* (New York: Knopf, 1993), pp. 22–30.

52. John J. Michalczyk, *Costa-Gavras: The Political Action Film* (Cranbury, N.J.: Associated University Presses, 1984), pp. 217–35, 252–53.
53. Cited by Barry Grey, "The Pinochet Coup and the Death of Charles Horman," at <*http://www.wsws.org/news/1998/Oct1998/horm-023.shtml*>.
54. *Covert Action in Chile, 1963–1973,* a Staff Report of the Select Committee to Study Governmental Operations with Respect to Intelligence Activities (U.S. Senate), December 18, 1975, p. 39.
55. William Blum, *Killing Hope: U.S. Military and CIA Interventions Since World War II* (Monroe, Me.: Common Courage Press, 1995), p. 214. This is a revised and updated version of *The CIA: A Secret History* (London: ZED Press, 1986).
56. Mark Mulligan, "CIA 'Partly to Blame' for Reporter's death," *Financial Times* (London), October 11, 1999, p. 15; Vernon Loeb, "CIA May Have Role in Journalist's Murder," *The Washington Post,* October 1, 1999, p. A15; Jonathan Franklin, "Memos Tie Us to '70 Coup Try in Chile," *Boston Globe,* October 9, 1999, p. A12.
57. Mary Dejevsky, "U.S. Implicated in 'Missing' Death," *The Independent* (London), October 9, 1999, p. 6.
58. For a discussion of the coup in Chile and the U.S. role, see James Petras and Morris Morley, *The United States and Chile: Imperialism and the Overthrow of the Allende Government* (New York: Monthly Review Press, 1975), which presents a detailed account of the complex economic destabilization engineered by the United States.
59. For an overview of film portraits of the U.S. role in the region, including an excellent discussion of *Missing,* see Prince's *Visions of Empire.*
60. On Pinochet, the man whose name became a virtual synonym for state-sponsored terror during his seventeen-year regime, see Peter Kornbluh, "Prisoner Pinochet: The Dictator and the Quest for Justice, *The Nation,* December 21, 1998; available online at <*www.thenation.com/1998/issue981221/1221kom.htm*>.
61. On Kissinger's role in the Chilean events, see Seymour Hersh, *The Price of Power: Kissinger in the Nixon White House* (New York: Simon & Schuster, Summit Books, 1984), pp. 258–96. See also Christopher Hitchens, "The Case Against Henry Kissinger—Part II: Crimes Against Humanity," *Harpers* 302, no. 1810 (March 2001): 49–74.

## 6. FAMILY VALUES? THE VIEW FROM RONALD REAGAN'S CLOSET

1. Rosalind P. Petchesky, "Anti-abortion, Anti-feminism, and the Rise of the New Right," *Feminist Studies* 7, no. 2 (Summer 1981): 208.
2. Susan Faludi, *Backlash: The Undeclared War Against American Women* (New York: Doubleday, Anchor, 1992).
3. Michael Rogin, *Ronald Reagan The Movie, and Other Episodes in Political Demonology* (Berkeley: University of California Press, 1987), p. 305.
4. See Jane Mayer and Doyle McManus, *Landslide: The Unmaking of the President, 1984–1988* (New York: Hougton Mifflin, 1988); Hedrick Smith, "The Image Game: Scripting the Video Presidency," in his *The Power Game: How Washington Works* (New York: Bantam, 1989), pp. 388–440; Mark Hertsgaard, *On Bended Knee* (New York: Farrar, Straus & Giroux, 1988).

5. Stephen Prince, *Visions of Empire: Political Imagery in Contemporary American Film* (New York: Praeger, 1992), p. 9.
6. Gary Wills, *Reagan's America* (New York: Penguin, 1988) and Rogin, *Ronald Reagan: The Movie,* analyze Reagan's unusual ability to quote movie images to support his positions or literally to make up scenes. Given that propensity, Edmund Morris' fictionalized treatment in *Dutch: A Memoir of Ronald Reagan* (New York: Random House, 1999) seems very much in character.
7. See Robert P. Kolker's insightful and comprehesive critical treatment of Spielberg's body of work in *A Cinema of Loneliness,* 3rd ed. (New York: Oxford University Press, 2000), pp. 247–328.
8. In addition to Rogin and Wills, see also Douglas Kellner, *Television and the Crisis of Democracy* (Boulder, Colo.: Westview Press, 1990) and *The Persian Gulf TV War* (Boulder, Colo.: Westview Press, 1992) on the use of "good versus evil" in Reagan's and Bush's speeches (many of which were writtten by the same people). Robin Wood's "Papering Over the Cracks," in his *Hollywood from Vietnam to Reagan* (New York: Columbia University Press, 1986), pp. 162–188, contains perhaps the most perceptive analysis and devastating criticism of Reaganism in the films of the 1980s.
9. The image appears in Wills, *Reagan's America.*
10. Stephanie Coontz, *The Way We Never Were: American Families and the Nostalgia Trap* (New York: Basic Books, 1992).
11. Rayna Rapp, "Family and Class in Contemporary America: Notes Toward an Understanding of Ideology," in *Rethinking Family: Some Feminist Questions,* ed. Barrie Thorne and Marilyn Yalom (New York: Longman, 1982), p. 162.
12. Jimmie L. Reeves and Richard Campbell, *Cracked Coverage: Television News, the Anti-Cocaine Crusade, and the Reagan Legacy* (Durham, N.C.: Duke University Press, 1994).
13. See Faludi's interview with Reagan advisor Gary Bauer in *Backlash,* pp. 263–67.
14. Betty Friedan, *The Feminine Mystique: Twentieth Anniversary Edition* (New York: Dell, Laurel, 1983), p. 189.
15. David Spiegel, "Mothering, Fathering, and Mental Illness," in *Rethinking Family,* p. 95.
16. His comments on the family as "utopia" were made in connection with the film *The Godfather,* "Reification and Utopia in Mass Culture," *Social Text, I* (1979); rpt. *Signatures of the Visible* (New York: Routledge, 1990).
17. See Kolker, *A Cinema of Loneliness,* pp. 301–2, following Terry Eagleton on this point.
18. Terry Eagleton, *The Function of Criticism: From the Spectator to Post-Structuralism* (London: Verso, 1984), pp. 121–22; Kolker, *A Cinema of Loneliness,* p. 325.
19. See Donald Spoto's analysis of the film in *The Art of Alfred Hitchcock,* 2nd ed. (New York: Anchor, 1992), pp. 115–27.
20. Ibid., p. 326.
21. Noted by Peter Bogdanovich in *Who the Devil Made It?* (New York: Knopf, 1997), pp. 302–3.
22. See William Arnold, *Shadowland* (New York: McGraw Hill, 1978), p. 221.
23. Gordon Thomas, *Journey into Madness: The True Story of Secret CIA Mind Control and Medical Abuse* (New York: Bantam, 1990), p. 221.

24. Ibid., p. 220.

25. That Freeman was only one among thousands performing psychosurgery is detailed in Thomas, *Journey into Madness*, pp. 219–25.

26. Arnold, *Shadowland*, p. 221.

27. These events are described by Arnold, *Shadowland*, and Thomas, *Journey into Madness*.

28. Walter Freeman, quoted by William Arnold, *Shadowland, p.* 223.

29. This page is reproduced in Arnold, *Shadowland, p.* 121.

30. Arnold, himself a *Seattle-Post Intelligencer* reporter, presents one of the most harrowing tales involving the destruction of a public celebrity ever written. The book obviously served as the basis for much of the screenplay, though it was uncredited. Arnold subsequently sued for compensation. See the account in Joshua Hammer, "A Shadowy Figure Says He Was Frances Farmer's Lover, But a Lawsuit Claims Different," *People Weekly*, March 21, 1983, pp. 38–40.

31. (New York; G. P. Putnam's, 1972; reprinted, New York: Dell Books, 1973).

32. Michel Foucault, *Madness and Civilization* (New York: Vintage, 1973), pp. 253, 255.

33. Hammer, "A Shadowy Figure," p. 38.

34. Quoted by Arnold, *Shadowland*, pp. 145–46.

35. Harry M. Cheney, "Frances: Prisoner in an American Gulag," *Christianity Today*, April 22, 1983, pp. 46–47.

36. Robin Wood, "The American Nightmare," in *Hollywood from Vietnam to Reagan*, pp. 70–94.

37. For the most comprehensive analysis and critical discussion of the film, see Michael Atkinson, *Blue Velvet* (London: British Film Institute, 1997).

38. These are developed by Sylvia Harvey, "The Absent Family of Film Noir," in *Women in Film Noir*, ed. E. Ann Kaplan (London: British Film Institute, 1980), pp. 35–46.

39. Atkinson, *Blue Velvet*, p. 11.

40. Quoted by Lizzie Borden, "The World According to Lynch, *The Village Voice*, September 23, 1986, p. 62.

41. The notion of Lynch writing a "secret history" of American life has been noted by many critics. See Danny Peary, *Cult Movies 3* (New York: Fireside Books, 1988), pp. 38–42; Betsy Berry, "Forever, In my Dreams: Generic Conventions and the Subversive Imagination in *Blue Velvet*," *Literature Film Quarterly* 16, no. 2 (1988): 82–90; Howard Hampton, "David Lynch's Secret History of the United States," *Film Comment* 29 (May–June 1993): 38–49; and Atkinson, *Blue Velvet*.

42. For an analysis of this and other rarely noted aspects of *Blue Velvet*, see Fred Pfeil, "Home Fires Burning: Family Noir in *Blue Velvet* and *Terminator 2*," in *Shades of Noir*, ed. Joan Copject (New York: Verso, 1993), pp. 227–59.

43. Lynch interview in *Cinéaste* 15, no. 3 (March 1987): 36.

44. Atkinson's analysis of these events in his study of *Blue Velvet* is insightful and detailed, yet everything about this amazing scene is open to a variety of interpretations.

45. Ibid., p. 54.

46. Ibid.

47. The madness of Norman Bates, Donald Spoto suggests in *The Art of Alfred Hitchcock*, while described onscreen by a psychiatrist, is never satisfactorily explained and almost mocked by the screen images. Uncle Charlie's behavior in *Shadow of a Doubt*

is explained away by a detective with the phrase "things go crazy from time to time" (p. 326). Dennis Hopper as Frank Booth apparently replicated some of his own wild, drug- and alcohol-crazed behavior ten to fifteen years earlier if the accounts of those who knew him then—related in Peter Biskind's *Easy Riders, Raging Bulls* (New York: Simon & Schuster, 1999)—are anywhere near correct. According to his ex-wife, who was interviewed by Biskind, his behavior in the 1970s was not far from that of the Booth character, including threats to shoot people.

48. Atkinson, *Blue Velvet,* pp. 44–45.
49. See Lynn Layton, "*Blue Velvet:* A Parable of Male Development," *Screen* 35, no. 4 (Winter 1994): 374–93.
50. Quoted by David Chute, "Out to Lynch," *Film Comment* 22 (Sept.-Oct. 1987): 32.
51. Especially insightful here is Howard Hampton, "David Lynch's Secret History of the United States," *Film Comment* 29 (May–June 1993): 38–49.
52. See Atkinson, *Blue Velvet,* p. 32.
53. Kolker, *A Cinema of Loneliness,* p. 302.
54. Patricia Brett Ehrens, review of *The Stepfather, Film Comment* 41, no. 2 (Winter 1987–88): 48. See also Kathie Maio's *Feminist in the Dark* (Freedom, Calif.: Crossing Press, 1988).
55. Ehrens, review of *The Stepfather,* p. 50.
56. Ibid., p. 48.
57. Wood, *Hollywood from Vietnam to Reagan,* pp. 90–93; Ehrens, review of *The Stepfather,* p. 49.
58. Ibid., p. 50.
59. Ibid., pp. 50–51.
60. Ibid., p. 52.
61. See Ellen Willis, "Sins of the Fathers: *Fatal Attraction* Snaps the American Family Portrait," *The Village Voice,* December 15, 1987, p. 89; "The Rabbit Died: Eight Capsule Comments on *Fatal Attraction,*" *The Village Voice,* December 15, 1987, pp. 90–91; Susan Faludi, "Fatal Distortion," *Mother Jones* (February–March 1998): 27–30. James Conlon, "The Place of Passion: Reflections on *Fatal Attraction,*" *Journal of Popular Film and Television* 16, no. 4 (Winter 1989): 148–155. The most comprehensive overview of all aspects of the film, consisting of nine essays, is the special issue edited by Liahana Babener, "*Fatal Attraction:* Feminist Readings,"*Journal of Popular Culture* 26, no. 3 (Winter 1992).
62. *Film Noir: An Encyclopedic Reference to the American Style,* 3rd ed., ed. Alain Silver and Elizabeth Ward (Woodstock, N.Y.: Overlook Press, 1992).
63. Richard Corliss, "Killer," *Time,* November 16, 1987, p. 72.
64. On this point, see Conlon, "The Place of Passion."
65. For a discussion of Robin Norwood's book and the groups it spawned, see the chapter entitled "Therapy for the Overly Feminine Woman" in Susan Faludi's *Backlash: The Undeclared War Against American Women* (New York: Anchor/Doubleday, 1991), pp. 347–56.
66. Susan Faludi makes references to audiences screaming "kill the bitch" in her definitive demolition of the director and the film; see her article "Fatal Distortion," pp. 27–30, 49–50. Also see Faludi's discussion of Adrian Lyne and *Fatal Attraction* in *Backlash,* pp. 117–23.

67. John Rohrkemper, "The Politics of Terror," *Journal of Popular Culture,* 26, no. 3 (Winter 1992): 83–90. For an article linking the film to the film noir tradition, see, in the same issue, Liahana Babener's "Patriarchal Politics in *Fatal Attraction,*" pp. 25–34.
68. For a comprehensive essay placing the film among other films on this subject and tracing the development of its screenplay, see Elaine Berland and Marilyn Wechter, "Fatal/Fetal Attraction: Psychological Aspects of Imagining Female Identity in Contemporary Film," *Journal of Popular Culture* 26, no. 3 (Winter 1992): 35–45. Also see Faludi's "Fatal Distortion" and related material in her *Backlash,* pp. 112–39.
69. See Kathe Davis' discussion of this point in "The Allure of the Predatory Woman in *Fatal Attraction,*" *Journal of Popular Culture* 26, no. 3 (Winter 1992): 47–58.

## 7. "SHE WAS BAD NEWS": MALE PARANOIA AND FEMMES FATALES

1. On this subject, see Amelia Jones' article "'She Was Bad News': Male Paranoia and the Contemporary New Woman," *Camera Obscura* 25 (1991), 297–320.
2. One of the most engaging and comprehensive studies of the fatal women of film noir is James F. Maxfield's *The Fatal Woman: Sources of Male Anxiety in American Film Noir, 1941–1991* (Cranbury, N.J.: Associated University Presses, 1996). E. Ann Kaplan, ed., *Women in Film Noir,* rev. ed. (London: British Film Institute, 1999) is still the standard collection of studies, revised and with an extensive updated bibliography.
3. Elizabeth Cowie, "Film Noir and Women," in *Shades of Noir,* ed. Joan Copjec (New York: Verso, 1993), p. 135.
4. Janey Place, "Women in Film Noir," in *Women in Film Noir,* p. 54.
5. Jackie Byars, *All That Hollywood Allows: Re-Reading Gender in 1950s Melodrama* (Chapel Hill: University of North Carolina Press, 1991), provides an excellent overview of the theoretical issues discussed here.
6. Laura Mulvey, "Visual Pleasure and Narrative Cinema," *Screen* 16, no. 3 (Autumn 1975): 17. This article is reprinted in her book *Visual and Other Pleasures* (Bloomington: Indiana University Press, 1989), pp. 12–28. Also see, in the same volume, "Afterthoughts on 'Visual Pleasure and Narrative Cinema,'" pp. 29–38.
7. Here and throughout this section I rely on Byars' perceptive critical exposition and discussion in *All That Hollywood Allows.*
8. Jonathan Rosenbaum's essay on *The Manchurian Candidate* in his *Placing Movies: The Practice of Film Criticism* (Berkeley: University of California Press, 1995), pp. 117–23, is the only one to note the Hollywoodian unreality of the Leigh character and her exchanges with Sinatra, juxtaposed against the darkly omnious plot.
9. See the interview with director John Waters in the PBS American Cinema Series *The Star* for an interpretation of these women of the 1950s as projecting a kind of "drag" persona. That was the case with Jayne Mansfield, who loved playing the star, but even more true of Marilyn Monroe.
10. See Paige Baty's *American Monroe* (Berkeley: University of California Press, 1996) for insightful commentary on this dimension of Monroe. For my review of her book, see *Political Theory* 25, no. 4 (August 1997): 602–7. For other biographies, see Anthony Summers, *Goddess: The Secret Lives of Marilyn Monroe* (New York: Pen-

guin, Onyx, 1986); Barbara Leaming, *Marilyn Monroe* (New York: Random House, Three Rivers Press, 1998); and Donald H. Wolfe, *The Last Days of Marilyn Monroe* (New York: Morrow, 1998), who presents much new material and makes a compelling case that Monroe was murdered.

11. See Maxfield, *The Fatal Woman,* pp. 84–94, for an excellent discussion of this character.
12. See Byars' "Cultural Studies: An Alternative for Feminist Film Studies," *All That Hollywood Allows,* pp. 25–66, for useful summary of the arguments.
13. For a definition of "reading against the grain," see Lisa Lewis, "Form and Female Authorship in Music Video," *Communication* 1 (1987): 355–77.
14. This line is spoken by Michael O'Hara at the end of Orson Welles' *The Lady from Shanghai* (1948).
15. On this point, see Frank Krutnik, *In a Lonely Street: Film Noir, Genre, Masculinity* (London: Routledge, 1991), p. 112.
16. See note 61 in the preceding chapter for the extensive critical literature on *Fatal Attraction.*
17. See John Blaser, "Film Noir's Progressive Portrayal of Women" under the general website listing "No Place for a Woman and Other Essays," at *<http://www.lib.berkeley.edu/MRC/noir/html>.*
18. Some of the most memorable quoted dialogue (Kathie: "I don't want to die." Jeff: "I don't want to die either, baby, but if I do I'm gonna die last") reflected additions by Frank Fenton. For an engaging exploration of the multiple versions of the screenplay, see Jeff Schwage, "The Past Rewritten," *Film Comment* 27 (Jan.–Feb. 1991): 12–17.
19. See Michael Walsh, "*Out of the Past:* The History of the Subject," *Enclitic* 6, no. 1 (1982): 6–16.
20. On the underemphasized importance of passion in neo-noir films, see James Conlon, "The Place of Passion: Reflections on *Fatal Attraction,*" *Journal of Popular Film and Television* 16, no. 4 (Winter 1989): 16–23.
21. Maxfield's analysis of this scene (*The Fatal Woman,* p. 59) is easily the best among all the published discussions of the film.
22. Walsh, "*Out of the Past:* The History of the Subject," p. 10.
23. Krutnik, *In a Lonely Street,* p. 112.
24. Maxfield, *The Fatal Woman,* p. 62.
25. Krutnik, *In a Lonely Street,* p. 112.
26. Eddie Muller, *Dark City: The Lost World of Film Noir* (New York: St. Martin's Press, 1998), p. 78.
27. Leighton Grist, "*Out of the Past,*" in *The Book of Film Noir,* ed. Ian Cameron (New York: Continuum, 1992), p. 211.
28. See Christopher Orr, "Genre Theory in the Context of the Noir and Post-Noir Film," *Film Criticism* 22, no. 1 (Fall 1997): 21–38.
29. Orr, "Genre Theory," p. 28.
30. Jonathan Buchbawn, "Tame Wolves and Phoney Claims: Paranoia and Film Noir," in *The Book of Film Noir,* p. 97.
31. It is prescient, in this respect, that in 1999 researchers found that PCB levels in ducks collected along the Housatonic River near Woods Pond, Massachusetts, were among

the highest biologists had ever seen. Reported in *Ducks Unlimited* magazine (Nov.–Dec. 1999): 12.

32. I am indebted to Danny Peary's discussion (p. 339) in *Guide for the Film Fanatic* (New York: Simon & Schuster, 1986) and the entry (pp. 271–73) in his *Cult Movies* (New York: Delta Books, 1981) for several details and insights on both films, and to George Lipsitz for suggesting its inclusion. I also wish to thank the Mystery Channel for screening it in 1999, since it was not available for purchase on video during this period.
33. For an extensive analysis of the film, see Celestino Deleyto, "The Margins of Pleasure: Female Monstrosity and Male Paranoia in 'Basic Instinct,'" *Film Criticism* 21, no. 3 (Spring 1997): 20–43.
34. Roger Ebert, review of *Basic Instinct, Chicago Sun-Times,* March 20, 1992, p. 1; also available online at <*http://www.suntimes.com/ebert.html*> or <*www.imdb.com*>.
35. Deleyto, "The Margins of Pleasure," p. 20.
36. Edwin Jahiel, review at <*imdb.com*>.
37. Laura Mulvey, *Fetishism and Curiosity* (Bloomington: Indiana University Press, 1996), p. 12.
38. Ibid.
39. Kaplan, "Introduction," *Women in Film Noir,* p. 17.
40. See Daphne Patai's wide-ranging critical study *Heterophobia: Sexual Harassment and the Future of Feminism* (Lanham, Md.: Roman & Littlefield, 1998).
41. Jeffrey Rosen, "Heterophobia," *The New Republic,* June 28, 1998, p. 35.
42. John Fekete, *Moral Panic* (Toronto: Robert Davies, 1995).

## 8. WOMEN AND SEXUAL PARANOIA

1. Andrea Walsh, "The Women's Film," in *The Political Companion to American Film,* ed. Gary Crowdus (New York: Cinéaste/LakeView Press, 1994), pp. 493–94.
2. Walsh, "The Women's Film," p. 494.
3. For a detailed discussion of *Gaslight* see Andrea Walsh, "'The Weeds Grow Long Near the Shore': Madness, Suspicion, and Distrust in Popular Women's Films of the 1940s," in her *Women's Film and Female Experience, 1940–1950* (New York: Praeger, 1984), pp. 176–85.
4. An excellent British production, closer to the stage play upon which the story was based, was suppressed by MGM for nearly fifty years, languishing in a vault until it was finally broadcast by Turner Classic Movies in 1999.
5. For an analysis, film stills, and production data on *The House by the River,* see Lotte Eisner's *Fritz Lang* (New York: Da Capo, 1986), pp. 285–94, 411–12. Additional context on this least seen of Lang's American films is provided by Patrick McGilligan, "1948–1952," in his *Fritz Lang: The Nature of the Beast* (New York: St. Martin's, 1997), pp. 368–70. A more extensive analysis of the film appears in Tom Gunning's essay "Coda: *House by the River,*" in his *Films of Fritz Lang: Allegories of Vision and Modernity* (London: British Film Institute, 2000), pp. 368–88.
6. As background to these developments, see Robin Wood's discussion of the American horror film in *Hollywood from Vietnam to Reagan* (New York: Columbia University Press, 1986).

7. For an extended analysis of the novel, including its urban context and reception, see Sharon Marcus' "Placing 'Rosemary's Baby,'" *differences: A Journal of Feminist Cultural Studies* 5, no. 3 (Fall 1993), 121–154.
8. These stories were undoubtedly based on Maria Monk's alleged captivity memoir *Awful Disclosures by Maria Monk of the Hotel Dieu Nunnery of Montreal* (New York, 1837), which is still in print and serves as fodder for anti-church conspiratoral rants.
9. Kim Newman, *Nightmare Movies* (New York: Harmony Books, 1988), p. 39. I am indebted to Newman's book for several insights on *Rosemary's Baby* and its influence on subsequent horror films, especially regarding women's paranoia about the family. See Newman's chapter "Devil Movies," pp. 37–49.
10. See the chapters "The American Nightmare" (pp. 70–94) and "Normality and Monsters" (pp. 95–134) in Wood's *Hollywood from Vietnam to Reagan*. Newman's *Nightmare Movies* traces the influence of *Rosemary's Baby* and *The Exorcist* (1973, William Friedkin) through the succeeding two decades of horror movies.
11. For an extensive and revelatory discussion of *Klute*, see the essay by Christine Gledhill, "*Klute* 2: Feminism and *Klute*," in *Women in Film Noir*, ed. E. Ann Kaplan rev. ed. (London: British Film Institute, 1999), pp. 112–28. See also Robin Wood's review essay of *Klute* in *Film Comment* 8, no. 1 (Spring 1972), 32–37.
12. Alan Pakula interview in *Positif*, no. 36 (March 1972), 36; cited by Christine Gledhill, "*Klute* 1: A Contemporary Film Noir and Feminist Criticism," in *Women in Film Noir*, p. 20.
13. Wood, *Film Comment*, p. 33.
14. One that comes close is John Rignall's "Alan J. Pakula's *Klute*," *Monogram* 4 (1972), 26–27.
15. For a revealing interview, where Fonda discusses her politics during this period, see Barbara Zheutlin and David Talbot, eds., *Creative Differences: Profiles of Hollywood Dissidents* (Boston: South End Press, 1978), pp. 131–43.
16. See Gledhill's essay "Feminism and *Klute*" on this point.
17. Jane Caputi, *The Age of Sex Crime* (Bowling Green, Ohio: Popular Press, 1987); see also her revelatory essay "American Psychos: The Serial Killer in the Contemporary Imagination," *Journal of American Culture* 16, no. 4 (Winter 1993): 101–12.
18. Caputi, "American Psychos," p. 102.
19. Caputi, "American Psychos," p. 103.
20. Among the extensive reviews, see: "Writers on the Lamb: Sorting Out the Sexual Politics of a Controversial Film," *The Village Voice*, March 5, 1991, pp. 49–56; Elizabeth Young, "*The Silence of the Lambs* and the Flaying of Feminist Theory," *Camera Obscura* 27 (1992): 5–35; Janet Staiger, "Taboos and Totems: Cultural Meanings of *The Silence of the Lambs*," in *Film Theory Goes to the Movies*, ed. Jim Colins, Hilary Radner, and Ava P. Collins (New York: Routledge, 1993), pp. 171–82; Diane Fuss, "Monsters of Perversion: Jeffrey Dahmer and *The Silence of the Lambs*," in *Media Spectacles*, ed. Marjorie Garber et al. (New York: Routledge, 1993), pp. 181–205; David Sundelson, "The Demon Therapist and Other Dangers: Jonathan Demme's 'The Silence of the Lambs,'" *Journal of Popular Film and Television* 27, no. 1 (Spring 1993): 12–18; Sabrina Barton, "Your Self Storage: Female Investigation and Male Performativity in the Woman's Psychothriller," in *The New American Cinema*, ed. Jon Lewis (Durham, N.C.: Duke University Press, 1998), pp. 187–216.

21. Thomas Harris, *Red Dragon* (New York: Bantam, 1981).
22. The reference to Coleridge was suggested by Harvey Roy Greenberg, "Psychotherapy at the Simplex: le plu ça shrink (psychotherapists in American films)," *Journal of Popular Film and Television* 20, no. 2 (Summer 1992): 9–16.
23. Mark Goodman, "Cops, Killers & Cannibals: Real-Life Role Models Give *Silence of the Lambs* a Chilling Authenticity That Generates the Wages of Fear at the Box Office," *People Weekly* 35, no. 12, April 1, 1991, pp. 62–65.
24. See Caputi, "American Psychos," for a striking discussion of this interactive process.
25. Ibid., p. 105.
26. For a review of Thomas Harris' *Hannibal,* see Annie Gottlieb, "Free-Range Rude," *The Nation,* July 19, 1999, pp. 28–31.

## 9. BAD COPS AND NOIR POLITICS

1. See Marc Cooper, "L.A. Not So Confidential," *Salon.com News,* Sept. 28, 1999; available online at *<http://salonmag.com/news/feature1999/09/lapd/print.htm>*.
2. Police pay varies widely across the United States. In 1999, according to articles in the *Detroit News,* police there went on strike over annual pay rates, which started at twenty-five thousand dollars. By comparison, the lowest-grade officers in Los Angels were paid nearly forty-two thousand dollars.
3. Eric F. Goldman, *The Crucial Decade—and After: America, 1945–1960* (New York: Vintage, 1960), p. 198. Also see David Halberstam, *The Fifties* (New York: Villard, 1993), pp. 188–94.
4. See Athan G. Theoharis and John Stuart Cox, *Boss: J. Edgar Hoover and the Great American Inquisition* (New York: Bantam, 1990), who describe the Apalachin, N.Y., mafia convention that forced Hoover to change his position.
5. On the circumstances surrounding the initiation of the Production Code, see Leonard J. Leff and Jerrold L. Simmons, *The Dame in the Kimono: Hollywood, Censorship and the Production Code from the 1920s to the 1960s* (New York: Anchor, 1991). See also Jonathan Munby, *Public Enemies, Public Heroes: Screening the Gangster from "Little Caesar" to "Touch of Evil"* (Chicago: University of Chicago Press, 1999).
6. On the film's powerful critique of capitalism, which is equated with organized crime, see Christine Noll Brinckmann, "The Politics of *Force of Evil,*" *Prospects* 6 (1981), 357–86.
7. The best discussion of *The Big Heat* is Colin McArthur's *The Big Heat* (London: British Film Institute, 1992).
8. On Lumet's films and personal vision, see Frank R. Cunningham, *Sidney Lumet: Film and Literary Vision* (Lexington: University of Kentucky Press, 1919). See also Jay Boyer, *Sidney Lumet* (New York: Twayne, Macmillan, 1993).
9. Larry Beinhart, *American Hero* (New York: Ballantine, 1994), p. 297. This novel was the original source for Barry Levinson's film *Wag the Dog* (1997).
10. Charles Mills, *The Racial Contract* (Ithaca: Cornell University Press, 1997).
11. Dan Flory, "Black on White: Film Noir and the Epistemology of Race in Recent African-American Cinema," *Journal of Social Philosophy* 31, no. 1 (Spring 2000): 107.
12. The terminology is borrowed from James Naremore's "The Other Side of the Street," in his *More Than Night: Film Noir in Its Contexts* (Berkeley: University of California

Press, 1998), pp. 220–53; Eric Lott, "The Whiteness of Film Noir," *American Literary History* 9 (1997): 542–66.

13. Carl Franklin, Harold Lloyd Master Seminar, American Film Institute, available online at <*http://www.afionline.org/haroldlloyd/franklin/script.6.htm*>.
14. In his review of the film Ed Guerrero points out why—the O. J. Simpson trial, among other reasons—this otherwise excellent film had limited box-office appeal. See *Cinéaste* 22, no. 1 (1996): 38–42.
15. On this argument, first presented by Du Bois in 1897 and published in *The Souls of Black Folk* (1903), see August Meir, "Booker T. Washington and the 'Talented Tenth,'" *Negro Thought in America, 1880–1915*, 2nd ed. (Ann Arbor: University of Michigan Press, 1988), pp. 206–45.
16. According to Cornell economist Duane Chapman (private communication), the cost-of-living index increased 745 percent from 1947 to 1999, making that hundred dollars a significant amount in today's terms.
17. See Mike Davis, *City of Quartz: Excavating the Future in Los Angeles* (New York: Vingtage, 1992).
18. See Paul Arthur, "Los Angeles as Scene of the Crime," *Film Comment* 32, no. 4 (July–August 1996): 20–28.
19. See Mike Davis, *Ecology of Fear: Los Angeles and the Imagination of Disaster* (New York: Henry Holt, Metropolitan Books, 1998).
20. See the following works by Kevin Starr: *Americans and the California Dream, 1850–1915* (New York: Oxford University Press, 1973); *Inventing the Dream: California Through the Progressive Era* (New York: Oxford University Press, 1985); *Material Dreams: Southern California Through the 1920s* (New York: Oxford University Press, 1990); *The Dream Endures: California Enters the 1940s* (New York: Oxford University Press, 1997); and *Troubled Dreams: California in War and Peace, 1940–1950* (New York: Oxford University Press, forthcoming).
21. Arthur, "Los Angeles as Scene of the crime," p. 20.
22. Interview in *Spliced* (Sept. 2, 1997), available online at <*http://www.splicedonline.com/features/a_hanson.htm*>.
23. "*L.A. Confidential*," *Cinéaste* 23, no. 3 (1997): 42.
24. Robert Conot, *Rivers of Blood, Years of Darkness* (New York: Bantam, 1967); Frank Donner, "The Los Angeles Police Department: Defenders of the Free Enterprise Faith," in his *Protectors of Privilege: Red Squads and Police Repression in Urban America* (Berkeley: University of California Press, 1992), pp. 247–89; Joe Domanick, *To Protect and to Serve: The LAPD's Century of War in the City of Dreams* (New York: Pocket, 1994); and Lou Cannon, *Official Negligence: How Rodney King and the Riots Changed Los Angeles and the LAPD* (New York: Random House, 1997).
25. James Ellroy, interview in *Salon* (Dec. 1996), available online at <*http://www.salon1999.com/dec96/interview2961209.htm*>.
26. "Politics as a Vocation," in *From Max Weber: Essays in Sociology*, ed. H. Gerth and C. Wright Mills (New York: Oxford University Press, 1946), pp. 121–22.
27. Steven Marcus, "Dashiell Hammett," in *The Poetics of Murder: Detective Fiction and Literary Theory*, ed. Glenn W. Most and William W. Stow (New York: Harcourt Brace Jovanovich, 1983), p. 207.
28. James Ellroy, *L. A. Confidential*, p. 156.

29. Gunnar Myrdal, *An American Dilemma* (New York: Harper & Row, 1944).
30. It was also one of the most inventive periods of the African-American musical tradition. Charlie Parker, Dizzy Gillespie, Kenny Clarke, Max Roach, Thelonious Monk, and Bud Powell, among others, developed bebop jazz, a form that reached its peak during the film noir period, though it was rarely represented in movies of the time.
31. In addition to Lott ("The Whiteness of Film Noir," pp. 542–66) and Flory ("Black on White," pp. 107ff.), see Manthia Diawara, "Noir by Noirs: Toward a New Realism in Black Cinema," in *Shades of Noir,* ed. Joan Copjec (New York: Verso, 1993), pp. 26–78; see also Ulrike Liskowski, "Bad White Men: *L.A. Confidential* and Film Noir," *Node 9* 3 (May 1999), available online at <http://*Node9.Phil3.uni-freiburg.de*>.
32. Charles Mills, *The Racial Contract* (Ithaca: Cornell University Press, 1997), p. 18.
33. Ellroy, *Salon* Interview.
34. Stephen Hunter, "Film's Dark Victories: *L.A. Confidential* Harks Back to Noir's Best and Bleakest," *The Washington Post,* September 21, 1997.
35. James Ellroy, "Introduction" to *L.A. Confidential: The Screenplay* by Brian Helgeland and Curtis Hanson (New York: Warner Books, 1997), p. xv.
36. See Domanick, *To Protect and to Serve,* pp. 70ff.
37. Quoted in Ronald Burns and Jason Seals, "*L.A. Confidential:* A Review," *Journal of Criminal Justice and Popular Culture* 6, no. 1 (1998): 19.
38. Burns and Seals, "*L.A. Confidential,*" p. 20.
39. Edward Herman and Noam Chomsky, *Manufacturing Consent* (New York: Pantheon, 1987), passim.
40. Liszkowski, "Bad White Men."
41. Davis, *City of Quartz,* p. 21.
42. Lott, "The Whiteness of Film Noir," p. 551.
43. In an ironic postscript, in the spring of 2000 two African-American men were arrested in New York City for the alleged execution of five employees in a backroom of a restaurant at which they were once employed.
44. Donald Lyons, review *L.A. Confidential* 33 *Film Comment* (Nov.–Dec. 1997): 10.
45. See Jonathan Munby, *Public Enemies, Public Heroes.*
46. Flory, "Black on White," p. 90.
47. On the Zoot subculture as a paradigm for successive oppositional movements ground in the black underworld, see Robin D. G. Kelley, "The Riddle of the Zoot: Malcolm Little and Black Cultural Politics During World War II," in *Malcolm X: In Our Own Image,* ed. Joe Wood (New York: St. Martin's, 1992), pp. 155–82. On the evolution of the black underground and its cultural manifestations, see Ben Sidran, "The Evolution of the Black Underground, 1930–1947," *Black Talk: How the Music of Black America Created a Radical Alternative to the Values of Western Literary Tradition,* 2nd ed. (New York: Da Capo, 1981), pp. 78–115.
48. Diawara, "Noir by Noirs," p. 266.
49. The title of the film is the same as that of undercover narc Michael Levine's memoir *Deep Cover* (New York: Delacorte, 1990), a scathing indictment of the Reagan-Bush and earlier drug wars that considers the whole U.S. effort—essentially the background to the film—a grotesque failure. Although there is no direct connection between the book by Levine and the screenplay by Tolkin and Bean, one must surmise

that any attentive student of the "drug wars" in the late 1980s and early '90s could not have avoided Levine's appearances on virtually every network talk and news show. The passage is quoted by Michael Levine in the opening pages (p. vii) of his memoir.

50. The name John Hull might resonate in some readers' minds as a character out of the 1987 Iran-Contra hearings. He was a U.S. citizen with a ranch in Costa Rica, near the Nicaraguan border, purportedly involved in smuggling arms to the CIA-controlled Contra rebels.

51. This marginality is effectively described in Waheenma Lubiano's "Don't Talk With Your Eyes Closed: Caught in the Hollywood Gun Sights," available online at *<http://www.tiac.net/users/thaslett/lubiano/deepcov.htm>*.

52. See Alfred McCoy et al., *The Politics of Heroin in Southeast Asia* (New York: Harper & Row, 1972); Alfred McCoy, *The Politics of Heroin: The Complicity of the CIA in the Global Drug Trade* (New York: Lawrence Hill, 1991); Gary Webb, *Dark Alliance: The CIA, the Contras, and the Crack Cocaine Explosion* (New York: Seven Stories Press, 1998); Alexander Cockburn and Jeffrey St. Clair, *Whiteout: The CIA, Drugs, and the Press* (New York: Verso, 1998). Cockburn and St. Clair's book is especially useful in providing extensive bibliographies following each chapter.

53. Flory, "Black on White," p. 93.

## 10. FROM ASSASSINATION TO THE SURVEILLANCE SOCIETY

1. These words are spoken by the narrator of Don Delillo's fictional treatment of the JFK assassination entitled *Libra* (New York: Viking, Penguin, 1988), p. 181.

2. The notion of distinguishing "knowing" from" believing" or "sensing" truth comes from Christopher Sharrett's perceptive review of Fredric Jameson's book entitled *The Geopolitical Aesthetic: Cinema and Space in the World System;* see *Film Quarterly* 46, no. 4 (Summer 1993): 39–41; the distinction also appears in E. Martin Schotz's *History Will Not Absolve Us: Orwellian Control, Public Denial, and the Murder of President Kennedy* (Brookline, Mass.: Kurtz, Ulmer & DeLucia, 1996).

3. The term "dangerous knowledge"—which is also the title of Art Simon's revelatory study of cultural images, *Dangerous Knowledge: The JFK Assassination in Art and Film* (Philadelphia: Temple University Press, 1996)—comes from Ron Rosenbaum's essay "Oswald's Ghost," which first appeared in the November 1983 issue of *Texas Monthly* and is reprinted in his *Travels with Dr. Death* (New York: Penguin, 1991), pp. 55–91.

4. Don DeLillo, "American Blood," *Rolling Stone,* December 8, 1983, p. 22.

5. See former Senator Daniel Patrick Moynihan's *Secrecy: The American Experience* (New Haven: Yale University Press, 1998). I do not share his conclusion deprecating conpiratorial implications of such massive secrecy.

6. One of the best examples of this dynamic is Judith Grant's "Trust No One: Paranoia, Conspiracy Theories, and Alien Invasions," *Undercurrent* 6 (Summer 1998): 1–45, which is available online at *<http://darkwing.uoregon.edu/^ucurrent6/6-grant.htm>*. It demonstrates how, through its own statements spanning fifty years since the Roswell events of 1947, the U.S. government has admitted systematic deception

and withholding of information in ways that support all aspects of the arguments of the most extreme advocates of a long-term conspiracy to hide the truth about possible encounters with extraterrestrials. See Marita Sturken's "Re-Enactment, Fantasy, and the Paranoia of History: Oliver Stone's Docudramas," *History and Theory* 36, no. 4 (December 1997): 64–79.

7. See Jeff Swartz, *PostModernity, History, and the Assassination of JFK,* available online at <*http://www.gslis.utexas.edu/~jeffs/thesis.html*>.
8. Attorney Vincent J. Salandria published three lengthy critiques of the *Warren Report:* "The Warren Report Analysis of Shots, Trajectories, and Wounds: A Lawyer's Dissecting View," *Philadelphia Legal Intelligencer,* November 2, 1964; "A Philadelphia Lawyer Analyzes the Shots, Trajectories, and Wounds," *Liberation* 9, no. 10 (January 1965): 13–19; and "The Warren Report?" *Liberation* 10, no. 1 (March 1965): 14–33. They have been reprinted as Appendix III in Schotz's *History Will Not Absolve Us, pp.* 87–172. Jay Epstein's influential work, *Inquest: The Warren Commission and the Establishment of Truth,* first published by Viking Press in 1966, immediately became a best-seller. It was most recently available in a collection of Epstein's assassination writings entitled *The Assassination Chronicles: Inquest, Counterplot, and Legend* (New York: Carroll & Graf, 1992). Mark Lane's *Rush to Judgment* (New York: Holt, Rinehart and Winston, 1966) was the most widely read of the critiques of the *Warren Report* and one of the best-selling books of that year.
9. Quoted by Arthur Schlesinger Jr., *Robert Kennedy and His Times,* vol. 2 (Boston: Hougton Mifflin, 1978), p. 643.
10. Ibid., pp. 643–44, citing the Senate Select Committee to Study Government Operations with Respect to Intelligence Activities (Church Committee), *Final Report,* Bk. V, *The Investigation of the Assassination of President John F. Kennedy: Performance of the Intelligence Agencies,* 94th Cong., 2nd sess., 1976, pp. 23, 33.
11. Mark Lane, *Rush to Judgment* (New York: Holt, Rinehart & Winston, 1966).
12. Josiah Thompson, *Six Seconds in Dallas: A Micro-study of the Kennedy Assassination* (New York: Bernard Geis Associates, 1967; rpt. Berkeley Medallion Books, 1976). See Rosenbaum's essay "Oswald's Ghost" for his account of an interview with Josiah Thompson.
13. Anthony Summers' *Not in Your Lifetime: The Definitive Book on the JFK Assassination* (New York: Marlowe & Company, 1998) is the best single-volume treatment of all aspects of the JFK assassination conspiracies. (Earlier editions were simply entitled *Conspiracy.*).
14. Gallup Poll 12/4–6/1993. See George Gallup Jr., *The Gallup Poll: Public Opinion Index 1994* (Wilmington, De.: Scholarly Resources Press), 15: 193.
15. See Sheldon Appleton, "The Mystery of the Kennedy Assassination: What the American Public Believes," *The Public Perspective* 9, no. 6 (Oct.–Nov. 1998): 12–17.
16. Their motivations are perceptively analyzed in Barbie Zelizer's *Convering the Body: The Kennedy Assassination, the Media, and the Shaping of Collective Memory* (Chicago: University of Chicago Press, 1992).
17. See Philip Melanson, *Spy Saga: Lee Harvey Oswald and U.S. Intelligence* (New York: Praeger, 1990); Epstein, *Legend: The Secret World of Lee Harvey Oswald* (New York: McGraw-Hill, 1978); John Newman, *Oswald and the CIA* (New York: Carroll & Graf, 1995); and Norman Mailer, *Oswald's Tale: An American Mystery* (New York: Random

House, 1995). After reading these works, I am left with the distinct impression there were *many* individuals who went by the name "Oswald," and that the latter was a probable asset of multiple intelligence agencies, was under FBI surveillance in addition to several other secret networks, including the mafia and anti-Castro Cubans. Also see Christopher Sharrett's brief profile of Oswald's probable status as a U.S. intelligence agent, which appears as appendix V in Schotz, *History Will Not Absolve Us,* pp. 193–98.

18. See Michael L. Kurtz, "Introduction," *Crime of the Century: The Kennedy Assassination from a Historian's Perspective,* 2nd ed. (Knoxville: University of Tennessee Press, 1993). Kurtz at first seemed to believe that Fidel Castro's security service was responsible for JFK's death, but his more recent comments suggest that his perspective has shifted. See his essay "Oliver Stone, *JFK,* and History," in *Oliver Stone's USA: Film, History, and Controversy,* ed. Robert B. Toplin (University Press of Kansas, 2000), pp. 166–77.
19. Timothy Melley, *Empire of Conspiracy: The Culture of Paranoia in Postwar America* (Ithaca: Cornell University Press, 2000), pp. 133–37.
20. Author's transcription of Stern's remarks.
21. Marita Sturken, "Reenactment, Fantasy, and the Paranoia of History: Oliver Stone's Docudramas," *History and Theory* 36, no. 4 (Dec. 1997): 74. Emphasis added.
22. *U.S. Statutes at Large* 106 (1992): 3443–58.
23. The *Final Report of the Assassination Records Review Board* was issued in 1998 and is available online at <*http://www.fas.org/sgp/advisory/arrb98/index.html*>.
24. On Stone's film, see *"JFK": The Book of the Film,* ed. Oliver Stone and Zachary Sklar (New York: Applause Books, 1993); Kurtz, "Oliver Stone, *JFK,* and History," pp. 166–77; Susan Mackey-Kallis, *Oliver Stone's America: "Dreaming the Myth Outward* (Boulder: Westview, 1996); and Sturken, "Reenactment, Fantasy, and the Paranoia of History," pp. 64–79. One of the finest arguments for Stone's film and for conspiratorial dimensions of the Kennedy assassination is made by Christopher Sharrett, "Conspiracy Theory and Political Murder in America: Oliver Stone's *JFK* and the Facts of the Matter," in *The New American Cinema,* ed. Jon Lewis (Durham, N.C.: Duke University Press, 1998), pp. 217–47.
25. Douglas Kellner, "Hollywood Film and Society," *Oxford Guide to Film Studies* (New York: Oxford University Press, 1998), p. 355.
26. For a negative evaluation of Garrison, see Edward Jay Epstein, *Counterplot* (New York: Viking, 1969; rpt. in *The Assassination Chronicles*); James Kirkwood, *American Grotesque: An Account of the Clay Shaw–Jim Garrison Affair in the City of New Orleans* (New York: Simon & Schuster, 1970). Defenders of Garrison include James DiEugenio, *Justice Betrayed: The Kennedy Assassination and the Garrison Trial* (New York: Sheridan Square, 1992); and William Davy, *Let Justice Be Done: New Light on the Jim Garrison Investigation* (Reston, Va.: Jordan, 1999).
27. See Zelitzer, *Covering the Body,* for a discussion fo this theory.
28. Historian Michael Kurtz's discussion of *JFK* in *Oliver Stone's USA* presents the best overview of contending theories among historians.
29. William Blum, *Killing Hope: U.S. Military and CIA Interventions Since World War II* (Monroe, Me.: Common Courage Press, 1995); Frank J. Donner, *The Age of Surveillance: The Aims and Methods of America's Political Intelligence System* (New York:

Knopf, 1980); Robert J. Goldstein, *Political Repression in Modern America: 1870 to the Present* (Boston: Schenckman, 1978; rpt. Champaign: University of Illinois Press, 2001).

30. This point is related in Thomas Powers' *The Man Who Kept the Secrets: Richard Helms and the CIA* (New York: Knopf, 1979). The Diem family is also sugested by onetime CIA agent Charles McCarry in his novel *The Tears of Autumn* (New York: Fawcett, Crest, 1976).
31. Michael Rogin, "Body and Soul Murder: *JFK*," in *Media Spectacles*, ed. Marjorie Garber, Jann Matlock, and Rebecca Walkowitz (New York: Routledge, 1993), p. 15. Also see Roy Grundmann and Cynthia Lucia, "Gays, Women and an Abstinent Hero: The Sexual Politics of *JFK*," *Cinéaste* 19, no. 1 (1992): 20–23.
32. This is how the situation is described by the narrator of DeLillo's *Libra*, p. 181.
33. "The Mystery of the Kennedy Assassination," Appleton, p. 17.
34. Ibid.
35. See Robin Ramsay, "Of Conspiracies and Conspiracy Theories: The Truth Buried by the Fantasies," available online at <*http://www.magnet.ch/serendipity/eded/laconspir.htm*>. Ramsay is the editor of *Lobster*, a British investigatory journal.
36. Fredric Jameson, *The Political Unconscious: Narrative as a Socially Symbolic Act* (Ithaca: Cornell University Press, 1981). The most useful exposition of Jameson's concept for this discussion is to be found in his book entitled *The Geopolitical Aesthetic* (Bloomington: Indiana University Press, 1992), especially the first section entitled "Totality as Conspiracy," pp. 9–84. Also useful is the preface by Colin MacCabe, which clarifies some of Jameson's difficult, obtuse prose. See Christopher Sharrett's review of *The Geopolitical Aesthetic* in *Film Quarterly* 46, no. 3 (Summer 1993): 39–41.
37. For example, see Rick Martin and T. Trent Gegax, "Conspiracy Mania Feeds Our Growing National Paranoia," *Newsweek*, Dec. 30–Jan. 6, 1997, pp. 65–66, 71; Jonathan Alter, "The Age of Conspiricism," *Newsweek*, March 24, 1997, p. 47.
38. The Arts & Entertainment network repeatedly broadcast a two-hour special entitled *Conspiracies* during 1997 and 1998. Network news magazine programs like *60 Minutes*, *Dateline*, and *Primetime Live* routinely feature stories involving a plot or conspiracy, such as the Vince Foster death/suicide or the Martin Luther King Jr. assassination.
39. Jonathan Vanken and John Whalen, *The 70 Greatest Conspiracies of All Time* (New York: Citadel, 1996). See their website at <*http://www.webcom.com:80/~conspire*>. Robert Anton Wilson, *Everything Is Under Control* (New York: HarperCollins, 1998). Wilson's website is available at <*http://www.wawilson.com*>.
40. See the website of the Center for Conspiracy Culture at <*http://www.wkac.ac.uk/research/ccc/academic%network.htm*>.
41. See John Marks, *The Search for the "Mancurian Candidate": The CIA and Mind Control—The Secret History of the Behavioral Sciences*, 2nd ed. (New York: Norton, 1991); and Gordon Thomas, *Journey into Madness: The True Story of Secret CIA Mind Control and Medical Abuse* (New York: Bantam, 1990).
42. The MAJESTIC (or MJ-12) allegations are covered in Howard Blum's *Out There: The Government's Secret Quest for Extraterrestrials* (New York: Pocket Star, 1991). A novelistic account is Whitley Stieber's *Majestic* (New York: Berkeley, 1990).
43. See the discussion and analysis of several themes and dimensions of *The X-Files* in David Laver, Angela Hague, and Marla Cartwright, eds., *"Deny All Knowledge": Reading "The X-Files"* (Syracuse: Syracuse University Press, 1996). Especially useful

is Allison Graham's "Are You Now or Have You Ever Been?: Conspiracy Theory and 'The X-Files,'" pp. 52–62. Douglas Kellner's unpublished manuscript "'The X-Files' and Postmodern Thought" (1998) was full of insights and I want to thank the author for sharing it.

44. For a brief historical background on CIA involvement in the Congo and the Dominican Republic, see Blum, *Killing Hope*, pp. 156–63, 176–84.
45. This particular subscenario was demonstrated in a 1993 History Channel update of the 1988 Nigel Turner video series *The Men Who Killed Kennedy* entitled "The Truth Shall Make You Free," which is the sixth tape supplementing a five-tape boxed set. The five-part series was reedited and narrated by Bill Kurtis and has been broadcast over the A&E Network several times.
46. The complete text of the speech is reprinted in Arthur M. Schlesinger Jr.'s *Robert Kennedy and His Times* (New York: Hougton Mifflin, 1978), 2: 913–14.
47. On the Doolittle Report, see the relevant section of the PBS documentary *The Secret Government: The Constitution in Crisis,* which aired in 1986–87.
48. William R. Corson, *The Armies of Ignorance: The Rise of the American Intelligence Empire* (New York: Dial Press, James Wade Books, 1977), p. 347. According to Corson, the report on the CIA's cold war mission "ominously encouraged illegal activities" (p. 346).
49. National Security Council memorandum 5412/1 officially sanctioned the destruction of international communism no matter where it might appear and authorized "all compatible activities" necessary to accomplish the objective. See Corson, *The Armies of Ignorance,* pp. 347ff.
50. See Grant, "Trust No One," pp. 1–16.
51. "Quagmire" aired May 3, 1996.
52. See Jonathan Romney, "The New Paranoia," *Film Comment* 34 (November 1998): 39.
53. Ibid.
54. The best recent work on the CPI is Stephen Vaught's *Holding Fast the Inner Lines: Democracy, Nationalism, and the Committee on Public Information* (Chapel Hill: University of North Carolina Press, 1980). Also see Noam Chomsky's "Media Control: The Spectacular Achievements of Propaganda," *Open Magazine* Pamphlet Series, Open Media: Pamphlet no. 10, February 1992. Available online at <*http://www.mcad.edu/classrooms/POLITIPROP/palace/library/mediacontrol.htm*>. An information online profile of the CPI was available at <*http://weber.u.washington.ded/~scmuweb/propag/war2.htm*>.
55. See David Chute, "Is 'Secret' Truman's Precursor?" *Los Angeles Times,* June 8, 1998, Hollywood Online, available at <*http://www.1hollywood.com/news/topstories/og-08-98/htm12-3.htm*>.
56. See Freud's "A Case of Paranoia Running Counter to the Psychoanalytical Theory of the Disease," in *Sexuality and the Psychology of Love,* ed. Philip Rieff (New York: Collier Books, 1963), pp. 97–106. The case is discussed in Mary Ann Doane's *The Desire to Desire: The Woman's Film of the 1940s* (Bloomington: Indiana University Press, 1987), pp. 131–35. See also Naomi Schor, "Female Paranoia," *Breaking the Chain* (New York: Columbia University Press, 1985), pp. 149–155.
57. See Jonathan Rosenbaum's perceptive review "The Audience Is Us: *The Truman Show*" in the *Chicago Reader* online film review archive, available at <*http://www.chireader.com/movies/archives/1998/0698/06058.htm*>.

58. "*Network* cut with *Blue Velvet* or *It's a Wonderful Life* on the Brink of Being *Invasion of the Body Snatchers*" is how David Thompson begins his review in *Esquire,* May 1998, p. 46.
59. See Neal Postman's comments on why the Hebrews were forbidden to make images of their god in *Amusing Ourselves to Death: Public Discourse in the Age of Television* (New York: Penguin, 1985), pp. 9ff.
60. It's all true, it's all real. Nothing you see on this show is fake. . . . It's merely controlled!" These words are spoken by Truman's best friend "Marlon," played—according to the opening cue cards—by Louis Coltrane (actually Noah Emmerich playing Louis Coltrane portraying Marlon).
61. Richard Alleva, "Two Kinds of Paranoia: 'The Truman Show' and 'The X-Files,'" *Commonweal,* August 14, 1998, pp. 20–22.
62. This aspect of the film was perceptively noted by Arthur Taussig in his film commentary on *The Truman Show* available online at the C. G. Jung, Analytical Psychology & Culture website (June 26, 1998) at *<http://www.cgjung.com/films/truman1.htm>.*
63. Jonathan Rosenbaum, "On Film—Crass Consciousness *(Ed TV),*" *Chicago Reader,* March 1999, online film review archive available at *<http://www.chireader.com/movies/archives/1999/0399/03269.htm>.*
64. Romney, "The New Paranoia," p. 22.
65. Max Weber, "Politics as a Vocation" in *From Max Weber: Essays in Sociology,* ed. Hans Gerth and C. Wright Mills (New York: Oxford University Press, 1946), p. 128.
66. Guy Debord, *The Society of the Spectacle* (1967; rpt. New York: Zone Books, 1994).
67. See Duncan Campbell, "NSA Builds Security Access Into Windows," available online at *<http://www.techweb.com/wire/story/TWB19990903S0014>.* According to Campbell, in every copy of Windows sold, Microsoft has installed a "back door" for the NSA—making it much easier for the U.S. government to access individual computers.
68. See the FAQ on Echelon at the American Civil Liberties Union website at *<http://www.acul.org/echelonwatch/faq.htm>.*
69. See Vernon Loeb, "NSA Admits to Spying on Princess Diana," *The Washington Post,* December 12, 1998, p. A13, available online at *<http://www.washingtonpost.com/wp-srv/national/daily/dec98/diana12.htm>.*

**AFTERWORD**

1. These figures are taken from National Election Studies (NES) surveys at the University of Michigan. Cited by Ronald Inglehardt, "Postmaterialistic Values and the Erosion of Institutional Authority," in *Why People Don't Trust Government,* ed. Joseph S. Nye Jr., Philip D. Zelikow, and David C. King (Cambridge, Mass.: Harvard University Press, 1997), p. 217.
2. Ibid., 316n.
3. Ibid., pp. 217–37.
4. Timothy Melley, *Empire of Conspiracy: The Culture of Paranoia in Postwar America* (Ithaca, N.Y.: Cornell University Press, 2000), p. 14.
5. George Ritzer, *Enchanting a Disenchanted World: Revolutionizing the Means of Consumption* (Thousand Oaks, Ca.: Pine Forge Press, 1999).

6. Carl Boggs and Thomas Pollard, "Postmodern Cinema in an Age of Corporate Colonization," paper presented at the annual meeting of the American Political Science Association, Washington, D.C., August 30–September 2, 2000. Reprinted in *Democracy and Nature* 7, no. 1 (2000): 109–31.
7. See E. Martin Schotz's perceptive comments on the JFK assassination and public knowledge in his *History Will Not Absolve Us.* E. Martin Schotz' *History Will Not Absolve Us: Orwellian Control Public Denial, and the Murder of President Kennedy* (Brookline, Ma.: Kurtz, Ulmer, & DeLuca, 1996).
8. Robin Ramay, editor of *Lobster,* a British journal investigating conspiracy/covert operations, has noted the genuine disquiet that should, in his view, come from "the objective reality of U.S. political practice," which much academic American history "manages to skip over unsolved." See his thought-provoking essay "Of Conspiracies and Conspiracy Theories: The Truth Buried by the Fantasies," available online at *<http://www.magnet.ch/serendipity/eden/laconspi.htm>.*
9. The role of the Internet in furthering discourses outside the mainstream is perceptively discussed by Jodi Dean in *Aliens in America: Conspiracy Cultures from Outerspace to Cyberspace* (Ithaca: Cornell University Press, 1998).
10. Hedrik Smith's PBS television series *The People and the Power Game,* which aired in September 1996, presented an excellent analysis of the pressures on the major network news programs that led to their reporting of the Flowers story. The rapid emergence of the Clinton-Lewinsky scandal in January 1998 calls attention to the transformation of traditional news outlets and their gatekeeping roles.
11. The original *USA Today* report on the Russell e-mail appeared in the *Salt Lake Tribune* on Monday, November 25, 1996. That the TWA 800 story never quite went away is discussed in Elaine Scarry's "Swisair 111, TWA 800, and Electromagnetic Interference," *New York Review of Books,* September 21, 2000, pp. 92–100.
12. On the emergence of electronic communities, see Joshua Meyrowitz, "The Merging of Public Spheres," *No Sense of Place* (New York: Oxford University Press, 1985), pp. 73–92.
13. Guy Debord, *The Society of the Spectacle,* trans. Donald Nicholson-Smith (New York: Zone Books, 1995), pp. 12, 14. This work was originally published in France in 1967.
14. Jean Baudrillard, "Requiem for the Media," in *For a Critique of the Political Economy of the Sign,* ed. and trans. Charles Levin (St. Louis, Mo.: Telos Press, 1981): pp. 164–84.
15. For an exegesis of Baudrillard's notions, see Madan Sarup's *An Introductory Guide to Post-Structuralism and Postmodernism,* 2nd ed. (Athens: University of Georgia Press, 1993), pp. 165–67.
16. Fredric Jameson, "Postmodernism and the Consumer Society," in *The Anti-Aesthetic,* ed. Hal Foster (Port Townsend, Wash.: Bay Press, 1983), p. 125. See also Steven Best and Douglas Kellner, *Postmodern Theory* (New York: Guilford, 1991); idem, *The Postmodern Turn* (New York: Guilford, 1997).
17. Jameson, "Postmodernism and the Consumer Society," p. 125. Emphasis added.
18. For a study of the iconization and functions of the construct "Marilyn Monroe," see Paige Baty's *American Monroe: The Making of a Body Politic* (Berkeley: University of California Press, 1994).
19. In the closing days of the Reagan administration, numerous studies of the politics

of illusion appeared, including Neil Postman's *Amusing Ourselves to Death: Public Discourse in the Age of Show Business* (New York: Penguin, 1986); Joshua Meyrowitz's *No Sense of Place* (New York: Oxford University Press, 1985); Hedrick Smith's discussion of the "Image Game" in his book *The Power Game* and the related PBS series; Mark Hertsgaard's study of Washington news reporters in *On Bended Knee: The Press and the Reagan Presidency* (New York: Farrar, Straus & Giroux, 1988); and especially Bill Moyers' four-part PBS series *The Public Mind,* which aired in 1989. These studies were preceded by Todd Gitlin's fascinating and revelatory analysis of media construction and manipulation of the New Left in *The Whole World Is Watching: Mass Media in the Making and Unmaking of the New Left* (Berkeley: University of California Press, 1980).

20. On the "hypodermic" model, see Denis McQuail, "The Influence and Effects of Mass Media," in *Media Power in Politics,* ed. Doris Graber, 2nd ed. (Washington, D.C.: CQ Press, 1990), pp. 19–36.
21. Baty, *American Monroe,* p. 47. Baty's is just one out of nearly a hundred book-length studies of Monroe. Among the most recent, Donald H. Wolfe's *The Last Days of Marilyn Monroe* (New York: Morrow, 1998) presents the most comprehensive survey of past literature and reveals many new dimensions, including what now appears to have been genuine—and obviously successful—conspiracies to eliminate her involving the Kennedys, the CIA, and the FBI.
22. The reference comes from Rousseau's *Discourse on Inequality:* "Far fewer words than these were needed to win over crude, easily seduced men who had, furthermore, too many difficulties to clear up among themselves to be able to do without masters for long. All ran headlong into their chains, hoping to secure their liberty. . . ." *Rousseau's Political Writings,* ed. Alan Ritter and Julia Conway Bondanella (New York: Norton, 1988), p. 45.
23. Gallup poll figures cited by Jonathan Alter, "The Age of Conspiracism," *Newsweek,* March 24, 1997, p. 47.
24. See Joseph S. Nye Jr., Philip D. Zelikow, and David C. King, eds., *Why People Don't Trust Government* (Cambridge, Mass.: Harvard University Press, 1997). See also Gary Wills, *A Necessary Evil: A History of American Distrust of Government* (New York: Simon & Schuster, 1999).
25. Baty, *American Monroe,* p. 129.
26. Michel Foucault, "Truth and Power," *Power/Knowledge* (New York: Pantheon, 1981), p. 118. Emphasis added.
27. Baty, *American Monroe,* p. 129.

# Bibliographic Essay

Rather than present an extended formal bibliography of sources, I refer readers to the extensive endnotes for complete bibliographical citations of specific works cited in relation to the themes, topics, issues, and films mentioned in each chapter; these are simply listed by title here if previously cited in an endnote. Basic data on films, revenues, and awards have been drawn from the following sources: Cobbett Steinberg, *Reel Facts: The Movie Book of Records,* updated ed. (New York: Vintage, 1981); Leonard Maltin's *Movie & Video Guide* (New York: Signet, 2000, 2001); Ephraim Katz, *The Film Encyclopedia,* 2nd ed. (New York: HarperPerennial, 1994); and the Internet Movie Database.

The Internet has changed the way one views and studies American films. Two websites that have proven invaluable in charting comments and opinion on more recent films and many classic reissues are the Internet Movie Database <*http://www.imbd.com*> and the Movie Review Query Engine <*http://www.mrque.com*>. One must proceed with caution when reading the reviews posted at these sites. Most—especially those posted by reviewers with no affiliation to print sources—generally lack depth and are quick, often trivially shallow takes on recently released films; a few do provide useful background information, insights, and perspectives, and make comparisons with other films.

While the Internet has grown rapidly since the mid-1990s, films from earlier periods (1940–1990) are only occasionally reviewed in online sources. With the growth of the digital video disk (DVD) medium, reviews of DVD versions of classic films have increasingly become available, though most tend to focus on the technical quality of the product. Vivid, strikingly improved and restored versions of many of the films discussed in this study are rapidly coming on the market. Such films as *Invasion of the Body Snatchers, Bullitt, The Parallax View,* and *Chinatown* in DVD and equivalent new wide-screen VHS reissues have restored wide-screen perspectives for home cineasts and may change contemporary critical perspectives on the films themselves. Regular surfing of the Internet film/video sources will reveal the availability of restored versions of many films mentioned here. Most of them were at one time presented on Turner Classic Movies, American Movie Classics, the Encore Channel, or the Mystery Channel. Among commercial sources, Amazon.com is a good place to start searching for commercial releases. The Internet Movie Database provides updated information on availability in different formats.

Several collections of reviews and commentary on films have shaped my own perspectives. *Halliwell's Film Guide,* 3rd. ed. (London: Granada, 1981) and the eighth edition, edited by John Walker (New York: HarperCollins, 1991) were helpful with capsule comments. Gary Crowdus, ed., *The Political Companion to American Film* (Chicago: Lakeview Press, 1994), with its scores of essays by *Cinéaste* contributors on the political dimensions of

American film provides an indispensable introduction to interrelationships between history, politics, and society. The first collection that stimulated my desire to teach and write about the political implications of American film was by John E. O'Connor and Martin A. Jackson, eds., *American History/American Film: Interpreting the Hollywood Image* (New York: Ungar, 1979). Danny Peary's *Cult Movies* (New York: Delta, 1981); *Cult Movies 2* (1983); and *Cult Movies 3* (New York: Simon & Schuster, Fireside, 1988), as well as his *Guide for the Film Fanatic* (New York: Simon & Schuster, Fireside, 1986) suggested a wealth of interpretations and ideas. I first started reading film criticism by Stanley Kauffman in *The New Republic* nearly forty years ago and then followed Pauline Kael's *New Yorker* reviews for most of her tenure there from 1967 on—the best of which are collected in *For Keeps: 30 Years at the Movies* (New York: Penguin/Plume, 1996). John Howard Lawson, *Film: The Creative Process* (New York: Hill & Wang, 1964) and his *Film in the Battle of Ideas* (New York: Masses & Mainstream, 1953) were some of the very first film books that influenced my thinking. Robert Kolker, *A Cinema of Loneliness* (New York: Oxford University Press, 2000), which has gone through three editions from 1980 through 2000—is perhaps the best single book on contemporary American film.

**CHAPTER 1**

This chapter began as a paper presented by the author at the American Political Science Association in September 1997, entitled "Conspiracy and the Quest for Coherence in Popular Culture." Jonathan Vankin and John Whalen, *The 60 Greatest Conspiracies of All Time* (New York: Citadel, 1996) provide an excellent introduction—sympathetic yet with a touch of postmodern humor—to the hidden aspects of diverse historical mysteries, cover-ups, and possible cabals in the historical background to many of the films I discuss. Additional cases are discussed by Doug Moench, *The Big Book of Conspiracies* (New York: Paradox, 1995) and Robert A. Wilson, *Everything Is Under Control: Conspiracies, Cults, and Cover-ups* (New York: HarperPerennial, 1998). George Johnson, *Architects of Fear: Conspiracy Theories and Paranoia in American Politics* (Los Angeles: Tarcher, 1983), provides a good historical background going all the way back to the alleged Illuminati conspiracy of the 1700s. On conspiracy culture generally, see the website of the Centre for Conspiracy Culture at <*http://www.wkac.ac.uk/research/ccc/index.htm*>. In the large and growing literature on conspiracy theory and paranoia, many of the publications in the form of critical essays or books seem to identify paranoia with mental illness and delusion, with the exception of the revelatory exploration in cultural studies and literary criticism by Timothy Melley, *Empire of Conspiracy: The Culture of Paranoia in Postwar America* (Ithaca, N.Y.: Cornell University Press, 2000), which goes beyond the simplistic identification of conspiracy theories and theorizing with personality disorder, instead exploring the growth of anxieties arising out of a sensed loss of autonomy and individuality described as "agency panic." Similarly eye-opening is Mark Dery, *The Pyrotechic Insanitarium: American Culture on the Brink* (New York: Grove, 1999). Among those taking the mental-illness approach to filmic and literary paranoia is a paper by Robert S. Robins and Jerrold M. Post presented at the 1997 meeting of the American Political Science Association entitled "Political Paranoia as Cinematic Motif: Stone's *JFK*," available online (Jan. 2001) at <*http://macadams.posc.mu.edu/robins.htm*>.

## CHAPTER 2

Douglas Kellner and Michael Ryan, *Camera Politica* (Bloomington: Indiana University Press, 1988) and Douglas Kellner, *Media Culture* (London: Routledge, 1996) have both influenced my thinking. Kellner's "Hollywood Film and Society," in *The Oxford Guide to Film Studies,* John Hill and Pamela C. Gibson, eds. (New York: Oxford University Press, 1998) is the most succinct statement of this subject. John Belton's *American Cinema/American Culture* (New York: Corporation for Public Broadcasting and New York Center for Visual History, McGraw-Hill, 1994), which is the companion volume to the PBS series *American Cinema,* provides an interesting perspective on the interplay of the film industry and society. Robert Kolker's *Film, Form, and Culture* (New York: McGraw-Hill, 1999) effectively demonstrates how film affects the society of which it is a part.

## CHAPTER 3

This chapter grew out of papers presented by the author at the Popular Culture Association in 1994 and 1996. Among the vast body of literature on the subject, mention should be made of the following: Victor Navasky's *Naming Names;* Thom Andersen's "Red Hollywood"; Larry Ceplair and Steven Englund's *The Inquisition in Hollywood;* Mike Davis's *City of Quartz;* and James Naremore's *More Than Night: Film Noir in Its Contexts.* Paul Arthur's "Shadows on the Mirror: Film Noir and Cold War America, 1945–1957" (Ph.D. diss., New York University, 1985), suggested by Robert Sklar, proved illuminating, as have Arthur's subsequent reviews and articles in *Cinéaste* and diverse publications. Dan Flory's lucid "Black on White: Film Noir and the Epistemology of Race in African-American Cinema" helped immensely in clarifying the distinctive epistemology of film noir and introduced me to the "black noir" subgenre, as did his book-length study *Black on White.* In addition to the usual film noir "suspects" cited in the endnotes, mention should be made of Alain Silver and Elizabeth Ward, eds., *Film Noir: An Encyclopedia of the American Style,* rev. ed. (Woodstock, N.Y.: Overlook, 1992), which has been the most consistently useful tool for several years. Among the less-often cited recent sources, definitely worth reading is Eddie Muller's *Dark City: The Lost World of Film Noir* (New York: St. Martin's, Griffin, 1998), which presents a striking collection of stills and color reproductions of posters that complement an engaging descriptive narrative emulating classic hard-boiled pulp prose. David N. Meyer's *A Girl and a Guy: The Complete Guide to Film Noir on Video* (New York: Avon, 1998) contains a series of incisive, stylishly written, often unique takes on noir classics, with canny psychological and social insight. Nicholas Christopher's *Somewhere in the Night: Film Noir and the American City* (New York: Henry Holt, Owl Books, 1997) communicates personal enthusiasm and makes one want to review the films. James Maxfield's *The Fatal Woman: Sources of Male Anxiety in American Film Noir, 1941–1991* (Cranbury, N.J.: Associated University Presses, 1996) presents unique and unconventional insights on fourteen films, from *The Maltese Falcon* through *Thelma and Louise.* Robert Sklar's *City Boys* contains memorable portraits of the careers of Bogart, Cagney, and Garfield. Worth reading is the biography of Abraham Polonsky by Paul Buhle and David Wagner, *A Very Dangerous Citizen: Abraham Polonsky and the Hollywood Left* (Berkeley: University of California Press, 2001). George Lipsitz's *A Rainbow at Midnight: Class and Culture in Cold War America,* 2nd ed. (Champaign: University of Illinois Press, 1994) provides an outstanding overview of the historical context of film noir. Jonathan Munby's *Public Enemies, Public Heroes: Screening the Gangster from* Little Caesar *to* Touch of Evil (Chicago: University of Chicago Press, 1999) provides numerous unique insights. The critical literature on film noir style is extensive and growing. *The Book of Film Noir, Film Noir Reader* and *Film Noir Reader* II, and *Shades of Noir* provide essential background information.

#### CHAPTER 4

Morris Dickstein's *Gates of Eden: American Culture in the Sixties* (New York: Basic Books, 1977), and David Farber, ed., *The Sixties* (especially George Lipsitz's essay on popular music) provide essential material. See Ray Pratt's "There Must Be Some Way Outa Here" for a discussion of anti-Vietnam themes in popular music of the period; see also his *Rhythm and Resistance: Political Uses of American Popular Music,* 2nd ed. (New York: Praeger, 1990; rpt. Washington, D.C.: Smithsonian Institution Press, 1994) for a more extensive discussion of music of the 1960s. Todd Gitlin's *The Sixties: Years of Hope, Days of Rage* remains one of the finest historical accounts, displaying great sensitivity to the ways film and music both reflected and shaped the popular consciousness. The essays by Lawrence Suid and Charles Maland on *Dr. Strangelove* were important in confirming my personal judgment on the importance of the film in the context of its time. Robert Kolker's discussion of Kubrick in *A Cinema of Loneliness,* 3rd ed. (Oxford: Oxford University Press, 2000) contains important insights on *Dr. Strangelove.* See John Cawelti, ed., *Focus on "Bonnie and Clyde"* (Englewood Cliffs, N.J.: Prentice-Hall Spectrum, 1973); and Sandra Wake and Nichola Hayden, eds., *The "Bonnie and Clyde" Book* (New York: Simon & Schuster, 1977) for the screenplay and collected critical commentaries and interviews. Arthur Penn is interviewed at length on *Bonnie and Clyde* and several of his films of this and later periods in Gary Crowdus and Richard Porton, "The Importance of a Singular, Guiding Vision: An Interview with Arthur Penn," *Cinéaste* 20, no. 2 (spring 1993): 5–12. Lee Hill's *Easy Rider* (London: British Film Institute, 1995) provides a good overview of the film and critical commentary. Peter Biskind's *Easy Riders, Raging Bulls: How the Sex-Drugs-and-Rock 'n' Roll Generation Saved Hollywood* (New York: Simon & Schuster, 1999) presents a harrowing series of portraits of Dennis Hopper and associates, including the making of *Easy Rider* and several other films of the 1960s and '70s. The FBI surveillance of Martin Luther King Jr. throughout the 1960s is outlined in searing detail in David J. Garrow's *The FBI and Martin Luther King, Jr.* (New York: Viking Penguin, 1983), which also provides one of the strongest, most concise statements of King's profound radical challenge to American society to live up to its values.

#### CHAPTER 5

Katheryn S. Olmstead's *Challenging the Secret Government: The Post-Watergate Investigations of the CIA and FBI* (Chapel Hill: University of North Carolina Press, 1996) is an outstanding study of the failure of the government's investigations to uncover the secrets held by the national security state. For a view from the inside of such an investigation—the House Special Committee on Assassinations—that describes its difficulties and ultimate failures, see Gaeton Fonzi's *The Last Investigation* (New York: Thunder's Mouth Press, 1993). Thomas Powers's *The Man Who Kept the Secrets: Richard Helms and the CIA* is really a history of the secret state that was the CIA during the cold war; it reads like a novel but is meticulously documented. See Biskind's *Easy Riders, Raging Bulls* for extensive stories on the making of *Chinatown.* The first edition of Kolker's *A Cinema of Loneliness* discusses Francis Ford Coppola's work; the second and third editions provide perspectives on Arthur Penn and *Night Moves,* increasingly regarded as one of the important films of the 1970s.

### CHAPTERS 6 AND 7

James Maxfield's *The Fatal Woman* and E. Ann Kaplan's *Women in Film Noir,* 2nd ed. (London: British Film Institute, 1998) were both strong influences. On *Pretty Poison,* see Floyd Conner, *"Pretty Poison": The Tuesday Weld Story* (New York: Barricade, 1995). Jane Caputi's *The Age of Sex Crime* and "American Psychos" both shaped my understanding of women's well-reasoned paranoia. Daphne Patai's *Heterophobia: Sexual Harassment and the Future of Feminism* and John Fekete's *Moral Panic* deserve wider attention.

### CHAPTER 8

For histories of the Reagan era, see Jane Mayer and Doyle McManus's *Landslide: The Unmaking of the President, 1984–1988* (New York: Houghton Mifflin, 1988); Gary Wills' *Reagan's America;* Michael Rogin's *Ronald Reagan: The Movie;* and Thomas B. Edsall and Mary D. Edsall's *Chain Reaction: The Impact of Race, Rights, and Taxes on American Politics* (New York: Norton, 1992). Elaine Tyler May's *Homeward Bound: American Families in the Cold War Era* (New York: Basic Books, 1988); Stephanie Coontz's *The Way We Never Were: American Families and the Nostalgia Trap* (New York: Basic Books, 1992), and Susan Faludi's *Backlash: The Undeclared War Against American Women* (New York: Anchor Press, 1991) deconstruct the images of "family" that emerged in the popular culture of the Reagan-Bush (Sr.) period.

### CHAPTER 9

Frank Donner's *The Age of Surveillance* and *Protectors of Privilege* were important works that shaped my perspectives on the police system, as were my first viewing of the films *Serpico* and *Dog Day Afternoon* and my reading of Peter Mass' *Serpico* (New York: Bantam, 1974). Lou Cannon, *Official Negligence: How Rodney King and the Riots Changed Los Angeles and the LAPD* (New York: Random House/Times Books, 1997), provides historical context for *L.A. Confidential.*

### CHAPTER 10

Ron Rosenbaum's "Oswald's Ghost," published on the twentieth anniversary of the JFK assassination and reprinted in *Travels with Dr. Death* (New York: Viking, 1991), is not a study of Oswald but an intense reappraisal of favorite theories about the assassination. Rosenbaum offers new takes on enduring mysteries, including fascinating interviews with Josiah Thompson, author of the influential *Six Seconds in Dallas,* which made many readers into Warren Commission critics. Rosenbaum introduced the concept of "dangerous knowledge," which was appropriated by Art Simon as the title for his extensive study of

JFK assassination films. On the latter—especially Stone's *JFK*—see Christopher Sharrett, "Conspiracy Theory and Political Murder in America: Oliver Stone's *JFK* and the Facts of the Matter," *The New American Cinema,* ed. Jon Lewis (Durham, N.C.: Duke University Press, 1998), which shaped and sums up my own perspectives on the film and the events as much as any single source. Marita Sturken's "Reenactment, Fantasy, and the Paranoia of History: Oliver Stone's Docu-dramas," *History and Theory* 36, no. 4 (December 1997): 64–79, provides one of the strongest arguments for the revelatory power of Stone's work. Stone's collection *"JFK": The Book of Film* (New York: Applause, 1993) collects hundreds of positive and negative reviews and provides an annotated version of the screenplay of the film, with links at crucial and disputed points to an extensive body of assassination research. *Oliver Stone's USA Film, History, and Controversy,* ed. Robert B. Toplin (Lawrence: University Press of Kansas, 2000), an excellent and comprehensive collection of essays, provides a scholarly overview of the body of Stone's work and is especially valuable in containing the director's own responses to each chapter. Anthony Summers' *Not in Your Lifetime: The Definitive Book of the JFK Assassination* (New York: Marlowe, 1998) is the best one-volume overview, though Michael L. Kurtz's *Crime of the Century: The JFK Assassination from a Historian's Perspective,* 2nd ed. (Knoxville: University of Tennessee Press, 1994) is also outstanding, especially (with Summers) in raising many reasonable doubts on the question of Oswald's guilt. Phillip Melanson's *Spy Saga: Lee Harvey Oswald and American Intelligence* (New York: Praeger, 1990) and John Newman's *Oswald and the CIA* (New York: Thunder's Mouth Press, 1995) pursue one of history's most enigmatic characters; Newman presents an important take on revelations found in materials declassified after the JFK Records Act. Among the many websites on the JFK assassination, see: "The Kennedy Assassination for the Novice" *<http://pages.prodigy.net/whiskey99>*; "The Academic JFK Assassination Site" *<http://karws.gso.uri.edu/JFK>*; and "The JFK Lancer Site" *<http://www.jfklancer.com>*.

The TV series *The Prisoner* was released in various home-video formats in the fall of 2000. The National Security Agency (NSA) Project ECHELON is discussed at length on scores of websites; especially the ACLU ECHELON Watch site at *<www.echelonwatch.org>*.

## AFTERWORD

This chapter grew out of a review of Paige Baty's *American Monroe: The Making of a Body Politic* (Berkeley: University of California Press, 1996) in *Political Theory* 25, no. 4 (August 1997): 602–7.

# Index